KNIGHT: *My Story*

Bob Knight
with Bob Hammel

THOMAS DUNNE BOOKS
St. Martin's Griffin ⚜ New York

To my mom, dad, and grandmother, and to Orrville.
To Tim and Pat.
To Karen.
And to all those assistant coaches who have helped me,
and to all those players and all those teams
that I have totally enjoyed coaching.

THOMAS DUNNE BOOKS.
An imprint of St. Martin's Press.

KNIGHT. Copyright © 2002 by Bob Knight and bob Hammel. All rights reserved. Printed in the United States of America. No part of this book may be used or reproduced in any manner whatsoever without written permission except in the case of brief quotations embodied in critical articles or reviews. For information, address St. Martin's Press, 175 Fifth Avenue, New York, N.Y. 10010.

www.thomasdunnebooks.com
www.stmartins.com

All photos courtesy of Bob Knight unless otherwise noted.

Book design by Michael Collica.

Library of Congress Cataloging-in-Publication Data

Knight, Bob.
    Knight : my story / Bob Knight and Bob Hammel.
        p. cm.
    ISBN-13: 978-0-312-31117-9
    ISBN-10: 0-312-31117-6
    1. Knight, Bob. 2. Basketball coaches—United States—Biography.
I. Hammel, Bob. II. Title.

GV884.K58 A3 2002
796.323'092—dc21
[B]
                                                            2001048990

10 9 8 7 6 5 4 3 2

Books by Bob Hammel

Knight with the Hoosiers (1975)*

•

NCAA Indiana All the Way (1976)*

•

The Champs (1981)*

•

Beyond the Brink with Indiana (1987)*

•

Super Scout (1992)
(autobiography of baseball scout Jimmy Russo)

•

A Banner Year at Indiana (1993)*

•

Silver Knight (1997)*

•

Hoosiers: Classified (1997)
(anecdotal history of Indiana high school basketball)

•

Glory of Old IU (1999)
(century review of IU athletics)

*Books on Indiana University basketball

CONTENTS

ACKNOWLEDGMENTS

Standard procedure in this section is to say thanks for—to acknowledge—vital assistance in researching and processing a book. I had lots of that from many people, and I do want to express my appreciation.

More than that, though, I acknowledge the great fortune I've had in the people I've met and gotten to know so well over my long basketball trail.

I've been blessed with mentors, with friends who have and have earned great renown in sports and in other roles, and with friends not so well-known but every bit as dear and as close to me.

I'm sure I've left out or greatly shortchanged some who qualify in each of those categories. The mentioned, the undermentioned, and the unmentioned all are part of the mosaic of people who have helped me in ways they might not remember, but I always will remember the people and their acts, and appreciate them deeply.

I acknowledge that there are some people I've run into along the line that I'm not so big on. Their number is vastly exceeded by the long, long list of people I'm indebted to for their help and their friendship.

Many of those showed up in Lubbock, Texas, the night of November 16, 2001, to see and help me get started in a new season, at a new location. The effort those people made to get there touched me deeply. I've never felt more honored. We were all entertained by the unmatched humor of Abe Lemons, one of my favorite people and one of the best and most underrated college basketball coaches ever. John Havlicek was there one more time and helped me once again, by talking to my Texas Tech team. I won't go on with names, but every one of the people who interrupted their own lives to get to Lubbock that special weekend will always have my appreciation.

A major purpose of this book is to acknowledge the privilege I've had to have spent my life in basketball, in America. I've always had an awareness, a sense of debt to so many who fought for and protected our country, but I think all of us elevated our national pride and determination in support of our citizen and military efforts to see that what happened on September 11, 2001, will never happen again.

The dedication and national response to the tremendous losses suffered by the New York City Police and Fire Departments and all the other victims at the Trade Center and the Pentagon will forever be a part of the greatest tradition of all: the ability to rise and unite to overcome adversity and tragedy.

ONE: *The Eight Greatest Words*

For the first time in thirty-six years, I don't have a basketball team.

I remember very clearly the thought going through my mind that day:
Only in America . . .

I'm a pretty appreciative guy, especially where my country is concerned. It's nothing I have to think about. I've always felt that way. In the summer of 1984 when I was coaching the U.S. Olympic team, every stop I made, every group I talked to, I mentioned the eight greatest words any American ever put together: *America, America, God shed His grace on thee...*

Through the winter of 2000–01 when I was speaking to different groups across the country, I made it a point virtually every time to ask World War II veterans to stand, then all people who had served in the military in service to our country. I did it because I enjoyed seeing those people stand and hear applause, and I enjoyed being one of the people applauding. I strongly feel we are all blessed by being where we are when we are, and there are some specific people and generations who deserve to feel proud and appreciated—like the New York City firemen and policemen of September 2001.

But this late-summer day in 1991 when I was pleasantly into my "only in America" reverie, I was wading in a river, fishing. The river was the Umba, in northern Russia. What I was thinking was that only in America could a guy like me, through a game like basketball, be standing there, having such a great experience.

Because fishing that same day in that same river, just around a bend, was my friend, Ted Williams. Ted was as close to a lifelong hero as I had, outside my family. As a boy I sat in the stands at Lakefront Stadium in Cleveland and marveled at his swing. I was all for the Indians, but when I saw that classic Ted Williams swing send a baseball screaming into the stands and watched that head-down Williams lope around the bases, I felt privileged.

The more I learned about him, the more I revered him—not only as a great baseball player but also as a genuine hero of two American wars; as a master fisherman; as one of the rare national figures who absolutely God-damned refused to knuckle under to a hostile press.

Here I was, a kid from a small Ohio town, a town not far from Cleveland where my parents had taken me on a few special Sundays to watch the Boston Red Sox and the great Ted Williams play against the Indians. All these years later, I clearly remember the chill I felt when he just stepped into the batter's box, and when he swung, and the unbelievably special times when I was there and that swing and a loud crack sent the ball out of the park. . . .

And here I was, fishing with him . . . because of basketball. I'm not too sure I've had another moment in my life when I felt more keenly, sharply aware of how much that game I loved had meant in my life.

I met Ted Williams because basketball introduced me to some people who could make it happen—me, the son of two small-town Americans: an Ohio railroad man and a schoolteacher.

I learned to fly-fish, my second-greatest sports passion, because of basketball. I was picked to make the trip, because of basketball. And I could afford to do it, because of basketball.

I've spent most of my life trying to give things back to the sport, because so many people in it have given so much of it to me. That day, on that river, in that special company, I knew as I always had that I owed the game more than I could ever give back.

But I was damned sure trying.

Jerry McKinnis of ESPN's *Fishin' Hole* show lined up the Russian trip. I had fished several times in the United States for shows Jerry did. I enjoyed them all, because Jerry is a hell of a guy and the best fisherman (Ted would take exception) I've ever met.

But he outdid himself by drawing up this trip. Jerry knew it, too. He's a big fan of both baseball and college basketball, a lifelong Cardinals fan who played the game well enough himself that he signed a professional contract coming out of high school. He knew from our previous travels and talks just where Ted Williams stood with me, and Ted had been Jerry's idol, too.

I couldn't say yes fast enough when Jerry suggested the trip. And I couldn't have been happier when I called Ted and he said, yeah, he could do that—he'd be glad to. Ted and I had already met. I had mentioned to Minneapolis sports columnist Sid Hartman how much I thought of Ted Williams, and Sid got him to call me. The first time I met him face to face, Jimmy Russo set it up.

Jimmy, an Indiana native who was the "superscout" for the Orioles during their great years in the '60s and '70s, was as strong an Indiana University basketball fan as I ever met. He lived in St. Louis and always got over to Bloomington at least once during the season, and I looked forward to those visits because we had some great baseball talks each time. Jimmy was still with the Orioles when I went to spring training after we had won the NCAA championship in 1981. Ted happened to be at a game both Jimmy and I attended, and Jimmy took me over and introduced me to him. We had maintained some contact over the years, so his agreement to go to Russia with me had some background.

So did the trip itself. The summer of '91, baseball's All-Star Game was played in Toronto. President George Bush brought Ted and Joe DiMaggio to the White House for a ceremony, then the three of them got on a plane and went to the game. On the way, the president asked Ted about his summer plans. Ted told him about the fishing trip he and I were taking to Russia. "You and Knight?" the president said. "Jeez-us." History will record that we hadn't been out of the Soviet Union for a week before the government fell. We'd both like to take credit for that, but . . .

Ted and I met in New York for the flight over. We were sitting together on the airplane, not too far into the flight, when he said:

"Okay, who do you think were the five most important Americans, in your lifetime?"

The first thing that strikes you about him is how smart he is. You are not dealing with a guy with ordinary intelligence. He is well-read, extremely opinionated, and he backs up his opinions with reasons. A mutual friend, broadcaster Curt Gowdy, had told me to be ready to argue with him, because there was nothing Ted liked better than that. It wasn't the worst news I'd ever heard; I don't mind a little debate myself, now and then.

And I knew from the way he asked me that question he had his own five.

I mentioned Franklin Roosevelt, and he agreed, finally. I knew he was an arch-Republican, but I thought he'd have to come around on Roosevelt.

He came in quickly with Richard Nixon, Joe Louis, and General Douglas MacArthur.

I said Harry Truman, and he didn't totally agree. His contention was, "Goddammit, you have The Bomb. Anybody can decide to drop The Bomb." I'm a big Truman man. We argued about that point. Yes, anybody could have made that decision. I don't think just anybody would have.

I picked George Marshall, the World War II general and the post-war secretary of state who came up with the Marshall Plan that revived Europe. Ted didn't disagree with that.

We both talked about Dwight Eisenhower. One guy I mentioned was Will Rogers.

Ted was very big on Richard Nixon. He knew and liked Nixon. I wasn't inclined to argue. I think even some of Nixon's political critics feel he will go down as one of the better presidents. The negative was obvious: all the things represented by "I am not a crook."

I mentioned, for personal reasons, William Simon. He knew Simon and thought he was a brilliant guy. We were talking twentieth century, so Henry Ford was another one we both picked. I don't remember if Thomas Edison came up or not, but he surely should have. This went on for a while.

Then he wanted the five most overrated.

I said John Kennedy, and I got out of the hole I had dug with FDR. "You're a hell of a lot smarter than I thought you were from our other discussion," he said.

We both agreed that Robert McNamara and General William Westmoreland were on that list of five—three out of the same era.

And we discussed baseball. He thought the best player ever was Babe Ruth. Period. He didn't think anybody was even close.

He called Joe DiMaggio the best player of his era. I heard him say that many times. However, I wasn't going to accept that one without raising a point.

I told him in 1947 when DiMaggio edged him out for MVP because one Boston writer didn't even put Ted in his top ten, DiMaggio shouldn't have accepted the award. He didn't say anything, just went to talking about something else, which was all I needed to feel that was exactly the way he would have handled the '47 situation.

That was the quality that stood out for me during that whole conversation and has in every one I've had with him: how genuinely unfailingly gracious he is to players of his era who were supposed to be his rivals. Stan Musial, for example—"a great hitter and a great person," Ted called him.

Williams quit playing after the 1960 season—after he homered in his last time at bat and gave John Updike the material for what may be the greatest sports story I've ever read. Updike was a graduate student at Harvard when he attended that game, sitting not in a press box but in the stands, as a fan. In an article entitled "Kid Bids Hub Fans Adieu" that he wrote for *The New Yorker*, Updike described Williams's eighth-inning home run, on a one-and-one pitch, off the Orioles' Jack Fisher, and his run around the bases: "He ran as he always ran out home runs—hurriedly, unsmiling, head down, as if our praise were a storm of rain to get out of." Updike was part of the crowd roar that ran for minutes in an attempt to get Williams to step out from the dugout and tip his cap. "The papers said that the other players, and even the umpires on the field, begged him to come out and acknowledge us in some way," Updike wrote, "but he never did and did not now.

"Gods do not answer letters."

What a perfect line.

Updike also said Williams, by declining to go with the team to New York for a meaningless three-game series closing out the season, "knew how to do even that, the hardest thing. Quit."

But that almost wasn't Ted's last at-bat. In Russia he told me the Yankees tried to get him to play the next year, as a pinch-hitter and part-time out-fielder—for the same salary he made with the Red Sox. Imagine what that would have been. "The next year" was 1961, the year Roger Maris hit sixty-one homers, and Mickey Mantle hit fifty-four. Now factor in Ted Williams, playing eighty-one games in the perfect stadium for a left-handed power hitter.

I thought about all that and had to ask him, "How could you *not* play a year in Yankee Stadium?" He just decided he had played enough.

"It was really tempting," he said. "But I'd had my day."

I had met Maris and become good friends with him. I think it's a shame that he died without ever being admitted to the Baseball Hall of Fame. I still think he will be, some day. Ted liked Maris, thought he was a great player, and worked hard to get him elected to the Hall of Fame.

He's proud that he has the highest on-base percentage in baseball history—"so I got on base all the time, but I hit 500 home runs." That's why he liked Musial and DiMaggio, because they hit for average but hit with good power, too. Lou Gehrig also. Ted played against Gehrig, and he saw Ruth in batting practice a few years after Ruth's playing career ended in 1935.

His teammate when he first came to the majors, Jimmy Foxx, was "a hell of a powerful hitter," Ted said. "There was a different sound to it when Foxx hit a baseball—like a cannon going off. Mantle was almost like that. He was a great player."

He called Bob Feller the best pitcher he faced. I couldn't resist saying: "Yeah, sure—I listened to those Indians–Red Sox games and you must have hit .500 against him." He just glared.

Feller, Virgil Trucks of Detroit, and Bob Lemon of Cleveland were his top three. The Yankees' Allie Reynolds and Vic Raschi, he said, were good pitchers but they played on a great team. He thought the Indians' Herb Score had a chance to be a great pitcher, until a line drive hit him in the face and he never was as good again.

I just listened most of the time, fascinated. But occasionally I'd make a comment. And sometimes he would say, "God-dammit, you're not dumb. You aren't dumb."

I told him of a conversation I had with Bill Dickey, the Hall of Fame catcher for the Yankees. I asked Dickey who was the fastest pitcher he faced. Before I could say the name, Ted cut right in: "He told you Lefty Grove was." He was right.

And I was right in crediting basketball for providing me with this opportunity with Ted, one of the richest experiences of my life.

Ten years later, I still feel indebted to basketball. My address has changed, but not my gratitude toward the game. In fact, in the months after the initial shock of being fired in my thirtieth year as Indiana University's basketball coach, I still was thinking of the next step I wanted to make, the next experiment I wanted to try, in the search for improving my basketball team.

I was fired September 10, 2000. I had already begun working with my team—a maximum of four players at a time, under NCAA rules, before full practice begins. October 15 was the first day that college basketball teams could practice in the 2000–01 season. The evening of October 14, the thought ran through my mind:

For the first time in thirty-six years, I don't have a basketball team. . . .

It was the first time in a lot longer than that since a new season approached and I wasn't excited about getting it started. Add two years as an assistant coach at West Point; a year before that as a high school assistant at Cuyahoga Falls, Ohio; four years before that as a player at Ohio State; four years before that as a varsity high school player at Orrville, Ohio; and two years before that in junior high.

I hadn't quite turned sixty, and it had been forty-nine years since a fresh, new basketball season arrived without my being involved with a team.

The truth is I resented it like hell. I knew what I had set out to build at Indiana University. Winning games and championships was part of the dream going in, and not just as a by-product. I wanted to win those games and build those championship teams the way some people, primarily in the press, were saying could not be done anymore—by following NCAA rules; by recruiting kids who could and would be genuine students and four-year graduates as well as excellent basketball players and teams. I wanted to make the INDIANA they wore across their chests an identifying symbol that meant to people throughout the state, the Big Ten, and the country that inside that jersey was a kid who would compete like hell and represent his school on the court and off it, during his college years and after them, in a way that would make the most important judges of all, that kid's parents, as proud as they could be.

To do all that and to win was the goal.

To win without doing all those things would have been to fail.

When they took direction of the Indiana University basketball program away from me, it didn't change my feeling about those twenty-nine years.

I had met my goal.

And I hadn't failed.

I was fired as Indiana University basketball coach while on a fishing trip in September 2000—fired in part *because* I was on a fishing trip, the spin later said. My being there supposedly proved my "insubordination."

Let me describe for you that "insubordination."

Late on Friday, September 8, at about 10:30 P.M., Myles Brand, the university president, called my home to advise me that he was going to be meeting with the university Trustees the next day. He knew I was planning to leave on a fishing trip to Canada at 5:00 the next morning. He asked me to cancel the trip so he could call me after he had met with the Trustees.

He wanted me to stay there so he could talk to me on the telephone after meeting with the Trustees. If he would have asked me to talk personally to the Trustees, I would have considered it, but I wasn't going to cancel the trip and disappoint people who had planned and made arrangements six months ago and already paid for the trip—not so he could talk to me on the telephone. There were telephones where I was going.

I called him about 7:30 that Sunday morning, and he told me I was fired.

We hadn't talked for thirty seconds when he said: "Well, Bob, the time to talk has passed. We're going to terminate you and move ahead.

"It really saddens me to do this."

By this time, I knew there were personal agendas. I said, "No it doesn't. It doesn't sadden you at all. The one thing left is that I want the financial considerations worked out as they should be."

"We'll take really good care of you, Bob."

I hung up the phone before I could say what I wanted to say. I wish I hadn't. I had already spent way too much time—certainly since May and actually for six years—holding myself back from instincts that had been reliable for me all my life. That's what disappointed me most about the ending to my relationship with Indiana University. Long before that telephone call, I hadn't done what I knew I had to do.

Quit.

In March 2000 when I was trying to get a pretty good team ready to play in the NCAA tournament, CNN carried a story that accused me of choking a player during a 1997 practice. In future pages, I'll get into details of what all happened next, but the net result was that I was told by Brand in May that I could stay on as coach under what the president called "zero tolerance."

Obviously, I should have quit right there. *I* know I should have quit years before, but certainly there.

Walter Byers, the retired executive director of the NCAA, was appalled by Brand's "zero tolerance" terms. He asked Wayne Duke, the retired Big Ten commissioner, to get in touch with me immediately and say that under no circumstances should I stay at Indiana with that held over me. His thoughts didn't get to me. I can't say I would have done anything different from what I did, but—as much respect as I have for Mr. Byers—I might have.

For twenty years I have felt no man has been anywhere close to Walter Byers as an administrator in athletics. One day in the early '80s, more on a whim than anything, I called the NCAA office in Kansas City and asked to speak to him. He came on the phone and said, "Coach, what can I do for you?" I said, "Really, nothing. I've heard about you all my life and I've played in your tournament several times—in fact, we've won it a couple of times. I just wanted to see if there actually *was* a Walter Byers."

He laughed, and we talked about several things.

From that moment on, I've had a very good relationship with him. He asked me to take part in several NCAA discussions or functions. One was special. The night before the 1988 semifinal games at Kansas City, the NCAA held a dinner celebrating its fiftieth tournament. I was invited, along with Pete Newell and Ray Meyer, to sit at Walter's table. That was one of the things in my coaching career that meant a lot to me.

Instead of sounding out people like Walter Byers, I tried to go on, just taking care of the basketball program figuring things would eventually work out. This was before I became aware of the agendas different people in the administration and the athletic department had. I tried right up through when—because of my fishing trip "insubordination" and other justifications just as flimsy—with a few hypocritical words I was fired.

I had a hard time accepting what happened. How could I believe that after twenty-nine years of turning out basketball teams and kids who followed the rules, went to school, graduated, and won championships, a university president and a lawyer-filled Board of Trustees could use a baseless case to rush to my firing?

More unbelievable to me was that I was still around to let them do it to me, four months after they couldn't find the reason to fire me but suited me up in the phony "zero tolerance" straitjacket so, in their minds, I could fire myself.

I was never even told what exactly was meant by "zero tolerance." Did it mean I couldn't get a technical foul? That I couldn't dispute something in the press? That I had to go through life without saying anything to anybody at any time? Brand said he made it clear. That's absolute bullshit. He never told me one thing about what mattered most in the situation he created: his interpretation of what those two words meant.

Zero tolerance was their term for what they would tolerate from me after Brand told the world in May that I had done a lot of terrible things but they were going to give me one last chance.

Last chance? Once these people—the president, his assistant, and enough members of the Board of Trustees—had started playing to the national media by building a flimsy case for firing me, I didn't have *any* chance. The idea of a last chance greatly irritated me because none of them had discussed with me the things they thought I should have been doing. When Bill Orwig, Paul Dietzel, Ralph Floyd, or John Ryan—men I had worked for and with most of my years at Indiana—thought I should do something, they told me what it was they wanted.

Instead, these people sought out and listened to everyone who had an accusation against me during the last twenty-five years and never—I mean never— got around to the very basic justice of confronting me with their charges and asking my version. I certainly would have had a response. When, after their May verdict was delivered, I finally heard or read in print their claims against me, I was as astonished as I was angry. I simply didn't do a number of things the world was given to believe as absolute fact.

And still I tried to coach. I remember talking with Dick Vitale months before any of this and telling him: "All I want to do is coach." That was so true that I let it affect my instinctive judgment.

At the end, I remembered something I had said to a friend just after I came to Indiana. They had hired me because they knew they had a major problem to clean up, and they cheered and praised me for getting it done—and, of course, for winning while doing it. But what I said to my friend even then was: "I'm like the marshal brought in to clean up Dodge City. After a while when things have gone well, they always turn on the marshal."

So, yes, almost from the start I knew there would be a time when I should hand in my badge and ride away.

But quitting is a hard thing for me to do, and it became all the harder because I let myself get soft. I was just too comfortable in the life I had created for myself in a town that had been special to me.

My first six years as a head coach were at Army. When I left there, I could have spent a year searching out every college town in the country and not found a spot better for me at that time than Bloomington. I had the places and the friends to go fishing with me anytime I wanted. I could hunt birds in season, play golf whenever I wanted, go to lunch and talk with people I liked, go to dinner and enjoy the foods that appeal to me—great steaks, Mexican food, Italian food, Chinese food. All of that was right there, in a comfortable and friendly small town.

And I was coaching basketball at a big university in the most basketball-conscious state in the country, playing in the kind of conference that gets a team that is good enough to win a national championship tested and experienced and sharp enough to get it done. I don't just say that in theory. My years there produced three national championships, and—although as a history major I'm quite aware that all history ever cares about is battles won—at least three more championship banners could have been hanging in Assembly Hall if particularly devastating injuries had not come to teams that were good enough to win. I had done a pretty good job in Dodge City.

That morning as I dialed the call to Brand, I also thought of the tantalizing future that was so close out there. I thought of the group of kids I would be coaching in another month—great kids, the kind I knew I could win with. Four of them were 6-foot-10, and they could do some things. I already was working out ways to play all four of them together at times. And it would work, because two of them, freshman Jared Jeffries and sophomore Jeff Newton, could handle the ball and they could shoot, pass, and drive well enough to move out on the court and cause problems for any defensive players who were big enough to cover them when they were close to the basket. The other two were Kirk Haston, second-team All–Big Ten as a sophomore and, I thought, the best big man—maybe the best player—in the Big Ten in the season coming up; and George Leach, a sophomore center who was going to be the best shot-blocker I ever coached.

I had high hopes for this team; I felt we could win more than sixty games over the next two years with a real shot at the 2002 NCAA championship. Through my twenty-nine years at Indiana, I knew what good teams looked like, and what they had to have to be really good. Seven of my twenty-nine teams at Indiana were either ranked No. 1 in the country at some point during the year or won the NCAA championship. Fourteen others—twenty-one in all out of the twenty-nine—were ranked in the Top Ten at some point in the season.

None of those teams ever had four big guys as good as these kids.

Jeffries grew up right in Bloomington, far and away the best player produced there in my twenty-nine years. He was so strong academically he could have gone anywhere he wanted. Duke, which has grown into the premier program in college basketball under a player I once coached, Mike Krzyzewski, was the other school he considered before making his choice known.

I felt all along he would choose Indiana. His dad and mom were strong, supportive people for him, people I liked a lot, and they were doing what they should have done: leaving the final decision up to Jared. I'm sure he didn't surprise them any more than he did me when he chose Indiana. And I'm sure they were as happy about it as I was.

In Atlanta, Georgia, A. J. Moye was a straight-A student who physically resembled one of our great players of the past, Quinn Buckner—a different type of player but just as bright, just as good a kid, with leadership potential, like Buckner. A. J. also picked Indiana.

In picking Indiana, those kids were picking me. They each said it in a dozen different ways: I want to play for Bob Knight.

They said that to a national media pack that was kind of shocked. My detractors in the media have never been able to believe that anyone would *want* to play for me. These kids did, and they didn't want to play for me a bit more than I wanted to coach them and the other kids we were blending together into this new team.

No, I damned sure didn't want to turn my back and quit on kids like those incoming freshmen.

Or on Haston, who had lost his mother in a horrible Tennessee tornado disaster a year before and even more than most kids we've had over the years thought of our basketball team as family.

Or on Leach, whose first college season was set back a year by inept scholarship-processing procedures at his high school and within our own coaching staff, and by the infuriating, mind-boggling stubbornness of NCAA committees.

But even with all of this, I should have walked away. And that's what bothered me the most. I hadn't done what I knew inside I had to do. Walk away. From a rotten mess.

I wasn't ready even then to walk away from basketball. I felt strongly that surely somewhere there was a school and an environment where I could enjoy coaching again.

TWO: *Cornerstones and Credos*

The will to win is not as important as the will to prepare to win.

For thirty-eight years as a college basketball coach, my thinking was focused on getting players to be as good as they could be. This, I knew, would give us a chance to have a team that was as good as *it* could be.

My thoughts on coaching came from my own studying and experimenting, and from discussions with coaches and phone calls I made over the years in search of answers and ideas about basketball.

Ultimately, I came up with four cornerstones for player and team development. And I owe these cornerstones to a lot of people.

I coached for eight seasons at West Point. In those years, I developed an interesting relationship with probably the three most prominent people in New York City basketball history—Clair Bee, Joe Lapchick, and Nat Holman.

Joe Lapchick had played on one of the first great professional basketball teams. There were two in New York in the '20s—an all-black team called the Rens, or the Renaissance, sponsored by the singer Kate Smith, and the other an all-white team called the Original Celtics. Lapchick was the Celtics' center, and he later became a great coach at St. John's, then with the Knicks, then back at St. John's.

When he retired in 1965, he was the most revered coach I had ever known, until I became acquainted with Henry Iba.

Mr. Lapchick passed away August 10, 1970, two weeks after my dad's death.

I took Coach Holman and Coach Bee to Mr. Lapchick's wake. He had loaned me the scrapbook he had put together on the 1950s college basketball gambling scandal. He showed the scrapbook to every player who ever played for him after that happened. I gave it back to Mrs. Lapchick that night; several months later she sent it to me to keep. At the wake, she took me into a little side room and told me, "I know you didn't play for Joe, but I want you to understand, you were one of his two favorites." No comment ever meant more to me. And I never asked her about the other one.

Every time one of my Army teams played in Madison Square Garden, when I would walk out on the floor I would look over to where he always sat. He'd put his thumb under his chin, which was telling me: "Lift your head up." He had a phrase: "Walk with the kings." And he lived it. This was a man whose schooling had stopped in the sixth grade, and he had the intellect, the great vocabulary, of a doctor of philosophy. He also dressed well, and economically.

I rode on an elevator with him once on our way to a Metropolitan Coaches Association luncheon. I can still see him, wearing a blue and yellow plaid sport coat, gray slacks, a blue shirt and a dark blue tie. I said, "Boy, Mr. Lapchick, you look awfully good."

"What do you think this cost, my boy?" he said.

"This is New York—that's got to be pretty expensive."

"Thirty-five dollars," he said. "That's what I paid for this."

"Wow," I said. "Where could you get a coat like that for thirty-five dollars?"

"That's the coat *and* the slacks, my boy. Thirty-five dollars."

He gave me the name of his tailor, Evy Levinson, whose shop was in the Garment District. The first time I went there, Mr. Levinson showed me some bolts of cloth. I'd never seen anything like it. I picked out six patterns for him to use in making sports coats for me. I picked them up a couple of weeks later. My bill for six coats was $108.

He was a great friend and tailor for me as long as I was at West Point. One day he pulled out a wine-colored piece of very soft material and told me, "I saved this out of a suit I made for somebody. I wanted to make a jacket for you out of it, if there's enough left." There was. I got a Mongolian cashmere coat for $22. That was 1968, and I still have it.

When I first went to Indiana, all the coats I had were from Mr. Levinson. I did buy some on my own, including the red-and-blue plaid coat that I wore in the 1976 finals against Michigan. For years, I kept in a pocket of that coat the room key from the hotel where we stayed—in fact, I kept the hotel keys from all three of our national championships, but I honestly don't know where they are now. I gave some of those jackets away. I gave one to the Basketball Hall of Fame, and others to people to auction off for different causes.

The first time I really got to know Coach Lapchick was a significant moment in my coaching career. At another of those Metropolitan Coaches Association luncheons, as I was getting ready for my first season as a head coach, I asked him if I could sit down and talk with him sometime. He gave me his home address, which I've never forgotten: 3 Wendover Lane in Yonkers.

I was twenty-four, and I was looking for some guidance. I went to Yonkers just as soon as we could work it out.

We hadn't talked very long before he said:

"What kind of training rules are you going to have?"

"That's one thing I wanted to talk to you about," I said.

What his recommendation amounted to was no training rules at all.

I'm sure people would think I'd have a rigid set of rules kids would have to live by—be in by this time or that time, don't do this, don't do that.

All those years as a coach, because of that evening I spent talking with Coach Lapchick, I had one training rule: If you do anything in any way, whenever or wherever, that I think is detrimental to the good of this basketball team, to the school, or to you yourself, I'll handle it as I see fit.

I think that was absolutely the best plan, and certainly he did. He told me why: "You're going to have a kid who is a pain in the ass, and you're going to be happy to get rid of him. And you're going to have a good kid who screws something up. You can't set down rules and then treat guys differently. You decide, based on your knowledge of the situation, what you're trying to do with it, what's best for the kid, and go from there."

His second question to me that night was:

"How important is it to you that people like you?"

I hadn't thought about that. I did for just a minute or so and said, "I'd like to be respected as a coach, but I'm not concerned about being liked."

He said, "Good. If you worry about whether people like you or not, you can never make tough decisions correctly."

Of the four cornerstones I have about coaching basketball, that was one of them: the whole idea of running a basketball team—team rules, my approach to training, and clearing away inconsequential matters to allow good decision-making, all of those things influenced by talking with and observing a master of the game: Joe Lapchick.

The second cornerstone came from one of the game's first truly great coaches, Clair Bee. It was the critically important role of teaching in basketball—teaching the game's fundamentals and philosophies, including all things involved in a team approach and a determination throughout that team not just to play well but to win.

Clair Bee dominated 1930s basketball as the coach at Long Island University, where he also coached football and baseball. His career as the basketball coach there carried into the early 1950s, and he has the best won–lost percentage of any coach in major-college history.

I was fortunate enough to meet him in my very early coaching years, and he willingly became a mentor to me.

His .826 winning percentage did not just happen. The sustaining, significant thing with him was his determination to win. One summer he and I were relaxing at a camp he ran at Kutsher's up in the Catskills. Without having any point to make, but just musing out loud, he said, "You know, there was a nine-year period when my teams lost twenty games."

I could tell how proud he was of that. Winning was a very important thing to him—not winning by breaking the rules in any way, shape or form, but winning, by working harder, being better prepared, and teaching better than the other guys.

He pounded into me that the very first thing you had to be was a teacher, and you had to *teach* kids how to play basketball. You had to teach them the *game*. You couldn't ever assume that they knew what they needed to know, or that they were going to do the right thing, unless you had taught them the right thing. This was a man who early in his coaching career developed a way to teach the two-handed set shot, which up until World War II was the basic method of outside shooting in basketball. People familiar with the history of basketball know a landmark game was December 30, 1936, when a player named Hank Luisetti introduced the one-handed shot when Stanford came out East. He scored fifty points in a game against Duquesne (still the Stanford record), but the news bombshell of that Stanford–Luisetti trip came when he scored fifteen points and Stanford ended a forty-three–game winning streak for Clair Bee's Long Island University team before 17,623 people at Madison Square Garden, 45–31.

Almost immediately, the loser in that game became one of the best teachers of the one-handed shot. His explanation of the mechanics and his phraseology of those mechanics were exceptional. He had a great phrase, the "elbow squeeze": catch the ball, and when you're getting ready to shoot, squeeze your elbows in. It puts your shooting elbow right under the basketball.

The jump shot put basketball into the game's modern era. This occurred between 1953 and 1956. Players entered the '50s shooting the two-handed set shot, went to the one-handed shot, and then the jump shot. By the mid-'50s, the jump shot had taken over basketball and made it the exciting, fast-paced offensive game that we've enjoyed since.

Coach Bee's college coaching career ended in 1951, before there was such a thing as a jump shot. But without ever coaching it, by the time the jump shot became a part of the game, he could teach a kid how to shoot it as well as any-body I've ever seen.

Coach Bee's ability to go from being victimized by the one-hand shot to being a master teacher of it and its successor, the jump shot, was just one more illustration of his ability to observe details and break down a facet of the game to its essential steps and parts—its "fundamentals."

He watched a game on television once, and a team working against a press had its best player take the ball out of bounds. "No", he almost shouted, "get him in the middle of the press where he can make all the decisions and handle the ball." It was one illustration of his advice that I heard more than once and can still hear today: make sure your best players are in their absolute best roles. Then use your supplementary players in just that, supplementary roles—against a press, they make the in-bounds pass, or they catch the in-bounds pass, then they get it to the guy who can do the most with it.

Coach Bee was inducted into the Basketball Hall of Fame at Springfield, Massachusetts, in 1967. That was my second year as a head coach. I felt hon-ored: he asked me to take him to Springfield for the induction. I accepted, with a condition. At something like that, he had a tendency to drink too much—not often, but on occasion. I made him promise that if I drove, he wouldn't have a drink there. At the dinner, the two of us sat with Harry Litwack, Frank McGuire, Adolph Rupp, and a couple of other guys, around a table. The waiter taking drink orders came to me first, and I said, "I'll have a Coke, and so will he." Coach Bee looked at me and snarled a little bit but he didn't say anything.

After a while, the waiter came back for a second round. Same thing: "I'll have another Coke and so will he." Rupp said, "Well, god-damn, Clair, are you gonna let that boy tell you whether you can drink or not?" The Coach rose out of his chair—I thought he was going over the table after Rupp. Frank McGuire reached out with his left hand, put it on Coach Bee's shoulder, and said, "Now, now, Clair, just sit down and relax." The Coach was seventy-five at the time. He wasn't a big fan of Rupp's to begin with.

At the time, only one recipient spoke for the whole class going in. Three out-standing coaches—Howard Cann, Doggie Julian, and Slats Gill—went in with Coach Bee, who was the group's designated speaker. He did a fantastic job.

Coach Bee qualified as a lifelong inspiration for me in other significant ways, including the most significant of all—human relations.

On Thanksgiving Day 1939, his LIU football team played Catholic Uni-versity at Ebbets Field and lost, 35–14. LIU's end, Dolly King, caught a touch-down pass. That night, at Madison Square Garden, King played in LIU's season basketball opener. Coach Bee coached both games and was honored at an alumni reception in between.

Dolly was black. LIU played Marshall in basketball at Huntington, West Virginia. At the hotel where the LIU team stayed, Dolly was told he couldn't eat with the team in the hotel's dining room. Coach Bee marched his entire team into the kitchen, sat everybody down, and said, "Serve us."

There never was a thought in Clair Bee's mind about color or religion or anything like that. I've tried to follow him in that way, too.

My third coaching cornerstone was an appreciation of basketball as something never to be mastered but always, every day of every year, to be studied with an unflagging zeal for answers—and a duty to pass them on. That was brought into focus for me by playing at Ohio State for another Hall of Fame coach, Fred Taylor, and it also gave me a better understanding of some things I learned from a couple of other coaches as I was growing up.

As a basketball coach, Fred Taylor was very well organized, and he was articulate in his explanation of how to play and what he wanted done. Somebody told me once:

> *All my life, I've had six honest serving men.*
> *They taught me all I knew.*
> *Their names were What, Where, and When;*
> *How, Why, and Who.*

As a college basketball coach, Fred Taylor put every one of those "serving men" to work for him. The how and the why are so important in basketball. When I was a freshman at Ohio State, we practiced against the varsity almost every night, so I saw him work daily. That was his first year as a head coach, and obviously—having played the game himself and having coached the Ohio State freshman team under Floyd Stahl before succeeding him—he went into it with some ideas and thoughts on how to play. But after that first year, he knew that he had to make his teams better on defense to have the kind of success he wanted to have. Maybe as important as anything I ever learned from him was that a coach should never be afraid to ask questions of anyone he could learn from. That's what he did to improve his defense to the point where he raised the level of the whole Big Ten through his teams' consistent success. Other teams had to try to match him if they ever hoped to beat him or compete with him for championships.

Maybe he's the reason I have never been hesitant about asking questions or calling people, or watching somebody else to find out about techniques—in flycasting, or attacking a press, or whatever.

I was lucky in getting a chance as a very young man to learn from—and then get to know—a couple of other excellent coaches.

I played football, basketball, and baseball at various stages from junior high school through high school for a great coach, Bill Shunkwiler.

He happened to be, basically, a football coach, but he could coach anything, because he just knew how to coach. I always felt the best coaches I ran across had that ability. Whatever sport that coach had chosen as his field, he would have been outstanding in any sport because of his attention to detail and his ability to see and figure out what to do.

My high school basketball coach the first three years I played was Jack Graham, who was a very tough and demanding guy. His practices were always well organized, pushing you to improve and become the best player you could be. I understood and liked that approach. Coach Graham was passionately determined that you would be good and the team would win.

My first year out of Ohio State, I worked as an assistant coach for Harold Andreas, a great coach who was another man who could have coached anything.

And I enjoyed working for two years at Army for Tates Locke. He had been a good player at Ohio Wesleyan for Frank Shannon, another tough, demanding coach who had good teams in the Ohio Conference.

All of that—valuable things I picked up from coaches I played for or worked under, symbolized by Coach Fred Taylor—made up my third coaching cornerstone: an unyielding, untiring passion for teaching kids to understand the game of basketball and carry this understanding and sense of commitment into all walks of life.

Pete Newell was the fourth cornerstone in the construction of my philosophy of coaching.

I met Pete for the first time in December 1969 when my Army team was playing in the Cable Car Classic in San Francisco. It was the beginning of my fifth year at West Point, when, coincidentally, I probably had the best of the six teams that I coached there.

Stu Inman introduced us. Stu was in on the organization of the Portland Trail Blazers as the team's first general manager, and he had a great grasp of basketball. He was a good friend of Coach Taylor's, and he helped me and befriended me in many ways. I got him to come to West Point a couple of times and to Indiana almost every year. He was articulate, and he always had a basketball message for our kids. He'd talk with each player—about what that kid could and should do, and what he had to work on.

The three of us—Stu, Pete, and I—had lunch that day in San Francisco. After lunch I sat, kind of enthralled, with Pete in the coffee shop and we talked about basketball for five hours. We were playing California that night in the Cable Car tournament and I damned near missed the pre-game meal.

That long conversation was to be the start of one of the greatest relationships of my life.

Pete was then in his second year in the NBA as an executive with the San Diego Rockets. He had been the athletic director at Cal from 1960 through 1968—after he had retired from coaching when he was just forty-four. He coached his last game more than forty years ago, yet, to this day, he maintains a great knowledge of what's happening and how to play, a terrific understanding of the game of basketball.

I didn't learn much about recruiting from Pete. When he was the coach at California, he picked up the telephone one day and a lady told him her nephew wanted to go to school there and she was looking for housing for him. Pete told her she'd have to talk to university housing and was about to hang up when she said, "I thought you might be interested. My nephew is 6-foot-10." That's how Pete "recruited" Darrall Imhoff, who was the center on his 1959 national championship team, played on the 1960 Olympic team, and had a good career in the NBA.

Credos

Among all the things I believe, and all I've gathered from the people who have influenced me, I think one tops the list:

The importance of preparation.

We talk in coaching about "winners"—kids, and I've had a lot of them, who just will not allow themselves or their team to lose.

Coaches call that a will to win.

I don't. I think that puts the emphasis in the wrong place.

Everybody has a will to win. What's far more important is having the will to *prepare* to win.

I've said that often enough that there's a man on the Supreme Court now, Justice Clarence Thomas, who told me he saw that quote attributed to me in a newspaper or a magazine years ago, clipped it out, and carries it—to this day— in his billfold. I'm flattered, but credit for it should go to Bud Wilkinson, the great Oklahoma football coach. I grew up an Oklahoma football fan, because that's where my dad was born, and Coach Wilkinson was one of the great middle-of-the-century football coaches that I later got to talk to about coaching. Somewhere along the line I read that Wilkinson said, "The will to win is not as important as the will to prepare to win." Ralph Waldo Emerson said that next to the author of a good phrase is the first to quote it. So, though I'm sure I wasn't the first, maybe I deserve a little credit. But certainly not full.

That feeling hasn't changed for me and I'm sure never will, but a whole lot of other things have changed in basketball since I first began to coach.

Certainly, the pay is enormously better. But that's about the only change I'd consider a positive.

I hate the elements that recruiting has brought into college basketball—the know-it-alls but know-nothings who have made fortunes by feeding the national recruiting frenzy with gossip and guessing that is passed off as inside information; way out-of-control AAU (Amateur Athletic Union) summer programs; shoe-company financial involvement that attracts unqualified and sometimes undesirable people in. The worst effect of all this may be the damage done to the egos of sixteen- and seventeen-year-old kids, in way too many cases convincing them they're far better than they are.

I don't like the three-point shot and the shot clock. Those two changes take away some of the control I felt I had on the outcome of the game.

The three-point shot exclusively favors raw talent—the ability to shoot the basketball, period. I think the intent of the rule was to take the zone defense out of college basketball: by awarding three points for an outside shot over the zone.

I don't think rules should ever be made that favor the team with the most talent. And both the shot clock and the three-point shot are talent-oriented rules.

I say these new rules reduce my control of the game as a coach. It's not truly a matter of control; it's a matter of teaching a game in which intelligent play is rewarded by giving it an edge.

Playing smart, in discussing how to play basketball, is a function of percentages. Playing smart is a function of positioning, of placement, of recognition. Playing smart is a major key to winning in all sports.

We try to teach our players to play intelligently. A key to that is getting them to understand not just *that* something works but why.

Identifying what each player can do and can't do is important. I can't expect any player to do everything well.

I consider it my fault if one of my players who can't shoot the ball shoots it.

I think it's my fault if the ball is in the hands of a poor free-throw shooter at a critical time at the end of the game and he's fouled.

I think it's my fault if I don't have the right defensive match-up. Not every kid can guard every opponent.

I have to understand the strengths and the weaknesses of every player who plays for me, and make sure they understand them, too. What a player can't do is every bit as important for him to know as what he can do.

Part of my teaching process is to tell our players:

"Learn what you do well. Learn your strengths and weaknesses. You can, on occasion, improve your weaknesses. You can work to steadily improve your strengths, but there will be some inherent weaknesses that you have as a player—or as a team—that you just can't improve greatly. In your play, stay away from weaknesses like those.

"Learn your shot range, what kind of shot you can take effectively. Then, don't shoot out of your range. Take shots that have a fifty percent chance of going in, not thirty percent.

"Don't try to make passes that you can't make. Play to your strengths and away from your weaknesses, while at the same time understanding each team-mate's strengths and weaknesses. Help them to play to their strengths and away from their weaknesses. If one is a big man who doesn't handle the ball out on the floor, don't throw him the ball when he's moving toward the bucket on a break, thirty-five feet out. Give him the ball where all he has to do is catch it and lay it in. It's just as important to know the strengths and weaknesses of your teammates as it is to know your own.

"Great players maximize their talent and make everybody around them better. It's no accident that they do this. They understand the game, and they understand the strengths and weaknesses of their teammates and their opponent. That comes from thinking. There's nothing more important that a basketball player can do. *Above all else, think!*"

The worst phrase ever used in teaching kids how to play a sport is, "Don't think, just do it."

If you can't think, you can't play.

A quick way for any player to make himself better is to think about what he himself doesn't like to play against. On offense, no one likes to play against a guy who's in his jock, all over him, making it tough for him to do anything. No one likes to play against a guy who won't let him get the ball, who makes it tough for him to get a good shot.

And it's the same thing on defense—no one likes to play against a guy who is moving all the time, a guy who goes to the offensive board on every shot, a guy who makes good fakes and takes the ball hard to the bucket. "Be hard to guard" is one of the things we continually emphasize to our players on offense.

"Think about those things that you don't like to play against," we tell our players.

"Then do them yourself, at both ends of the floor."

I use the word "understand" often. I want my players to understand why teams lose: poor shot selection, bad passing, failure to block out defensively, lack of pressure on the ball. Often the reason players and coaches give for losing a game is how well the other team shot, when the actual reason is how poorly their own team played defensively in giving up so many good shots. Another extremely poor excuse for losing a game is that "we just couldn't hit anything tonight," when in actuality the team that lost didn't work hard enough to get good shots and took a lot of bad ones.

To me, concentration is basketball in a nutshell. Concentration leads to anticipation, which leads to recognition, which leads to reaction, which leads to execution.

The concentration I'm talking about involves four key words.

The first two are "look" and "see." Everybody who plays basketball looks, but very few players see. Very few players train themselves to use their eyes. Not everybody has the same shooting ability as everybody else, nor the same size, nor the same quickness. But each person who's playing this game can develop the ability to see what's happening on the court—see the open man, see where to take the ball, see the guy who's being defended, see who's open on the break.

"Hear" and "listen" are the next two words. Most people only hear. The key is listening to what you're being told, what's being said, what is expected of you in your role as part of any team.

A basketball player who learns to see and to listen has improved tremendously without doing a single thing involving physical skills. Once learned, "seeing" and "listening" are valuable traits for anyone doing anything.

We all want to win. We all talk about winning. But I'm a great believer in understanding what goes into losing, because if we know how we can lose, if we know those factors or reasons that cause us to lose, and we eliminate those things, we stand a much better chance of winning.

I don't apologize to anybody for really wanting to win or for hating to lose.

Win at any cost?

No. Absolutely not. I've never understood how anybody who cheated to get a player, or players, could take any satisfaction whatsoever out of whatever winning came afterward.

We play our game with our own additional rules—*my* rules on how I want the game played. Our defensive rules are based on each player's knowing where the ball is and trying to keep it from going where we don't want it to go. People know me as a man-to-man defensive coach. The ones who really know me are aware that Clair Bee, one of the true coaching greats I've mentioned as having influenced my thinking, was renowned for the zone defense his Long Island University teams played.

However, he used to tell me that you couldn't ever really play zone unless you could play man-to-man. That was a cardinal thing with him, and I never heard him deviate when he talked about playing defense. I had two reasons for essentially staying away from the zone for so long: I didn't think it enabled a defense to put enough pressure on the ball, and I felt it made blocking out on the defensive backboard difficult. That blockout point came up frequently when Coach Bee and I argued about the merits of a zone.

I look back over the years now and think I should have used a zone more than I did—which was maybe ten or eleven games. When we used it, we had a high percentage of success.

I think a combination of the two, within the same possession, could be very good—show zone when the opponents bring the ball downcourt, let them set up against it, then after about ten seconds, come out after them man-to-man. Then they'd have to recognize and change. It's always to your advantage if the other guys are worried more about what you're doing than what they want to do.

The truth is the standard defense we play is pretty similar to a zone on the help-side—the side of the court opposite where the ball is. I've never said that differs much from zone defense.

If kids have worked harder at anything since adoption of the three-point shot, it's shooting. And we've had to alter our help-side rules, because of the extra damage a three-point shot can do. When we're playing against a really good shooter, we don't help from him at all (drop our defender several feet off him to help jam the center area when the ball is on the side of the court away from him).

We used to want the middle as clogged as we could get it. In more recent years at Indiana, as one reaction to the new value of the outside shot, we developed a phrase, "Don't help red-on-red or white-on-white," which meant don't automatically drop back in there if a teammate—another guy wearing a red shirt like yours or a white shirt if we're at home—is already where you would be going. "Stay wider when help is already there." Simplicity and clarity in teaching are essential in getting kids to understand what you want.

The team-preparation facet of coaching boiled down for me to trying to figure out two seemingly simple and obvious things:

Number one, how to stop somebody—different things you could do on defense: switches we could make and switches we couldn't—all kinds of specially tailored tactics you could use to try to take away things that the team you were preparing for liked to do and did well.

Egos inflated by the modern recruiting process can be a plus, if they're on the opponent's team. We opened the Big Ten season against a big-name recruit in the 1980s. From the start of the game, we backed off him completely when he was outside, in jump-shot range. It clearly bothered him; we weren't showing him a star's respect. The first few times he had the ball outside, he looked around, wondering where his man was. He had a very mediocre game and I don't think he ever did hit a jump shot.

The second thing to think about in getting ready for every game was, of course, offense—how could we score on that opponent?

That's what coaching is all about. There are fundamentals that have to be adhered to and mastered in any business. Some people grasp those fundamentals, and teach them or learn them, and others don't. And those who don't are never as successful as those who do.

In coaching, it's a matter of having a sound fundamental base, both offensively and defensively.

On offense, your players don't take bad shots. They don't throw the ball away. They move without the ball. They help each other get open.

On defense, your teams don't give up easy points on conversion, on fast breaks. They don't commit bad fouls—unnecessary or dumb fouls that keep the other team on the free-throw line. Your guys never foul a guy who is in the act of taking a bad shot or a three-point shot. And they have to control the lane, and know where the ball is at all times. A good defensive player can never lose sight of the basketball, because it is the ball that has to be stopped, not a particular player.

When a shot goes up, they have to be consistently good at blocking out, because that one thing eliminates a lot of problems. There's nothing more demoralizing to a defense than playing well and forcing the opponent to take a shot that he misses, then giving up a point-blank basket because a guy who wasn't blocked out sneaked in and got the rebound. The first thing you have to do defensively as a coach is eliminate cheap points, and nothing is cheaper than that.

The intriguing part of coaching is that those fundamentals—those basic mechanics of basketball—are there for everybody. They apply to both teams, and they can be utilized by one team as well as the other. Here, concentration is the key, not athletic ability.

And many times the difference in a game is not so much the basket at the buzzer but something one of the coaches figured out that his team could do to take something away from their opponent—maybe throughout the game, maybe just at a critical time—almost invariably involving one of those simple, fundamental things at his and the other team's disposal.

Then: how do we score against them?

I always started with the two basic defenses the opponent was likely to play: a man-to-man or a zone.

Either way, as a coach you are seeking the same thing: the advantage that comes to a well-taught team. A primary goal of teaching anything is the advantage that learning gives to people over their competitors who haven't been as well taught.

As a coach in building a game plan against an opponent, there are certain things to understand. If the opponents play some form of man-to-man defense, *they* can determine who will guard our particular players, but I will determine *where* our guys are going to play, and consequently where theirs will play. That was true twenty years ago, and it is true today. In the 1981 NCAA championship game, I could put a guard like Isiah Thomas in the post if I wanted to—as I did in the second half against North Carolina—and he was outstanding. Or, I could put a center like Ray Tolbert of that 1981 team on the high post, where he could drive—as he did, frequently over his career, about as well and as effectively as any center I remember.

The key was I could determine where our players were going to have to be played by whoever was guarding them, always looking for whatever would give us an advantage.

Or, if the other team played a zone defense, the opponent could determine *where* their players were going to be—which of their players would be in each spot of the zone. But, in 2002 at Texas Tech just as in 1962 when I was coaching a high school jayvee team, I get to decide who's going to be there for them to guard. That meant playing against Minnesota in 1980, I could match 6-foot-5 Mike Woodson up against 6-foot-10 Kevin McHale. That put a player who was hard to guard in the best possible situation to drive and get shots and, maybe, get their best player into foul trouble.

I spend hours looking at tapes as preparation for a game. I've always felt that preparation is much more important than anything else you do. If you have prepared correctly, your team plays well, but you can't make adjustments once the game is played that cover up lack of preparation. Maybe you have to change something a little bit, or something doesn't go well, but you have to be able to go into a game with a very good idea of what you have to do to win this game, what you have to do to stop them, what you have to do to score against them.

That's a point I've tried to make in almost every talk I gave during my winter out of coaching. You can't go into a sales situation or a negotiation and try to run it by the seat of your pants. In any walk of life, the best-prepared person creates advantages that help him or her be the most successful.

In all of sports and pretty much in all of life, the mental is to the physical as four is to one. And one thing more almost supersedes everything else.

Enthusiasm.

Emerson said, "Nothing great is ever accomplished without enthusiasm." Norman Vincent Peale said "Enthusiasm makes the difference."

In coaching, I want to be enthusiastically critical: "Dammit, we can't *do* that." I try to teach that you can do something wrong enthusiastically and it can turn out right. You can execute something with the right technique and lose the play.

I'm constantly posting things in the locker room. One was:

> *Enthusiasm.*
> *That certain something that pulls us out of the mediocre and commonplace, and fills us with power.*
> *If we have it, we should thank God for it.*
> *If we don't have it, we should get down on our knees and pray for it.*

In the part of game preparation time that I devote to studying tapes of the upcoming opponent, what I'm looking for isn't very original: I want to see what they have and what they do. As I'm watching, I'm deciding: what can we stop and how can we stop it? I just want an overall picture. Or: They're counting on three or four things to score. What can we do to disrupt those things?

In planning our offensive approach, I'm thinking: What are they doing on defense? If they're playing a zone, which side is weaker in the one they play? If they press, where can we put our people to make it difficult for them?

If they're a man-to-man team, what do we have to do? If it's a sloughing man-to-man, we've got to get shooters in position to be shooting from seventeen feet. If it's a pressuring man-to-man, we've got to take the ball to the bucket—*catch the ball, face, fake, and drive!* Do that, do it well, and you'll be on the foul line. Almost invariably.

Kids have to understand that *you*—you, the coach—aren't going to be satisfied with just winning. Play can be sloppy, things can be poorly executed in games you win, but before you can be good and beat better teams, that kind of play has to be straightened out and eliminated. Kids will be satisfied with what you tolerate. If a coach tolerates mistakes, kids will be satisfied with mistakes. Steve Risley, who played for us at Indiana from 1978 to '81, once said of me in an interview, "He's after the perfect game. Maybe he'll coach forever and not get it." I thought, that's probably true. There have been times I was more upset after we won than when we lost.

The most essential thing in a team's being ready for a game is that the coach is ready—that the coach understands the importance of keeping everything on an even keel. Kids react in very, very funny ways to things that are said. From just the inflection in the coach's voice, they can pick up, "This game isn't very important," or "This game is important."

You don't want to—you've got to be careful *not* to—convey either of those messages. You have to be sure your kids know that to you every game is important, and they have to play hard and well game-by-game. You work at doing that with every kid and every team.

I was lucky enough to coach one of the best groups college basketball ever saw in that matter of reaching and maintaining a steady, even approach to games throughout a season. In the 1974–75 and 1975–76 seasons, we did several things that no college team has been able to do since then—two straight unbeaten regular seasons (including the only 18–0 Big Ten records in the league's history), losing just one game in two straight seasons, and—in 1975–76—going unbeaten all the way through to the national championship.

Even that smooth a ride, even that consistent a team, had some relative highs and lows, for an unusual reason. The kids on those teams knew what I wanted from them and genuinely tried to give it to me, but they were smart and they were human. They understood just how well they had to play to win each game, the tip-off for me being that they almost always played better on the road than they did at home. At home, they sometimes let human nature creep in—"these guys can't beat us here." But on the road, they were tough, always tough; they fed on the noise of those road crowds—always a sellout, always fired up to a season peak. The worst play we had, basically, came at home.

Still those teams were the best I've ever seen at leveling out the peaks and valleys to a consistent, high plane. Human nature did slip in when they were playing at home and almost got us beat a couple of times. *Just* a couple of times, though—in two full years.

If you're a pretty good team, you're going to play some teams that aren't nearly as good as you are. When that happened, I tried to be honest. I'd tell my players: "Hey, unless you guys just decide to go out and do nothing, there's no way we should lose this game. This is a game that's going to be determined by your attitude." It's something you as a coach have to stay with all the time.

You can't make every game out like it's the national championship game. But over the course of a season you've got to develop a sense of pride in performance. Winning just isn't enough. You win on Wednesday playing sloppily against a mediocre team and you go out on Saturday and play the same way against a good team and you get your ass beat.

Winning is the last of all criteria that I think you should use to determine how well you're playing. When the way you've won a game just isn't good enough, you show your players why: you talk about turnovers, missed block-outs, fast-break points allowed, fouls committed—to show your team, "We just didn't play well."

I do that, and then I point out some games that we still have left to play where we can't play poorly and win. You're trying to get players to understand that how they play is a hell of a lot more important than whether or not they win.

I've been criticized for that approach. We'd be ahead late in a game, sure of winning, and I'd let a player know—as I can—when he let his concentration drift or he made a slipshod play. I'm sure people would go out of the arena saying: "God, what was he so upset about? We won."

I don't subscribe to that line of thinking. My job is to get us to play as well as we can as often as we can. More than anything else, that's what I have to do, and it will have a direct carry-over to whatever each kid winds up doing in life.

It can be harder when your team has been playing well than when it hasn't. When we've won a game where we have played well—maybe a game we weren't expected to win, or a big game between two top teams—I've always said: "Okay, this was a hell of a win. You guys did a great job. But, if we turn around and get beat, then we lose what we've won here." I use the word protect: "We have to protect this win with the next game we play."

I always try to get players who have just played well thinking "next game." The phrase I use is "Last Game, Next Game." You can't stay with big wins. You can't be thinking of the last game when the next game is coming up.

During the 2000 college football season, Minnesota was going along pretty well, and Indiana wasn't having a very good year. The week before playing at Indiana, Minnesota won a big game over Ohio State.

The morning of the Minnesota–Indiana game, I told Sid Hartman, a great friend of mine who has been a sports columnist at the Minneapolis *Tribune* forever, that Minnesota was going to lose. Sid just laughed and said, "No way."

Indiana won the game.

Give the Indiana kids and their coach, Cam Cameron, all the credit in the world—especially their quarterback, Antwaan Randle El, an enthusiastic, competitive kid who, like Cameron, played some basketball for me in addition to his football. That day against Minnesota, Randle El did something nobody else in Big Ten football history has ever done: he gained two hundred yards passing and two hundred running in the same game. But I still strongly suspect that another factor in Indiana's winning was that Minnesota had waited too long to forget about beating Ohio State.

Ironically, the same kind of thing had happened in another Minnesota–Indiana game, in 1977. Michigan was number one in the country when Minnesota shut them out, 16-0—the first shutout for Michigan in ten years. The Monday after that game, I ran into Lee Corso, the Indiana football coach, and he said: "What a hell of a note that is. Now we play Minnesota." I really liked Lee—I enjoyed him then and I still do. We didn't go about things in the same way, which happens a lot in coaching, but he brought a real enthusiasm to his job and genuinely liked coaching.

That day, though, I think I shocked him. My response to his "hell of a note" fretting was: "Hey, if you can't beat them *this* week, you can't coach. They'll come in here still thinking about having beaten Michigan. They won't even be thinking about you till the kickoff. You'll beat them three touchdowns." That

Saturday, Indiana won the game, and if Minnesota hadn't put across a meaningless touchdown in the last two minutes, my three-touchdown comment would have been right on the button. As it was, Indiana won 34–22.

As with Cameron twenty-three years later, I'm not taking anything away from the coaching achievement. Corso is a very bright, imaginative guy, and that's evident when you see him on TV today.

Failure to forget about a past victory certainly isn't the only thing that can beat you. It isn't even the number one thing. In any close game that we've lost, I've always felt—and emphasized to my team—that mistakes we made beat us, more than good things the other team did. When I was a kid, Ash Hall, an outstanding Ohio high school coach at Rittman near my home town of Orrville, told me, "Basketball is not a game of great plays and great shooting, it's a game of mistakes and errors. If you ever see a state championship game, you'll see errors and mistakes made, and the team that makes the most of them will be the team that gets beat, almost without exception." At that point in my life, a state championship game meant basketball being played by the very best teams. But I've watched every level of basketball there is and Ash's point is absolutely right. It's a game of not making mistakes. The more you cut down on mistakes, the better your chance of winning is—in basketball or in any other sport, and in just about anything in life.

Sometimes you play awfully well and you still lose. My evaluation of what is good play and good effort in a losing game maybe isn't quite so lenient as the average person's, but it happens. Then I could tell our players, "Okay, we got beat today, by probably a better team than we are. But, if you had played with this efficiency and execution, it sure as hell would have been good enough to win a lot of games before this. We can beat an awful lot of teams coming up if we stay at this level and continue to improve."

In all the years I've coached, I've never worked in preparation for an opponent until it is the next team we play. I do always have an assistant coach assigned to work ahead, so when we're done playing Team A, I can immediately switch to planning for Team B—and the assistant assigned to that game will already have prepared the tapes he knows I'll want to study. I never talk to the players about upcoming games beyond the one we're playing.

What I would occasionally do, heading into a weekend when we were going to play two games, was say, "All right, we have eighty minutes of basketball to play this week. This is an eighty-minute game divided into four twenty-minute periods." If we came in at the half of the first game and we had played pretty well, I would say, "That's the kind of play that will sustain us through all four of these periods."

I would do that so that when we won the first game, there was no real celebration. Now they'd know: "We still have forty minutes to play." I always tried to do things like that, particularly in a Christmas tournament or the NCAA tournament. I would never start with the players, though, on the next game with personnel or strength of the team until the previous game had been completed. Now, what I have done on occasion when the score was decidedly in our favor was go to the starting players already out of the game and say: "Okay, let's start thinking about who we're going to play next. You're going to guard so-and-so . . ." right on down the line. So while they're watching their teammates finish up this game, the players who are going to start the next game are already thinking about it. At least I've put that in their minds.

It's hard to get through to a kid who has played well in a big game that he and his team have just won. Kids like to think about plays they made: I stopped this guy, I blocked that shot, or I took the ball to the bucket. As long as the game has been played, that's the way kids have reacted to playing well. They all want to sit around and pat themselves on the back, or let somebody else do it. They walk across campus and everyone tells them how well they played. At Indiana, that was always something that I felt we had to fight, because the whole campus, the whole state, watched every game and cared deeply about how our team did.

We opened the 1998–99 season by beating Seton Hall and South Carolina, two teams that were pretty good but not great. Our people had us in the NCAA finals—after two games. The expectations at Indiana, Kentucky, Duke, or North Carolina are usually so high they're ludicrous.

I have never allowed myself to dwell on games we won. I've always felt winning is what you're supposed to do. Winning is a by-product of preparation and work at practice, all the things leading up to a game. I get away from games that we won and into the next game right away, and I'll do it as long as I coach—for myself as well as the players. I think it's important for the guy who's running the operation to be able to do that. I was so conscious of getting on to the next game that over the years I'm sure I didn't publicly give kids as much credit as I should have for games they won. I shortchanged kids in that regard. And if we got beat, I might bleed that to death in going to the next game. I always felt we had to learn something out of the game. It can't just be a total loss.

• • •

I think when you coach, and you like the game of basketball, you develop an appreciation for how it's played—not just by your own team but also by opposing teams and certainly by players.

I always try to let coaches know when I think they have done a good job with their team, or that their team was difficult to play against, or that their team has played well against us.

I did the same thing many times with individual players from teams we played. The last time we played against kids (usually from Big Ten schools) who were seniors I thought had showed a great competitive spirit and attitude over the years, I liked to tell them how I felt about them. I'd say something very quick to a kid like that just as pre-game warm-ups were ending or after the game.

I particularly liked to do that on his team's home floor, so that school's fans could know a player was appreciated by someone other than his own people. I did that to players like Kevin McHale, Greg Kelser, Danny Jones, Jerry Sichting . . . the number has to be in the dozens.

The school the kid played for didn't matter. Sichting, for example, was from Purdue. You're bound to make some mistakes in recruiting, and Jerry Sichting was one I made. He was from Martinsville, about twenty miles from Bloomington, and he wanted to come to Indiana. I liked him, too—he was a tough, hard-nosed kid who did everything I want players to do. But we recruited other kids that year, and it was a major recruiting mistake.

Danny Jones was the opposite case. We recruited him hard, but he chose to go to Wisconsin instead. I ended up feeling very bad for him, because I thought with us he would have wound up being a high NBA draft choice. He never got that chance. I should have recruited him better.

My approach to recruiting is a little different from the norm. I know what kind of kid I want. I know what kind we need to have teams that perform and produce at the level I expect. Through recruiting, even some times when we didn't end up taking or getting the player, I've met some great parents, some terrific high school coaches, and a lot of great, great kids.

And I've met some I didn't care for all that much.

The former greatly outnumber the latter.

I said once that recruiting Steve Alford cost us about forty-seven cents. He had always wanted to go to Indiana, and we mailed him a scholarship form.

It was similar when we recruited Randy Wittman. Randy attended our summer camp as a seventh-grader, and during the camp, my assistant coach Bob Donewald told me we had a kid who looked like someday he would be an outstanding player. He told me the name, and I said, "Bring him over." He did, and here's how he and I conversed:

"You're Randy Wittman?"

"Yes, sir."

"When you get old enough if you're good enough, are you coming to Indiana?"

"Yes, sir."

Four years later, when he was going into his senior year of high school, I visited his home. His mom, dad, and sister were there. After saying hello, I said to Randy:

"Do you remember when you were at camp and I asked you if you were coming to Indiana if you were good enough?"

"I sure do."

"Do you remember what you told me?"

"Yes I do."

"Have you changed your mind?"

"No, sir."

"Okay, I'll see you."

And I got up and walked out. I thought his mother was going to have a heart attack. But not only did he turn out to be a great player, his mom and dad, Shirley and Bob Wittman, became two of our greatest parents, too.

Alan Henderson's mom, Annette, asked me one time: "If you had five Alan Hendersons, what could you do?"

"Win the national championship," I said, "if we could teach one of them to dribble."

She got to worrying once about Alan hurting his NBA chances by being branded a center. I said, "Don't you worry about that. He's a forward."

So we introduced him as a forward and played him at center.

A lot, anyway.

She was pleased. And he was a first-round draft pick. Annette and her cardiologist husband Ray are high on our great-parents list, too.

If I make a home visit, I'm serious about recruiting the kid. I've been convinced by my own observations, by what I've seen on tapes, or by strong recommendations from my assistant coaches that this player is good enough to play for us. The home visit theoretically is designed for the coach to sell himself and his program. That works two ways. I want to do some observing, too. I want to be sold.

Not many years ago I was in the home of a top-rated recruit. I had been there just a few minutes when I heard him talk to his mother in a way I couldn't tolerate. As of right then, that night and that moment, Indiana was no longer recruiting the kid, though he wound up playing in our league and doing some things pretty well. On the basketball court, he also wound up showing the character that had come through that night. It always does.

Joe Falls of the *Detroit News* came down to Bloomington in January 1994 to cover our game with Michigan, and he sat down with me the night before the game. He wrote in his newspaper what I said to him that night:

> *I like our system. I like the way we do things. We're always looking for new ways to be better. I'm forever drawing up diagrams. Every day, every practice. We try everything. Some of my ideas are pretty good, but some are pretty bad. I tried a couple the other day and they were awful. But when they work in a game, when you see the players execute what we've been working on—there is no finer feeling in the world.*
>
> *Our team is like a ball of putty. It is always changing form. We might look one way for Iowa, then we roll the putty around and look a little different for Michigan. After Michigan, we'll work it around again and have still another look for Purdue. When you get right down to it, that's the joy of this game.*
>
> *The hardest part of my job is waiting to play—the final preparation. Once the game starts, I'm fine. No problems, even when things aren't going right. It's the time leading up to the games that gets me. This part is getting harder and harder. I can't wait until the games start.*
>
> *I know what my problem is. The difference between winning and losing is so great for me—such a tremendous emotional difference—that it really works at me just before we play.*

Joe followed what I had to say with an observation of his own that was as nice a compliment to our Indiana program as anything I ever read in a newspaper:

> *Knight is the king of all he surveys. And what he surveys—what he is the absolute ruler of—is the finest basketball program in the land. The Dukes come and go. North Carolina is always a threat. Michigan has its moments. Keep an eye on Kentucky. But year in, year out, this is the place they respect, the place they envy, for it is here that success is defined in ways that no one else has been able to match for nearly a quarter of a century.*

That was 1994. That would have been the perfect time for me to leave.

THREE: *Early Life in Orrville (1940–1954)*

*Even then I had a little problem with people not quite
understanding things I said.*

As proud as I was of the no-frills, no-names uniforms my teams at Indiana wore for all those years, I may have been even prouder of another uniform. You should have seen the Mizer Tykes.

I grew up in Orrville, in northeastern Ohio. It was an active sports community, but we didn't have organized, uniformed sports teams in fifth and sixth grade, never mind third and fourth as they do in Indiana. So, the first organized thing I ever did in sports was play baseball, when I was nine years old. Frank Mizer, who operated a beauty parlor along with his wife, loved baseball and did a lot of good things for kids. When I was growing up, Orrville had only one diamond and they later named it for him, which shows the impact he had on the entire community.

Frank had major league aspirations for his son, Ronnie, who was a year younger than I was.

Because of Ronnie, he formed a youth baseball team in Orrville, and I benefited. All I'd ever done until then was play flies-and-grounders in the street and pick-up games on the playground. Now, here I was, nine years old, with a real team, a schedule, and a uniform that I can't begin to describe how thrilled I was to put on. It carried that great name: Mizer Tykes.

I was always pretty tall, so I played first base. We played other youth teams from around Orrville—Rittman, Wadsworth, Wooster—and eventually there was a second team in town.

I heard my first hassling from the stands when I was the Tykes' first baseman. At Rittman, I told Ronnie Mizer to throw the ball over to me the first time they got a man on base. This wasn't true Little League; in our league a base runner could lead off. They got a man on, Ronnie threw over, I slapped at his foot with a hard tag, and of course he was safe. But I hit the base hard enough that it was knocked out of line a little. I was already leaned over, and I told the kid, "Lift your foot so I can straighten out this bag." He did, I slapped the ball on him, the umpire said, "You're out"—and the kid's grandmother, who had sat there in the stands and watched all that happen, called me names I hadn't heard up until then.

She *really* got mad when we did it to the same kid again later in the game.

By the time I was eleven, we played in an official Little League: our Orrville team and five teams from Wooster (ten miles away). Our team's sponsor was a group of Orrville merchants, and we each wore uniforms with different names on them—not our own names, and no numbers, just the name of one of those sponsoring merchants. I was Johnson Hardware. We won the league, and I played on an all-star team that went to Canton and played in the Little League eliminations. We got beat in the first game, 6–4.

After that year, Orrville dropped Little League and our team moved into the Hot Stove League. When I was thirteen, we beat a team from Elyria to win the state championship. The next year, we played Elyria on their field. I hit a home run and a triple, but the last time up in the game was one of the most memorable at-bats of my life.

I took three straight outside pitches, so I was ahead in the count, 3 and 0. Right there, they changed pitchers. Against the new guy, I stood with the bat on my shoulder while three strikes went right past me. I can remember it to this day—I walked back to the dugout in disbelief. I didn't even make a move to swing, I just stood and watched, and, boy, that wasn't me. I was up there to swing, always. That sure wasn't the best but it's the most remembered at-bat I ever had. I'll never understand how a kid who liked to swing as much as I did stood there and took three straight strikes. I learned right there that it's much better to make things happen than wait for things to happen.

Orrville was then a town of six thousand, about twenty-five miles from Akron and fifty miles from Cleveland. It was a terrific place to be a kid. It had all the qualities Norman Rockwell used to build into his *Saturday Evening Post* covers—the barber shop characters, the family doctors—he could have set himself up in Orrville and found people representative of whatever point he wanted to make. The town's commitment was to its kids, to giving them a great start in life. The community's pride was its school system. Another was Orr Park, a big recreation area with the town's baseball and softball diamonds and the best swimming pool in the whole county—again, primarily for the town's kids. Running across the back of our lot was a railroad, and on the other side of the railroad was the town's greatest identification: the Smucker's preserves plant. I didn't know any Orrs in Orrville, but I did know several Smuckers. The plant was a good neighbor; we weren't overwhelmed with sickeningly sweet smells or anything like that. And I think most people in town were like me, genuinely proud that the whole country was familiar with something that was Orrville's. There was a neat humor to their TV sales line: "With a name like Smucker's it *has* to be good." It always gave me a kick when I'd be in New York or some place a long way from Orrville and, at breakfast in a hotel or restaurant, the little jelly containers that they'd serve would be Smucker's, with mention, always, of its point of origin: Orrville, Ohio.

My mom was a schoolteacher and my dad was a railroad man. They had been married in 1934 in her parents' backyard in Akron, and they never owned a home until they built one in 1956. It had two bedrooms: one for my mom and dad and one for my grandmother. I slept on a pullout couch, all the way through high school.

My father was born in Oklahoma, and his jobs with railroads brought him to Orrville. Railroaders are conscientious people, none more so than my dad. I saw that as a boy. On too many rainy, cold, or snowy nights to count, I walked through the railroad yard with him, me holding a lantern so he could check the seals on boxcars to make sure none had been broken into. "If you're going to accept pay for something, do it right," he said. When a player I've had says he learned a work ethic by playing for me, I'm thrilled, because I know it's not really a reflection on me but on the man who instilled it in me: my dad. He bought only two cars, a 1951 Ford Victoria and a 1961 Nash Rambler, and he paid for both with cash. That was another of his maxims: "If you can't pay for it, do without until you can." The only time he ever owed anybody a cent was when—after twenty-two years of marriage—he and my mom paid $1,500 for a lot and $22,000 to build a home on it. Dad took out a twenty-year mortgage on the house, gave up everything he liked to do, and had that mortgage paid off in just over four years. He's the most honest man I've ever known.

I've made a lot of money over the years, and I've always thought of it in comparison with what my dad made and how hard he worked for it. I never in my life thought things were more out of whack than the first time I was paid $8,000 for making a speech. The thought went through my mind: Dad never made more than that in a year.

My first experience with fishing came when I was in grade school, fishing with my dad for bullheads on Sugar Creek near Orrville.

We took a couple of cane poles with line tied around the end and a can of worms we had dug up in a pasture field across the street from our house.

It wasn't very sophisticated fishing, but we had a lot of fun together doing it.

Years later, when fishing with one or both of my own boys, I always thought back to those cane poles and that can of worms with my dad.

My dad and I eventually graduated to casting rods and lures. I never saw him more excited than he was when he caught a four-pound smallmouth bass on a trip we took to Canada.

The last happy memory I have of being with him was a visit we made to a lake—still with those old cane poles. I can see him yet baiting his hook, and catching bluegill, and every time the bobber went down and he pulled up another fish, Dad smiling like it was the first he'd ever caught.

My dad had two great passions other than his family and his job: one was playing golf and the other was walking. They went hand-in-hand, because I'm not sure I ever saw him in a golf cart.

He thoroughly enjoyed playing golf and would always tell me about two pars in a row he had made, or the rare occasion when he made a birdie, which was the same thing for him as winning a big game always was for me. My dad was about six feet tall and weighed 200 pounds, with very little flexibility in his upper body, so golf was not an easy game for him to play.

He got every bit as much fun out of looking for lost golf balls as he did playing the game. The first thing he'd do when he came home after a round of golf was pull a ball out of his pocket and show me a new Sweet Shot or Kro-Flite or some other premier ball he had found.

When I'd go with him to play, I'd always make him promise that we'd just play golf—no wandering off to hunt for golf balls. He'd promise he wouldn't do that, and he wouldn't—until the second hole, when he would hit his drive, then walk straight off the tee into a cornfield, looking for sliced drives.

He taught me a lot of things about life, most of them the best way—by example. But there's nothing I'm more grateful for than the time he took to introduce me to fishing. That was very much in my mind when I first taught my son, Tim, to fish, then his younger brother, Pat.

My sons and my wife, Karen, all learned to fly-fish with me. Karen says the thrill of fishing is not catching the fish but the serenity and beauty of a stream and its surroundings. I know what she's saying, but I'm not going to short-change catching the fish. I remember on my trip to Russia with Ted Williams, he caught a good-sized Atlantic salmon, and as I was getting it out of the water for him, I yelled, "Hey—would you rather catch a big salmon like this or hit it in the seats with two on?" He laughed and said, "Well, you know how much I like fishing, but I think I'd take hitting it in the seats." The fact that he even thought about the comparison says a lot for the thrill of catching a fish.

On family trips, though, that is only part of the fun. I haven't found anything in life that offers families the pure joy that comes with planning, then taking a fishing trip together—the time, the precious hours, spent together as a family.

We make those trips now with the latest and very best equipment, but I never step into a stream without thinking of those old cane poles my dad and I used. I couldn't be more pleased than if, as time passes, my own boys have the same kind of memories of good times fishing with me.

Karen's right, though: one of the great appeals of fishing is that it's nice just to be outdoors, usually in weather that is pleasant, sunny and warm—sometimes lousy, but usually nice.

I like hooking a fish, fighting a fish, trying to read where the fish is going to be, and catching a fish . . . the thrill of feeling the fish on the hook, landing it, and then, after the battle, releasing the fish and letting it go back into the stream.

I also like to hunt birds, because the bird flies and darts, and there's real skill involved in bringing one down. I just wish you didn't kill the bird—that you could down it and release it as you do with a fish. I don't enjoy killing anything.

It's been a long, long time—since I was a kid—since I ever shot a rabbit or a squirrel or a ground animal. Some guys, when they're bird-hunting, will shoot a rabbit just to be shooting. I've never done that.

As a kid growing up, I was undoubtedly influenced more by my mother than by anybody else. She was a schoolteacher with very strong convictions that I would go to college, but she didn't try to influence what I should major in or what I should be preparing myself to do. She was a very bright person, well-read; she followed current events around the country and the world with great interest.

She was also my second-grade teacher. I don't recommend that for any kid. But she was a great teacher. She was always concerned that I paid at least as much attention to what I was studying as what I was playing. She supported my involvement in sports, right through my coaching, and after my dad passed away, she made a lot of trips to see us play at Indiana. That can't have been more of a thrill for her than it was for me.

Two women I went to high school with told me about the time my mom was sitting at a lunch counter in the supermarket in Orrville where she always shopped, and the two of them came up and sat down with her. One of them said, "Hazel, Indiana and Kentucky are on TV Saturday. Aren't you excited?"

Her only comment:

"I just hope he behaves."

My mother and my grandmother loved to go to Akron and shop on Saturdays. I had to go with them, and I always dreaded it. O'Neil's and Polsky's were the two department stores in downtown Akron, on Main Street right across from each other. They'd drag me through every department at O'Neil's and then across the street to Polsky's, instead of just letting me stay home.

Another department store, Yeager's, was about five blocks away, and if my mother and grandmother had time, they'd also drag me down there. Television saved me. My mom discovered she could leave me in front of a TV set in O'Neil's appliance department—say, on a fall Saturday—and come back three hours later and I'd still be sitting there watching Red Sitko and Leon Hart and Notre Dame play football. The next great discovery I made at O'Neil's was Chip Hilton books written by an author named Clair Bee. My mom, as a teacher, was a stickler for getting me to read. I read before I ever played anything. Of all the great things my mom did for me, nothing was better than making me be a reader. The library in Orrville ran a winter-long book-reading contest, for different age groups. The top ten in my group—always—were nine girls and I.

At the library, I read John R. Tunis, the Jack Armstrong books, the whole Hardy Boys series, and biographies of great Americans. I can still see those biographies, in orange binding—George Washington, Thomas Jefferson, Benjamin Franklin. However many the library had, I read 'em all. I bought all the Chip Hilton books. I had about fifteen by the time I was in high school. Twenty-three were published, and I have them all now, plus the manuscript of one that was never published. In 1999, Cindy and Randy Farley, Bee's daughter and son-in-law, arranged for the entire series of Chip Hilton books to be updated and reprinted. One of the greatest honors I've ever had was being invited to write the introduction to several of them. As a youngster reading and enjoying those books, I could never have imagined something like that— nor that the author of those books and I would become about as close as father and son.

I didn't know when I was a boy that Clair Bee was a famous basketball coach. The jacket probably said he was the coach at Long Island University—it may have said he was one of the greatest and most innovative and influential coaches in the history of the game, because he was.

But none of that would have meant anything to me then. All I knew was that he created Chip Hilton, Biggie Cohen, Soapy Smith, and Taps Browning, and a coach, Henry Rockwell, who was brilliant, tough, and almost never lost.

Coach Bee told me later that he patterned Chip Hilton after Bobby Davies, a real-life blond-haired kid who was an All-American player at Seton Hall and one of the all-time great players for the Rochester Royals in the NBA. When I was at Army, I got to know Davies as a Converse shoe representative. He's in the Hall of Fame, but as good a player as he was, he was a better person.

I always thought it was interesting that in real life he played against, not for, Coach Bee. He watched him as a rival player and through him envisioned Chip Hilton.

After I got to know Coach Bee, we talked about his books and his characters. I couldn't resist kidding him.

"Who'd you pattern Coach Rockwell after?"

He'd say, "God-*dammit*, God-*dammit*, who do you *think* I patterned him after? I patterned him after *me!*"

I said, "Ohhh, Coach, he's too mild-mannered for you."

Or, "Coach . . . Rockwell *never* made a mistake."

He once got a letter from a Harvard graduate student:

> *Dear Mr. Bee:*
> *When I was in the seventh grade, Chip Hilton was a senior at Valley High School.*
> *I'm about to complete my doctoral thesis at Harvard, and Chip Hilton is still a senior at Valley High School.*
> *What's wrong with Chip Hilton?*

The books cost $1.25 each. My mother would give me enough money to buy a book and it would take me two hours to decide which one I wanted.

One day I bought my book at O'Neil's and we all went on to Polsky's. Mom and I got separated, but I didn't care. I was too excited about my new book to wait until I got home to read it. I found a chair behind stacks of slacks back in a corner, opened my book, and started reading, all wrapped up with Chip.

All of a sudden, I looked up from my book and my Mom was in front of me—livid, madder than I'd ever seen her. She had looked for me and couldn't find me. She thought I was lost, and when they announced my name on the store loudspeaker system, and I didn't show up, she got more and more panicky.

Until she found me.

I hadn't heard a thing. Chip Hilton was beating the hell out of someone and I was totally oblivious to everything else. As irritated as she looked, I was kind of pleased that she'd liked me well enough to keep looking for me.

But I mean she was *mad*.

My lifelong status as a hero-worshiper started in those days. I had a lot of heroes, and most played for the baseball Indians or the football Browns.

The summer of 1948, before I turned eight, there weren't many TV sets in Orrville and we didn't have one. The appliance stores as a sales gimmick would have a TV set going in their front window, so you could see it from the sidewalk. That's how I first watched baseball games.

And what a perfect year it was to be rooting for the Indians. They beat the Braves, four games to two, in the '48 World Series.

My favorite Indian was Joe Gordon, who hit thirty-two home runs that year. I had a hard time understanding how a guy named Joe Gordon had also played for the Yankees. Trades were beyond my comprehension then. I figured the guy who had played for the Yankees must have been another guy named Joe Gordon.

I can still name Cleveland's starting lineup: Jim Hegan catching, Eddie Robinson at first base, Joe Gordon at second base, Lou Boudreau at shortstop, Kenny Keltner at third base, Dale Mitchell in left field, Larry Doby in center field, and different guys in right field—Bob Kennedy, Allie Clark, Walt Judnich, and Thurman Tucker. The pitching rotation was Bob Feller, Bob Lemon, Gene Bearden, and Steve Gromek. Satchel Paige, who was supposed to be forty-two and may have been lots older after a long and great history in the old Negro League, came on as a "rookie" in the middle of the year and went 6–1. They also had Sam Zoldak.

Boudreau was the playing manager. That was the first team I became interested in, and I lived and died with them for the next seven years.

Maybe partly through me, my mom also became a big fan of the Indians. We listened to them every day on the radio; Jimmy Dudley is still among my favorite baseball announcers, with Marty Brennaman, Jack Buck, and Curt Gowdy.

For seven or eight years, as soon as the American League schedule came out in the winter, we'd pick out games we could go to—my parents, me, and two friends of theirs, Stanley and Rita Marquard. We always saw the Yankees, the Red Sox, the Tigers, and on occasion some other teams.

I mentioned seeing Ted Williams hit some home runs against the Indians.

That was on those trips with my parents and the Marquards, when I was a kid. In 1960, when I was in college, on a weekend I went to Lakefront Stadium for his last game there. Cleveland was ahead 5–2 in the top of the ninth. He pinch-hit with the bases loaded, and they walked him on four pitches.

That may be the greatest gesture of respect I've ever seen.

The Marquards didn't have any children, so they kind of attached themselves to me. Stanley took me fishing with him—sucker-fishing in creeks. She was a schoolteacher like my mother, and he had been a student at Michigan when Tom Harmon and Forest Evashevski played football there. The five of us went up to Ann Arbor three years in a row, 1950–52, to see Michigan play football. The first Big Ten football games I ever saw were Michigan against Minnesota, Northwestern, and Michigan State.

It was a big thrill going into that stadium. I knew I was going only once each year so I especially looked forward to it. The Minnesota game in 1951 was two days after my eleventh birthday, and Paul Giel was a great star for Minnesota; I was excited as we were driving up. Then my mom and Mrs. Marquard had to stop to go to the bathroom, and we missed the first two and a half minutes of the game. The score was 14–7 when we got to our seats; I couldn't believe we had missed three touchdowns. and I wasn't very happy about it. But the game ended up 54–27, so I did see a lot.

The coach who had the most influence on me when I was a boy had my name. Dave Knight wasn't a relative, but he took me under his wing.

He was with the Army Corps of Engineers in World War II. He landed on New Guinea on his nineteenth birthday. After the war, he played football at Wooster College. He came to Orrville to teach and coach when I was in the sixth grade.

He must have been about thirty and I was about twelve, so he seemed old to me. He played basketball in a Church League in West Salem, and he'd take me to those games. Sometimes I'd play if they needed another player; sometimes I'd keep score; sometimes I'd referee. Thinking back, I'm not sure I wasn't a better referee as a twelve-year-old than several I ran into later on.

I baby-sat for Dave's kids, who were a lot younger than I was. His home had a double garage with a concrete square in front of it, and he put up a basket—for his boys, he told his wife Ruth, but it was for him and me. We used to have great games there on Saturday and Sunday afternoons.

As a sixth-grader, I was probably 5-foot-10 and Dave brought me over to practice a season with his seventh- and eighth-graders. My first basketball lesson came from an eighth-grader named Bob Shonk, who became an outstanding high school and college athlete. My first night, I was guarding him and I lined up wrong on defense. He put his hand on my shoulder, placed me in front of him, and told me, "On defense, you always have to be between your man and the basket." It was valuable instruction that I appreciated, even though several years later as a coach I altered the whole principle slightly, to keep the defensive man between his man and the ball.

After that season I had my own two years of junior high basketball under coach Bill Shunkwiler. Those years were the only organized basketball I had before high school. Ohio wasn't Indiana, where basketball is concerned. In Indiana there are goals and courts everywhere. When I was growing up, there wasn't one blacktop court in Orrville, not on a playground or anywhere. There was one outdoor court at the high school—the buckets were about twelve feet high. And there was a goal on the playground at the grade school where my mom taught. That one had no nets, just a wooden backboard, a goal, and a gravel court that was dusty, dirty, and painful. The ball got all gouged-up—they didn't make a ball with a coating tough enough to survive on gravel. Kids, either. I got skinned and bruised more playing basketball on gravel than I ever did sliding in baseball or playing football. One of my buddies, Ronnie Birkbeck, had a backboard in his garage driveway. I learned to shoot and play Horse there. Those were the days when I first fell in love with the game.

In high school, I became a big fan of Kentucky's basketball team, because of their radio broadcasts. I remember to this day George Walsh coming on: "Good *evening*, ladies and gentlemen, welcome to *Kentucky Wildcat* basketball, brought to you by *Citizens Fidelity*, the bank and trust of all Kentucky, and your nearby *Sinclair* dealer."

Saturday afternoons in the '50s and early '60s, Midwestern states used to get a Big Ten basketball *Game of the Week* on TV. My freshman year in high school, I was in the home of my best buddy, Norman Douglas, watching Ohio State play Minnesota. Dick Garmaker and Chuck Mencel were the big stars for Minnesota, and the center was Bill Simonovich.

Something exciting happened on-screen and I shouted to Norman, "Boy, is that Simonovich big!"

Mrs. Douglas came running out of the kitchen and said, *"Bobby Knight, what did you just say?"* Even then I had a little problem with people not quite understanding things I said.

Heroes

A continuing kick for me in later life was one more thing that basketball has given me: the opportunity to get to know some of those players I had watched as a boy. Paul Giel was one of them. I got to know him and liked him when he was athletic director at Minnesota.

Maybe the greatest of all, in that sense, were Lou Boudreau and Otto Graham. Four or five times at Chicago Cubs games in the '70s and '80s I sat in the radio booth with Lou, when he and Vince Lloyd were the announcers. He had been a great basketball player at Illinois; we would talk about basketball and Vince would try to do the baseball game around our talking. Because as a kid I had idolized him as the Indians' player-manager, getting to know him was just a treat for me. Some of those boyhood feelings came back for me when he died at the age of eighty-four in the summer of 2000.

As a big Browns fan, I considered Otto Graham a special hero. He was one for just about everybody in northern Ohio at that time—more than idolized, he was revered, the biggest Browns star of that whole era. Later as athletic director at the Coast Guard Academy, he invited me to speak once at their year-ending athletic banquet. He couldn't have had any idea of how big a thrill I got out of that, because of the way I had felt about him as a boy. I also developed a friendship with Dante Lavelli, who was a great receiver on those early Browns teams and became a big fan of the Indiana basketball teams I coached.

In my adult years, I got to know Paul Brown. He epitomized coaching to me—and I'm happy I was able to let him know that. I played golf with him a couple of times, and as we played I asked him questions about coaching—about organization, how long he practiced, that kind of thing. I'm always interested in what coaches try to do in practice—Paul Brown above all, because he was the first to plan practices right down to the minute.

One time when I was talking with him, I asked, "How many times did you take Massillon to the state finals in basketball—wasn't it four?"

I'm not sure he had ever been asked that, certainly not for a long while. I sensed he got a huge kick out of my knowing how good he was in my sport, as well as in his.

He was one of those rare coaches who, like Doc Counsilman at Indiana, could have coached anything. Doc built an incomparable swimming program at maybe the last place you would expect to see great swimmers. He brought in the best swimmer in the world, Mark Spitz, and made him even better. He built whole teams of championship swimmers from California, Arizona, Florida, and even other countries. He's the only coach ever to win six straight NCAA swimming championships, the last three of those coming after I had gone to Indiana.

From watching him and getting to know him (I bought his house shortly after moving to Bloomington), I always figured the sport Doc coached was swimming only because as a young athlete he was a swimmer, but he would have put the same thought and ingenuity into anything else that he might have coached or done. Doc Counsilman was one of the truly, truly great coaches who ever lived—in any sport.

He also could send great notes:

> Bob:
> Congratulations on Monday night's game. It was the greatest game I've ever seen.
> Another game like that and I'll be convinced you are the second-greatest coach Indiana University has ever had.
>
> Doc

I haven't saved many things, but I kept that.

I make the connection between Doc and Paul Brown because I think those two were exactly alike in how meticulous they were with detail, and in how they experimented and explored in ways other coaches hadn't even thought about.

That's why, considering how important the Browns were in the sports culture in northern Ohio at the time I was growing up, being able to talk to Paul Brown and spend time with him was an unforgettable experience for me. Just as pleasing for me was the chance, as an adult, to tell him how influential and elevating to our shared profession I considered him to be.

I'm not sure the Cleveland area ever had a sadder or more catastrophic day than when Art Modell fired Paul Brown, unless it was the day Art Modell moved the team to Baltimore.

Brown was fired after the 1962 season. That was my first year out of college, and I was an assistant coach under Harold Andreas at Cuyahoga Falls High School, just outside Akron. That wasn't just a normal coach firing. This was an owner firing the man who built the franchise into one of the most respected in all sports—the only coach I know of whose team was named for him. The Browns and Paul Brown had some extremely loyal fans, so that was a black day in northern Ohio for all of us fans. My mind went back to Paul Brown and those dark days after I was fired at Indiana.

Several years ago, I met Art Modell at a golf course in Palm Springs, California. I had spoken with him prior to that—I called him to give a recommendation when he was looking for a successor to Jim Shofner after the 1990 season. I had been impressed with the job Bill Belichick had done as the defensive coordinator under Bill Parcells with the Giants. They had just won their second Super Bowl in five years. I recommended Bill, and— I'm sure there were a lot of other reasons and recommendations—he got the job.

It was at the end of the 1995 season that Modell moved the beloved Browns to Baltimore. He may have been ripped even more for that in Cleveland than when he fired Paul Brown.

Just five years later, in the playoffs of the 2000 season, Baltimore met Oakland for the AFC championship and a spot in the Super Bowl.

I had a tough time with that game. By then I knew Modell much better and liked him a lot, so I wished the best for him. But Jon Gruden, the Oakland coach, had been a ball boy with our Indiana teams—the great ones in 1975 and '76. I saw where Jon said one of his most enjoyable boyhood memories was his association with those teams and kids and with me. Jon's dad, Jim, was an assistant on Lee Corso's Indiana football staff at the time, and Jon also was a good friend of my son Tim.

I can't say I ever did resolve my personal dilemma on the AFC championship game; I just knew I would have somebody to root for in the Super Bowl.

Baltimore beat Oakland, so I went from my feelings on the day when Paul Brown got fired to rooting like hell for Art Modell's team to win the Super Bowl.

Damned if it didn't.

Kids have heroes. Boudreau, Lavelli, and Graham were certainly three of mine. Not to mention Paul Brown.

But the biggest of all for me was Ted Williams. Why? I honestly can't say. There was just something about his presence: the way he stood at the plate and absolutely dared pitchers to throw him a strike.

FOUR: *High School Days (1954–1958)*

*Being right and being quiet never has been a combination
I was very good at.*

High school basketball actually started for me when I was in the eighth grade. Maybe, in a way, coaching did, too.

The high school coach, Jack Graham, occasionally called me to ride with him to scout a game. It was unusual, but I was pretty big, probably 6-foot-1 even then, and I was a good enough junior high school player that I think he knew I was eventually going to play for him.

I grew up imagining myself as a major league baseball player, as most boys do. Graig Nettles once said every kid wanted to either play baseball or be in the circus, and playing for the Yankees he got to do both.

But I really wanted to be a basketball player, as very few Orrville or even Ohio boys of my era did. I don't even know why I liked basketball so much. I'm sure part of it was that it was a sport you could work at by yourself. And I did that, by the hour, year-round. I was a good player at all the levels growing up, although when I got into the level I played at in college, I was very average.

Once I got to ninth grade, Coach Graham moved me right onto the varsity. I think I practiced one day with the jayvee team.

We played Mansfield Madison in our first game my freshman year. I was announced in the starting lineup, but I didn't start and Coach Graham told me, "I wouldn't do that to you." (And I was thinking, *Why not, Coach? I'd love to start.*)

My memory is that in that first game I shot five times and made three baskets. Breaking into a lineup dominated by seniors is never easy for a freshman, but I got valuable help that year from two senior players, Don Ault and Warner Harper. First and foremost in their minds was what I could contribute to the team. Don later served in the Marine Corps in Vietnam, and because of a lot of things that happened to him there, he died at an early age. I still consider

Warner one of the best athletes I've ever been around. I played both basketball and baseball with him in high school and fast-pitch softball the summers I was in college. He was one of several Orrville people who came to Bloomington every year to see us play.

When I was inducted into the Orrville High School Sports Hall of Fame, I focused most of my remarks on Warner Harper and what an omission it was that he wasn't included in the first group to be inducted. But I was doubly pleased the next year: not only was he in the second induction class but also he asked me to present him for induction. I felt as honored by that as I did by my own induction.

Playing for Coach Graham for three years was a great experience.

No one tried harder to do everything he asked us to do. One night my junior year, my mom had her bridge club at our house. Someone asked where I was, and she said she didn't really know but she never had to worry about it because the basketball coach had a curfew of 10 P.M. and she knew I'd always be home by then.

That night I went to a movie with a guy in my class that I played football with, Jerry Brubaker, and his older brother. It was January—colder than hell, snow on the ground, wind whipping. We came out of the theater and Jerry's car had a flat tire. My house was only three blocks from the theater; I could have made it home before 10 easily by just walking. But I didn't think I could just leave those guys, so I stayed to help.

At 10:30, not only wasn't I home yet, but the bridge women still were around, teasing my mother. And, for the first time ever, Coach Graham called—not to check on me but to ask me a question. Mom very sheepishly had to tell him no, I wasn't home yet.

When I finally got home and explained the situation, my mom—because of her confident assurance to her bridge friends and the kidding she got—was nowhere near as quick to understand as Coach Graham was.

Jerry Brubaker went on to a distinguished career. In the period after the Gulf War, he was one of America's leading arms inspectors in making sure Iraq was living up to its war-ending agreements.

I averaged about nineteen points a game as a sophomore. As a junior, I was averaging about twenty-five points a game when I broke a bone in my foot. I played a couple of games before they decided to put the foot in a cast for four weeks. I was in such a hurry to get back I broke four casts trying to shoot while wearing it. The cast came off the twenty-sixth day, rushed forward a little because we started tournament play the next day against Massillon at the Canton Fieldhouse. My foot was so weak I could hardly walk. But I played, and the ankle—not the foot but the ankle—was so sore at the half that I didn't even go out to shoot before the second half started. I played until I fouled out.

After that season Coach Graham had an offer to be an elementary school principal in Orrville. As any kid would, I thought only about me when I heard of that. I felt he should hold out for a year, because of the team we were going to have. But he didn't. Although that was a big disappointment to me then, it didn't alter the warm relationship between Jack Graham and me that exists today. Every time my Indiana teams played at Iowa, he and his wife came to the game from where they live in Colorado Springs.

His leaving coaching did have an impact on my basketball life—as both a player and a coach. Orrville brought in a man named Bob Gobin to coach the team. Of all the coaches I had from Little League through high school, he was the only one I didn't like or get along with.

Gobin wanted everybody to take the same number of shots and everybody to score ten points a game. My senior year we scrimmaged Wadsworth right after the football season was over, and I scored forty-some points. I had worked hard to get ready for that senior year. No kid ever worked any harder at basketball. But Gobin didn't like my scoring like that. He told us, "We won't have that happen again."

Basketball is the ultimate team game, but no game built around a team principle utilizes individual skills more. You don't have to score to be a good basketball player. There's some role for everybody. And one thing I have always said is that basketball is not an equal-opportunity game, where shooting is concerned. My teams work to get shots for our shooters.

I'm sure one reason we do is the lifelong influence that I got from that year under Gobin. We've had some kids who weren't great basketball players who have been really good scorers, because of the way we used them. As a player my senior year in high school, I felt I was misused, to the detriment of my team. It was a team that greatly underachieved. We finished 11–9.

I played basketball for Bill Shunkwiler in junior high and football and baseball for him in high school. During my senior basketball season, he knew how frustrated I was getting and he tried to intercede with Gobin for me. It didn't work. Shunkwiler came back to me and said, "You're just going to have to keep quiet and play."

Being right and being quiet never has been a combination I was very good at.

I did find one release during that year. Both my junior and senior years, on Saturday mornings I was the volunteer basketball coach for a group of sixth-graders. One of those kids was Bobby Weltlich, who was later an assistant coach for me at Army and Indiana and went on to be an outstanding head coach.

Each of those two years, we found some other teams and played six or seven games a year. We went on the road to play some of them.

That was an ideal way to coach. To this day, nobody has any idea whether we won or we lost. And not one of those games was covered by a newspaper.

Bill Shunkwiler enjoyed coaching, whatever the sport, and I thoroughly enjoyed playing for him. We had a great player-coach relationship that became a strong, lasting friendship, starting with him playing third base and me short-stop on the Orr Park fast-pitch softball team while I was in college.

In football, I played for him as an end on both offense and defense—right end on offense, left end on defense—and I was also the punter. I could kick pretty well—just ask any of my Indiana players who ever saw me launch a bas-ketball high into Assembly Hall to make a point at a practice.

For some reason, I remember several punting experiences better than I do anything I did at end. During one game played in an unbelievably strong wind, I was back to punt and I hit the ball pretty well. But as the ball got up in that wind, I saw it just turn around and start blowing back toward me. I fell on it behind the line of scrimmage, gave it to an official, and he said, "Son, you could have run with it."

I said, "I was just happy I stopped it right here."

I was sick with flu all week leading up to a game we played at Uhrichsville. Ohio rules said you couldn't play if you hadn't gone to school the day of the game. My teacher-mother knew the rules. I went to school in the afternoon so I could play.

Because I wasn't feeling great Coach Shunkwiler restricted me to defense and punting. It was a big game—both teams were good. In the first half, punt-ing from the goal line, I dropped the ball, picked it up, and in my hurry to get it off, shanked my punt out of bounds on our seventeen. That didn't please my coach, I'm sure, but he didn't say anything to me.

However, in the fourth quarter we had a two-touchdown lead when we again had to punt. On the sidelines, Coach Shunkwiler made a special point of telling me, "Just kick it out of bounds—don't let them run it back!"

I lined up my usual twelve yards deep and did just what I was told to do. I kicked it out—of the stadium, high, long, over the track, over the bleachers, and into the parking lot.

It was an impressive kick. For six yards. They got the ball at their 44.

I didn't even want to look at the sidelines, I knew how upset he'd be. I was usually the left defensive end. This time, I just switched with our other end and lined up on the right—opposite the sideline where Coach Shunkwiler was, rather than being right in front of him.

Playing defensive end I usually stood upright at the line, so I could see the play develop. Standing up, I glanced over to see what Coach Shunkwiler was doing. For just a second, he had his back to the field while he talked with his coaches, then he wheeled around to say something to me, thinking I'd be right there in front of him. When he saw I wasn't, from clear across the field I heard, "Dammit, where the hell *is* he?"

Very quickly I changed my approach. I dropped down in a three-point stance, hiding.

As it happened, they came my way three straight times, I made three tackles and forced a fumble, we got the ball back—and he didn't even know I was in the game.

I was just as happy he didn't.

I love Shunkwiler, and with a few personal incidents from my high school days I can describe why. At baseball practice on a cold, windy spring day, he had a kid throwing batting practice who wasn't very good at it. Shunkwiler—he was the one coach we called "Chief"—had an unbending batting practice rule: when your turn came, you got four pitches, and then the next guy was up. You got four *pitches*, not necessarily four swings. I argued with him: "Chief, you can't want us to be swinging at bad pitches." He said, "You get four pitches like everybody else. Get your four pitches and get the hell out of there."

This day during my second time up, I did just what I had done the first time: I took all four bad pitches that came in—eight pitches and I hadn't swung at one yet. This time, I just stood in the batter's box waiting for another one. "Get out of there," Shunkwiler yelled. "I told you, you get four pitches. Get the hell out of there."

As I left, I turned my head away from him and mumbled something less than complimentary about the pitcher. I didn't mumble low enough. Shunkwiler was standing on the mound, feeding the pitcher balls. All of a sudden he just unloaded on me—firing baseballs at me, giving me hell for what I said and telling me to get out of practice.

The baseball diamond was about two blocks from the gym. I just ran up to the high school, put my basketball stuff on and, in a nice warm gym, went out to shoot by myself.

When baseball practice ended, he walked into the gym and said just three words: "Horse or 21?"

I said "Horse."

He thrashed me.

Then he left without saying a word about baseball practice. He had made his point, outdoors and indoors. And I got it. He had chewed me out but he wanted me to know that he still liked me. I also got a second message; I knew he could beat me at Horse or 21 anytime he wanted to.

My senior year playing for him in his primary sport, football, we went to Mentor, Ohio, to scrimmage. The coach there was Lee Tressel, whose son Jim is the new coach at Ohio State.

This was in the heat of August, after ten days of two-a-day practices. It was a three-hour trip by schoolbus, and we stopped halfway to Mentor for a break. When we got back on the bus, somebody—I *really* don't think it was me—had bought a package of condoms. They got blown up, like balloons. We devised a game kind of like volleyball, and we were batting the condoms around in the back of the bus. One sailed up to the front where Shunkwiler was sitting, his back to us. The inflated condom landed in his lap.

I whispered to my wide-eyed buddies, "This is not going to be good."

He never said a word, just looked at it, threw it on the floor, and stomped on it.

And I was right.

It had to be a hundred degrees that day. I was one of four guys on that team who played both offense and defense. I was the only one of the four who never came out that day. I scrimmaged ninety-four consecutive plays, with an occasional gulp of water, of course, but no other kind of break. Subs would come in, but never for me. My conclusion after about seventy plays was that he thought I had something to do with the condom caper.

I was so tired that night I didn't even go to a big potluck supper the Mentor mothers put on for the two teams.

The next morning, we went from Mentor over to Fairport to scrimmage. Same thing: I scrimmaged from beginning to end. I damned near had to crawl off the field.

The scrimmage ended about noon. The one thing I knew was that on the way home I didn't want to see any part of that bus. Our duffel bags and equipment had come up in a pick-up truck. I looked at that loaded truck and I looked at the bus. I asked Coach Shunkwiler: "Would you have any objection if I rode home in the back of that pick-up truck?" He looked at the bus, looked at the pick-up truck, looked at me, and said, "I think that would be a *great* place for you." That's all he ever said. Or had to say.

Shunkwiler left Orrville not long after I graduated and coached at Harding High School in Warren, Ohio. That was an excellent football job; Paul Warfield, the great Ohio State and Miami Dolphins star, had played there. One of Bill's Warren teams came within a fumble of beating Massillon for the state championship. He went from there to Kent State as an assistant to Dave Puddington, who quit with about six games to go that season and left Bill out of a coaching job.

He got back into football as a scout for the Philadelphia Bell in a pro league that didn't last long, the USFL. Jim Mora was the team's coach, and they won two league championships. When the USFL died, I passed Shunkwiler's name along to Gil Brandt, a guy I know because, hell, he knows everybody.

With the Dallas Cowboys, Gil was the first guy in pro football to develop a truly national comprehensive approach to scouting. He even sent out questionnaires to college basketball coaches, asking if we knew of any basketball players with high school experience in football who might be good receivers or defensive backs. His no-stone-unturned approach paid off for him with Cornell Green and Pete Gent, among others, and soon the rest of the NFL was also doing it. Before I ever got to Bloomington, Indiana had gone to the Rose Bowl for the first time, with a lot of sophomores getting the headlines. What few people realize, even in Indiana, is that the athlete from that 1967 sophomore class who by far had the best NFL career was a basketball player, Kenny Johnson, who was a defensive end with the Bengals for seven years. His first NFL contract was with Gil Brandt and the Cowboys.

Gil hired Shunkwiler as a scout, and later on a guy I really like and respect, Bill Polian, took him on with the Indianapolis Colts where—in the fiftieth year since I first played for him—he's still working in football.

My summers in Orrville during my college years were educational, too. We lived about three blocks from the Municipal Plant, and I worked there for the water superintendent, Ray Carney.

He knew every water pipe in Orrville. If we had to dig up a valve, on a blacktopped street, he'd walk around in the street intersection and finally say, "Okay, Bobby, dig right here."

I asked him once, "Are you ever wrong about these?"

"Rarely," he replied.

I'd start digging with a pick or a jackhammer and, I'll be damned, there'd be a valve.

I was on a two-man crew painting fire hydrants. I'd paint the top yellow and my partner Harry would paint the bottom red. It would take me a minute. Then Harry would paint the bottom like it was the Mona Lisa. One time a lady called in to report me for sleeping in the shade of her bushes. She was right—I was lying in the shade, my head propped up with a towel, while da Vinci painted a fire hydrant.

Mr. Carney let me paint them all myself from then on.

I loved the guy. I'd come home from Ohio State in the summers, go to the shop, and he wouldn't bother with handshakes, he'd just put me to work: "Bobby, you do such-and-such."

At night and on weekends I played a lot of basketball and fast-pitch softball.

One of the things I loved about fast-pitch softball was the sixty-foot bases and—unlike the slow-pitch softball that is so popular now—you could steal bases. It was a real challenge. In softball, you can't lead off—you're out if you leave the base before the ball leaves the pitcher's hands. To steal a base, you had to time it just right—and that made it fun.

We played in the championship game of one tournament, late at night. The game went fourteen innings, and I was thrown out twice trying to steal. In the bottom of the fourteenth, I hit the ball up the middle, the grass was wet, and I stretched it into a double.

By now it was about two in the morning, and we had a good hitter up, Nelson Fejes. I was on second, and before there was another pitch, a guy in the stands screamed, *"Chain him down!"*

Everybody laughed, including me. And the guy was right: I *was* sizing up third base, where I could score a lot of ways.

Before I could try to steal, Nelson hit the first pitch for a home run.

Ernie Demlow was my batting coach. He was older than me, although his dad worked with my dad on the railroad. Ernie had been an outstanding softball player himself and he taught me to hit fast-pitch, which requires a much shorter, quicker swing.

He was a machine-gunner on a bomber out of England in World War II. He flew thirty-five missions into Germany. In the same squadron, Clark Gable was a gunner on a bomber. Ernie couldn't have been more impressed with Gable because—as big a name as he was—as a soldier he was perfectly happy being treated like everybody else. He was just there doing a job for his country. In part because of Ernie's feelings about him, Clark Gable became my all-time favorite actor, a guy whose screen presence was as commanding as was Ted Williams's on a baseball diamond.

Ernie became one of our Indiana teams' biggest fans. He came to games every year in Bloomington.

While I was still at Army, I brought him out to our boys' basketball camp one summer, and on that trip he and I went to New York City once. We saw a Mets game, and we took a walk downtown. Just off Broadway on 42nd Street at Times Square, approaching us may have been the first same-sex couple Ernie had ever seen. He grabbed my arm and said, "Jesus Christ, Bobby, would you look at that?" Ernie wasn't quite ready for New York, but he was a hell of a guy.

In basketball the spring after my senior year in high school, I played some with Gus Johnson, the future NBA star who graduated from Akron Central High School that same year. Gus deservedly was the most publicized high school player in that part of the state, but in these independent tournaments at the Akron Community Center and around northeastern Ohio he was used to playing with guys who couldn't *spell* pass. The first time I played with him, I hit him in the head with a pass. Then, a second one. As we walked off the floor at the half, Gus put his big arm around me and said, "You know those other guys aren't ever going to throw the ball to anybody. But I'll be ready for you now. Just keep throwing it to me." I didn't run into him a lot after that, but every time I did, I'd say, "Gus, who's your all-time favorite passer?" And he'd come back, "You, my man, you."

I played baseball under Shunkwiler for three years—first base. I really wanted to play a fourth year, too, but I think, given how my senior year of basketball had gone, even Shunkwiler knew it was best for me to take advantage of the chance I had to play some extra basketball, with good players.

But I've always regretted losing that senior year and not putting more into my baseball career because that was my most natural sport.

I would have been on an excellent team with two good pitchers. The year before, we had beaten Barberton and Canton McKinley, two traditionally outstanding teams. Canton McKinley's shortstop was Wayne Fontes, who later was a defensive back at Michigan State, an NFL player, and the Detroit Lions' head coach. We got to know each other long after high school, and I occasionally—maybe always would be a better word—brought up that game, to the point where, if he saw me coming, he would say, "I don't want to hear a damned thing about that Orrville–McKinley baseball game."

Dean Chance, baseball's Cy Young Award winner in 1964 when they named only one from the two leagues, played for Northwestern in my home county. That was a small school but a great program. His coach, Roy Bates, won more than 900 games in baseball and basketball, and was inducted into the Ohio High School Hall of Fame. After I was out of school, Roy became a longtime good friend of mine and often came to Bloomington to help with the basketball team. My junior year, we beat Northwestern in baseball but didn't beat Chance. He started the game, but he'd pitch a while, then go to the outfield, then come back and pitch. Ronnie Walko, a really good football player, doubled in the winning run in the ninth inning and we won, 3–2.

Although the schools and towns are nowhere near the same size, Orrville's biggest athletic rival has always been Wooster, about ten miles away. In my class, Wooster had a hell of an athlete and a really tough competitor, Bill Musselman. We first ran across each other in Little League baseball. He always lorded it over me that our senior year in high school they beat us in all three of the sports we shared—football, basketball, and (though I didn't play it that year) baseball.

Bill was damned good—a fullback on the football team (they beat us our senior year, 6–0); a guard in basketball (they beat us 81–64 in the sectional basketball tournament, then went to the regional finals in the state tournament that year), and an outstanding catcher in baseball.

The only time we played together on a team was in basketball the summer of 1958, after we graduated from high school. We played a lot then, and became very good friends.

Our relationship cooled when he took over the basketball program at Minnesota in the 1971–72 season, the same year I went to Indiana. He cheated like hell and didn't make any bones about it. He was one of those rule-breakers who always puzzled me the most. Most chronic cheaters do it because they can't coach. Musselman was a damned good coach. He did the two things that are most important in coaching basketball—he paid attention to defense, and he worked like hell to get good shots. There's no way he had to cut corners to win.

He went to college at Wittenberg, where he was obviously influenced by the coaching style of the basketball coach there, Ray Mears—very patient, very low-scoring, and very successful. Mears went from Wittenberg to Tennessee, a huge coaching jump. I'm not sure Bill even played basketball at Wittenberg. He basically was a football player—for a great small-college coach, Bill Edwards.

Musselman coached first at Ashland College, where his teams played exactly like Mears's had. They played good defense and they just wouldn't shoot. Their scores were always around 39–35. And they almost always had the 39.

He jumped from there to Minnesota, where things got out of hand for him because of all the stuff he did recruiting. But he and I, after a pretty stormy first few years together in the Big Ten, again became good friends. So of course his death at fifty-nine in May 2000—though I knew he had cancer and he'd had a stroke—was a jolt for me.

• • •

The whole out-of-control AAU summer-basketball thing represents the dramatic way things have changed for today's kids from the way it was when I was at Orrville.

The first time I was ever on an airplane was as a sophomore at Ohio State. For high school kids today who have been all over to play, there isn't anything new for them in college.

In basketball now, kids—boys *and* girls—from middle school–age through high school are permitted to join what basically are all-star teams and play an unlimited number of games anywhere they can go to play as soon as their scholastic season ends. There is very little regulation of how their expenses are paid, who coaches them, or how teams are put together.

Too often their summer coaches can't coach. They're "basketball bennies"—guys who have had a taste of the game as a fan and think they're experts—guys who have no background or training as a coach and have no idea how to direct and lead and channel kids.

The worst victim of the runaway AAU program is the high school coach. The kid has spent his summer playing however he wants to, trying to get himself noticed. Then he goes back to school and his high school coach has to try to coach him. That's an impossible situation.

I think the only hope for correcting the problem is the state high school athletic associations. They need to make rules that limit a kid to playing on a summer team within a twenty-five-mile radius of his own high school. If that isn't available to him, then he has to go to the next-closest team. And whatever team he plays on has to be coached by a high school faculty member from within that area.

So, if I were growing up today, would I be one of those guys caught up in AAU playing? Sure. I don't fault the kids for playing. But the people who handle the games too many times have an awful lot of ulterior motives in their involvement.

The first time I was on the Ohio State campus I was a senior at Orrville and I was brought in as a football recruit—one of about five hundred. I saw a game and met the freshman coach, Ernie Godfrey. I did not meet Woody Hayes. I was smart enough to know that if I wasn't one of the guys who met Woody, I was probably not real high on their football list.

From a basketball standpoint, that spring post-season independent play was good for me. I played for three different teams, maybe forty games, in independent tournaments with and against some really good players and coaches.

One of those players was Clair Muscaro, who played at West Virginia Tech under an outstanding small-college coach, Neal Baisi. Clair was coaching at Ravenna at the time, and we became friends. Now he's the commissioner of Ohio high school athletics.

That spring, Ohio State brought several of us to an outing at Merrybrook Farms on the Scioto River in Columbus. Jerry Lucas and John Havlicek were there, and so were Mel Nowell and Jack Landis, who also wound up at Ohio State. Bud Olsen, who went to Louisville, and Gordon Mickey, who went to Indiana, also played that day.

By then, I had already seen some of my future teammates play. My senior year, I was the guest of Ohio State at the state finals, at St. John Arena in Columbus. Gary Gearhart played for New Lebanon–Dixie against Northwestern and Dean Chance in the Single-A tournament. For the Double-A championship, Columbus North beat Middletown, the only high school game Lucas ever lost—and the only time I saw him play in high school. I had gone to the state finals at Cleveland Arena in 1956 and couldn't get tickets to see the Double-A game. Middletown won and Lucas as a sophomore scored something like ninety-nine points in the semifinals and finals.

Even before the outing I had met Coach Taylor, who was just thirty-three and hadn't yet coached his first game. He was a good basketball player at Ohio State but even better in baseball. He made it to the major leagues with the Washington Senators for parts of three seasons before he gave up baseball and became an assistant basketball coach under Floyd Stahl at Ohio State. When Coach Stahl retired after the 1958 season, Coach Taylor got the job.

Recruiting then was nothing like it has become. My neighbor, dentist, and lifelong friend, Dr. Don Boop, was the reason I was recruited by Ohio State. He had gone to dental school there. He called the basketball office and told them about me. They were interested, so Doc sent them some films. That's just one of many, many things Doc Boop—just a wonderful man and friend—did for me. He had served as a navy corpsman in the first marine division in World War II, in some of the toughest Pacific fighting. He was wounded, and he was awarded several combat medals. The rest of his life, he had to suffer through innumerable operations because of his war wounds, but as much as I was around him I never heard the first complaint. He passed away last year.

On the home visit that Doc Boop arranged, I was impressed by how articulate Coach Taylor was. Something set him aside. He was big, always very well dressed, and he could tell stories—he was just impressive, and a good guy. My dad really liked him, too.

He talked about the team he was trying to put together, but I didn't have any idea—and I'm not sure he did either—how good a first recruiting class he was going to have. Start off with two Hall of Fame players, Lucas and Havlicek. How many other college basketball coaches ever recruited two of those in one class, let alone in his first recruiting class?

Two years later, after our first season of varsity eligibility, we were all sophomores on the best team in the country.

But the thing Coach Taylor from that day on has talked most about regarding his spring recruiting visit to Orrville was my grandmother's strawberry shortcake.

My grandfather on my mother's side died before I was born. My grandmother—Sarah Montgomery—was a unique lady, a great person. Just being around her and her friends taught me a lifelong respect for older people. This was particularly helpful for me in meeting, getting to know, and learning from older coaches.

I was as close to my grandmother as any kid ever got to a grandmother. I used to go with her when she shopped in the country for eggs, peaches, corn, and whatever else she could find.

When I got old enough to drive, I became her chauffeur. She belonged to a couple of clubs, one in Orrville and a Bingo club in Akron. I'd make sure all the ladies got home from the club in Orrville. And I'd drive my grandmother to the club in Akron for the ladies' Bingo game there. I had a great time with them. I used to call the Bingo numbers, and once in a while they'd let me play. But if I won, they'd make me quit playing and go back to calling numbers.

One day at home I was lying on a couch watching a baseball game, and my grandmother was in a chair in the corner of the room. She looked asleep, her hands folded in her lap, but I heard her say, "Some people simply serve as an example for others of what *not* to do."

I looked around the room, and I was the only other person there. I don't know what she thought I should be doing, but it obviously wasn't lying in the house watching a baseball game.

My senior year, I was recruited in basketball by Dick Shrider, the coach at Miami of Ohio, and he set it up for me to visit there the day after the senior prom. I was out all night for the prom, so when we left Orrville for Oxford early in the morning, my grandmother was the driver and I slept in the backseat.

She had a 1950 Pontiac, and on two-laned Route 42 somewhere in south-central Ohio I looked up over her shoulder once and saw the speedometer was matching her age: a little past eighty.

All I did was lie back down and say, "Lord, if it's time, I guess it's time."

I guess it wasn't.

She was eighty-two when she died. That day she had driven uptown by herself to do some shopping and then driven back home. I used to kid her about her parallel-parking skills, "Grandma, there aren't enough corners in Orrville for all you ladies to park on." But she was still driving.

She had come in from her car that day, sat down in a chair—her hat and coat still on—and passed away in the chair. It was late May, I was home for the weekend, and I found her there. I was a nineteen-year-old sophomore at Ohio State.

Way too many kids grow up today with just one parent in the house. I, in effect, had three. Having my grandmother around all those years, in addition to my parents, was a great advantage for me growing up. I'm sure it wouldn't work that way for all families and all kids, but it did for a kid in Orrville, a very lucky kid.

FIVE: *Playing for a National Champion* (1958–1962)

Coach Taylor and I differed in a lot of ways, and I'm sure he's glad. I don't think he'd want me to be thought of as his clone— or for everything I've done over the years to be attributed to him.

Over the years, my Indiana teams played against a great many coaches I liked. Dean Smith in his years at North Carolina was certainly one of them. In all our coaching years, we scheduled just two games against each other, in 1979–80 in Bloomington and in 1980–81 in Chapel Hill. They won both games.

But that didn't have anything to do with why we didn't schedule each other any more. Dean didn't like to play friends. I preferred to, because then I didn't feel nearly so bad if we lost—I knew a good guy had won.

Understand that losing, even to friends, was never easy for me to take. As long as I've coached, winning never did anything for me or to me that in any way compared to what losing did. The loss was far, far worse than the win was good. The two never evened out in terms of emotions involved or emotions spent.

But, for me, the hardest games that I coached in or ever expect to coach in were against Ohio State when my college coach, Fred Taylor, was coaching.

Ohio State had been good to me. I had a lot of friends there, and all of them were Ohio State fans. I had some "friends" there I'd never met—they always filled St. John Arena for Indiana–Ohio State games. At one of those, something happened on the floor and I wasn't happy about it. I slammed a towel down and things quieted just as I cut loose with a loud "*Jeee-zus Christ!*" Instantly, from way up high, a voice yelled back, "Hang on, Bobby, I'll be right there!"

Who wouldn't enjoy an atmosphere like that?

But coaching against Ohio State my first five years at Indiana was tough because of the respect I had for Coach Taylor.

When he moved up from assistant coach to become the Ohio State basketball coach, instead of just saying, "I've got the job, so now I am a coach," he analyzed himself and said, "What does it take to win?"

After he recruited our class in the spring of 1958, his first Ohio State team went 11–11, while we as freshmen sat in the stands and watched.

We felt a little closer to the varsity than any other freshman group I knew of during that period when freshmen couldn't play varsity ball. About seven of us practiced against the varsity every night. We rarely practiced as a freshman team.

That was an exciting year, especially for me, coming from a small town and a small high school. A lot of kids today come to college expecting to move right in and play. One of the interesting things each year at the start of practice is watching freshmen go through a period of shock—these guys they're on the floor with now, guys who looked so average when they watched them the year before against Big Ten or other major-college opposition, are operating on a much higher plane than they're used to. There's a relativity to it all; the college game is faster, stronger, and played much harder than high school basketball. Everybody who has a major-college scholarship was probably the best player on his team and maybe the best of all the players on his team's whole high school schedule. There's almost an instant realization of that once all-out competition begins the first day of practice. It was true when I stepped up from Orrville to Ohio State in the 1950s and it's true today, even with all the AAU and all-star high school competition kids go through today. They've played against better players now, but not under the discipline and against the defensive pressure of holdover players on a well-coached college team.

I didn't know going in how I would compare with the other guys in my own class, let alone on the whole team. The period between the start of fall classes and the opening of practice wasn't a great deal different from today, in the sense of what went on every day. We'd do our running, then go to the gym for pick-up games. Those gave me a little more realistic picture of where I was. By the time my sophomore year came and I was eligible to play on the varsity, I thought I'd get to play, but I never harbored any thoughts of being a great player. I knew I couldn't play like Jerry Lucas or John Havlicek or Mel Nowell from my own class and Larry Siegfried, Joe Roberts, and Dick Furry, who were holdovers on the varsity, but I thought I could play with anybody else. And that is pretty much the way it worked out.

During that freshman season, Coach Taylor many times used us as a demonstration team against the varsity—just like in football, we'd get a quick introduction to what the upcoming varsity opponent liked to do and we ran their offense and simulated their strengths as well as we could. Northwestern came into St. John Arena ranked No. 11 in the country. We freshmen worked three days as Northwestern, and after our varsity had beaten them 88–77, Coach Taylor told me my shooting in practice had really helped them win that game. Hearing that from him may have been my highlight for the whole year.

Years later, the thought crossed my mind that I'd have been a lot better off if my defense was what had impressed him. It wasn't. After he was out of coaching and working with the Big Ten TV network, we went into St. John Arena for a game he was doing. He came to our shooting practice the morning of the game, and after the players had finished and gone to shower, someone asked Coach Taylor what kind of defensive player I was.

"Well, I'll say this: he was tough," he said. He walked to a position on the court, about fifteen feet from the basket along the baseline, pointed to the floor and said, "Right here was where he would foul guys. He'd either shove them out of bounds or foul them, but they wouldn't get by."

I didn't get the feeling he was particularly endorsing my approach, but he liked the competitiveness.

He actually played us as a freshman team against the varsity twice, in about the middle of that 1958–59 season. I think we played on a Friday and again on a Monday and we beat them both games. Coach Taylor didn't let anybody outside the basketball program come to the games, which meant they certainly weren't covered by the media. The first time we won 109–91. The second time it was back-and-forth the whole way and we ended up winning 91–82. Jerry Lucas scored in the forties for us both times.

Going into the next season, I think Coach Taylor was as excited as I was—as all of us sophomores were. I think he knew he had a chance to have a much better team, but he also felt it was important that his teams got better defensively. That summer he went to the Concordia Clinic in Moorehead, Minnesota, to spend a week with Pete Newell, whose California team had won the 1959 NCAA championship.

He came back with Pete's thoughts on defensive play. They pretty much became our thoughts and our ideas on defensive play. But it took a while.

We opened my first varsity season at home against Wake Forest, which had a couple of very good sophomores, too—Lennie Chappell, a 6-8, 240-pound center, and a 5-10 guard named Billy Packer. They had us down 47–39 at halftime but John Havlicek—the only time as a college player that he didn't start—came off the bench to help us win, 77–69. Packer, whose dad was a very good coach at Lehigh, scored eighteen points in his first college game and to this day I think really feels they were better than us and wishes they could have played us again, in the NCAA tournament. Maybe I saw the game better than Billy did—I sat on the bench and never got in that one; he was a much better basketball player than I was, and I guess, judging by our differing appraisals of those teams, I was a better analyst—then. I'll guarantee you that by NCAA tournament time, they would not have beaten us.

This was basketball at a level I had always dreamed about. Every day was exciting. Our fifth game that year and our first road game was at St. Louis. Our flight there was the first time I had ever been on an airplane. Toward the end of the first half, I missed a shot, followed it up, got the rebound, and scored. At the half, Coach Taylor told me what a good play I'd made. He was great at that—when you made good plays, he let you know about it. It was a thing I picked up from him that first year and always tried to do in my own coaching—in practice or in games, just as he did.

We won our first six games and jumped up to No. 3 in the country. Around Christmas, we took a two-game trip to Utah. Utah beat us 97–92 at Salt Lake City. The next night after we beat Brigham Young (91–79) and were back at the hotel, Coach Taylor gave some sort of Christmas gift to each of us, but he wasn't a very cheerful Santa Claus. He delivered the gifts personally to each of our rooms, and he damned near threw them at us. We knew why he wasn't happy: our defense. Just after Christmas we lost at Kentucky, 96–93, and he told us, "It's sad when you can score ninety points on the road and still not win." Over the holiday break, he had his assistant, Jack Graf, go to California with a few more questions for Pete Newell.

Our second Big Ten game was at home against the best team we played all year, Indiana. It was a hell of a game; the lead changed hands fourteen times. They led us 95–90 with about a minute to go, but we won 96–95. Larry Siegfried, a great competitor, had not scored a point in the game, but here's where coaching comes in. Coach Taylor had what he called an "emergency score" play—set up for Siegfried. We ran it, he came off a double-screen, took an in-bounds pass as he drove down the right lane, and from about eight feet banked the ball in with just a few seconds to go.

That was a huge win for us—the first really big conference test that we had faced as a team, and we had passed it, barely. As players, the main thing we noticed was that we won, and we were thrilled, jubilant. As was the case with me many times in my own coaching career, simply winning did not satisfy Coach Taylor. He was trying to make us a defense-conscious team, and we had just given up ninety-seven, ninety-six, and ninety-five points in a five-game stretch. His attitude toward those scores I think was the most decisive factor in that team eventually winning the national championship. He left no doubt in our minds that the success of this team was going to depend not on players' ability but how well we learned to play defense, and how hard we became to score against. From that point on, we just didn't give up many points, and we got better and better as a team.

I had never thought much about defense, and I wasn't alone. That's what set Havlicek apart from all of us. He just realized, better than anybody else on our team or anybody on any team I ever was on, that "this is how I can play on this team"—by playing defense. He was ideally suited for it—quick, long-armed, with big hands.

And Siegfried, who had averaged forty-one points a game in high school and led Ohio State in scoring his sophomore year, went from being a scorer to being an extremely good defensive player and an excellent passer his junior year.

We were locked in on winning the Big Ten championship—that's the only way you could get to the NCAA tournament then. And we were in a very tough league, the one that at the time had more players in the NBA than any other conference.

We just kept winning. We beat Michigan State at St. John Arena by thirty-two points, but we had a tough game against them later in the year. Forddy Anderson was a very good offensive coach, and they had some excellent players—Lance Olson was a forward who was tough for even John to play against, and Horace Walker was good. We won, 83–82. And a week later when we beat Wisconsin, 93–68, we clinched the Big Ten championship—12–0, three games ahead with two games to go.

By then, we were No. 2 in the country, behind Cincinnati and Oscar Robertson. Our first game after clinching the championship, we lost at Indiana, 99–83.

After that game, the Indiana coach, Branch McCracken, told Coach Taylor: "That just shows the wrong team is going to the NCAA tournament."

We all heard about that. Coach Taylor told us. The year before, Indiana had set a Big Ten scoring record by winning at Ohio State, 122–92. It would be hard to call it a true case of running up the score. The game was tied 48–48 at halftime, and they had an unbelievable second half—seventy-four points. But I do know this: Coach Taylor never forgot either the point record or the McCracken comment after our 1960 game.

That loss to Indiana dropped us to No. 3 in the national polls, but we were safely into the NCAA tournament. That brought a whole new level of excitement. We found out right away other teams were excited, too. In our first game, we were behind Western Kentucky 43–37 at the half but we came on to win, 98–79. I scored three buckets and felt great about it—it was always a terrific feeling just to make a contribution. Then we beat Georgia Tech and we were in the Final Four at San Francisco.

We won our first game there, 76–54, over New York University. That was the first semifinal game. The second was between California, the defending champion, and Cincinnati, which had been No. 1 all year. After our loss to Indiana, California passed us for No. 2.

As a high school senior, I had made a recruiting visit to Cincinnati. While there, I got a chance to play a pick-up game in an old gym with Oscar and Jack Twyman, a former Cincinnati player who by then was an outstanding NBA player with the Cincinnati Royals. It was one of my greatest days as a player—a high school kid, playing with those guys. Oscar was just a great, great player—"The Big O," one of the first real basketball nicknames.

At the semifinals that night, Coach Taylor did something I almost never did as a coach—he allowed us to come out after we had beaten NYU and watch the first half of the California–Cincinnati game. I went back to the hotel that night not sure which team we were going to play but convinced that neither one of them could beat us. I think everybody on our team felt the same way—and probably for the same reason I did. I played with and watched Lucas play every day, and I thought, *Man, there's nobody this good.* Oscar could control a game one way, but Lucas could really control it another way—around the basket.

Then, we had just one day to prepare—the semifinals were on Friday night and the finals on Saturday night. But we were prepared. California, which had beaten Cincinnati for the second year in a row in the NCAA semifinals, had a little guard named Bobby Wendell, who was not a good shooter. We just didn't guard him. Mel Nowell dropped off him, jammed things up inside, and the movement they were trying to get there was rendered ineffective. Wendell went 0-for-6. I thought at the time, as a player, what a great coaching move that was, and I copied it a lot over the years with my own teams. I asked Pete Newell later, and he said we were the first team to do that to them. This pointed out the value of preparation and the role of assistant coaches. Frank Truitt had suggested that after watching California game films.

Winning that championship game wasn't all just a matter of strategy. We also played pretty well.

I say "we." I wasn't greatly involved in it. The first half we missed just three shots—we were 16-for-19 and led, 37–19. It was a night when our shots were just going in. Joe Roberts made a hook shot from the top of the key. I had never seen him even try that. We won, 75–55.

That was to be Pete Newell's last year as a coach, and our game was his last game. I knew what Coach Taylor had done the previous summer and with Jack Graf over the Christmas-break that season. When I was out on the floor in the final minutes of that championship game, I remember thinking that one reason this was happening for us was that the coach of the other team shared what he knew with our coach. His doing that allowed our coach to become much more knowledgeable about defensive play, and that enabled us to become a much better defensive team than we would have been. He shared this knowledge, and it came back to cost him in the most important game of the season, the national championship. And I knew that part of it didn't bother him in the least.

That gave Pete Newell a special stature for me long before I ever met him or coached a game. What he represented to me in this case was the responsibility a teacher has to share with others whatever he has come up with that he found to be of some benefit. When later I was in a position to do that, I always did. If we were doing something that people were interested in, I never held anything back at clinics or in conversations with fellow coaches, especially young ones.

As a team, of course we were elated. We cut the nets down and jumped around and hugged—all the things championship teams do. And eventually we were showered, dressed, and ready to celebrate some more.

We were in San Francisco. Havlicek, Gearhart, Siegfried, and I went out on the town to celebrate. The very first place we went to wouldn't let us in. None of us was twenty-one. Siegfried was our spokesman. He argued, "Whaddya mean we can't come in? We just won the national championship." The guy at the door looked at him and said, "I don't give a shit what you won, you're not coming in."

And not very long after that we were back at our hotel.

The next day at Columbus there was a big celebration—at the airport, then at St. John Arena.

And there wasn't a guy on our squad who had a doubt in his mind that we would win that thing three years in a row.

We had great teams each of the next two years, but the team that won the 1960 national championship was our best. Joe Roberts and Dick Furry, excellent players, were seniors on that 1960 team.

Furry as a senior was the ultimate team player. He went from season-opening starter to the best sixth man in college basketball. Coming off the bench never outwardly bothered him. He gave a great effort in every minute he played. He was particularly good to me as a sophomore; he took me under his wing like an older brother. We always wore a coat and tie when traveling; Dick Furry taught me to tie a tie.

The other co-captain, Joe Roberts, has remained close to me ever since that year. He was an outstanding player and one of the best people I've ever been around. I roomed with him several times on road trips and I always looked forward to that, because it meant we were going to have some great discussions. When I roomed with him at the regional in Louisville, I suggested one night that we go to a movie. It never entered my mind that blacks and whites couldn't sit together or go to the same movie in Louisville. Joe was aware of it and just said he didn't care to go that night. My respect for Joe goes way beyond his ability as a player.

Three other seniors—Howard Nourse, Dave Barker, and John Cedargren—didn't play a lot but they were great to have on a team. I learned a lot from Dave Barker, who played more as a sophomore and a junior than he did as a senior. That didn't change his attitude at all. In practice, every day he got all of us nonstarters fired up to go against the first team. And we weren't bad. The only team in the Big Ten better than Ohio State's nonstarters was Indiana.

The next year, Richie Hoyt and I played a lot of the minutes that Joe Roberts and Dick Furry had played, and we just weren't as good as those guys. But as far as the rest of the country was concerned, there wasn't a fall-off from that national-championship season. We were unbeaten and ranked No. 1 all year until we lost in overtime to Cincinnati in the NCAA championship game.

We had a couple of close games during the season, but not many. One of them was definitely not against Indiana—at our place, the first time we had played them since Coach McCracken's remark to Coach Taylor after they had beaten us the year before.

We won, 100–65. We blatantly ran up the score. And nobody—including McCracken—could have been angrier about it than I was. I was the sixth man, and neither I nor anyone else off the bench went into the game until we had reached 100, with about a minute to go. I was pissed—but certainly not on Indiana's behalf. I just thought the game had long since passed the point where guys on the bench who had worked hard deserved a chance to play. That was the thing from that game that became a hallmark in my own coaching: let the bench guys play whenever you can.

When we played Indiana the second time that season at Bloomington, we had a hell of a time with them before winning, 73–69. I remember one play from that game. They had a center, Walt Bellamy, who had played for Pete Newell on the 1960 Olympic team. He was the first player taken that spring in the NBA draft, and he was the NBA Rookie of the Year with scoring and rebounding totals that still are the best by any rookie ever, except Wilt Chamberlain.

Bellamy was 6-foot-10½, 240 pounds. They ran a play with a guard throwing the ball into him in the post and cutting off him for the basket. Bellamy had the ball above his head, and I came in from behind, went up, and grabbed the ball. The problem was he had a good hold on it, too. He shook me like a dog shaking off fleas, but I held onto the ball, and that wasn't a good idea. He was so strong he ripped the ball away and in the process sent me flying through the air—I ended up on my ass, out of bounds. This whole thing started at the free-throw line. I can remember sitting on the sidelines and saying to myself, "Wow!"

The Pittsburgh Pirates' radio broadcaster, Bob Prince, went with us on that trip to do the telecast back to Columbus. The game was played on Monday night, and we arrived in Bloomington on Sunday. Sunday night, we ate in a hotel there, and Havlicek, Gearhart, and I—all of us baseball fans—sat in the hotel restaurant with Prince and he told us one baseball story after another.

At Michigan State that year, we won pretty easily and Lucas set a Big Ten scoring record with forty-eight points. Don Schlundt of Indiana's 1953 national champions had set it with forty-seven—he did it twice, both times against Ohio State. Lucas came out of the game with forty-six, and Coach Taylor put him back in to get the record. I had the ball out of bounds at mid-court, and I told him to break for the basket. He did, I lobbed him a pass, he got his record-setting basket, and came out again. In the locker room, I told a *Columbus Dispatch* sports writer, Dick Otte: "The headline tomorrow should say: KNIGHT AND LUCAS SET BIG TEN SCORING RECORD."

It didn't.

But I still liked Dick Otte. We had a good relationship then, a newspaper guy and a kid, and later he became far more than a newspaper guy to me. He was very good at what he did; he advanced to managing editor of the *Dispatch* and made one of Ohio's best newspapers better. He's a lifelong friend who over the years has given me advice about how to deal with a lot of things, including the press—more of which I probably should have followed.

Our teams at Ohio State were always pretty close and we players did a lot of things together. Havlicek and I were movie fans, and conscious of our money. If one of us owed the other a quarter from the time we had gone to the movies last week, we'd sure as hell bring it up—"Hey, *I* bought the popcorn last time. You owe me." We weren't operating with a huge budget. We knew the football players—not the basketball players, but the football players; this was Columbus—could go to the movies free. From our freshman year on, Havlicek and I would give the names of a couple of football players when we came through and it worked every time, right up through our senior year. I never worried about me, but I was afraid sooner or later someone was going to recognize Havlicek and call us on it. But it never happened.

We won all four of our NCAA tournament games by double-figure margins our first year. Our junior year we got a hell of a scare against Louisville in our first game. Lucas had an awful game—nine points—and they played us tough. We were tied in the final seconds when Havlicek hit the longest jump shot I ever saw him take in college. The shot went through with four seconds to go—now we were up 56–54, and I was on the court, guarding a forward. At a time-out, and after the time-out when we were back on the floor, if Siegfried told me once he told me eight times—"Bobby, don't foul! Whatever you do, don't foul. Remember, don't foul." They passed the ball in, Havlicek and Siegfried had Louisville's best player, John Turner, trapped in mid-court with his back to the basket as the last seconds were running out . . .

And Siegfried fouled him, with one second left.

I remember thinking, "Siegfried, you may be one of the smartest players I've ever been around, but that's gotta be one of the dumbest plays I've ever seen."

Turner hit his first free-throw, missed his second, and we won, 56–55.

I've watched the Big Ten for forty years now, and Jerry Lucas is the best player I've ever seen in the league.

He was a three-year All-American for us. He had that rare off-night against Louisville, but, boy, did he bounce back. The next night, he had thirty-three points and thirty rebounds and we beat Kentucky, 87–74. Think how excited the media would be today about a "thirty-thirty" game, involving two name teams. It *was* exciting; that's the only time it's been done in NCAA tournament history—counting Bill Russell, Wilt Chamberlain, Elgin Baylor, Lew Alcindor, Elvin Hayes, Larry Bird, everybody, ever. He was unstoppable. I got a tip-in and there was a time out right after it. When we got to the sidelines, Coach Taylor grabbed me and said, "Boy, that was a *heck* of a rebound."

I said, "Coach, the way Lucas is playing you've got no idea how good that rebound was." I didn't just have to out-rebound Kentucky to get that one, I had to out-rebound Lucas.

Back at the Final Four, though, we lost the championship game to Cincinnati, 75–70, in overtime. We shouldn't have. We were better than they were. One of the biggest contributions I made as a player in that whole era was scoring the basket that tied the game and sent it into overtime.

I remember how ecstatic we all were the night in San Francisco when we won the year before. What I remember of this game is how stunned and devastated we all were. And I remember John Havlicek and I walking the streets of Kansas City for three hours that night, trying to deal with that loss.

Our senior year, we had to play without Larry Siegfried, who had graduated. Siegfried was one of the best competitors I've ever seen, and as good a guard as I've ever seen in the Big Ten. He was a great defender. Of course we missed him.

But still we were No. 1 all year long and unbeaten again until, in our twenty-third game, after we had already clinched a third straight Big Ten championship, we lost at Wisconsin, 86–67. That night, I was on the floor late in the game and Havlicek, our captain, had been taken out. George Ellis, who had refereed some high school games I'd played in and was a National Football League official, walked over to me and said, "Taylor told me you're the captain—I guess he's given up."

We were 40–2 in Big Ten play those three years, both losses coming after we had clinched the league championship. And both of those last two years we reached the NCAA finals—the only time a Big Ten team ever made it to three straight Final Fours, let alone the championship game each time. Our class, the first one Coach Taylor recruited, in our three varsity years went 78–6.

Unlike the first time they beat us, in 1962 Cincinnati was just better than we were. Where we had lost players—Roberts and Siegfried off our 1960 championship lineup—they had added Ron Bonham and George Wilson.

Had there been freshman eligibility when we played, Lucas obviously would have started as a freshman and done very well. I'm not sure that Havlicek would have, even though he became one of the greatest Boston Celtics ever, a Hall of Fame player along with Lucas.

John was able, as a shooter, to change. He averaged over thirty points a game in high school. He used to kind of laugh about it. He said, "I'd just shoot it, go get it, and put it in."

But even as a freshman, the guy was just tireless. I mean *tireless*. He developed into a really good fourteen-, fifteen-, sixteen-foot shooter as a college player, and as a pro he was a very good eighteen- or nineteen-foot shooter.

He made great adjustments at every level where he played. I never did see him as high school player, but obviously I saw every game he played as a college player and I watched him play a great deal over the course of his career as a pro. He just got better and better every year.

There's a world of difference between John Havlicek, future Hall of Famer, as he left Ohio State and these kids who go into college today dollar-struck by all that NBA money and thinking it's just logical, really inevitable, that they're going to make it there. They look at the money without even thinking about what they have to do to get there.

When Havlicek got drafted by the Celtics, he asked me, "Can I make that team?" Remember, there were only nine NBA teams then, and Boston had just won its fourth straight championship.

I told him, "That's the best team in the world for you to play on. You don't know how lucky you are." I think Havlicek could have been drafted by some teams and not really fit in. He was perfect for the Celtics and became one of basketball's all-time best.

I admired John as much as any player I was ever around, because of his competitiveness and his willingness to do anything he had to to win.

I always got kind of a perverse kick out of reading newspaper references to me as a bench rider or a substitute. Any kid who's on scholarship at a major Division I basketball school can play. I played a lot as a sixth or seventh man and started a few games, on a very good team for a great coach.

I worked hard for Coach Taylor, but—not outwardly but inwardly—I'm sure I was kind of a pain in the ass for him because I always thought I should play more. That in no way lessened the feeling I had about being part of a good team. Because of my own experience, as a coach it never bothered me when one of my kids felt that way. I'd like to think all kids want to play more.

As a coach, I always try to tell a kid what he has to do to get more playing time—"you've got to become a better rebounder," or "you've got to see people open and get them the ball," or "right now we have guys who are doing the things that have to be done better than you." I always have empathy for guys like that.

Coach Taylor and I differed in a lot of ways, and I'm sure he's glad. I don't think he'd want me to be thought of as his clone—or for everything I've done over the years to be attributed to him.

I'll give an example of one difference.

My senior year, we played Wichita State on Friday night at Columbus. I had played as sixth man and scored a couple of baskets. We beat them and flew out that night for a Saturday game against Wake Forest. We were No. 1 in the country at the time and they were No. 3—Lennie Chappell and Billy Packer now established as stars.

We were down six points when I went in with ten minutes left in the half and we were six ahead at halftime. I hadn't turned the game around, but I thought I had played pretty well. Coach Taylor started the second half with his same starting lineup. I was disappointed. I felt I deserved a chance to start that half, but he just didn't believe in altering his lineup. When I was a sophomore, he started Dick Furry in the first game. The next twenty-six games he started John Havlicek. That one move, Havlicek replacing Furry, was the only time all year that he changed the lineup, unless there was an injury. And the starters also started the second half. Always.

When I started coaching, that Wake Forest situation was something I remembered. It has definitely influenced my feeling about picking a starting lineup for the second half.

I would guess that over the years I've changed starting lineups maybe more than any coach in basketball—usually as a reward for a kid for what he did in practice or for his play in a game. I can look at things the way a substitute player does, when he has that moment when he plays well and helps his team. Maybe he's not a better player, but that situation is a chance for the coach to reward that kid in the way that means the most to him—by starting him the second half, maybe, or the next game, or playing him a little more.

I think if players look back over their careers at Indiana, they would all have to feel, "I had a lot of chances to play." By the same token, I'm sure there are probably circumstances where justifiably kids thought, "He's given so-and-so more chances to play than he's given me." And maybe in doing so I went against my own best instincts—maybe I felt we were a little bit stuck with our offensive play and needed a little more scoring, or . . . whatever.

When I look back on decisions I made against my defense-first instincts, I second-guess myself. When I stay right down the line with things that I believe in, I think the team and the coach are better off. Defense is obviously one of those.

In the years since we played together at Ohio State, Gary Gearhart has been one of my closest friends. I can't count the number of times he has come to Bloomington to see us play—or gone to a number of places on the road, or to NCAA tournament games around the country.

And John Havlicek and I have always been close friends. We never roomed together, but we got along well right from the beginning and retained that friendship. We played freshman baseball together. I didn't go out for baseball until a month after they had started. John played first base—he was agile, a good fielder. John went on to play one year of varsity baseball. I remember seeing him hit an inside-the-park home run one Saturday afternoon, and it was against Indiana.

John and I took several classes together. One was in physical education:

canoeing. We got to class late one day, and everyone was already out on the Olentangy River with the instructor, Charlie Mann. We couldn't see them, but we knew where they had to be, so we got in our canoe and paddled like hell to catch up. One thing about those canoes: they don't have a brake. We came charging around a curve and saw our class—but not in time to avoid ramming right into the canoe the instructor was in.

Our senior year Ohio State won the Big Ten football championship but had to turn down the Rose Bowl bid because the faculty refused to approve the trip. The reaction among the students was predictable: protests everywhere. The papers mentioned that as part of the protest some students took over a street-car downtown and commandeered it. John and I were in on that. Today, we'd be all over television news. Then, nobody paid any attention to us.

I'm sure John would say both of those times were my fault. He might be right.

Joe Roberts ranks right with John and Gary as the three I've stayed closest with from the teams I played on at Ohio State. College days are why John and Gary, in particular, and a few others from Ohio State frequently call me—to this day—by a nickname:

"Dragon."

When we first got to know each other, I told John, Gary, and some other guys that back home in Orrville I was a member of a motorcycle gang called The Dragons. I don't want to say they were gullible; I'd rather think I was pretty damned convincing, to get anybody to believe that in those days in Orrville I was in a gang.

Long after they all realized there wasn't any such thing, they stuck with it as a nickname for me. The idea of a fire-breathing dragon—there could have been a little bit of that involved in why they maintained it.

I do think it was neat that 1940, the year I was born, was a Year of the Dragon on the Chinese calendar.

And so was 1976, the year our Indiana team went unbeaten and won the NCAA championship.

I had four different roommates at Ohio State. As a freshman, I started out with John Banks, a football player from Hamilton, Ohio, and Gearhart, who was an outstanding basketball player from the Dayton area.

My sophomore year I roomed with Frank "Moose" Ambrose, a lovable character who went to Notre Dame on a football scholarship, decided he didn't want to play, and went to Ohio State. He was the best imitator of Art Carney

I've ever seen. When we'd go to the Union to shoot pool or play cards, he'd wear a white T-shirt, a vest, and a hat, and he sounded just like him. I handled the fun we had just a little better in the classroom than Frank did. He went back to Dayton to live, and his son, Frank, eventually went to Indiana to play football.

My last two years, my roommate was another basketball player, Dick Reasbeck, from Martins Ferry, Ohio—one of the best shooters I ever saw.

My first exposure to Olympic basketball came my sophomore year at Ohio State.

America used an altogether different selection system then from what we used in 1984. Because we won the 1960 NCAA tournament, we were invited that spring to the U.S. Olympic trials to compete as a team in an eight-team tournament with the Akron Goodyears, Phillips Oilers, and Peoria Caterpillars from the AAU league, and all-star teams from the NCAA University Division, NCAA colleges, NAIA, and Armed Forces.

We lost in our first game to the NAIA team, then won two to finish fifth. The winning team automatically got six players on the team and the other spots were picked at large.

Pete Newell's University All-Stars won the tournament, and that made him the coach. From his University All-Stars, he was able to put on the Olympic team Oscar Robertson of Cincinnati, Jerry West of West Virginia, Terry Dischinger of Purdue, Walt Bellamy of Indiana, Jay Arnette of Texas, and Darrall Imhoff of his own California team.

AAU players who made it were Les Lane, who had played at Oklahoma (and later coached at Oklahoma—he was just over forty when he died of a heart attack in 1975, and that's the job Dave Bliss got when he left our Indiana staff), Burdette Haldorson (who also played with Bill Russell on the 1956 team), Al Kelley (who played on the Kansas team that Indiana beat in 1953 for the NCAA championship), and Bob Boozer, who had played at Kansas State.

Adrian Smith, who had played at Kentucky, came off the Armed Forces team, and Jerry Lucas was the only Ohio State player who made the Olympic team.

I think John Havlicek came very close, but the second guy on our team who should have made it was Larry Siegfried. He outscored Lane something like 21–3 when we played the Phillips Oilers. Lane later became the guy who ran the Olympic team for Pete. And there were a couple of other guys on the team who in just no way were better than Siegfried.

But Havlicek also was very good at the Trials. And Jimmy Darrow of Bowling Green, playing on the University All-Stars, absolutely should have been on the team. He had three excellent games coming off the bench but he didn't make the team.

It didn't matter much, as far as winning the gold medal. Pete Newell coaching and West, Robertson, and Lucas playing guaranteed it would be a damned good team.

SIX: *The Army Way (1962–1971)*

*His mother would have sent him to a monastery if she could
have. I and West Point were the next-best thing.*

After I graduated from Ohio State, I had a pretty good idea what I wanted
to do: teach and coach in high school for a year, then go to law school
somewhere where I could work in basketball as a graduate assistant coach. My
Ohio State coach, Fred Taylor, was working that out.

When we played in the NCAA finals at Louisville my senior year, Harold
"Andy" Andreas, the coach at Cuyahoga Falls High School outside Akron and
one of the most respected coaches in Ohio, asked me if I'd be interested in
being an assistant coach for him the 1962–63 season.

That certainly appealed to me, but I didn't commit one way or the other. I
had an invitation from Celina High School in western Ohio to apply for their
head coaching job in basketball. The job also included being the line coach in
football.

I went to Celina for the interview, although as much as I had enjoyed playing football, I had no desire to coach anything but basketball. I didn't think I
could put together a good basketball program at any level without having all
year to work on it. When I told them that, whatever chance I had to be Celina's
head coach went out the window, as I knew it would.

So I took the job with Andy. It may have been the best decision I ever made,
and the most valuable year I ever spent. I learned about coaching basketball. I
learned the difference between coaching and playing, and all the decisions a
coach has to make, all the things that he has to factor into his decisions. Andy
was one of the best coaches I was ever around.

I was the junior varsity coach, but our varsity and jayvee teams practiced
together. So I was with Andy every night.

He had a certain way he thought the game had to be played. About
halfway through the season, we played Barberton, and they had a hell of a

good jayvee team. I thought we could beat them, but I wanted to be a coach. So I figured out how we could beat them with a one-three-one half-court trapping zone. I was kind of proud of it, and I explained my thinking to Andy. He listened to everything I had to say, and then said, "Well, if you're ever going to be a coach, you'd better figure out how to beat 'em man-to-man."

I didn't know whether that meant if I was ever going to be a coach with him, or a coach period.

I took his hint. We played them with a man-to-man and won. It was a long, long time after that before I ever again seriously considered using a zone.

One of my best moments that season came the first time I went back to Canton Fieldhouse, where my high school playing career had ended.

Cuyahoga Falls played Canton Lincoln there as part of a doubleheader, which meant there was no jayvee game. It was a tough game between two very well-coached teams (Kenny Newlon was Lincoln's coach) and we won, 54–51. With about two minutes to go, I suggested to Andy that we spread Lincoln's defense out and put our center, Bob Forte, on the high post and work to get lay-ups. Andy took a time-out and set that up. When we were walking off the floor after the game, Andy put his arm around my shoulder and said, "That was a really good suggestion." An assistant coach can live on a moment like that for a long time.

That year with Andy convinced me how much more there is to basketball than any player understands. When you're playing, you're wrapped up with yourself. Andy showed me what goes into the decisions a coach has to make, and I had a much different perspective on my own career. Anybody who ever plays always thinks he's a good player and, particularly in a competitive situation where you or somebody else could be playing, you always think it should be you. After that season with Andy, I felt that if every player had an opportunity to coach for a year, he'd look at himself as a player in a much different light.

The NCAA finals were in Louisville again in the spring of 1963, and I went down to see the games with Bob Fee, a Cuyahoga Falls math teacher who became a lifelong friend of mine. I was standing in the Brown Hotel lobby, talking to Coach Taylor about my graduate school situation—he had talked to some coaches about it the day before—when George Hunter, the Army coach, walked up. He was a friend of Fred's, and he listened to our conversation for a while. When I left, Hunter told him, "If he ever goes into the army, be sure to let me know and we'll get him transferred to West Point to do some coaching with our plebe team."

Had it not been for George Hunter coming into that conversation at exactly the point he did, I probably wouldn't have gone into coaching.

The early stirrings involving the United States in Vietnam had not even begun by then, and it wasn't yet on everybody's mind. There was a draft, though, so when I heard what Coach Hunter had told Coach Taylor, I started thinking about getting my military obligation out of the way and doing some coaching, too. I volunteered for the draft. My dad didn't think anybody should go to college to be a coach in the first place, and when I told him I had volunteered for the army, he thought for sure he had raised an idiot. So did I, when not more than a week after I had done it, Coach Taylor called to tell me George Hunter had been fired at Army.

I didn't know what the hell was going to happen.

Coach Taylor went to work for me then. He talked with the new coach, a twenty-six-year-old guy named Taylor "Tates" Locke, who had been Hunter's assistant for two years.

Then he called to tell me everything was still on.

I thoroughly enjoyed my two years as Tates's assistant. They were his first two years as a head coach, and he was feeling his way—which was good for me. It meant I got to be involved in the basic things—should we do this? Should we do that? I was much more involved in decisions than most assistants are, and that made it a great learning situation. Tates believed in defense-first, and he had a lot to do with my own thinking in that regard.

I had all kinds of experiences at West Point as an assistant coach and a recruiter and scout under Tates, and even later when I was head coach.

The second year I assisted Tates, we played in the National Invitation Tournament (NIT). Tates had gone ahead, and I was on the bus with the team going down to New York for our first tournament game.

I always wanted to use time well, so while we were riding along, I stood in the front of the bus with a clipboard and went through a scouting report with the players listening.

Our center was John Ritch, who did a hell of a job for us. This was his senior year, and he was a Rhodes Scholar.

As I was talking to them about the other team's personnel and what we wanted to do, I noticed Ritch wasn't even looking at me. He was staring out the window.

That kind of irritated me, so I said in my best slightly irritated voice:

"Dammit, John, pay attention to what I'm saying—forget the window. Now, *what did I just say?*"

John turned his head, looked at me, and casually repeated verbatim the last five things I had said.

As I said, John was a Rhodes Scholar.

While I was still an assistant I had an unforgettable scouting trip that showed me how gracious great veteran coaches could be.

I was scouting St. John's. My trip started in Milwaukee where St. John's lost big to Marquette, and then I was to see them a second time two nights later in Chicago against Loyola. I ran into the legendary St. John's coach, Joe Lapchick, who knew what I was doing. He said, "If you're going to scout us, you might as well go to Chicago with us." He gave me a train ticket, I rode to Chicago with them, I stayed at their Chicago hotel, and as we were checking in, he said, "Be back down here in the lobby in fifteen minutes. You're going with us to the Diamond Grill for a steak."

The next night, I watched St. John's beat Loyola, and at the game I sat beside Ray Meyer, the Hall of Fame coach at DePaul who was coaching there before I started first grade. It was the first time we had met, but he asked me how I was getting back to New York. I had a midnight flight to catch, and he went considerably out of his way to take me to the airport to catch that flight.

As both an assistant coach and a head coach, I would leave West Point when school started in early September and not get back until the tenth of October. I'd go all over the country looking at kids and talking to kids—every once in a while slipping back to make sure my kids were working.

A record I'm not particularly proud of is that I once figured out that I'd had speeding tickets in every state on a straight line from New York to Kansas. Once I had my driver's license confiscated in Illinois and the next day got another speeding ticket in Ohio, which was not a good idea without a driver's license.

As an assistant coach I watched a Friday night high school game in Washington, D.C., and a Navy game on Saturday afternoon. Tates was supposed to pick me up at the Newark airport and the two of us would go scout St. John's. We got the communications screwed up; there was nobody there to meet me and it was snowing like hell.

The clock told me to give up on the St. John's game, so I went out to hitchhike back to West Point. The first ride I got took me a few miles in that direction. Then I was back out in the snow, trying to get up on the Palisades Parkway.

Walking along, I came across two young women whose car was stuck in the snow, and they were frightened. I walked up and actually got the car out for them. They were very grateful, and they asked me, "Where are you going?" I told them about missing connections and how I was trying to get to the Parkway. A little reluctantly—and I certainly didn't blame them, in a snowstorm—they took me to the Palisades Parkway. Then another young guy and his wife, returning from their honeymoon in Florida, took me to West Point.

After I became head coach, I was driving west on the Pennsylvania Turnpike to speak at a clinic in Mercer, Pennsylvania. It was late at night. I wasn't going to get in there until one or two in the morning. At about midnight, I ran out of gas. Nobody has run out of gas more times or in more difficult places than I have. This was one of them. There's nowhere to buy gas on that turnpike except at some spread-out Howard Johnson's service plazas.

I had seen a service plaza not too far back on the eastbound side—the other side for me. I walked over to that side and hitchhiked. Before long a Greyhound driver picked me up. I stood in the well of the bus and he let me off at the service plaza. I bought a can of gas and crawled over the median rails to get to the side headed west toward my car.

It was too far to walk—ten or twelve miles. I had to hitchhike. Eventually, a young woman with a baby picked me up—in a Volkswagen. She had the little baby strapped into the backseat.

As I rode with her, I explained to her what had happened. Then when we got to my car and as I was getting out, boy, did I give her a hell of a lecture, "Don't you ever pick up anybody at night. You're out of your mind doing that. I can't tell you how much I appreciate your giving me a ride, but don't ever, ever—by yourself, in particular with your baby—give anybody a ride."

She may not have cared much for my style, but I hope she listened.

The man who gave me my first head coaching job, Colonel Ray Murphy, was one of the five most influential people in my lifetime. I loved the guy like a father—I loved just being around him, the way he handled things. He's retired now, living in Colorado Springs, and he's still as good a friend and as big a booster as I have.

As Army's athletic director he went out on a limb offering me the job. I was twenty-four. I had coached the Army plebe team. Not everybody there thought I was the right guy to coach at West Point. I was tough and aggressive—too tough and too aggressive for some.

But not for Colonel Murphy.

After two great years as head coach at Army, Tates Locke left in the spring of 1965 to go to Miami of Ohio. On a Friday morning, Colonel Murphy called me to his office and told me:

"I'm going to make you the next basketball coach at West Point."

I said, "I'll let you know on Monday. I've got to think some things through."

I don't think it was the answer he was expecting. If he'd had a rifle in his hands, I might not have made it out of that office.

I wasn't just being coy. Back in Orrville, Tony Yonto, who has been one of my good friends all my life, told me how Ara Parseghian had handled his first contract negotiations when he went from Northwestern to coach at Notre Dame. Tony's brother Joe was Ara's line coach at Notre Dame, so I was sure Tony knew what he was talking about.

As the Northwestern coach, Ara's teams beat Notre Dame four straight times. Then the Notre Dame job opened, and he wanted it. He went to South Bend, he agreed to take the job, and then Notre Dame backed down on something—maybe reneged. Ara left. He wanted the job, but he would take it only under his terms.

And, after a few days, that's what he got.

That happened in 1964. This was just a year later. That story was on my mind when Colonel Murphy offered me the job, and I thought, *I don't want them to think I'll take this job under any conditions*. It wasn't a pure bluff. I had a couple of other offers to be an assistant coach. Cincinnati was one. Tay Baker, who succeeded Ed Jucker, offered me the freshman job. I wasn't absolutely sure that I wanted to coach. Even at that point, I still had some thoughts about going to law school.

On Monday, I went in and accepted the job. But first I did get agreement on things I thought I had to have to continue the improvement of the basketball program that Tates had started—like setting up the floor in the Fieldhouse so we could practice there in October, not after the football season was over. Tates's first game as head coach we played Lehigh in the second-floor central gym in the physical education building. The gym was a rectangular box, no windows, two doors; it had maybe six rows of bleachers on each side seating about 400 people. The wall was right behind the basket. It was the worst place I ever saw a major college game played.

We played there because the policy was to keep the Fieldhouse available if the football team had to practice inside. The court wasn't put down until after the Army–Navy football game, which was in December.

As big as football was at Ohio State under Woody Hayes, that would not have happened there—by Woody's preference. Before I ever got there, a tackle named Dick Guy was a guest on Woody's TV show after they'd had a week of bad weather and practiced outside in it, prior to the Michigan game. Woody was proud of practicing in those tough conditions and he said, "If you're going to fight in the North Atlantic, you train in the North Atlantic, isn't that right, Dick?" Guy said, "If it's all the same to you, Coach, I'd just as soon fight in Florida."

But at West Point then, basketball gave way to football.

My first year, Colonel Murphy promised me that the floor would be down on October 15. Something happened. I never asked what. He called me in one day in the fall of 1965 and said, "I know what I promised you, but I can't get this done for ten days." I could see that whatever it was, he had a problem. I said, "Fine." I trust people who have given me reason to trust them.

After I had coached one year at West Point, I had a chance to go to the University of Florida to coach. Norm Sloan had left Florida to go to North Carolina State. Ray Graves, who had been an outstanding football coach there, was the Florida athletic director. When he interviewed me for the job, we hit it off well.

He offered me the job, and I was excited. Florida had gone 21–4 the year before and had everybody back, including a good center, Neal Walk. Gainesville obviously was going to be a nice place to live. I was just twenty-five and I had a chance like that.

I went in on a Thursday morning and told Colonel Murphy I was going to Florida.

That night I called Columbus, Ohio, to tell Coach Taylor what I was going to do.

He didn't tell me what to do. He heard me out, then said, "You know, you're a young guy. They gave you a chance at West Point without your ever having coached anywhere."

He was right. I had coached for three years but I had never been a head coach when I got that job.

"I just want you to think about the fact that they gave you a chance and nobody else was going to," he said. That's all he said, and that's all he needed to say.

I went to see Colonel Murphy the next morning. I can see him now, sitting behind his desk, signing some letters. He looked up and kind of acknowledged me when I came in.

I said, "I just came in to tell you I'm going to stay. I'm not going to Florida."

I guess I expected him to jump over the desk and hug me. All he did was look up at me and say, "I knew you would."

And he looked back down and went right back to writing.

I walked out of there kind of stunned. Then, as I got to thinking about that,

I realized it was one of the greatest compliments I ever had. He was telling me that staying was the right thing for me to do, and he knew I would do the right thing.

It became an extremely special moment in my life.

Other than that, the closest I ever came to leaving Army before I actually did was after the 1967–68 season, when I was interviewed at Wisconsin. I considered it an attractive job. They indicated I was their choice, but I asked for time to go back to West Point and think about it. Almost as soon as I left, they announced me as their new coach. When I arrived home at West Point, I heard what they had done.

Now, I was in a hell of a spot. I was up all night trying to figure out what I should do. Everybody was telling me, "You have to do what you think is best." Of course you're going to do that. You want to know what *they* think.

The only guy I could think of to run this by was Bo Schembechler, who was coaching then at Miami of Ohio. He had been an assistant to Woody Hayes when I was in school at Ohio State. I knew he had gone through a situation similar to mine at Wisconsin the year before, involving the football job. When we were both at Ohio State, I didn't know him well, but he was an assistant coach who mixed well with kids. One time John Havlicek and I were standing and watching the state high school baseball finals at the Ohio State diamond. Bo came up, elbowed his way in between us, and said in his staccato speaking style, "This reminds me of when Naragon and I brought Barberton down here for the state finals." Barberton was close enough to Orrville that I knew a little bit about that. Bo was a damned good high school pitcher, and the Naragon he mentioned was Hal, who made it to the major leagues as a catcher. I couldn't resist a needle. I said, "Coach, is that the time you got knocked out in the seventh inning and you lost the game?" He said, "Son-of-a-bitch, how did you know about that?"

After Tates Locke had gone from Army to Miami and Bo was still there, I got to know him a little better. So, about six in the morning, I called Bo at Miami. He said, "Damn. Let me wash my face and wake up a little bit and then tell me the story."

I told him how Wisconsin had released my name as the new coach before I'd had a chance to talk to them about what was necessary for them to do—that I'd have liked to take the job but I didn't think I could, under those circumstances. He listened to everything I said, then told me, "Just call them and tell them you have no interest in the job." I did.

About twenty years after that, an alumnus of Wisconsin came up to me at a golf course and asked for my version of what happened when I almost became Wisconsin's coach. I told him about my situation and the one the year before with Bo, and said if Wisconsin had handled both situations a little better, Bo and I might have been coaching there together for a long time.

I think the football part bothered him the most.

An irony of the situation was that my pulling out let Wisconsin give the job to outgoing coach John Erickson's assistant, John Powless. Powless was still on the job when I came into the league at Indiana, and we formed a friendship that has lasted. He lives in the Madison area, and through my last year at Indiana, he would always come by our hotel and have breakfast with me on the day of our game up there.

After I was at Indiana and Bo was at Michigan, we developed a great relationship. One day, my locker room phone rang, I picked it up, and a voice said:

"It's a hell of a thing when my best friend in this league is a God-damned basketball coach."

Click.

That was Bo, another of my coaching teachers. He taught me the responsibility of a coach to demand from his players the best they could give.

When he retired from coaching and became president of the Detroit Tigers, they had a banquet in Ann Arbor honoring him, and I was a speaker. When it was my turn to talk, I put on a dark blue Michigan baseball cap and dark sunglasses and walked, Bo-style, to the microphone. And then I said, in as close to his voice and speaking style as I could muster, "I'm paying millions of dollars for guys who can't hit, and millions of dollars for guys who can't get the ball over the plate—Christ Almighty, I feel like I'm coaching at Illinois."

Late in my fourth year at Army, the Texas Tech coaching job opened. The president of the school, Grover Murray, came out to New York City to see me about the job. We met at the Plaza Hotel, and I was really interested. I thought at the time Texas Tech and SMU were the two best basketball programs in the Southwest Conference, and I fully intended to go out and talk to him further after the season.

That week, we played at Navy. At the time, TV was carrying only one regional game a week, and this was the Eastern game, with Jim Simpson as the announcer. Navy held the ball on us and the score at halftime was 24–17. We got ahead 28–17, Mike Krzyzewski and Jimmy Oxley were my guards, and I told them, "If they want to hold the ball, we'll show them how it's done." The final score was 51–35, and I was happy. What I didn't know was that Texas Tech's athletic director, J. T. King, had come to the game. He went back out to Lubbock and told Dr. Murray, "We can't hire that guy. The way he plays, we'd *never* sell any tickets."

Ever since then I've never gone by the Plaza Hotel without walking through the lobby, where I can see the restaurant and even the table where we sat. When Gerald Myers called me about the Texas Tech job last spring, that whole experience in 1969 was the first thing that went through my mind.

That one game may have set me back thirty-two years. But I'm finally there.

I'll always cherish my eight years at West Point. Anyone as fond of history as I am would have to love spending that long a period surrounded by the aura and the tradition of the Academy.

And the kids I was fortunate enough to coach there added to all that.

Vince Lombardi once talked about power—football power, manpower, Packer power—and he said, "All of these dwindled into insignificance when one thought about heart power." Napoleon said the power of the spirit was far superior to the power of the sword.

Our Army teams won 67 percent of their games my six years as head coach though far more times than not they gave away an edge in attributes most people consider vital for a basketball team. They never met a team, though, that had an edge on them in Lombardi's "heart power" or Napoleon's "power of the spirit." They taught me how much of a privilege coaching is when kids want to win without thinking of individual goals.

People think the toughest thing about coaching basketball at Army is the military academies' height restriction—nothing over 6-foot-6 seems to be the common understanding. First of all, that's not true. Much tougher to sell were the restrictions inherent in a service academy, starting with a four-year military obligation after graduation which later became five years, and I think is now six. It was a highly regimented type of life. A kid then was up at ten to six every morning, he had to go to breakfast and to lunch and stand in formation to do so, he didn't cut class, and classes went through to Saturday at noon. They had weekly academic checks to determine each cadet's eligibility; they didn't go semester by semester. Cadets got only one month off each year, in the summer. During my years, there were no female cadets. Because everyday life was so demanding, I felt I had to be more demanding as a coach than anybody there. It was the only time during the day when the players could relax—on the practice field or floor, they got away from military regimentation. I felt if I was going to be successful, if we were going to win, I couldn't allow them to let down.

My first game as a head coach was at Princeton. Ed Pillings was our trainer. He also was the football trainer and I enjoyed him immensely. Ed was a great storyteller, and he had worked for one of college football's all-time great coaches, Colonel Earl (Red) Blaik.

We were getting ready to go out on the court to start that first game at Princeton. I wasn't sure what to do, so I thought we should say a little prayer. I said, "Let's bow our heads and say The Lord's Prayer."

As we were walking up the stairs, Ed put his arm around my shoulders and said: "For whatever it's worth, let me tell you: you and prayers just aren't a good mix."

We never did that again.

We were behind Princeton at the half, 26–25. John Stevens, who was an American League baseball umpire from Scranton, was one of the referees, and I had been on him a little bit.

As we were walking off the court at halftime, I went up to him and said, "Mr. Stevens, I'm sorry. I'm excited. This is my first game. I don't mean to be getting on you guys like I have."

He looked at me a second, then said, "Son, when you've heard everything I've heard coming out of those dugouts, you sound like an angel."

I always had a soft spot in my heart for John Stevens.

Mike Silliman, who may still be the best player I've ever coached on a college team, was on the first team I coached. Mike was the best basketball player West Point ever had. If there had been a McDonald's All-America team in his high school days at Louisville St. Xavier, if there had been a Gatorade National Player of the Year, Silliman would have been picked. He was Kentucky's "Mr. Basketball," and obviously it was quite a feat for Army to get him. George Hunter was the Army coach involved, but I think the truth of the matter was that Kentucky recruited him hard and his mother wanted him to go to Notre Dame, so he went to West Point as a compromise.

Mike was a great player and a great person—captain of the Olympic team in 1968, three years after he graduated. Henry Iba told me later how much he enjoyed having Mike as a player and as his Olympic team captain. He was in the military for four years, then had a year in the NBA. Tragically, he died the summer of 2000—a week before he was going to come to Bloomington along with seventeen or eighteen other former Army players to take part in our annual Indiana Players' Golf Outing.

I coached him for just half a season, but there's no player I've had that I would directly compare with him. He was 6-foot-6, and he weighed 230. He could pass the ball, and handle it—he wasn't great with the ball on the dribble, but he was a tremendous passer. He was very smart reading defenses, he could go either way. He was a very, very adequate shooter, he defended well, and he couldn't jump but he rebounded well—he was a great all-round player.

An appendectomy kept him out of our first two games. We split those. In his first game with us, we beat NYU on a Saturday, then beat Cornell in overtime on Monday. Mike scored in the twenties in each of those games.

We were 10–4, on our way to becoming very good, when we played Rutgers, which, under Bill Foster, was always a tough game for us.

In the second half, Mike injured his knee, and his season and college career ended right there.

I ran the film over and over again that night, for an hour, and I couldn't see where anything happened. He was running down the floor—no cuts, no sharp moves, running straight ahead—and all of a sudden he pulled up limping. He must have had a partially-torn cartilage that just gave way. Had that been today, the surgery would have been done with an arthroscope and he might have been back in two weeks. But then, we lost him for the season.

We won the Rutgers game, but it didn't feel like a win. Not even close.

It was a midweek afternoon game—until my last year, West Point always started its midweek home games at four o'clock. Coach Bee was there. He hadn't let me know he was coming, but I saw him sitting by himself high up in the stands. I called him that night, and he asked me how Silliman was. I said, as glumly as I felt, "Coach, he has torn cartilage. He's out for the season."

I think everybody else I've ever known in my life would have said, "Oh, my. That's awful." That isn't what the Coach said. His immediate comment was, "Okay, who are we going to replace him with?"

I don't think there was ever a time I talked to Clair Bee, or ever a time I was around him, when I didn't learn something from him. By the same token, and I've always appreciated this: I don't think there was ever a time when we were together when he didn't try to teach me something.

What he taught me that day of the Silliman injury formulated my attitude toward injuries from then on—let's make sure the kid has the best care possible, let's make sure he goes through rehab as well as he can. But as a team—let's get on with it. Let's see what we can do to play better. No matter how much it takes out of you, or how much you wanted something to happen that didn't, you've just got to keep going.

In all the years since, I've rarely talked publicly about injuries. Against Pepperdine in the opening round of the 2000 NCAA tournament, which turned out to be my last game as Indiana's coach, we lost our best rebounder and inside player, Kirk Haston, in the first minute of the game. Obviously it hurt us badly; we thought we had a significant edge on them inside.

In the press conference afterward, I rejected that injury as a factor in the game. "We don't beat these guys if Haston *doesn't* get hurt," I said. I didn't believe it, but I've always handled it that way. I don't want to take anything away from the other team's accomplishment, and I don't want our team grasping at excuses. But the third and biggest reason was the lesson Clair Bee taught me that day we lost Mike Silliman.

I was very lucky that first year. Our captain, Dick Murray, was a tough, competitive kid who made himself a tremendous defensive player. Bobby Seigle handled the ball well and got the ball to people when they were open. Billy Schutsky was an outstanding player. Joe Lapchick called him "that wonderful son-of-a-bitch Schutsky."

Billy had a supreme confidence in his ability, and yet he played within his limits. He averaged over eighteen points a game for his three-year career. Schutsky might have been the best-prepared kid I ever saw come into college. Rollie Massimino coached him through his junior year and Jack Sayer his last year. They did a great job. He could put the ball on the floor well, he was a very good shooter, and he was excellent at reading the defense. He was only 6-foot-2 and he couldn't jump, but he could take it to the bucket and score against anyone.

One of the best games any of my teams ever played was against San Francisco in the NIT that first year I was a head coach. They beat Penn State easily in the first round, and their center, Erwin Mueller, who made the NBA All-Rookie team the next year, scored thirty-one points. At the same time, we'd had a very tough game with Manhattan (71–66).

Billy Helkie, one of the best shooters I've ever had, was one of the players who had stepped up when we lost Mike Silliman. Billy wasn't just a basketball player. He works now for the Federal Reserve System and is a member of the World Bank.

In the first half of the game with San Francisco, Billy scored twenty-five points and we led, 39–24. We played so well I didn't know what to do. Colonel

Murphy was so excited when he came into the locker room he was beside himself. He shouted to me, "I've never seen basketball played this well." I didn't want to hear that, with twenty minutes to play. I said, "Be quiet!" And I was so tight I stepped into the shower room and threw up. We went on to win, 80–68, and Helkie kidded me after the game, "Coach, we didn't mean to make you sick at the half. I thought we were playing better than that." That was as well as I've ever had a team play throughout a game.

In the semifinals, we led BYU by two points with about two minutes to go. Their All-America guard, Rich Nemelka, collided with Helkie at the top of the key—an obvious charging foul on Nemelka, which would have been his fifth. One official, Bud Fidgeon, came running toward the play with his hand behind his head, signaling a charge. Lou Eisenstein came from the baseline to wave Fidgeon off the play and called a blocking foul on Helkie. We lost 66–60. I thought that call cost us the game and said so very emphatically in the press conference after the game. That was my first major encounter with the press; I just got blistered in the newspapers. Eisenstein was from New York. I think he missed that call, but I always thought he was a good guy and good official.

The 1969–70 team (22–6) may have been my best at West Point. It also was involved in my biggest disappointment there.

It happened against St. John's in the NIT semifinals. We were leading 59–58 when the ball went out of bounds with four seconds to go. The game film clearly showed St. John's hit the ball out of bounds but the call went their way and they retained possession. They passed it in, Rich Lyons got off a desperation shot over Jimmy Oxley that had no chance of going in, but the whistle blew—Oxley was called for fouling the shooter, with one second to go. It was an awful call. Lyons hit the free-throws and instead of going to the finals for the first time, we were out.

I was so crushed I was excused from the postgame press conference. I went back into a room and sat there alone. That's where I was when I looked up and saw a man standing in front of me.

Howard Cosell.

"Bobby," he said, "don't forget: the sun will come up in the morning, and they'll still be fighting in Vietnam."

And he turned and left.

I can't begin to say how much I appreciated the thought and the kindness in that gesture by Howard. As long as he lived, he had no bigger fan than me. I knew him not only as a brilliant person but as a man who sincerely cared about friends. Frank Deford once wrote a long feature article on Howard and asked him to send three letters that had meant the most to him. Frank told me one of the letters he picked was from me, with a note on the side that said, "You know this man means what he says." When he passed away, I was touched and honored when his daughter Hillary invited me to a special memorial service for him.

Clair Bee knew how painful that St. John's loss was for me. A letter came in:

> *It was a heartbreaker and probably your last big test in the crucible of fire that molds a man into a man. I prefer to feel that way about it because now you have drained to the bitterest dregs an impossible defeat in your near-miss pursuit of glory and you will be stronger for it.*
>
> *Disappointments and heartbreaks strengthen a man. Your day will come; this I know. Your determination, desire and devotion to the game will carry you to new heights. I hope I am around to cheer for you and your team when that day comes.*

He was, and for that I'll always be grateful.

Being at Army was a great introduction for me to the pressures of coaching. Although basketball certainly wasn't a great priority at the Academy, getting to the NIT was a real objective for us—every year.

In fact, in 1968 I turned down a bid to the NCAA so we could accept an invitation to the NIT. Imagine someone doing that today.

We were good—20–4 at the time, the third-ranked team in the East, according to the NCAA selectors. Columbia was seeded first and should have been. They had a great coach in Jack Rohan and outstanding players in Jim McMillian, Heyward Dotson, and David Newmark—each of them drafted by the pros, and McMillian in particular went on to have an outstanding NBA career. St. Bonaventure, with Bob Lanier, was second. I couldn't argue with that one, either. We were going to be assigned to play in either Blacksburg, Virginia, or Kingston, Rhode Island. In neither place were we going to be able to take the corps of cadets along.

The kids in the corps loved going to New York. The academy would take 1,500 to 2,000 cadets to our games at Madison Square Garden—bus them down and they'd get to spend a day in New York. Whenever we played in the NIT, they took cadets down every game.

That was something I had in mind when I made the NIT-over-NCAA decision. As much as I would have liked to see us play in the NCAA, I thought what was involved was just bigger than our playing basketball—something for the whole corps.

So, in my infinite wisdom, I chose the NIT and we got beat right away by Notre Dame, 62–58. I've always felt that was a game where I hurt my team, not during the game but the day before it, and it was a lesson I never forgot.

We went into New York the day before we played. Something got screwed up—the timing of the practice or something, and I made some wise-ass comment I'd have been better off not making. But we practiced, and we couldn't have been any better—so good I stopped the practice halfway through.

We had always stayed at Loew's, up where the old Garden was, Eighth Avenue and 49th Street. This time we stayed at a place that had just been remodeled: the Penn Garden, right across the street from Pennsylvania Station. From the time we got there, it was chaos. Some of our players' rooms didn't have showers. We had two kids in one bed.

And we couldn't find a place for the team to eat that night. Chaos.

In the game, we were behind by two at the half, got down nine, and lost by four. I thought the key was just poor organization. And in looking back on that game, as I always have done after a loss, I felt my getting upset the day before had as much to do with it as the hotel screw-up did. I had done a lousy job.

Late in the 1968–69 season, we played at Rutgers, trying to get into the NIT. Rutgers was undefeated at the time. We got beat at the buzzer, 49–47.

We walked off the floor and down some steps to the locker room. I said some things to the kids. Bill Parcells, an assistant to Army football coach Tom Cahill at the time, had made the trip and sat on the bench with me. And after I was done talking to the kids, Bill whispered, "Come here, I've got to talk to you." We walked off by ourselves in a corner of the room, and Bill, still speaking as quietly as he could, told me, "When you were walking off the floor, some guy took a swipe at you with his program. He missed you. I just reached up and cold-cocked him. I think the cops are coming after me."

So, when we left, I had the team form a circle, and we put Parcells inside it and told him to duck. We got him out of there, with his own honor guard.

And thus was preserved the career of one of the greatest football coaches of all time, and one of my best friends.

At West Point, Bill and I spent endless hours in my basement or his living room discussing teams and coaches in all sports, and what each of us thought made coaches successful or kept them from being so.

Even as a young assistant coach, he had an extremely good mind that was well focused on what it took to win and what you had to do to prevent losing—up to a point. I've been unmerciful when he's gone to a prevent defense late in a game, and lost. Not at the moment but sometime afterward I bring up the game and tell him: "Will you ever learn that the only thing a prevent defense does is prevent you from winning?"

But Bill Parcells became one of the four or five all-time best coaches in any sport that I've been around.

With all the success he's had in professional football, with two Super Bowl championships, he has remained the same guy I knew as a linebacker coach at West Point. You can walk down a lot of dark alleys with Bill Parcells.

In college basketball, winning a national championship is a great thrill for players and coaches. But I got just as big a thrill out of watching friends win the biggest events in their field—Bill Parcells, his Super Bowls; Tony LaRussa, the World Series; Mike Krzyzewski, his NCAA championships; Wayne Lukas, the Kentucky Derby; or John Havlicek and Red Auerbach winning all those NBA championships with the Celtics.

Inclusion of Lukas on that list demands some explanation, but he belongs there. Before he became horse racing's most successful trainer, his background was in basketball. He was a graduate assistant coach at Wisconsin when I was playing at Ohio State, and he developed a weighted basketball shoe that Converse sold nationally. We used them at Army; most schools did.

I got to know Wayne through Pete Newell, who loves horse racing almost as much as he does basketball. Wayne became a big Indiana basketball fan as well as a great friend of mine—he got to Bloomington for at least one game almost every year.

It was an overwhelming moment for me in his box at Churchill Downs when he won his first Kentucky Derby with the filly Winning Colors in 1988.

Wayne also was my business partner. He trained my horse.

At an auction, he bought a five-year-old horse named Gogarty and told me he got it for me. I figured if anyone should know a good horse, it was Wayne, so I paid him $65,000 and I was a certified horse-racing owner.

I was right about Wayne; he had found a bargain. That horse won four or five races and earned $240,000. Don't mistake that for a $175,000 profit. The cost of feeding and training a horse runs $2,500 a month. On purses, the jockey gets ten percent, the trainer gets ten percent. But I still came out okay.

Wayne told a reporter I was "a great owner. He doesn't know when the horse runs, he doesn't know how it finishes, and he really doesn't care. If it wasn't for his wife Karen, he'd never know." All I know is I got out of the owner business when Gogarty went for $12,000 in a claiming race. I figure Wayne trained that horse down from a $65,000 price tag to $12,000 in about a year, at the same time he was winning six straight Triple Crown races.

I worked for great people at West Point. Colonel Murphy was head-and-shoulders over the other two athletic directors I had, but I got along okay with all three. The superintendents I worked for, with the exception of the last one, were good.

General John Jannarone was the dean, the head of the whole academic operation. I loved Jannarone. He was very smart, a Rhodes Scholar. He worked with General Leslie Groves on the atomic bomb Manhattan Project. Jannarone was a big basketball fan; he enjoyed going with me to games at Madison Square Garden.

Colonel Tom Rogers, one of the great people in my life, was a godsend for me as our basketball program's officer-representative. At West Point, every athletic team has an officer-representative who travels with them. Tom was great in that role. For a couple of years, I had a captain or a major as officer-representative. They were good guys, but in the military, it was amazing how much different it was when the officer-representative was a full colonel. Tom would say, "Major, we'd like to get out of here quickly." And the major would say, "Yes, sir, right away, sir." Everything was speeded up immeasurably.

Richie Cardillo was our officer-representative one year, and he has been one of my closest friends ever since. He retired as a one-star general. When he became a general, Norm Ellenberger—who was a friend of mine then and later an assistant coach for me—was living in New Mexico. I got Norm to have an Indian silversmith make Richie a pair of shoulder stars out of pure silver. Over the years I have talked more things over with Richie than anybody else. He and his wife Inez have been like a brother and sister to me, and I love them like they were.

Jannarone, Colonel Murphy, and Frank Kobes, head of the Academy's physical education department and athletics committee, were the three who saw fit to give me the coaching job, when I was a nonentity.

Kobes once told Richie Cardillo, "He means a lot to us, but he does need your guidance now and then." I stayed in contact with Frank until he passed away.

The superintendent at West Point my fourth and fifth years there was General Sam Koster, an absolutely outstanding person.

Dave Windom, a friend of mine who was his aide, told me, "Anytime you need to see the general, you let me know, but dammit, make sure it's important."

One day something was bothering me, so I called Dave for an appointment and he said, "Be in the office at seven o'clock."

I was there when the general came in. He hung up his uniform jacket, sat down at his desk, put his feet up on the desk and said, "Okay, Coach, let me have it."

So I started in. I suppose I went on for three or four minutes on what was bothering me. When I stopped, his feet came off the desk, he leaned forward, and he said, "Everybody tells me how smart you are, but there's one thing you obviously haven't figured out. There's only one guy here you have to please and you're looking at him. Have I ever, *ever* been upset with anything you've done?

"Now, before you say anything, let me say I don't agree with everything you do, but I know what you're trying to accomplish, and there's nobody here who does a better job of making sure how this place is represented."

Then he went on with as good a talk as I've ever had. It included, "This is not the place for you to stay. This is a stepping stone for you, and I'm well aware of that. But you've got to make sure that the next place is the right place for you to go."

I listened to him. And the next place was the right place, for twenty-four years.

Of the players I recruited for West Point, I think we got just one who was recruited by a lot of major basketball schools: Jimmy Oxley, who still ranks with the best guards I ever had.

I enjoy being around Jimmy to this day, but I can't say either one of us can take a lot of credit for his going to West Point. His mother would have sent him to a monastery if she could have. I and West Point were the next-best thing.

Jimmy was a smart player. He never weighed more than 155 or 160 pounds. He was not real quick but he was good with the ball. He could shoot, and he wanted to win. Along with his skills, he understood what we wanted done and how we had to play, and he worked at getting other people to play that way. The key to Jimmy's whole being is that as a West Point graduate, he ended up becoming a doctor, which is a very difficult proposition for any kid. He had not had the background for it as a student at West Point, but he investigated and wound up developing a career as a doctor.

I saw him play in high school in South Jersey—at Bishop Eustace High School in Pennsauken. His coach there was Don Casey, who later coached at Temple and in the NBA. Casey and I became good friends; he is one of the most knowledgeable coaches about the zone I have ever known.

Jimmy wasn't able to play freshman ball for us because he had two knee operations. Then, for three years, he was a hell of a player.

Mike Krzyzewski was in the Class of '69, a year ahead of Oxley. Gene Sullivan, later an assistant coach at Notre Dame and after that head coach at Loyola, was a high school coach on the north side of Chicago when he told me about Mike.

When recruiting, I always liked to ask high school coaches about other good players they knew of. When I asked Gene if he knew of any Chicago kids I should check out, he mentioned a good guard at Weber in the Catholic League.

I went to Weber, found Mike, and took him to lunch—at the school cafeteria. I made arrangements to meet with him and his parents at their home. I visited, and I talked about what we had to offer. His dad didn't say much, but when I was all done, he said, "Well, Mike, I think West Point is where you ought to go to school."

He had a great family. After I went to Indiana, his mom and his "Auntie Mary" used to come to our game at Northwestern every year, and his mom would always bring something for me to give to the team to eat on the trip home. She'd keep clippings about our team and mail them to me. We didn't have a bigger fan.

Mike lost his dad in his senior year at Army.

We hadn't had a great season that year. We were 10–8 but we won six straight games to be 16–8 and we heard that if we won our last two games—on the road at Colgate and Rochester—we'd get the last spot in the NIT, if Duke didn't beat North Carolina in the ACC tournament. North Carolina won; we were alive.

Our sixth win in that streak was over Navy, which never did beat us in the eight years I was at Army. It was at that point of the season—after Navy, before the closing road trip—that Mike's father died. Mike had called him Saturday night after the Navy game, and his dad was overjoyed. He told Mike if we got in the NIT, he'd go to New York for the tournament. The next night, he died.

Mike talked about that in 1975 for *Knight with the Hoosiers*, the first book Bob Hammel did:

> *I was just really shocked. There was a snowstorm that night. I couldn't even get down to the airport fifty miles away. About four in the morning, Coach picked me up and got me there. I don't know how; it was like Siberia. There wasn't anybody on the roads.*
>
> *We were in the airport waiting for a flight, and he gave me some money and said, "Just in case you need it." We had these big games coming up that weekend, but he told me, "Don't worry about anything. You go home and take care of your mom, and I'll be out there to see you."*
>
> *Anybody who has ever been around him knows how much a practice means to him—let alone one in this situation, when we were playing for the whole season, really. But he came out to Chicago that night, and he came right to the*

house. He came in and loosened his tie. He sat around the kitchen table—Polish people sit around the kitchen table and eat all the time. My mom had some Polish food on the table, and Coach would just grab it with his fingers. It was very relaxed—just the sort of thing my mom needed. He stayed around till Wednesday, when we had the funeral. He talked with my mom after the funeral, and he ate another meal with us. He didn't get away until that afternoon, and we were leaving for Colgate Thursday. I'm captain of the team and I'm starting at guard, and he told me to stay with my mom and take all the time I needed.

People say, "Boy, it was really nice of him to come out," but they don't realize just how nice. The NIT is what the coach and the whole team look for at Army. I know how much work had gone into it, but it was important for him to come out there and visit.

I got back in time to go on the bus up to Colgate. We won both games and we got the bid to the NIT, so it turned out great.

Everyone knows the success Mike has had as Duke's basketball coach. Most of those Army "kids" have done very well—not many of them in the military, but those who did stay in the Army had good careers. Dick Murray was on target for being a general when he got out of the Army. Wally Wojciechowski is a general. He played for me the last couple of years I was there, and he was a battalion commander in Desert Storm.

Bobby Seigle was a regimental commander in Desert Storm. He retired as a full colonel. The army has an efficiency report that's written by your commanding officer or somebody superior to you every year. If there was ever a guy who was cut out to be a general officer that I ran across at West Point, it was Bobby Seigle. Somewhere along the way a great injustice was done to him.

Eddie Jordan was a down-the-line player as a sophomore, and even as a junior until he eventually became the guy taking Silliman's place. He was from Montgomery, Alabama—the Sidney Lanier Poets. The next game after Silliman got hurt, we lost at Canisius, 81–77, and Eddie played pretty well. We had a game scheduled with Bucknell on Wednesday afternoon, and it got snowed out.

The next Saturday we played Penn State. John Egli, the coach at Penn State, coached zone defense as well as anybody I ever saw. We made a guard out of Eddie in a week and played him on top against the zone. He scored just five points in the game but handled the ball well and he was just great defensively. The halftime score was 24–7. We won 59–39 and Eddie Jordan wound up being one of the very best players I ever had at West Point.

The army gave him the same treatment it did Bobby Seigle. Eddie got nailed somewhere along the line by a bad efficiency report, and it stuck with him. He was in the army for eighteen years as a captain, and they were going to drop him two years short of retirement. He had a child who needed constant medication that was expensive, and he was going to lose his insurance. Bob Yerks, who was a regimental commander when I was at West Point and went on to be a three-star general, had retired in charge of army personnel. Bob was one of those rare people willing to do whatever possible to correct something that was wrong. And he wasn't afraid to take a lot of heat while doing so. He was just like Richie Cardillo in that regard.

He helped straighten out Eddie Jordan's situation. Eddie was able to retire as a lieutenant colonel.

Mike Gyovai was my all-time favorite player—and everybody who ever played for me knows it. I think I've finally learned to pronounce his last name right— go-*vay*. For a year at least I pronounced it *guy*-o-vie—just as I eventually figured out that it's Mike shuh-*sheffs*-kee when it always seemed to me that Krzyzewski, which looks to me like kruh-*zew*-ski, should at least be kruh-*sheffs*-kee.

Gyovai played at Marmion Military Academy in Aurora, Ill., and his dad was in the Bataan Death March. His name was Frank and they featured him once on Ralph Edwards's *This Is Your Life* TV show. I believe if Mike had gone someplace to play football he would have been a great defensive end in the NFL. He was 6-foot-5 when he played for us. He weighed 225 pounds and he looked like he weighed about 195. But basketball was his game, not football, and that was all to our benefit.

Once Mike Krzyzewski and I were in a car in Washington, D.C.; I was driving and he was in the passenger seat. Mike was the coach at West Point then, and he told me he had a kid coming in the next year who was "a lot like Mike Gyovai."

I just looked at him, and Mike understood, grinned a little bit and revised what he had said to, "Well, he's *close* to being like Mike Gyovai."

That tickled me, because Mike had played with Gyovai for a couple of years and knew how I felt about him. And the kid he was talking about was Gary Winton, who went on to be a hell of a player at Army. Just not a Mike Gyovai.

In the 1969–70 season, we got beat by Manhattan, 60–57—the only game we lost at home that year. Gyovai was our only guy who played that game; nobody else played well at all.

The next day at practice, he was there early. I said, "Mike, why were you ready to play yesterday and nobody else was?" He said, "Coach, I know I can't afford *not* to be ready. I'm not good enough to go into a game not ready to play."

He's the most competitive guy and the toughest person mentally I've ever been around.

We played up at Syracuse on a Saturday night in the 1969–70 season. On Thursday, anti–Vietnam War rioters at Syracuse had taken over the ROTC building. That was the atmosphere in which we—the United States Military Academy—went in to play this game.

Bob Kinney, who was the sports information director at Army at the time and was known around the country as one of the very best, still has a nut and a bolt that were thrown onto the floor—big enough that somebody could have been killed if hit in the head. Some Syracuse students were unscrewing the bleachers and throwing things at us.

We beat them pretty easily. With about two minutes to go in the game, I took Mike out. This was at old Manley Fieldhouse, which had a raised floor. Mike had chased the ball out of bounds, off the court. He retrieved the ball and gave it back to the official, then saw that a substitute was coming in for him. He was at the opposite end of the court but on the same side of the floor as our bench.

The Syracuse students had been on him all night, and when they saw he was going out, they booed him—loudly.

And how did he react to that?

Guys walking to the electric chair have walked faster than Mike walked to our bench. He just glared right at that whole student section and kept walking, just dared them—come one at a time, come all together, it didn't make any difference to him. There was a running-track between the bleachers and the raised court. Nobody came across that track.

Colonel Tom Rogers was on the bench with me that night. Tom had glasses that would slide down his nose, and he was constantly pushing the glasses back. He was talking to one of our players and had not seen Mike start his long, slow walk to the bench.

I couldn't let that happen. I said, "Hey, Tom, look at my boy." He looked down the floor, over those glasses, and said, "Jeee-zus Christ!" His head just dropped.

So, since he couldn't—or didn't want to—see what was happening, I couldn't resist giving him a play-by-play:

"Gyovai steps away from the foul line extended, he's moving toward our bench, but very slowly, Colonel, verrr-ry slowly. It may take five minutes for him to get here. . . .

"Ohhh, the crowd is looking at him. They're booing him."

Colonel Rogers certainly heard that.

Finally after what seemed like an hour, Mike got to our bench. Colonel Rogers reached up and grabbed him by the arm, pulled him down between us, and wrapped his leg around Mike's leg.

Now, Colonel Rogers weighed about 155 pounds, maybe. As he pulled Mike down, he said, "You son-of-a-bitch, if you're going anyplace, you're taking me with you." And I thought to myself: "*Colonel, I have a feeling that would be no real problem.*"

That incident was enough to show that Mike Gyovai was not an ideal peace-time soldier. But, boy, he could play for me. He played a lot in all three of his varsity seasons and started the last two.

He wasn't a perfect student. He was occasionally ineligible because of grades.

In fact, he finished last in his class academically, but they didn't officially declare him last on graduation day because in one class he had an incomplete. That cost him $750; at West Point at that time every graduating class member chipped in a dollar and the guy who finished last won the pot. That collision with bureaucracy irritated Mike. He felt he deserved to be last.

The fall after he graduated, he sent me a letter to give to that year's team, which turned out to be my last one at West Point. It was a great letter, encouraging the team, talking about what they had to do to get ready to play, that kind of thing. He was in Ranger School at the time—I think he finished first in his class there.

But he sent this nice letter and at the bottom, he signed it and added, "P.S.— This shit sucks."

How could you not love that kid?

After Mike completed his military service, he became the city engineer for Rolla, Missouri. The favorite scenario that all of us who knew him at Army imagine is what would have happened if some company along the way tried to do less than what a contract with Rolla called for.

He lives now on a farm near Rolla, and he frequently made it over to Bloomington from there to see our basketball games. Lubbock is a little longer trip, but I'll bet we see him a lot.

I formed several lifelong friendships with Eastern coaches while I was coaching at Army.

Not all were in colleges. Mickey Corcoran was one of the outstanding high school coaches on the East Coast. He had coached Bill Parcells as a high school player at Riverdale High School in Dumont, New Jersey. Pete Newell was one of many college coaches who had Mickey scout for them before their team came East to play at Madison Square Garden. Mickey knew as much about the game of basketball as anyone I knew, and he had a great ability to observe and evaluate what was happening in a game. A lot of coaches know X's and O's but don't see things well. Mickey was extraordinarily astute in both areas.

When Tates Locke was at Miami of Ohio and Rollie Massimino was at Lexington High School in Massachusetts, they had a camp so far up in New Hampshire I think it was in Canada. Al LoBalbo and I would eat like hell as we were driving up there knowing we wouldn't get much to eat after we got there. And we'd take whatever we wanted to drink in an ice bucket because all Rollie was going to serve us was Kool-Aid. Rollie went on to be an outstanding college coach, winning the NCAA in 1985. At Indiana, we played against his Villanova teams twice, and they won both times—in the second round of the 1978 NCAA tournament and in the 1982 Holiday Festival at New York. Never has a coach been more gracious in beating us than he was.

John Chaney at Temple is a throwback to the same era I came from—very demanding, probably as good for a kid as anyone coaching today. Kids who play for John have a head start on life. He's also the best teacher of zone defense that there is in basketball. He has no tricks. He just does a better job of getting his players to cover the floor than anyone else does. It's hard to get the game in a position that forces them to come out of the zone and go man-to-man. One reason is the shot clock. But, also, his teams can trap out of their zone, or press out of it. My guess is they could play pretty good man-to-man defense, but they certainly don't play it a lot.

A more recent Eastern coach, Dave Gavitt, deserves credit for a lot of good things that have happened in college basketball. He was a very good coach at Dartmouth and Providence—he was the U.S. Olympic coach in 1980, when unfortunately America didn't go to the Games. After his coaching, he almost single-handedly created the Big East Conference and made it into a major college basketball power. He made great contributions to basketball in a variety of ways.

If I could go back and coach those same Army teams today, I would use the offense that evolved at Indiana and I think we would have done even better.

The principal thing with that offense is reading the defense, and those West Point kids did that very well. What we tried to do there offensively was always give them an option. If you're coming off a screen, you could go high or go low or pop back—you had to read the defense. But the screen was going to be set, and from that standpoint, the reverse-action offense was not stereotyped because there was a lot of reading in it, but not nearly as much as utilizing to your advantage what the defense is trying to do, as we did at Indiana and now are doing at Texas Tech.

Against the press at Army, we wanted to beat it and then try to run our offense. What I changed at Indiana was beat the press *and* try to score—make the defense pay an immediate price for extending its pressure. We didn't do that at Army because I wanted to keep the ball in our hands as much as possible. I look back and think that was a mistake.

On defense, I don't think I would change much of what we did. Defensively we were ahead of what we were doing offensively.

My Army "kids" now are men in their fifties. Several of them honored me almost annually through the '90s by coming as a group to our game at Penn State, the easternmost Big Ten school. They'd arrive the night before the game so we could all go to dinner and talk, and talk, and talk. Many of them in the summer came out to play in our Indiana Players' Golf Outing fundraiser. And, in October 1992 when one of those kids, Tommy Miller, was the head coach at Army, they honored me with a two-night reunion of former players at West Point.

Dick Schaap was the master of ceremonies. He said:

> *Always, he is what he is. There is absolutely not one phony bone in Bob Knight's body. I don't always agree with everything he does, but I always know that he's doing it for a good reason.*
>
> *I have spent time with Coach Knight in many different places. We've had some wonderful meals at strange places—an Italian restaurant in Albuquerque, a Chinese restaurant in Manhattan, in the back of a gas station in Bloomington, Indiana.*
>
> *But for me, one of the best moments was a few years ago in Seattle, during the Final Four, when I had the opportunity to take Coach Knight to dinner with another friend of mine whom he had never met—Vince Lombardi Jr., who is a lawyer in Seattle. When the three of us got together, I said to Vince Lombardi Jr., "This is Vince Lombardi Jr." They both knew what I meant and I think both took it as a compliment.*
>
> *Like Vince Lombardi Sr., Bob Knight has a burning desire to win, and to do it within the rules. The first feeling is not an uncommon one, and the second one unfortunately sometimes is.*

Bob Knight not only has principles but he has passed those principles on to almost everyone who has played for him and has coached with him—like Mike Krzyzewski, who flew in here last night to say hello to Coach Knight and join in this tribute, and Tom Miller, who is now the head coach here. . . .

Both of those men, like almost everyone, would love to have their sons play for Bob Knight. He is The Coach today. My wife and I had dinner with Wilt Chamberlain just about four days ago. Wilt told us that someday he would like to have a son play for Bob Knight.

And, one by one, players stepped up to speak.

I had ridden to West Point from the Newark airport with Dr. Jimmy Oxley. "Then we got to talking about the old days," Jimmy told that banquet audience. "I can remember some things that happened. I can remember playing Notre Dame in Madison Square Garden on St. Patrick's Day. Coach Knight remembered playing Notre Dame in Madison Square Garden on St. Patrick's Day, and the names of the two Irish refs, and the play in the second half that changed the game. It was like turning a switch on. It was like a library of basketball. It was the shortest trip I ever made from Newark airport to West Point. He went through each of the teams that he coached and he had something to say about every player he coached.

"Then last night at the Hotel Thayer, Coach went around to everybody. We really felt close together. Some guys hadn't been back since they graduated, twenty-two or twenty-three years ago. They didn't come back for their class reunion, but they came back for this.

"Recently, my dad asked me, 'Do you think Coach Knight knows how many games you have won for him the last twenty years?' I said, 'What are you talking about? I haven't made a bucket for him for twenty-two years.' He said, 'I wonder if he realizes that when Scott May shoots a jumper or Kent Benson shoots a hook, all his players and his former players are twisting and helping that shot go in.'

"I know that when Keith Smart made that jump shot against Syracuse, every one of us willed it in."

Then "Colonel Murphy" who hired me as head coach was now retired Major General Ray Murphy said:

"I've never seen a period in my lifetime at the Academy when the student body was so buoyed by a team. You talk about *esprit*—the basketball team brought it on, but the corps was pushing the basketball team. I thought that was a good thing, and I haven't seen it since. Magnificent."

• • •

Tradition is such a powerful part of West Point, because of no man more than Colonel Earl "Red" Blaik, the coach during Army football's glory days during and after World War II.

During my West Point years, I got to know him and several times talked with him about coaching and winning. When Colonel Blaik would walk in a room, without ever saying a word, everybody knew he was there and everybody was conscious of him as long as he stayed there. He had a presence about him that exceeded any I've ever seen.

I played one round of golf with him at Palm Springs, California, and it's a memory I treasure. When he passed away, I called his son Bobby to tell him how much I enjoyed having known his dad. Bobby said, "I just want you to know that during the later years of Dad's life, you were one of his favorite people." That was extremely meaningful to me.

As long as I was coaching at West Point, my objective was to do with Army basketball what Colonel Blaik had done with Army football—make it representative of all the things for which the institution stood.

I think it was General Mark Clark in World War II who once said, "I need a man for a tough and dangerous mission. Get me a West Point football player."

I read about that while I was coaching there, and immediately my goal was that, through the way I handled the basketball program, the same thing could be said about a West Point basketball player. Our Army teams played all over the country, all up and down the East Coast, in California, and Texas— damned near all over. My ultimate objective was that whenever and wherever people saw our kids play, as they left the arena they could say to themselves:

"If that's an example of the kind of competitor—the kind of fighter—that West Point produces, our country is in great shape."

During the years that I was there, those kids lived up to that and more.

I had the same goal, in a different way, when I was coaching at Indiana and I've carried it with me to Texas Tech. I want people to watch us play and say, "Boy, this is what college basketball should be. Here are kids who work as a team, they're good students, and they show that good students can win."

The Indiana kids more than achieved that, and through the years I'm sure Texas Tech kids will, too.

The kids at Army and Indiana were great in one other way that is important to me.

When a coach is done, whoever he is, people talk about his won–lost record and the championships he's won, and whatever particularly notable things happened in his years as a coach.

That's why that reunion at West Point was so special to me, because the greatest reward that a coach can ever have is a kid coming back to see how he is doing. Absolutely nothing compares to that—a kid comes back to say hello, to play golf, to go out and eat with you, to watch practice, whatever it is—that's the best reward there is in coaching.

I have been richly rewarded.

SEVEN: *Welcome to Indiana (1971–1974)*

"... to this day, I've never opened another fortune cookie."

I knew when my sixth year as Army coach ended it would be my last one. I had been patient and passed up some very good offers. I had been interviewed a few times, by outstanding people like Ray Graves of Florida and Doyt Perry of Bowling Green, by a committee of seventeen at Wisconsin, and by four or five people at Minnesota. Sometimes I was offered the job; sometimes I wasn't. And sometimes I wasn't considered for jobs I'd have liked—Penn State, for instance. That position opened after my third year as Army's coach, and I was interested. I hadn't yet met Pete Newell and he recommended John Bach, who got the job. I needled Joe Paterno later that he didn't let them hire me because he didn't want a basketball coach coming in there passing the ball.

But through my first five years as a head coach, I stayed at Army, happy with the job I had.

After the sixth year I not only was ready to move, I fully intended to, because the situation at Army wasn't what it had been. I went to the 1971 NCAA tournament at Houston hoping to get the job I wanted.

That job was Indiana, which had opened about two weeks earlier.

The Indiana search committee consisted of four people: Ed Cady, the faculty representative; Bill Smith, the alumni representative; Schuyler Otteson, from the faculty; and Bill Orwig, the athletic director. When I met with them for my interview, Dr. Cady asked me, "Do you want to ask us questions, do you want us to ask you questions, or should we go back and forth?"

I told them, "If you'll give me fifteen minutes, I'll outline what I'll bring to Indiana to your basketball job, and how I'll do it. If you like that, I'll stay as long as you want to talk about it. If you don't like it, move right on to your next candidate and it will only cost you fifteen minutes."

I wanted the job but I wanted it under my conditions. I told them how we would play, how we would recruit, that I wouldn't accept interference from alumni or anyone else, that I would try to do, whenever asked, whatever I could do to help the university in any way, and I would not tolerate any breaking of NCAA rules.

I told them I would get kids who would represent the university well, who would be students and would graduate, and I would expect them to be part of the student body, not just basketball players.

We went on to discuss those things for three and a half hours.

Mr. Orwig told me they would invite one candidate to make the trip to Bloomington, and "We would expect the guy we invite to have a real deep and sincere interest in the job."

Thursday morning, the day of the NCAA semifinal games, Mr. Orwig called and invited me to Bloomington. I told him I had to do some coaches' committee work Friday and I couldn't come until Saturday morning. He said, "Fine," and I flew out on Saturday.

I'm always intrigued when I read about coaches and their agents and "negotiations" for contracts today. I'll tell you how our negotiating went that day.

Mr. Orwig asked me, "What do you think the salary should be for this job?"

I said, "You and I have both agreed that this is a good job, so I would think you will pay what the job is worth."

He said, "How would $20,000 be?"

I said, "That's fine." That was about half of what I made at Army, but money was not an object. Salaries were just lower then. Fred Taylor was making $17,100 at Ohio State, after seven Big Ten championships and a national championship. There was no excuse for that, even in those days. Ohio State, my alma mater, was being cheap with a great coach.

No more was said between Bill Orwig and me about a contract until we were in the parking lot at the Columbia Club in Indianapolis after the Monday press conference there announcing me as the coach. I was about to go on my first recruiting trip and I needed some money. He pulled out a huge roll of bills, gave me $300, and said, "You make damned sure you remember where you got that and bring receipts back." He didn't part with money easily.

That's when he said, "By the way, how long do you want your contract to be?"

He answered first, "I think it ought to be three years."

I said, "I was thinking five."

He said, "How about four?" That was it.

We couldn't have spent two minutes on all our "negotiating." Getting the expense money was the hard part.

Twenty-one years later, Indiana University gave me its Bill Orwig Award (for "outstanding contributions to Indiana University athletics" by a nonalumnus of the university) and he came down from Michigan to present it to me. I heard the Indiana version of my hiring, from Mr. Orwig in a newspaper interview.

> *We had an awful lot of applications, but we had researched it down to eight or nine. I had never met Bob until we met him in Houston. I remember talking to Gordon White of the New York Times and a couple of other people back there that I knew. They said he was a little tempestuous . . . but that has never bothered me.*
>
> *We had a little problem. We needed someone who was a strong disciplinarian. We knew that Bob, with his West Point background, certainly would give us that. We knew he had won a lot of games with scores in the fifties, and, yes, that was a concern. We knew with Assembly Hall opening, we had to have a pretty good group of people in there. We felt a winner would bring them in, and we felt Bob could win.*
>
> *In the interview with us, he was so well prepared. Some of the others stammered and stuttered around. We had a set of questions that we asked—what do you do about this, how do you handle that? The interview was just tremendous.*
>
> *After we had completed all the interviewing, we each had a rating sheet. Bob was No. 1 on every sheet. There was no question who we were going to invite.*
>
> *The day he came to Bloomington, after we had talked everything over and we were sitting in my living room, I asked him, "Why did you want to come to Indiana?" He said, "I can win there."*
>
> *I like a guy who says, "I can win."*
>
> *And he did it probably more so than anyone thought. I'm sure some of those other fellows we interviewed would have been winners, too, but I don't think anybody would have ever built the program the way Bob has built it. It's hard to improve on a Hall of Famer.*

He had read me pretty well in that conversation he mentioned. I did expect to win. I think the first thing you have to have—in coaching or anything else—is a confidence in your ability to do the job. If you don't have that, don't take the job.

I think you gain confidence by asking questions, by discussing things with people, and by learning about the job as you go along. Then it's up to you.

I've not always liked the rules that the NCAA has implemented, but I've had total confidence in my ability to coach and coach well within whatever rules they've set up.

Once I had the Indiana job, I had a very clear idea of what I wanted to do. And I wanted to put the pieces together as fast as I could. That's what those early days and years at Indiana were all about: building the kind of program I had dreamed about.

I knew how strong Bill Orwig was when, as he was walking with me up to President John Ryan's porch for my introduction to Dr. Ryan, I looked down and saw he was wearing a Michigan ring (he played both football and basketball there and he's on their "Wall of Fame"). Knowing the intensity of the feeling between the two schools, I said to myself, "If a Michigan guy has the guts to hire an Ohio State guy to coach at Indiana, he's going to be a great guy to work for." He was.

Mr. Orwig mentioned to me my first day in Bloomington that Indiana "had a little problem" with its basketball team. I wasn't surprised. Problems of one kind or another are usually the reason a job is open. Once I was on the job, I tried to find out what problems had existed regarding their recruiting. Don Luft, who in the early '50s was the last Indiana athlete to letter in football, basketball, and baseball, was the head of the Varsity Club (the athletic department's fundraising unit) when I came. He was very helpful to me. Brad Bomba, an All–Big Ten football end at Indiana before becoming a doctor, also was helpful, not necessarily about people but with thoughts and ideas. Archie Dees, who was one of Indiana's all-time greatest basketball players, was very good to me. Jim Strickland, one of America's best hand surgeons, was invaluable to us right from the start. Chuck Marlowe was my TV-show partner for all twenty-nine of my Indiana years. Both Jim and Chuck are still great friends of mine. And Lou Watson, the coach I replaced—I couldn't have found a guy who was more helpful or who became a better friend than Lou.

As I started my new job, the best Hoosier friend I had was a former ROTC teacher of mine at Ohio State, Jim Schneider. He was a retired air force colonel who was living in Fort Wayne. Both John Havlicek and I had taken his class. In my Indiana years, he was the very best of fan and friend, and through him I met some other great Fort Wayne people—Jim and Tom Kelley, Dick Inskeep, Charlie Robertson, and Tom Foy.

The people I met in my first few days at Indiana made everything fit together. Mr. Orwig and Dr. Cady from the selection committee were helpful from the start. Bill Armstrong headed the IU Foundation. He was one of the first people I met my first day in town and he was a close friend and unfailing supporter to the day he died in 1999. George Pinnell, head of the IU School of Business, succeeded "Army" at the Foundation; trustees like Danny Danielson, a baseball teammate of Mr. Armstrong's and a close friend of his ever after, Carl Gray, Dr. Joe Black, Dick Stoner, and Harriett Inskeep—everybody who was in a position to help did so in every way possible. By then, Carl Gray was in his eighties, but there was never a time when things weren't going well or we had lost a tough game when he didn't give me a call. He always knew how nice it was for a coach to hear encouragement at a time like that.

The helpers certainly included President John Ryan, and the most beloved leader the university ever had, Chancellor Herman B Wells. I must have received fifty notes from Dr. Wells over the years—always supportive, always thoughtful, always meaningful and appreciated. He died at ninety-seven in late-spring 2000.

I got enough of an indication from the athletic people of their "problem"— who was involved with players who didn't need to be. Ironically, one of those guys became a very close friend of mine: a doctor named Bill Howard, who died just a few years ago. Nobody was involved more with breaking the rules than he was, but we hit it off well as friends, after I got him out of the recruiting business.

All kinds of people came to me who had been giving money to players, or flying parents from one place to another—I'd heard that was going on at Indiana when I was at Ohio State.

The first thing I did was cut off access to practice for outsiders, including Bill Howard and his brother, Jim, another doctor who was the most intense fan of Indiana basketball I think I've ever met.

After a couple of months, Bill Orwig and Ed Cady were in Mr. Orwig's office. I walked in, closed the door, and said, "Okay, here are the people I've eliminated from basketball at Indiana, because of all the rules they've been breaking. Now, have I missed anybody that you didn't tell me about? I know you hired me as the sheriff to come in and clean up the town without telling me a whole lot about it. I just want you to know I understand my purpose. Have I missed anybody?"

They kinda chuckled, looked at each other, and said. "No, you've made a pretty good sweep."

In a state that loved high school basketball as much as Indiana did, I thought it was important right away to get to know some of the state's most respected sports people.

At the top of that list was the commissioner of the Indiana High School Athletic Association, Phil Eskew. I had never met him when I was coaching at West Point, never had any reason to talk to him. I met him at a dinner in Indianapolis. We grew to have a wonderful friendship. People over the next several years frequently said to me, "I've been one of your greatest supporters." He *was* one.

He was a rarity. He was never afraid to say what he thought. When he thought something was bullshit, that's what he called it.

When we played UCLA in St. Louis to start the 1975–76 season, he flew down there with us. I asked him to talk to the team after dinner. He was as good an after-dinner speaker as there was in Indiana—very funny, full of stories from a lifetime in athletics, always able to come up with something pertinent to the occasion. He talked to our players that night about honesty and playing within the rules—how they as Indiana University players had already become an example of how you could be very successful doing that.

Mr. Eskew had been the commissioner that very fall when—more than sixty years after the first state high school basketball tournament—Indiana had its first football playoffs. Indiana's association always had been concerned with giving small schools as much of an equality with the big schools as it could. For those first playoffs, Mr. Eskew's organization had limited the team rosters to thirty-three eligible players. He told of going to a playoff game in northern Indiana that first year, and a couple of people in front of him were saying, loud enough—maybe intentionally—for him to hear it, that they couldn't understand a rule like that. He didn't say anything. The game started, and on the kickoff a guy made a good return—for the team Mr. Eskew's critics were cheering for. They were up on their feet, roaring, and Phil looked at them and said, "Why are you so excited about that? Why didn't he catch the ball, run off the field around the stands, and come back in the field about the fifteen—he could have scored a touchdown."

"Hell," one of them said, "he can't do that. That's against the rules."

And Eskew said: "You're damn right it is, and so is having more than thirty-three players."

Our kids loved that.

Five Indiana high school coaches in particular became good friends of mine and greatly helped us for years and years, publicly and whenever they could— Ray Crowe; Oscar Robertson's coach at Indianapolis Crispus Attucks, retired from coaching by the time I came to Indiana; Bob Straight, an outstanding coach whom Mr. Eskew had hired at Huntington before becoming the IHSAA commissioner; Phil Buck, who had played basketball and baseball at Indiana and did a great coaching job at Madison Heights in Anderson; Bo Mallard, who ran one of the state's best programs at Gary Roosevelt and won the 1968 state championship; and Bill Stearman, a former IU baseball player who had a long and great career at Columbus High School, about forty miles east of Bloomington.

They're all in the Indiana Basketball Hall of Fame, and they all became not just good friends of mine but also highly supportive of our team, our players, and the overall operation we had. I think that was very helpful in getting us started.

Starting with that first season at Indiana, I taught a coaching class, and the first one included Steve Downing, a junior center on my team.

After we started practice, I brought in Mike Krzyzewski to speak to the class one day. Mike was at Indiana working on an MBA and helping us coach. He talked a while, then opened up for questions. Steve's hand was the first to go up.

"I don't really have a question," he said. "I just wanted to say how happy I am to see that someone survived what we're doing right now."

I knew right then Steve and I were going to get along pretty well.

I also knew I wanted to continue teaching that class, although even then I don't believe any other head football or basketball coaches in the Big Ten were doing any teaching. I had a great time with that class over the years. Every year, the first day I would ask them to write down the name of the best teacher they'd ever had. When they were done, I'd ask them to name the toughest, most demanding teacher they'd had. Invariably, the two names were the same.

I'd also say, "Raise your hand if you ever had a coach you really didn't like." At first, they'd be hesitant. Then someone would get bold and raise a hand—and I don't know what it says, but almost always the first to raise a hand was a girl. Once one was up, there'd be a rush to follow, until almost every kid in the room had his hand up. Then I'd say, "Here is your first lesson in coaching. We don't like all you little bastards, either."

Of the players we inherited that first year—Steve Downing, Joby Wright, and John Ritter, certainly, but also other kids like Rick Ford, Bootsie White, Jerry Memering, Kim Pemberton, and Frank Wilson—all did a good job of absorbing the culture shock of being recruited into one system and style and switching suddenly to a quite different approach.

Steve, I think, was the quickest of all in seeing the good things that could come from the way we wanted to play.

Up through his sophomore year at Indiana, I understand he had always been kind of quiet, and he had always played in the shadow of a great basketball talent, George McGinnis.

George and Steve were buddies all the way through high school at Indianapolis Washington. George was Indiana's Mr. Basketball, a high school All-American in football as well as basketball. I don't know that any high school team ever had two better players in one class than those two, and they played together on an unbeaten state high school championship team their senior year. All eyes then were on George, who set some scoring records that are still standing. They followed up their state championship as seniors by playing together in the two-game Indiana–Kentucky All-Star series, which has been going on for more than sixty years now. That's one of George's still-standing records: on a floor full of guys who became very good college players, he had fifty-three points and thirty rebounds—in one game.

At Indiana, they sat out their freshman season, then, in their one year of playing together in college, Steve had some injury problems but came on to play well the last several games. In his one college season, George became the only Indiana player ever to lead the Big Ten in both scoring and rebounding, averaging just under thirty points a game.

George cast quite a shadow. They listed him at 6-foot-7 and 235 pounds—a classic football build, and he was very good as a two-way high school football end.

At Indiana, George made All-American teams that sophomore season and, on the same day that an unknown player named Julius Erving announced that he was leaving Massachusetts a year early to turn pro, George McGinnis left Indiana two years early and signed with his hometown pro team, the Indiana Pacers of the ABA. He left just as I was coming in, but there was no connection. His father had been killed in a construction accident the summer before George entered Indiana. He had a chance to make some money for himself and his mother, and he took it.

Knowing he was likely to leave made it easier for me to take the news then, but as the years passed and I got to know George, I regretted it more and more—for him and for me. After he retired from pro basketball and went back to Indianapolis, I got to know him well, through Steve. I love the guy, and that's a big part of why I wish I could have had him play for us. I know he was a headstrong player, with a reputation of being hard to coach, and I have a reputation of not being the kind of coach a guy like that would want to play for. But I'd love to have coached George, and I think he would have thoroughly enjoyed playing for us, because we would have put his talents in a position in movement that would have made him damned near impossible to play against. If he had just waited two years, he could have made a lot more money.

But I was awfully blessed to have Steve Downing.

In my first Indiana game, and the first official game played at Assembly Hall, Steve set the one-game rebounding record that still stands there—twenty-six. He also had thirty-one points and we beat Ball State that night, 84–77.

That was on a Wednesday. That Saturday we beat Miami of Ohio and Downing hurt a knee. He played with the injury and scored twenty-two points two nights later when we went to 3–0 with a 59–56 win over Kansas, which had gone 27–3 and played in the Final Four the year before.

All three of those games were at Assembly Hall. The year before, even with players as popular as McGinnis and Downing, Indiana had averaged just over 8,000 people in a 10,000-capacity Fieldhouse. We had 16,666 seats to fill at Assembly Hall, and the crowds for those first three games were 14,853, 13,897 and—even with us 2–0 and Kansas coming in ranked fourteenth in the country—11,736.

Our style was not exactly welcomed at Indiana, where Branch McCracken had been one of the early champions of fast-break, race-horse basketball. They called Branch's teams the Hurryin' Hoosiers. My early Indiana teams were in no hurry.

One of the guards I inherited on that first team was Bootsie White, 5-foot-8 and 176 pounds. Every player I've ever had, at West Point or Indiana, called me Coach—every player but Bootsie, who called me Chief.

He tried to run the team the way I wanted it run, and that meant working for good shots every time down the court and putting the ball away in the last minutes when we were ahead. Bootsie was running our delay game late in one of those early games, and the crowd was so quiet that everyone in the building heard one lone voice scream in frustration at our delay game:

"Shoot the ball!"

Bootsie had the ball in his hands. Slowly, he dribbled over toward the sidelines, where I was sitting. Without looking at me, he whispered, "Don't worry, Chief. I can't hear 'em."

Another time—it may have been the Kansas game when the score was something like 50–48 and we had already put the ball away—another loud fan with a sense of humor and an ability to add bellowed out, *"We want a hundred!"*

Even I had to laugh at that one.

If the Indiana people weren't crazy about our offense, they did notice we won our first three games. Our fourth game, and our first on the road, was at Louisville against Kentucky, and Adolph Rupp.

Rupp and the man who coached Indiana to its first two NCAA championships, Branch McCracken, were not friends. Here were two of the most passionate basketball schools in America, from neighboring states, but they didn't sign on to play each other annually until Watson had replaced McCracken. And when we went to Freedom Hall that Saturday night, Indiana had lost five straight games to Kentucky.

That 1970–71 Kentucky game made a connection for our new program with old-line Indiana fans. We beat Kentucky 90–89, in double overtime, and Steve Downing was heroic. The cartilage problem in the knee he had injured the week before slowed him down, but he played. He played all fifty minutes. He scored forty-seven points, with twenty-five rebounds. In Indiana, they make legends of performances like that one, in a basketball victory over Kentucky. Hell, *it was* legendary. It was my fourth game at Indiana, and I consider it the best any player ever had for us. Steve was so tired the last part of the game and the two overtimes that he would walk to the offensive end. We could wait.

In the front-court with Downing we had another player built about like Steve: Joby Wright, 6-foot-8, strong and quick. When we played Kansas, I told Dave Bliss, "Look at the way those guys are going after the ball on the board. This is the first time I ever had two like that on *my* side."

Dave and Bob Weltlich were assistant coaches who came in with me right at the start. Dave had played basketball and baseball at Cornell, and he was very good at both. He was on my Army staff for two years, and after completing his military service he was in an executive training program with Procter & Gamble when I offered him a job at Indiana. He was an exceptionally bright and hard-working guy who had a big hand in helping set up what happened in 1976. The year before that, though, he was hired as head coach at Oklahoma, by the athletic director there, Wade Walker. He has gone on to have an excellent career at SMU, New Mexico, and Baylor after Oklahoma.

Bobby Weltlich also went with me to Indiana from Army. He was a good high school player at Orrville, six years behind me. He went to Ohio State and graduated there but didn't play basketball. He, Dave, and Don DeVoe, who had played with me at Ohio State, were all Army assistants who went to West Point the same way I did, as part of their Army duty. Our first two months at Indiana, Bobby took sort of a leave of absence from the army and worked like hell on our recruiting. I'm not sure the army knew he was gone, and if not, I'm not sure if that's more of an indictment of military organization or of Bobby's military value. Bobby has a good mind and a quick, sharp way of making points. He's a coach who has done a hell of a job of surviving in difficult circumstances. He went to Texas when I tried to talk him out of it. He wound up getting what I thought was a really bad deal there but survived and came back, and now he is doing an outstanding job at South Alabama.

Don DeVoe probably would have gone to Indiana with us but he got the Virginia Tech coaching job principally on a letter he wrote and letters of recommendation that Coach Taylor and I wrote. He did a very good job there and he has gone on to have good teams at four different places—Virginia Tech, Wyoming, Tennessee, and Navy. The last one is the irony: when we were together at Army, we always worked like hell to beat Navy and always did. Now, he's working like hell in the other direction and he's 22–1 in that series.

The Saturday after the Kentucky game, we came back to Assembly Hall for the building's dedication game against Notre Dame. We drew 14,992, which was considered great, a school record, at the time, but was still two thousand under capacity. We won the game, 94–29. Downing played less than ten minutes. John Ritter, another very good player whom we inherited, did something I've never seen another college player do—he personally outscored the opponent, 31–29, and he played just a little more than half the game.

Digger Phelps, who had coached at Fordham when I was at Army, was the new coach at Notre Dame and I wasn't at all happy about seeing that score climb. But counting Downing we had only nine players, and Digger—as good a friend as I had in coaching and a coach whose teams always were among the best-prepared of all our opponents—stayed with a press almost the whole game. So almost the whole game we were shredding it and shooting lay-ups.

The combination of the exciting win over Kentucky and the bizarre win over Notre Dame almost obscured to our fans a slip-up in between. We went over to Ohio University on the Wednesday night between the two big Saturday games and lost, 79–70. Maybe the fans and the people doing the national rankings hardly noticed it, but I sure did.

Here was the classic illustration of the Last Game–Next Game theory that was already ingrained in me. In no way had we gotten over our Last Game, the win over Kentucky, in time to get ready for the Next Game, Ohio University.

The game at Ohio U. also illustrated another thing I have continually tried to fight with my teams, not always successfully.

Players categorize teams and players. They did then, and they still do. My last year at Indiana before we ever got into the Big Ten we beat Kentucky, Temple, and North Carolina—and we lost to Indiana State, which wasn't as good as those other teams but was a lot better than our team gave it credit for, and played a lot harder that night than we did. It wasn't a fluke that they won. That night, on our floor, Indiana State—prepared very well by Royce Waltman, who had been an assistant coach on our staff—deserved to win. Royce was such a good coach and person that I could lose to him without getting too upset about the loss itself, though I was very much upset about our effort.

Sometimes no matter what you do, kids aren't going to think right. That brings defeat for more good teams than anything else. Poor teams can lose because they obviously aren't good enough to compete, but that isn't always the case. Poor teams sometimes have decent players, sometimes damned good players, and those teams become poor teams because they aren't taught well or aren't prepared well. And good teams lose to an inferior opponent, more often than not, because they went into the game feeling that opponent was inferior and they responded with an inferior effort. All of a sudden they were in trouble and they ended up getting beat.

That 1971–72 Ohio U. team was not a poor team. And we were never in the game. Jim Snyder was a hell of a basketball coach, and his team was every bit as good as ours. Yet, they probably would have had a very difficult time beating Kentucky, unless Kentucky approached the game as we did—just not ready to play.

Ohio University is in a conference that thrives on that kind of situation. Every year there are players in the Mid-American Conference who are every bit as good as players in the Big Ten—not quite as many, but certainly some. Players recruited by Big Ten schools seem to think Mid-American players are a level below them. That has caused a hell of a lot of Big Ten teams to lose to Mid-American teams over the years.

I used to use that in reverse at West Point. I'd say to Army kids, "Who all recruited you? Where did you have a chance to play?" I knew the answer—most of them were not highly recruited. Then, when we were playing against a team with highly touted players, I'd go on, "Here's a guy you're going to guard who thought he could go anywhere in the world to play. Now you can go out and shove all that stuff right up his ass." At Army, we beat South Carolina one time when they had seven high school All-Americans.

That first year for us at Indiana, those first six games came very close to being the highlights of our first season. In December, we did win the first tournament of any kind that one of my teams ever won—the Old Dominion Classic at Norfolk, Virginia. Usually we flew home immediately after road games, but we had to stay over that night so I took advantage of it. Tom Murphy, a New Jersey sportswriter who had been a friend of mine in my Army days, had come down for the tournament, so he and I went out in Norfolk to celebrate—with a bowl of chili and a chocolate milkshake.

The first night there, we had played Brigham Young, my first time to coach against them since the bitter loss with Army in the 1966 NIT semifinals. This

BYU team wasn't as talented as that one but they came into the tournament unbeaten and ranked eighth in the country. We led 26–25 at the half and I was tickled to death. When we walked back out on the floor together for the start of the second half, the BYU coach, Stan Watts, brought me down to earth. He asked me, "Wasn't that the worst half of basketball you ever saw?" I guess it may have been, but it hadn't *felt* like it to me until he said so.

Their center was one of the top international players, Kresimir Cosic of Yugoslavia, who later became Yugoslavia's national coach. In the finals, we beat Old Dominion, barely (88–86). They were a Division II team then but they had a great little guard, Dave Twardzik, who went on to be damned good in the NBA.

So, for our first game after the holidays, we went up to Northern Illinois 8–1 and ranked fourth in the country. Riding on the bus from the hotel to the game, I told Dave Bliss, "Boy, wouldn't it be great if we *really* had the fourth-best team in the country sitting behind us here?"

Northern Illinois killed us (85–71). And my first Big Ten season was about to begin, with four straight losses.

I couldn't have asked for a better group of coaches to "welcome" me. I met them all before the season began at the coaches' meeting the Big Ten always had. I was a new kid on the block, and I sat beside the one in there I knew best: Coach Taylor. The first few things that came to a vote, Johnny Orr of Michigan and Gus Ganakas of Michigan State voted the same way. Someone got on them a little for that—"Are you Michigan guys going to stick together on everything?" Gus looked at the guy, looked over at Coach Taylor and me, and said, "If you don't think those two guys are going to vote the same way, you've got another thing coming." And I think he was probably pretty close to a hundred percent right.

The needling around that table was choice. That first year, Orr mentioned that after just a few years in the league, he already had won the coaches' sportsmanship award twice. "Hell," John said, "Freddie Taylor hasn't ever even been nominated."

John and Coach Taylor were good friends, but they hid it well.

My first year also was the first for the Big Ten's pre-season press conference in Chicago—on the Sunday after the football season ended the day before with the Ohio State–Michigan, Indiana–Purdue, and other rivalry games.

When it was Orr's turn, he talked about taking a Big Ten All-Star team on a summertime exhibition trip to the South Pacific. They went unbeaten; there wasn't a whole lot of competition for them there. "I loved it," Orr said. "The best game of all was at Tahiti. We won 123–16. Now, that was fun. The only thing that would have made it better is if Freddie Taylor had been coaching Tahiti."

In the press questioning, I of course was asked about my reputation for low-scoring games. It wasn't a matter of not wanting to shoot, I explained. "We want to take more *good* shots than the opponent does." Orr, whose teams ran as hard and put up as many shots as any in the league, came next. He repeated my comment: "We want to take more *good* shots. . . . I never thought about it that way, but that's exactly what we've been trying to do all these years, too. I'll go back home and say it that way and they'll think I'm a genius."

John could take it, too. The next year at that meeting, Campy Russell was the most touted sophomore coming into the league season. He hadn't played a game yet, so John had some fun. "He's not bad," Orr said. "If he gets a little bit of coaching, he could be damned good." And Ray Marquette of the *Indianapolis Star* chipped in a classic line:

"Well, then, we'll never know."

Coach Taylor fired back after one of Orr's zingers to him: "You'd better win some games, John. Schembechler didn't build Crisler Arena for you to lose." And Coach followed up: "I've heard that one used on me a few times at home."

Right in that period is when I got to know Johnny Orr. I figured anybody with a sense of humor like that had to be a pretty good guy. I was right, and he also was one hell of a coach.

During that bad Big Ten start, we lost at home to Wisconsin. The night before, I went to a high school game in Indianapolis and then ate at a Chinese restaurant in Bloomington late that night. After the meal, I got a Chinese fortune cookie that said, "You will find success, but it will be slow in coming."

It proved right, of course. But the slow part damned near killed me.

I've probably eaten a thousand Chinese meals since that night. I love Chinese food.

But to this day, I've never opened another fortune cookie.

In that 0–4 Big Ten start, we also lost on the road at Minnesota, Ohio State, and Michigan State. After we lost by ten points at Michigan State, I unloaded on our kids pretty hard. We were 0-for-January and I was wondering if we would ever win a Big Ten game. It turned out that of our next seventy-four Big Ten games, we won sixty-eight. I wasn't seeing anything like that ahead when we were 0–4.

We won nine of our last ten regular-season games and in the process I was amused at watching a pretty profound change—in the stands as well as on the floor.

From those early "Shoot! Shoot!" yells, we actually reached a point where some people got upset when *they* thought we had taken a bad shot. And our players changed, too.

At Wisconsin, Joby Wright—who played hard and well for us all year—missed a free-throw but made the second to send the game into overtime. We jumped out in overtime to a seven-point lead, but Steve Downing fouled out with about two minutes to go. I was standing on the sidelines thinking about who we were going to put in for him, and Steve came running up behind me, grabbed me, spun me around, and shouted, "*Coach!* Don't let them take any *bad* shots now!"

Our strong finish got us the first NIT bid in school history. In fact, for all of its basketball success and prestige over the years, Indiana had played in Madison Square Garden just one time, and that wasn't even in my lifetime—December 19, 1936, when Everett Dean took his team out there to play Manhattan (and won, 42–34) in one of promoter Ned Irish's Garden doubleheaders that helped college basketball in the East so much. For many reasons I was tickled about getting the NIT bid, which wasn't officially announced until after our final game with Purdue. Word leaked out, though, and George King, who was coaching at Purdue, "congratulated" me before the game by saying, "They kinda like to pass that around."

I wasn't sure who "they" were, and I didn't care, because I was taking my first Indiana team to a tournament that had always been big for me—and to people who always had been nice to me.

It was an educational trip. When I went into coaching, there was a prevailing belief that play in the Big Ten was rough—"no harm, no foul"—and the East was a finesse area. Well, I had just spent a season in the Big Ten, and when we went back East to play in the NIT, Princeton manhandled us and won 68–60.

Pete Carril always did a great job with his players. He was an extraordinary teacher of basketball. And that day his team was far more physical than any team we played in the Big Ten.

We got off to a good start against Princeton—we were ahead 12–4. There was a time-out, they added a third guard named Reggie Bird, and they just throttled us.

I certainly wasn't happy about losing, but I did feel our first year had gone pretty well. The good finish had pulled us up to third in the Big Ten and 17–8 overall.

But the more I thought about it through the spring and summer, the more I thought about how we lost our Big Ten opener at Minnesota, 52–51, after we led 51–46—and if we had won that game and all other things had come out as they did, we'd have shared the championship with the Minnesota team that won it.

A curse of my life is that I always figure out those things, and then can never forget them.

That first full year at Indiana, starting with our arrival in late March 1971, was an interesting recruiting experience. The 1970–71 season had been an extraordinarily good one for senior prospects in the state of Indiana. It was actually about as good as we were going to find in all the years we were there, although there was nobody rating recruiting classes then and college basketball would have been better off if there never had been.

Our problem in spring '71 was that, arriving in March, we were coming in too late to have a good shot at a number of the best kids. I can remember Bobby Weltlich in particular was shocked and a little discouraged. In an interview a few years later, he said, "When Bob first talked about going to Indiana, I thought that was one of the most unbelievable coaching positions in the world, only to get out there and find that six of the All-State players who still had not made commitments—Pete Trgovich, John Garrett, Jerry Nichols, Tim Stoddard, Junior Bridgeman, and Mike Flynn—we couldn't even get to visit campus. I remember Bob and I sitting in Nichols's home in Greenwood, with Dick and Tom Van Arsdale—there were no greater idols in Indiana than the Van Arsdales. And still we couldn't get him to *visit*. I just couldn't imagine why people were not more receptive to the state school."

Trgovich went to UCLA, Garrett and Nichols to Purdue, Stoddard to North Carolina State, Bridgeman to Louisville, and Flynn to Kentucky—and all of them but the Purdue kids wound up starting on teams that played in the Final Four. If we'd had the whole season to recruit, I think we'd have done a lot better. Of the group, the one I think would have done us the most good—and I believe we'd have been able to get—was Bridgeman, who was the best of them all as a college player, and an outstanding NBA player at Milwaukee with Quinn Buckner.

Weltlich was right about the Van Arsdales being Indiana heroes. The situation with Jerry Nichols was unusual. They were the first people I got to help me recruit—they jumped in right away and they were good at it. The entire time I was there, anytime I ever asked them to do anything, they were very helpful. Their mom got involved with us, too, and I really liked her. More than any woman I've ever known with the exception of my wife, Karen, Hilda Van Arsdale understood athletics and what all went into it. She had a great grasp of the situation at Indiana. During my last months there, she was adamant about *not* wanting me to stay.

The Van Arsdales were two of several Branch McCracken players who stepped in right away to help us.

Frank Radovich, who played at Indiana when I was at Ohio State, helped in a lot of ways. Frank talked to me about past things at Indiana—about people he thought I should be involved with as well as those he didn't. We fished a lot, we played golf—he even helped coach that first year.

Archie Dees, who played just ahead of Radovich and me and was the first two-time Big Ten basketball MVP, was another guy I talked to about the circumstances in Bloomington. He was a big plus for us in getting things started and set up the way we wanted them. Sam Gee was another from the McCracken era who was very helpful. And there were many more.

Despite all those Indiana high school players who wouldn't even talk to us, our recruiting went all right that first spring in Indiana. At the end of my first week in Bloomington, we signed our first player—Steve Green, who played for his dad, Ray, at Silver Creek in southern Indiana and was debating between Kentucky and Vanderbilt before we got in.

I couldn't have picked a better kid to go down in history as our first Indiana recruit. Green was a great shooter and an extremely smart player. He had an outstanding three-year career as a starter for us, on very good teams, and he went on to the NBA and a career as a dentist. Steve's dad and mom were great people. While Steve was playing, his dad used to call me and discuss things, coach to coach. When Steve was the subject, Ray would always chuckle a little and say, "I know I think he's a little better than you do, but . . ." After his senior season ended, I was involved in negotiations for his first pro contract with the ABA Utah Stars, and when I called Ray to tell him the salary terms that had been agreed on, he laughed one more time and said, "I know I think he's better than you do . . . but *I'd* have never paid him that much."

Ray passed away in the fall of 2000, and I was at the funeral to hear his three sons eulogize their dad in a way all fathers should hope their sons would feel about them. Both Ray and Steve are in the Indiana Basketball Hall of Fame.

Still focusing on Indiana, in the next week we came up with two small-school guards who also were very smart—Steve Ahlfeld of Northfield, who is now an orthopedist, and John Kamstra of Rossville, now a CPA. John Laskowski of South Bend St. Joseph's signed with us; he also had a couple of NBA years. We added another smart, tough kid from Illinois, Doug Allen.

Doug was what all teams need, a great practice player. When Scott May was a senior, he gave a lot of credit for his development to Doug for how hard he was to play against in practice.

That class's freshman year was the last year of freshman ineligibility. We worked those kids against the varsity most of the time and sometimes by themselves. We knew we were going to get some vital help from them.

Meanwhile, besides playing that first season at Indiana, we had our first full year of recruiting, and it went well. We established the Ohio–Indiana–Illinois region as our recruiting focal point the next year. We got Quinn Buckner, Jimmy Crews, and Don Noort from Illinois, Scott May and Craig Morris from Ohio, and Bobby Wilkerson and Tom Abernethy from Indiana. May and Wilkerson had to sit out their freshman year because of test scores, but all the rest of those kids—our freshman and sophomore classes in 1972–73—became eligible for varsity play at the same time.

We were also making a major change in how we played the game, which made it an incredibly interesting year for me.

In the early stages of my coaching, I felt that utilizing deception and being unpredictable, unrecognizable, and difficult to scout were instrumental in offensive success. I've always felt that. When I've talked to football coaches, I've talked about deception. And in basketball, I have always wanted the offensive cutter to have options—so if the defense does one thing, the cutter can do another thing. It's not something that just goes one, two, three, four. In basketball, if you're running a set play, a smart defense doesn't have to react to what you're doing, they can do something prior to your move, because they know the movement as well as the offense does.

When Butch Van Breda Kolff was coaching there, Princeton was one of the best-coached teams I ever saw. Bill Bradley was playing then. Princeton's players were obviously smart, they played well defensively, and they were very good offensively. They played with keys—if the passer went inside, that was one thing; if he cut to the bucket, it was another thing. They didn't just run set plays, they keyed off movement. Pete Carril, Van Breda Kolff's replacement, carried that same approach to incredible success in his own career at Princeton. I tried to incorporate that into what I wanted to do at Indiana, but almost exclusively based on reading the defense.

So, in the spring of 1972, I went to Pete Newell's house and I sat down in the middle of the floor, with a stack of three-by-five cards that I used to diagram each separate option.

With Pete right there, thinking along with me, I started by wanting to utilize two people in the post, like a high-low post or a tandem post, with three people on the perimeter. I filled out seventy-four cards with what could be done from that. *If the guy in the middle passes left, here are all the things that could be done. If the guy on the side hits the post* . . . I wanted it to be something that was totally done by recognizing the opportunities that the defense gave you, and the position of the ball.

In putting that in with our team, we coaches constantly harped on spacing, how important it was to maintain fifteen- to eighteen-foot spacing among all the players. I think spacing is one of the two keys to utilization of the court in offensive play. The second is floor balance, keeping players in positions that maintain an ability to attack both sides of the floor. The ball is like a magnet. It attracts players. If you're not careful, you can have five players in half the width of the court.

Then we developed our approach to screening and cutting, with the screener always being on the inside and the cutter on the outside. And that led to the backscreen.

We quickly recognized seven things the passer could do. Three of them were: pass to someone, then (1) go behind that man and get the ball back, (2) go screen for the man who now had the ball, or (3) stand where he was.

We immediately eliminated those three. I didn't want congestion around the ball.

That left four other things the player who made the first pass could do: (1) make an inside cut to to the baseline; (2) cut to the basket; (3) screen away, or (4) replace himself. When we introduced this to the players, those four things are what we did with a four-on-four drill, to get them to see and understand what we were trying to do.

I originally called it Pass, Cut, and Screen, because those were the three things our players were going to do. I wanted to do away with excessive dribbling. I made some rules: "The dribble is to be used against man-to-man defense to bring the ball up the floor, to improve the passing angle, or to take the ball to the bucket—and that's it."

From the end of the 1971–72 season to the start of practice for the next one, I wanted to spend as much time on the new offense as I could, and talk to as many people about it as I could.

I read everything that one of the game's great coaches, Henry Iba, had written about defensive play and his passing-game offense. I met Mr. Iba when I was still coaching at West Point. He was the speaker at the Akron Touchdown Club's high school basketball banquet. I went to hear him talk.

Afterward, I was talking to somebody and I felt a hand on my shoulder. I turned around, and the fellow said, "Son, my name is Henry Iba."

I couldn't keep from chuckling, that a man of his stature felt he needed to introduce himself to anybody. I said, "Yes, Coach, I know very well who you are, and I really enjoyed listening to you."

He said, "I just wanted to tell you Doggie (Julian, who had coached Holy Cross to the 1947 NCAA championship) and the boys out East tell me you're doing a good job coaching defense."

That was praise from on high, at my first meeting with him.

So in the spring of 1972, I was looking for information, Coach Iba was going to coach the U.S. Olympic team, and I called him to ask if he needed any help with the Trials. He invited me to be one of the coaches there. It was great at those Trials—first, Coach Iba was clearly the man in charge, and second, which I suspect was related, there was no press coverage.

He assigned each of us a team of seven or eight kids, and we played games as part of the selection system. One time, just to needle a guy, I wore a referee's shirt when I was coaching my team in a game. The next morning at breakfast, I walked past the Coach while he was eating cereal. Without even looking up, he said, "I don't want to see that God-damned striped shirt today."

And he didn't.

My team included Swen Nater, a seven-footer who was probably the only back-up player there—he was second-string at UCLA to Bill Walton, but pretty good. We got along well there and had some great exchanges. He kidded me about something, and I told him, "Just remember I'm the only guy who ever started you." Walton was one of the great players who didn't attempt to play for the Olympic team in 1972. In Walton's case, he was going to get a free ride all the way through the Trials to the team, because of how good he was and an injury he'd had. If Walton had chosen to play on that '72 Olympic team, I don't think any kind of officiating would have let the Russians win the gold medal, and his not playing for his country left a sour taste in my mouth, and in many others'.

On my way home from the Trials in Denver, I drove through Oklahoma to stop and see Coach Iba and thank him for the experience. Just north of Stillwater, I got stopped for speeding.

I did my best to get out of it. I told the state policeman who stopped me that I had coached for Coach Iba at the Olympic Trials and I was on the way to Stillwater to see him. The officer said, "Oh, my, he is a popular man. He's a very big man in this state."

I found out his assistant coaches weren't. I got a ticket.

Another coach assisting at the Trials was Joe Cipriano, the coach at Nebraska. I hadn't known him before, but I spent a lot of time with him there. I was trying to learn all I could about Coach Iba's passing game and I knew—being in the same conference with him and playing his Oklahoma State teams two or three times a year—Joe would know it well. At Nebraska in his offense, he ran a play that evolved into the passing game.

He did help me on that, but more than that, he became one of the closest friends I ever had in coaching. Joe had been a damned good player at Washington—along with an All-America center named Bob Houbregs on a team that went to the NCAA finals in 1953. He coached at Nebraska for a long, long time. His teams were successful but never a national contender. He was a hell of a coach and a great guy to be around. We had eight or nine years of friendship before he passed away from pancreatic cancer.

About a year after his death, his wife gave me a watch, which she knew had a history. When Joe and I were in Italy together with our 1979 Pan American Games team in a tournament that included the Russian and Canadian teams, he was wearing a Big Eight watch. He traded it to a Russian coach for a Russian watch. I couldn't resist having some fun with that. After we had walked away, I got all over him: "Joe, that's like trading a steak for a hot dog. The Russians don't make anything that works. Why the hell would you do that?"

I have that watch to this day. It doesn't run, but every time I see the thing it brings back awfully nice memories.

I couldn't wait to get started installing our motion offense when fall practice started. It was the only pre-season in my coaching career when we merged three groups—our returning varsity players (including Steve Downing and John Ritter), the freshman team from the year before, and the incoming freshman class that, for the first time in college basketball since 1952, was eligible to play right away.

We spent a lot of October practicing four-on-four and five-on-five—without allowing a dribble. There we were truly playing Pass, Cut, and Screen; we didn't let anybody dribble. I always wanted to see a basket scored without the use of a dribble, and I'd react when we got one.

It turned out that the best player we had to run that kind of offense wasn't with us then. Freshman Quinn Buckner had come to school as a combined football-basketball recruit. His father, Bill Buckner, had lettered on the only unbeaten football team Indiana ever had (1945), and he was a close friend of a teammate from that year, assistant football coach Howard Brown, one of the nicest people in the world and so staunch a Hoosier people called him "Mr. Indiana." Buckner had been a tough recruit. Publicity for high school athletes had escalated but it still wasn't close to what it is today. Still, he was way ahead of his time in the national attention he got before he chose a college. In football at Thornridge in one of the toughest Chicago suburban leagues, he led the conference in scoring—and never played a down on offense. He got all his touchdowns with interceptions (as a defensive back) and kick-off and punt returns. Then he led Thornridge to two straight state basketball championships. He put off signing with us until the last allowable day—July 31, just a few weeks before he reported to start football practice.

For the hype he got, he was about as good to work with as a kid in those circumstances could be.

I'll tell you how good an athlete Quinn Buckner was. Since freshman eligibility went into effect thirty years ago, I'll bet he's the only major-college player who started the opening game of his freshman season in both football and basketball.

Think about how hard that is. He finished his football season at Purdue on November 25 and opened the basketball season on December 2—from one Saturday to the next.

I don't think starting that fast in basketball was even on his mind. He has said since then that he was planning to go home to Chicago after the Purdue game and enjoy the weekend, then report back on Monday. I sent word to him that I expected him to be suited up for our public intrasquad exhibition game at Assembly Hall Sunday night. I had talked with Ritter and Downing. They both felt he should play.

He was there. In those intrasquad exhibitions, we usually played three twenty-minute periods, and we did that night. The first one, I had him sitting with an assistant coach at the start so he could point out to Quinn what we were trying to do on offense. We sent him in to play with the second unit after about eleven minutes. He was so new to the basketball kids we had that when he was told, "Go in for Kim," he ran to the scorer's bench, was waved in, started onto the court, turned with a kind of embarrassed, confused look, and asked in almost a whisper, "Which one's Kim?"

He played out that first period with the second unit; then the second period I let him play some with the guys we expected to start. Halfway through the third period, he put the ball on his hip and told some of those starters where they should be.

I obviously wasn't expecting him to be a starter right away. By Wednesday,

I had seen enough that after practice, from Assembly Hall, I called the best person I could think of to talk this thing out with me: Clair Bee. I told him the situation, and how reluctant I was to move a kid who had been practicing only a few days ahead of kids who had been busting their ass for six weeks. Coach Bee, as he always did, got to the heart of it in one sentence, "The only obligation you have to your players is that they know you're starting the best lineup you have." By the time the week was over, that sure as hell included Buckner.

The first game we played was against Harvard, which had good talent, including three guys from the Washington, D.C., area who were very heavily recruited. The tip went to a Harvard player, and about two seconds into his college career, Buckner stole the ball.

We won, 97–76. Ninety-seven points with our new offense—I was pleased.

And I felt we had significantly strengthened ourselves at guard. The addition of Buckner gave us a rotation of three good guards—with him and Jimmy Crews learning how to play, and John Kamstra, who may have been the best of the three at that time. With Kamstra coming off the bench, we actually elevated what we did in some respects.

We won our first five games and just before Christmas went down to Columbia to play South Carolina and Frank McGuire. Frank had won an NCAA championship with a 32–0 team at North Carolina in 1957. He was a great guy who, with his style and his approach, was one of the early coaches to bring attention to basketball—and to move toward the national recruiting we have today, with all the New York kids he brought to North Carolina and South Carolina. On this team he had Alex English, who's in the Hall of Fame now, and three other guys—New Yorkers—who all played in the NBA: Kevin Joyce (who had played on Henry Iba's 1972 Olympic team), Brian Winters, and Mike Dunleavy. Frank loved his two-three zone defense, and we played well against it. We were ahead 56–40 six minutes into the second half. We got beat, 88–85. Those last fourteen minutes in particular but pretty much all night, Joyce just killed every guard we had—Buckner included, in fact, Buckner most of all. Joyce scored forty-one points, twenty-five in the last half.

We were way too passive in letting that game get away. On the flight home, I was at the front of the team plane and John Ritter, a senior, was in the back, seat belt on, asleep. I yelled, "*Ritter! Come up here!*" I let him know—loudly—that I expected a whole lot more from our leaders.

Our next game was in El Paso for a holiday tournament. When we got off the plane there, we didn't have a bus—they took us to our hotel in separate cars. Downing and Buckner weren't in the car with me, but I understand the subject of the flight back from South Carolina came up. Downing broke out in his great laugh and said, "Yeah, Coach got a pretty good piece of ol' Rit. I thought we were *all* going to get a little bit of that." "So did I," said my rookie, Buckner. "And I was just hoping he was going by class."

The first night of that El Paso tournament, we beat a good Houston team, which set us up to play UTEP in the championship game. Midway in the second half, I got thrown out—the first time for me at Indiana. There wasn't anything contrived about it; I couldn't believe the officiating I was seeing, and I said so, more than once. It took three technical fouls to get ejected then, and I qualified. A cop walked me off the floor, and to get to our locker room I had to go past the UTEP coach, Don Haskins, a good friend of mine. I had no idea what he'd say, or if he'd say anything, but I heard his gruff voice bark out, "You put up with that shit a lot longer than I would have."

I looked at him and said, "Come get me afterward and we'll go eat." And we did.

We were off to a 5–0 start in the Big Ten when we played at Michigan, which had Campy Russell and figured to be one of the primary contenders for the league championship. Right away in the game at Ann Arbor, John Kamstra tore his Achilles tendon. That was a tremendous blow, not just to that team but to John's career and Indiana's basketball future. John never regained his quickness after that. I've always believed Kamstra would have been one of the best guards I ever coached, and I just don't think his injury was properly handled. I was unaware at the time that they were doing a new procedure on him that was almost like a trial. They rolled the Achilles down and put it in a cast so it would adhere to the heel bone. The second day he was out of the cast, the tendon rolled right back up again.

A few minutes after Kamstra went down in the Michigan game we lost another key player, John Ritter, to a concussion. This was a big game for us, and right away we were missing two of our best players.

Tom Abernethy was a freshman forward from South Bend. I'll guarantee you prior to that day Johnny Orr and Michigan had no idea who he was. He hadn't scored a college point yet, and he wasn't even listed on our roster in the Michigan game program. But that day when we needed it, he came off the bench to score twelve points, and we won, 79–73. I was talking to the press after the game when I saw his mother down the hall. I yelled to her, "Hey, Mrs. Abernethy! Your kid earned his scholarship today!" We've always had a lot of great moms, and she was one.

That team came together well. The seniors—Jerry Memering and Frank Wilson, who were reserves, and Ritter and Downing as starters—did a great job as leaders, the South Carolina game notwithstanding. These were all kids who were recruited by Lou Watson to play a totally different kind of basketball, but they bought into what we were doing. That was the main reason I decided to honor them with a little ceremony on the floor after the last home game—to give them a chance to speak, and hear some appreciation from the fans.

It also gave me a chance to say what I felt about Watson, the man I replaced. It was a good idea, but Lou was just like I would have been—he had no idea what was coming, so when the game ended, he already was on his way to his car to beat the traffic. But, I was glad the people in the stands that day could hear how much I appreciated him and the kids he had left me.

The ceremony after the last home game was a spur-of-the-moment decision that became one of the nicest traditions we developed at Indiana. The next year, we didn't have any seniors, but from there on we had a "Senior Day," and that chance to hear the seniors and give them a last hurrah became the hottest ticket on our home schedule. It usually brought out terrific efforts from our kids as well. We did it twenty-six times and won twenty-three of those games.

Beating Purdue in that last game of the 1972–73 season meant we were sure of at least a co-championship. But a tie for first would have meant that to get to the NCAA tournament we were going to have to beat a very good team, Minnesota, on Monday night at Champaign in a playoff for the Big Ten's NCAA tournament berth—then get ready right away to play our first tournament game just three nights later. Minnesota's last-day game was at Northwestern, which was 1–12 in the league going into the game, so everybody assumed there would be a playoff game. A good little left-handed guard named Mark Sibley scored thirty-six points that day and Northwestern won. We were the Big Ten champions, outright, only the fourth time that had ever happened at Indiana, and we were in the tournament with ample time to prepare. I sent Sibley an Indiana blanket, from our team.

We still talk about Steve Downing's forty-seven-point, twenty-five-rebound, fifty-minute game against Kentucky his junior year, but he was almost as good in getting us past Marquette at Nashville in our first NCAA tournament game. Al McGuire's Marquette teams were known for their press, and we went against it with freshman guards, Buckner and Jimmy Crews. The way they handled the press was a big thing for us, but Al also had an outstanding player at center in

Maurice Lucas. Steve scored twenty-nine points in that game against twelve for Lucas, and that was the key to our winning. Marquette, which was No. 5 in the country, was probably as good as anybody in that tournament except UCLA.

We beat Kentucky to get to the Final Four at St. Louis, against UCLA—unbeaten, ranked No. 1, and trying for its seventh straight NCAA championship.

I think you can look back, especially your first time, and say, "It was a great thrill that we got to play in the Final Four." As a young coach, taking a team to the Final Four was one of those things I had thought about—*Wouldn't it be great to . . .*

But, starting with that first time I took a team to the finals, I was always too wrapped up in how we were going to play and what we had to do to be particularly thrilled by it. More than anything else, I was always kind of scared: I just wanted my team to play well. From a coaching standpoint, the greatest fear I've ever had—and it doesn't take a Final Four to bring it out—is that in some way I might not have prepared my team as well as I could have. I'm always afraid I've left something out, or overlooked something. If you've done that, you've shortchanged your players. They're not as well prepared as they should be.

Against UCLA, we played pretty well at the start. Then we missed some shots, and—as we did a lot of times, in concentrating our defense on particular guys—we didn't guard one of their guards, Tommy Curtis. He made some baskets and we got down by twenty-two points. Without those shots we missed and the way we played Curtis, maybe we'd have been down twelve, who knows?

But we came back because they didn't have anybody who could handle Downing. We had already started catching up with them when their All-American, Bill Walton, picked up his fourth foul and went out of the game. When we got from 46–24 to 54–47 with still 10:27 to go, they had to bring Walton back in. We got it to 54–51—we had scored seventeen straight points—when Walton posted up along the baseline, turned to his right shoulder to drive, and drove his forearm into Downing's chest. The call was a foul on Downing—not Walton's fifth, Downing's fourth. Within a minute, Downing had his fifth foul and was out of the game. UCLA won, 70–59. Downing outscored Walton twenty-six to fourteen, two nights before Walton's 21-for-22 shooting night and forty-four points when UCLA beat Memphis State for the championship.

I had a tough time swallowing that loss. I've always considered that fourth foul on Downing one of the two worst big calls my teams have ever had—the other one in the St. John's game in the 1970 NIT. But, as bad as I felt, I told two friends of mine from Orrville, Dick Rhoads and Tony Yonto, on the elevator that evening, "We weren't good enough to win it, but we'll be back with a team that *will* win it, soon."

I definitely thought that.

They were still playing a consolation game in 1973, and we came back on Monday night to beat Providence, 97–79, and finish third. I can't take any credit for how well we played that night.

John Havlicek won that game.

He got to St. Louis the day of the Providence game, and he told our kids, "Fellows, I came up here to see you win the national championship, and we all know you can't do that now. Since I came to see you play the best you can, I expect to see you win, because third is a hell of a lot better than fourth."

I can't tell you how great it was for John to come out there under those circumstances and give our kids the lift he did. He and the Celtics had played the night before and they were playing the next night. That says all that needs to be said about John Havlicek as a friend.

There's no player I've been closer to or appreciated more than Steve Downing. He was a tremendous captain for us in '73 and just a great player that year—the Most Valuable Player in the Big Ten and the NCAA regional, and, after completely outplaying Walton head-to-head, he was an obvious pick on the All–Final Four Team.

But while he was doing all that as our captain and a senior, he also did things for us in the way of leadership that nobody knew about. I'll mention one. Under the NCAA rules at the time, both Scott May and Bobby Wilkerson were considered academic nonpredictors, which meant they could come to school on scholarship but they couldn't play on our team or even practice with us that season, as freshmen. That's a tough adjustment for any kid who has been used to competing, and it was especially hard for Scott. Without a real basketball outlet, he got homesick more often than I'm sure he would have, and he went home to Sandusky—a six-hour trip one-way—fairly often. We tried to help talk him through that period, of course, but the one guy who could do it best was Steve, because he and George McGinnis had been through the same thing their freshman year—basketball, as big a part of their life as it was Scott's, suddenly denied them.

Later on that year, Scott got very close to Quinn Buckner, but in the fall months when Quinn was playing football, Steve was the one who stepped in as a friend and made a big difference with Scott. Steve did it knowing that he would never play with May but feeling that our program was the right place for Scott and that Scott would be great for our Indiana program. Boy, was he right.

After his own basketball career ended, Steve came back to Bloomington to work in the athletic department.

He was the most underappreciated person in the university, and grossly underpaid. No one there was more responsible for athletes getting straightened out when they had problems, or working with kids and helping kids, or setting an example for what athletes should be expected to do and how they should conduct themselves.

Steve is also at Texas Tech now, as an assistant to athletic director Gerald Myers, who has a great appreciation for Steve's value to our athletic department. Getting him was a great addition for us and far more of a loss to Indiana than the people there could ever understand. The little compensation and appreciation that he received for the contributions he made to the athletic program there was ridiculous.

Obviously we had a big rebuilding job to do in 1973–74, after losing Downing and Ritter. We got an invitation to play in a summertime tournament in Spain. The seniors from our Final Four team couldn't go, and Buckner was unavailable—he was playing in the University Games, with the first U.S. athletic team to go in to China, that barrier-breaking summer. But, I accepted the invitation to Spain anyway and took nine kids. The trip and the tournament did help us.

One night over there, in the first half we were cutting and screening, executing our offense well, and we were beating the best team in Spain, Real Madrid (their best player was an American, Walt Szczerbiak, whose son Wally had a great career at Miami of Ohio in the '90s and since then has done very well in the NBA). The second half, Real Madrid played as though our screens weren't even there. They ran over them or through them—just knocked the hell out of us. And they beat us.

The last two nights of the trip, we were playing in a tournament at Majorca. Nobody but me knew I wasn't going to be around for the last night of it. I was leaving the next morning. Dave Bliss and Bobby Weltlich were the assistants with me, and I hadn't told them. During the game, I found something to get upset about with the officials and I took the team off the floor. The crowd was going crazy, but we went outside and just sat. It was hotter than hell. They needed a break. And I was having some fun. After a while, we came back inside and won the game.

Our host was a buddy of Doc Counsilman, the great Indiana swimming coach—Alfonso was his name; I called him Fox. After the game, I told him, "Okay, Fox, I've got to have a ride to the airport at eight in the morning."

Alfonso shrieked, "Bobby! Bobby! *Why*? Where are you going?"

"I'm going home," I said. "I'm going fishing. But don't worry, Fox, you won't be able to find enough tickets for this game. I've put you in a great position." And I was right. I had the town so stirred up you couldn't buy a ticket for the finals.

"Fox" wasn't the only one shocked. Weltlich and Bliss almost had cardiac arrest when they found out I was leaving and *they* had to face the crowd. But they beat a team from Barcelona that was one of the best in Spain and we came away with the championship. Dave and Bobby had some fun of their own, taking our victorious team around the arena like a conquering matador after a bullfight.

My comment at St. Louis to my hometown friends Dick Rhoads and Tony Yonto about getting back to the NCAA tournament and winning it presumed one thing that hadn't officially happened yet, but did. Kent Benson, the best high school center in our primary recruiting area that year, signed with us in the spring. He was the final piece I thought we needed to go with what we had recruited our first two years.

When we started practice in the fall of 1973, Bennie was our new player, but we also were adding Scott May and Bobby Wilkerson, who'd had to sit out their freshman year.

I liked the possibilities for what we had, but I wasn't sure exactly where we were—and I certainly wasn't ready to talk much about anything.

The pre-season wire service polls came out and, before we ever played a game, we were ranked No. 3 in the country—behind UCLA with Walton and North Carolina State with David Thompson. In the fall, I spoke at an evening meeting of a Bloomington service club. Bob Hammel had been at practice that day, and after it was over, I told him where I was going. He had heard all the pre-season talk from me he wanted to hear, knowing I was pretty much going to dodge every question about the upcoming season anyway. So he wasn't much interested in going. "You'd better come," I told him. "You'll miss something."

We left practice in separate cars, but when I got there, I saw he was in the back of the room. The first question mentioned that No. 3 ranking. I said the people who did that must not have noticed that Downing and Ritter had graduated from our Final Four team. Then—knowing that everybody there that night also knew Bob was in the room—I added, "You know who makes up those polls: sportswriters. And we all know what sportswriters are. All of us learn to write in the second grade, but most of us go on to other things."

It was an unplanned thing, but the result was just what I expected: everybody laughed, Bob turned a little red—I enjoyed that line.

So did Bob. He ran it in his paper the next day, then sent it to a national magazine, which ran it as a "Quote of the Week," and paid him—*him*, not me—seventy-five dollars.

That's how and when one of my most-quoted quotes happened, and who really made out on the deal.

I'm really not so sure my line was wrong. My mom saved a ton of things from my school days, and one was an early English paper, a handwritten story titled, "The Saga of Stanley Dumwiddle." It was written when I was not really in the second grade but somewhere along the line in the Orrville school system. My "Stanley" was a Revolutionary War hero who, in my story, froze to death plugging holes, Little Dutch Boy style, in the boat that carried Washington across the Delaware. When I read it today, it seems to me to be literature far beyond what I see on most sports pages. A lot of writers I've read should study my spellbinding style, especially the sheer poetic artistry of the ending:

> *Stanley's unknown throughout the land,*
> *But he saved our country with his icy hand.*
> *I'd never have told of this brave creature*
> *If not for you, my English teacher.*

I got an A+, on the three-page paper, with no visible corrections. It was all prose until the poetic finish, which is probably where the A became A+.

All that aside, I *was* worried about replacing Downing and Ritter.

As is the case with most high school players, Kent Benson had done a lot there with his raw size—6-foot-10, about 230 pounds. His coach at New Castle, Cecil Tague, had worked well with him on playing in the low post. We worked hard to strengthen his hands, because in early games guys were taking the ball from him all the time. To show what kind of kid we were working with, when we were all going down the ramp at the Spectrum in Philadelphia for the 1976 national championship game, I was behind Bennie and I saw him—a two-year All-American by then—squeezing those two rubber balls we had given him as a freshman to strengthen his hands.

He was a workmanlike player—there wasn't anything flashy about him, he wasn't a great athlete, but he gave everything he had. He was hurt a lot in his college years, but he played hurt. He blocked out, he rebounded, he set great screens—he was a team-oriented kid. As a senior, things didn't go very well for him or our team, but he did a lot of things kids with the recognition he got wouldn't have wanted to do. Those things were a long way ahead of him when he started to work with us as a freshman. We didn't have much choice: he was our center. We restricted what he could do and where he could go and pretty much worked around him.

The best indication of how little he was doing for us in those opening weeks was that he was a pretty good shooter and he still didn't make his first college free-throw until our fifteenth game.

He was immature. We played a pre-conference game at Ball State—in Muncie, near his hometown. Our bus when we were on the way to a game was always quiet. I wanted it that way—not tense, but quiet, everyone thinking about the game. Near the arena, Bennie spotted someone he knew, so he rolled down the window and yelled, "Hey, so-and-so!" I didn't say a word. I didn't have to. The looks he saw around that bus when he put the window back up told him Indiana players didn't do things like that.

That year Scott May was just as new to us as Bennie, but right from the start we knew he would be special for us. The year away from organized basketball, though, had cost him some development, especially in footwork. In practice, we don't officiate tightly. We do constantly let them know about violations such as walking but it's not the same as losing the ball for a turnover in a game. Things got so bad with him that Dave Bliss, after we had played a game on Saturday, spent a whole Sunday afternoon working with Scott on nothing but footwork. That was after our sixteenth game of the season, and it paid off. The very next game, he broke out with his biggest game up to then, twenty-two points, and we beat Illinois. From there on, he was the outstanding player we thought we had.

And we were lucky to have him.

Scott was a great athlete in high school at Sandusky, Ohio. He was recruited as a football end by Nebraska, Ohio State, and Michigan, and he was third in the discus in the state track meet. In basketball, he was All-State, and he played in a very tough conference. He was intelligent, and he was in a great family. His mother and father made sure all three of their kids paid attention to education.

I determined very early that Scott wanted to play basketball, not football.

But, under a Big Ten policy at the time—a policy, not a rule—we couldn't give him a scholarship. Here was a kid who graduated in four years from Indiana with a 2.8 grade average as a speech major, without ever taking a summer-school course, but he was a kid who just couldn't take the standardized test well. So, he was a nonpredictor, and the Big Ten policy was you only took nonpredictors from your home state.

I looked into that policy a little. Doc Counsilman had been recruiting a nonpredictor swimmer from Pennsylvania who wanted to go to Indiana, but the policy said he couldn't—so he ended up going to Ohio State. Well, he sure wasn't from Ohio, either. Purdue took three great football prospects from Chicago—nonpredictors: Dave Butz, Otis Armstrong, and Darryl Stingley. Wisconsin had some athletes like that.

And Michigan and Minnesota were both going to take Scott May. I sat down with Bill Orwig and said, "The hell with this. If those two schools are going to take him, we're going to take him. We're not going to lose Scott May because of adherence to a policy that nobody else follows." Bill and Ed Cady, our faculty representatives, were great. With the guy we had as athletic director at the end of my years there, Scott May would have never played at Indiana.

We got to the Big Ten season not playing very well. Buckner was one of the reasons, and I thought I knew why. He had played football again as a sophomore, and Pete Newell told me when this all started that if he continued to play both sports, his basketball skills would deteriorate. After we lost a fifteen-point lead and got beat at Michigan in our Big Ten opener, we had a nonconference trip to Miami of Ohio. The day of the game over there, at the hotel where we were staying in an Ohio state park, I called Quinn to my room and told him:

"I know you don't want to play football. I'm going to give you an ultimatum, which puts it all on my shoulders. I'm going to tell you you're not going to play basketball if you play football. So no one will ever blame you for not playing football."

I announced it, and of course got some strong press criticism. But I thought it was crucial to him, and I think the way things worked out for him proved we both did the right thing; my making the ultimatum and Quinn picking basketball.

But that far into the season we still had a team that wasn't playing as well as I thought it could.

We won games—we beat Wisconsin, 52–51; Northwestern, 72–67, and Iowa, 55–51. But, obviously, we weren't getting things done offensively.

We had a week after the Iowa game before we played Northwestern again. I had never been a big believer in offensive "conversion"—the fast break. Al LoBalbo, with us at Army and later with his own Fairleigh Dickinson teams, used the phrase "defensive fast-break." It meant that you damned well concentrated on getting back fast to the defensive end. But we didn't have much of an offensive break—we would run on a steal or if we had real positive numbers on a break (two-on-one, three-on-one, three-on-two), but not much otherwise. I restricted outlet passes—from the man who got the defensive rebound to the man open to take the ball up-court—to fifteen feet.

I felt we needed to develop our running game far more than we had. I still wanted short outlet passes, unless somebody ahead was wide open. I told them, "Make sure it's a good pass. We're not just throwing the ball down there *hoping* somebody will be there. The most important thing in the break is to get there with the ball, and *then* work to get a good shot."

That open week we worked hard on all of that. Then we went to Northwestern and on their court, against the team we had beaten by five points at Assembly Hall, we won 82–53. Undoubtedly the change in our approach shocked Northwestern. The Hoosiers were actually Hurryin' again.

We also had thirty turnovers that game. Everybody says, "If you run, you're going to have more turnovers." I never accepted that. If you can handle the ball, you can handle the ball. If you can handle the ball under the pressure of good half-court defense, you sure as hell ought to be able to handle it in full-court play against very little pressure.

But where we had averaged 60.7 points and won four times in the seven games before the change, we averaged 90.4 in the next eight games—and won all eight. The change became permanent.

That opening Big Ten game we lost at Michigan hurt us badly. We lost just one more time, at Ohio State in the next-last game of the season, but we ended up tied for the Big Ten championship with Michigan at 12–2. That was the last year that the NCAA allowed only one team from a conference in the tournament, so we played Michigan at Champaign for the Big Ten's spot. They won.

I had wanted to take that team to the NCAA tournament, but if we weren't going to do that, I wanted to go to the NIT. That didn't happen, either. The Big Ten had been a leader in a group that set up its own tournament for teams not invited to the NCAA. It was called the Conference Commissioners Association tournament and it was played at St. Louis, bringing in eight major conference runners-up. I argued with Mr. Orwig about going; I didn't like anything about the CCA tournament, including the fact that it was a blatant attempt to kill the NIT. But he said I had no choice, we were going to St. Louis if we were going anywhere at all, and on the airplane to St. Louis I told our kids, "If we have to go, let's win the damned thing."

We didn't play very well in the early rounds. We beat Tennessee 73–71 and Toledo in overtime, 72–71. That put us in the finals against Southern Cal and a close friend of mine, Bob Boyd, one of the best coaches of my era.

When the NCAA tournament accepted only one team from a conference, nobody was hurt more than Bob. He had some outstanding teams that didn't get in, because those were the years UCLA was so dominant. In the 1970–71 season, Bob's Southern Cal team, with Paul Westphal and Dennis Layton, went 24–2 and finished the season No. 6 in the rankings. But, the two losses were to UCLA, which went to the tournament and won. There was no love between those two schools. I suspect it was someone from USC who said that hanging up there from the Pauley Pavilion roof with all those championship banners should have been booster Sam Gilbert's checkbook.

The 1973–74 Southern Cal team we were playing for the CCA championship was very good—runner-up by a game again to UCLA in the Pac-Eight, ranked as high as No. 7 late in the season, 24–4 going against us. They had an outstanding guard, Gus Williams.

But by then we were starting to see our own future.

Benson had been a much better player the last third of his freshman season. He had his first big game, twenty points, when we beat Michigan at home, and after averaging less than six points a game up to then, he averaged 15.4 the rest of the way. After we beat Southern Cal, 85–60, to win the tournament, Bennie was named the Most Valuable Player.

One other thing happened in that final game. Bobby Wilkerson, who had played up-and-down that year but had been more and more consistent in practice, showed how good he was going to be. Against Southern Cal, he played the best game a guard played for us all that year. It was important for him to wind up that way, just as it was for Bennie to play as well as he did.

I didn't want to go to that tournament, but winning it wound up the season on a good note for us. It got everybody thinking about what we could do, and what we had to do. And the three games there—in an ill-conceived tournament that drew about two thousand people per round—got us started on the longest winning streak a Big Ten team ever had.

The most important thing to me was we were playing basketball at last the way I wanted to play it, and we had the kids to play it that way.

Our "regular" offense was gone completely. We were running it in practice one day and Buckner was standing beside me. It wasn't going very well, and I said to him, "You guys don't like this offense, do you?" He said, "No—we love playing motion." We never used it again.

Clinics and Fishing

Before I ever got to Indiana, I was pretty heavily involved with coaching clinics. A lot of credit for that belongs to my college coach, Fred Taylor.

By the time I was a head coach, he had won a national championship and five straight Big Ten championships. Obviously, he was in demand for clinics. He didn't like to do them, but he had a deep respect for their role. Once I was coaching, he'd slip me in as a suggested alternative when he turned one down, which he did a lot. Those "referrals" helped me get started.

Before I ever spoke at one, he told me, "Always remember there have been, and there will be, a lot of people who help you, people who share basketball with you. When you're asked to come to a clinic, make sure you share what you do with them."

Because of the absolute honesty and the feeling for the game he and Pete Newell had and lived up to, I never held back anything we did when I spoke at clinics. I can tell you, not every coach feels that way.

From the beginning, the thing that I almost always talked about at clinics was defensive play. The coaches that I played for or worked for or with in college were always more emphatic about defensive play than the offensive end. Besides Coach Taylor and Pete Newell, Andy Andreas was first a defensive coach. The same was true of Tates Locke at West Point, and Al LoBalbo, who was a big part of our staff at Army the 1963 and '64 seasons. For years Al had been one of the great coaches in Eastern high school basketball—his teams at St. Mary's of Elizabeth won seven New Jersey championships. Al was way ahead of people at the defensive end of the floor, and I learned an awful lot from him. Now in his eighties, he has lost none of the passion he had while he was coaching. At Indiana, I brought him out to watch us practice every year, and our players always enjoyed his visits and his observations.

The first year I was at Indiana I spoke at a clinic Bill Foster had at Valley Forge, Pennsylvania. My subject was defensive play. But there were some clinics where I spoke several times, and then I would include offense—what we were doing at West Point, then in the early years at Indiana. At both places we ran "reverse-action" as Pete Newell had at California. Ed Jucker, whose Cincinnati teams beat the Ohio State teams I was on for the 1961 and 1962 NCAA championships, wrote a book called *Cincinnati Power Basketball*. He called his offense swing-and-go; it was a lot like reverse-action.

Pete didn't take credit for his reverse-action offense. He traced it all the way back to Jimmy Needles, whom he played for in the 1930s at Loyola of California.

At the end of my season of coaching under Andy at Cuyahoga Falls, we went to Warren, Ohio, where the coach, Dick Boyd, had invited Andy and me to their banquet. Ed Jucker, the Cincinnati coach, was the speaker. During his speech, he introduced me in the crowd, saying he was sure with the background I had playing under Coach Taylor at Ohio State and working with Andy I would develop into a fine coach. I thought that was an incredible thing for an opposing coach to do for a kid he didn't even know. I never forgot that, or him.

I had a similar experience earlier that year. Coach Taylor was a speaker at a pre-season clinic in Cleveland, and Andy took me to it. During Coach Taylor's talk, he was starting to demonstrate something when he looked up in the crowd and told me to come down to the floor. As I was headed there, he said, "If you're coaching and you have a kid to demonstrate, you don't have to do it yourself."

The next two hours, I did the best I could to illustrate what Coach Taylor talked about—proud that he asked me to help him. When I got home from that clinic, I wrote Coach Taylor a note thanking him for including me that day but also letting him know how much I appreciated all that I had learned about coaching from playing for him and from being around him for four years. Years later, his daughter Nikki told me that was a letter he had saved and was proud of.

After the great early years we had at Indiana, my clinic invitations picked up, to the point where I had to pick and choose.

Bob Murrey, a former coach and a close friend whom I met when I was the Army coach and on the MacGregor Sporting Goods advisory staff, was in charge of MacGregor's coaching clinics and he did most of the booking for me. The sport of basketball has no idea of all that it owes to Bob Murrey. For more than thirty-five years he has run clinics all over the country, bringing ideas and thoughts on the game to coaches of all levels from America's most successful coaches. In doing that, he has made a quiet, highly significant contribution to the development of teaching the game of basketball.

Bob liked just about everything about my clinic presentations except my fondness for working in a joke or two. I had my favorites; I'd tell one, my audience would always howl, and Bob would shake his head afterward and say, "Why do you *do* that? You don't *need* those jokes." Finally, after I had been at Indiana five or six years, I listened to Bob and quit telling jokes. But I'd embellish a basketball story occasionally; I always tried to entertain. And there are still clinics today where after I've spoken an older coach will come up and ask me to tell the guys he's with one of those old stories.

In the summer of 1970, I accepted a two-day speaking engagement at the national high school coaches' clinic in Jackson Hole, Wyoming. There I met the high school coach at Jackson Hole, Paul Kraft, who had played at Massillon Jackson just a little ahead of me. Orrville played Jackson in both football and basketball.

Paul owned about two acres on Jackson Creek. I stayed at a motel on the south side of Jackson Hole, and he told me I could come out and fish anytime I wanted.

I went there ready to fish. I had a little Garcia spinning rod and a Mitchell 308 reel. I still have them. As soon as I arrived at Jackson Hole, I got a box of nightcrawlers, kept them in my room, and each of my two mornings there I got up at dawn, went over to Paul Kraft's place and fished off a bank—with my nightcrawlers, on a little thing called a Colorado spinner. I caught some nice cutthroat trout, and that started me on a lifelong pursuit of trout.

Two years later, Joe Cipriano, the Nebraska coach I had grown to know and like, took me to Ennis, Montana, to fish—the first time I was ever in Montana. I hadn't even owned a flyrod when I went to Jackson Hole. By my Montana trip, I had one—a dentist and friend in Indianapolis, Karl Glander, had made a little flyrod for me.

In Montana I met Bob Cleverley, who is still a friend of mine, and Danny Glines, who coached at San Jose State before going into the guide business at Ennis. I fished for four days—the first three with my spinning rod, two on the Madison River and one on the Jefferson River. The fourth day, Danny— a great fisherman—took me fly-fishing on a creek, the first time I ever did that.

Nothing I've ever done or been exposed to has provided me with more enjoyment than fly-fishing has. I haven't missed a summer going out to Montana or Wyoming ever since. And that whole introduction to the sport started with that 1970 clinic at Jackson Hole.

Clinics are teaching, something I always enjoyed. When I was freshman coach at West Point, two publications for coaches were magazines called *Scholastic Coach* and *The Athletic Journal*. They always carried advertisements for coaching clinics. I remember going through those and thinking to myself, "Boy, that would be neat, to have coached to the point where people wanted you to come talk about what you did, and how you did it."

The summer when I was named head coach at West Point, 1965, Bill Foster—the coach then at Rutgers, later at Duke, Utah, and Northwestern—asked me to fill in for somebody who had canceled at the camp he and the Temple coach, Harry Litwack, ran near Stroudsburg, Pennsylvania, in the Poconos. That was my first clinic with them, and I went back a lot of times after that. I liked and respected both of them for all they did for basketball and the way they went about coaching.

The fall of that year, just before the 1965–66 season, the Michigan State coach, John Benington, was to speak at a clinic in Tarrytown, New York, and he had to cancel. This was the first time Bob Murrey used me at a major clinic. Benington, who had been a good player for Pete Newell at San Francisco, was an excellent coach and a genuinely witty guy. He told a group one night: "I was really thrilled when they retired my number at USF. Of course they didn't do it right away. A guy named Bill Russell wore it after me."

My annual fishing trips to Montana and Wyoming formed a whole long list of friendships I cherish. One at the top is with the great radio and TV broadcaster, Curt Gowdy.

Curt grew up in Cheyenne, Wyoming. In the early '80s, he was doing Cheyenne Days, the big rodeo, on ABC's *Wide World of Sports*. I was out there for a clinic and I went to the rodeo for the Sunday events. I sat with him in the booth, then—as we had agreed to do beforehand—we went fishing together on Monday, Tuesday, and Wednesday in Laramie, where he had played basketball and graduated at the University of Wyoming.

Curt then was the biggest name in television regarding hunting and fishing. Not many people knew anything about my fishing—including Curt Gowdy.

He owned a radio station in Laramie, and his son was married to the daughter of a rancher named John Morris. That day I was with him at the rodeo was Curt's birthday, and they invited me to go to a party for him at the Cheyenne country club. John Morris came up to me at the party and asked, "Bob, what kind of fisherman are you?"

"Why?" I asked.

He said, "Curt's afraid he's gotten himself into a baby-sitting situation for the next three days."

I said, "Don't let him think otherwise, John, but don't worry about me fishing. I can fish." By this time, I had been fly-fishing for ten years.

I had driven out there, so I had a car. I picked Curt up each morning those three days and drove us to our fishing spot. He always brought along a newspaper, and as I was driving along, he would open up the paper and say in his great radio voice, "Good morning, ladies and gentlemen, this is Curt Gowdy with the Gillette Cavalcade of Sports."

Then he'd announce the baseball scores and other sports news of the day—and he'd pause for a commercial, in the car, with me as an audience of one.

That was a neat experience, one of many I've had with Curt.

That first morning I knew he was apprehensive about the next three days.

When I parked close to the first stream that we were going to fish, I opened the trunk to get my stuff. I've got all kinds of flies, rods, enough stuff for a small fishing store. Curt looked in and said, "You've fished more than I thought you'd fished, haven't you?"

We talked about places where I had fished. He asked me, "How in the hell did you come up with all these places? You've got places out here *I've* never heard of."

I told him my secret. Fairly frequently, especially after we played a national TV game, I got letters from coaches who had a question about something they had seen us do on offense or defense. I'd always answer any coach's questions the best I could. But after I had caught the fly-fishing bug, I saw how I could help my fly-fishing with that kind of exchange.

I picked out five states—Utah, Idaho, Wyoming, Montana, and Colorado—and if the coach who called or wrote was from one of those states, I'd add to my answer: "Is there any fishing around where you are, and, if there is, would you be able to get me on some ranches?" By doing that, I built up a whole card catalog of fishing spots in those states.

The last night we were there, the people who ran his Laramie radio station had a big backyard party for him. Curt was talking to some people, with his back to me, and I was talking to some others. I heard my name come up and he told his group, "He led John Morris and me to believe that he couldn't fish worth a damn, but we had a great time. The guy loves it.

"And I'll tell you one thing—you've all watched Indiana play on television, and you know how good they've been, but I'll guarantee you if the guy spent as much time on basketball as he does on fishing, nobody would *ever* beat them."

Curt was NBC's No. 1 guy when they were doing the NCAA tournament and some major national college games in the early '70s. He still tells the story that the first time we ever met was at the 1973 Final Four at St. Louis, where we played UCLA. The way he tells it, I came walking toward him in the minutes just before the game started. "I didn't know Bob," he said, "but I'd heard he was hard to get along with. He comes up to me and says, 'Mr. Gowdy, my name is Bob Knight. You're going to do our game today. If you have an opportunity to do so, I'd appreciate it if you'd say hello to Clair Bee for me.'"

It wasn't my intention, obviously, but I couldn't have said anything that would have impressed Curt more.

That was a double–bull's-eye for me: I got a message to one close, long-time friend, and made another. Just before we started practice at Texas Tech last fall, Curt said in a national Internet column he writes:

It was on a trout stream where I really got to know my friend Bobby Knight. I want to say something here that is important. If you believe that I tell the truth, believe this: no coach in any sport ever cared more about his players than Bobby Knight. Winning is big to Bobby, very big. But what has always been bigger is that his players put forth their best effort. What happened at Indiana is really very simple. Bobby Knight just stayed too long at the dance.

I remember a night we spent with basketball guru Pete Newell in Hawaii, when Pete and I tried to convince Knight, who had won three national championships, to move on. A new administration had taken over at the school, and we felt that the altered atmosphere would not be hospitable to Bobby. He understood the logic of what we were saying, but he said he wanted to win one more championship. As things turned out, it was one bridge too far for Bobby, and he was defeated in one of the most humiliating battles any coach ever faced. In my opinion, the university didn't acquit itself well in its campaign to get rid of the man who brought it so much fame.

But delayed endings are never easy—and often bitter.

Not too long ago, after he had found new employment at Texas Tech, he called me and said, "Curt, I should have listened to you." I said nothing, except to offer encouragement in his new job. Then, he asked me to be the master of ceremonies at a fund-raising dinner. I agreed, of course.

It will be great to see Bobby again. Maybe we'll make a date for another fishing trip before the night's over.

He came, he was great, and we did get a fishing trip scheduled. I hope we have dozens more ahead. As much as I enjoy fishing, I enjoy being with Curt even a little bit more. Anytime I can put those two favorite things together, I have one more reason to feel deeply indebted to basketball.

EIGHT: *Perfection (1974–1976)*

*"Take a good look at these kids, because you're never going to
see the likes of them again."*

I t now has been more than twenty-five years since college basketball had an
unbeaten champion.

That's a long time to stand up there alone, and the Indiana team of 1975–76
that achieved that last perfect-season record was a great one—maybe even better than its 32–0 record says, because that team (1) did it wearing the target of
No. 1 on its back from the first game on, (2) won in the home arena of every
team in the strongest conference in the country that year, and (3) worked its
way through the toughest tournament lineup any high-ranked champion ever
has faced.

But I think even the players on that 1976 team know that the team they
played on the season before was a little bit better.

I think:

- The 1975 Indiana team was as good as any I've ever seen play
  college basketball.
- The 1976 team was as tough a team mentally as I've ever seen.

The players who made up the '76 team just weren't as talented, particularly on
offense, as the ones of the year before. But they were the toughest team mentally I can ever imagine.

Was either of those the best college team ever? I don't know how you can
compare teams from different eras. I know enough about Bill Russell to be
sure that his 1956 San Francisco team—the first NCAA champion to go
unbeaten—was extremely tough. So, of course, were the UCLA teams. And to
complete its 32–0 season North Carolina won triple overtimes on back-to-

back nights at the 1957 finals, the second of those against Wilt Chamberlain and Kansas. That's impressive.

But I think the two Indiana teams could have played well against any team that ever played. They dominated college basketball for two years.

The Big Ten was as strong as it always is in 1975. For three teams in the league—Michigan, Purdue, and Minnesota—the only home game they lost all year was to us. The closest game UCLA had in winning the '75 championship was a double-overtime escape against Michigan. We won the Big Ten championship that year by six games (still the league record, by two games). Until Scott May went out with a broken arm in our twenty-sixth game, our average winning margin in conference games was 25.9. That was unheard of; the 22.8 average margin that team finished with still stands as the Big Ten record, breaking one set by the Illinois "Whiz Kids" during World War II.

When we began practice for the 1974–75 season, I wasn't expecting to go 63–1 over the next two years but I did feel we had all the ingredients to be able to beat anybody. And "ingredients" to me was not just another word for talent.

The recruiting class from my first full year at Indiana turned out to be the best I ever had. Three of those players—Scott May, Quinn Buckner, and Bobby Wilkerson—went in the top eleven of the NBA draft their senior season. No college team ever has matched that.

Another player from that class, Tom Abernethy, also played in the NBA. Two players from the class just ahead of them, 1975 seniors Steve Green and John Laskowski, played in the NBA. And the last piece of the puzzle for those '75 and '76 teams, Kent Benson, the center, was a sophomore in '75 and the No. 1 pick in the whole NBA draft in '77.

So, obviously we had some talent. But to be as good as it can be, a team has to buy into what you as the coach are doing. They have to feel you're a part of them and they're a part of you. And we had that. In our fourth game of the 1974–75 season, we played at Notre Dame. In practice Bob Donewald, one of my assistant coaches, was setting up the Notre Dame presses that we would see and I was trying to show our players how to recognize the different presses.

Buckner had rotated out of the lineup and he was standing beside me. He said, "Coach, do you recognize which press it is every time?"

It was such a good question I didn't even take the time to answer it. I stopped play and said, "Let's don't pay attention to the press. Benson, stay deep. You other four guys, whoever gets the ball take it out, and the other three guys run triangle (a familiar, basic part of our offense)."

We lost the ball once to the press that game and won over a good team on its home court, 94–84.

In that situation, we simplified everything, and we did it because Buckner had no hesitancy to tell me what he thought. Players have to be able to do that. Players who know how to play have to be able to come to you with a suggestion, as he did.

Of course, there weren't many Buckners. Three days after that Notre Dame game, we played Texas A&M at Indianapolis in the first college game ever played at the new Market Square Arena.

The only guy who was playing well for us early in the game was Scott May. I called a time-out and got on them. I made them count to four—actually count, out loud: *one, two, three, four*—so, I told them, I could know that despite what I had been watching, they *could* count as high as the number of passes I wanted before they shot. I made them do it once, then a second time, louder. Finally the time-out ended and they went back out—to their relief, I'm sure.

We made two passes, and May—the one guy who had been playing well—took a shot and missed. We got the ball back, and Buckner—who was one of the main reasons I called the time-out, he had been playing so poorly—dribbled over in front of me, and just reamed May out, "Dammit! He told you *four passes!*"

May was his buddy.

And Buckner knew May was the one player on that team who had a green light to shoot.

That was leadership, Buckner style.

Another of our early-season games was against the Kentucky team that later was the runner-up for the NCAA championship. We led that team 78–44 before our starters were removed. The final score was 88–64.

The margin had nothing to do with it: I wasn't pleased that our reserves weren't playing up to their own capabilities, and I let them know that from the sidelines. A Kentucky assistant coach, Lynn Nance, shouted at me: "Attaway, Bobby, give 'em hell." I didn't appreciate it, and the head coach, Joe Hall, knew I didn't. We met at center court along the sidelines, I told him he should shut that guy up, and he agreed that he should and would.

He turned to go back to the bench, and I—as was my habit—gave him a gesture of approval by whacking him in the back of the head, as I had done with my players a number of times. I'm not going to say that it was a great move on my part, but I know Hall was aware it was friendly, not antagonistic. But Nance came off their bench and yelled, "Do that to me, Bobby."

And now it was an issue.

I had done a lot of things in defense of Hall, who was in his second year as

Adolph Rupp's successor and not at all popular with Kentucky fans. All he had to do after that game was say, "Hey, I know he didn't mean anything by that." But he didn't; he left me hanging. From that moment on, I had no respect for the guy, and as more and more things happened in his program, I came to have as little respect for him as any coach I've ever been around.

He was no longer coaching, but what had happened in that program under him certainly was in my mind when Cawood Ledford, an extremely popular, Hall of Fame announcer of Kentucky sports, interviewed me before an Indiana–Kentucky game. Cawood introduced me with a question about my feeling for "this great college basketball rivalry," and I shocked him by saying that "because of all the things going on down here" I didn't care as much for the rivalry as he thought I did.

None of my feelings reflected on him, and I went out of my way that night and ever after to make that clear to him. He was a gracious man who fully deserved the love and admiration Kentucky fans felt for him. He treated me wonderfully, as a coach and a friend, occasionally even as a broadcast partner, right up to his death in fall 2001.

We did a lot of things that year to try to make that '75 team as good as we could. We knew it was going to be damned good. We had everybody back, and May had improved dramatically over what had been a good sophomore season. Once we got into the Big Ten season—I'd say when we were about 15–0 overall and had played some very good teams—we knew this was a special team.

By the end of the season, everyone recognized that. We placed four players on the coaches' five-man All–Big Ten team. The one who didn't make it should have: Bobby Wilkerson. To this day, few people realize what a great college basketball player Wilkerson was.

I talked to Bobby the day before we played Nebraska in the final game of our first Indiana Classic four-team tournament in December. Nebraska had an all–Big Eight guard, Jerry Fort, who was about 6–3. Wilkerson was 6–7. He jumped center for us at the start of games, played guard on offense, and then played wherever I wanted him to play on defense.

I sat Bobby down that day and told him, "You're going to guard Fort tonight. Now, listen to me: if you'll do just what I want, you'll probably never average more than ten points a game, but your role on this team is to shut people out.

"I don't mean just hold them down. Whoever you're on at the start of the game, or during the game, they are not to score. You're to be the best defender in the country.

"If you do that, you'll wind up being a first-round draft choice. I know that's what you want to eventually do, and this is how you'll get there."

Fort didn't get shut out. He scored seven points, but we won 97–60. I would guess that he scored at least some of those points after we pulled Bobby out.

I have said that as a player at West Point, Mike Krzyzewski did a great job of doing what I wanted him to do. Wilkerson was another one who did that, and I think he is the best athlete I ever had.

He could guard anybody. We put him on Billy McKinney of Northwestern, who was little and quick, and on Mychal Thompson of Minnesota, who was big and athletic. Bobby did a great job on each of them. I've never seen a better defender in college basketball.

Scott May was our consensus All-American, and I'll always believe his arm injury at Purdue on February 24 is why the 1974–75 Indiana team isn't among the seven unbeaten NCAA champions.

May's injury was the same kind of team-devastating loss that the first team I coached at Army suffered when it lost Mike Silliman. And the first thing that went through my mind when it happened was what Coach Clair Bee had told me the night of the Silliman injury back in 1966: Okay, who are we going to replace him with?

You have no choice. You have to go on.

The only thing was, in 1975 I kept my mind on what I had to and I still made a big error.

The Purdue game was on a Saturday afternoon, and playing without May the whole second half we hung on to win, 83–82. Buckner and Wilkerson jarred the ball loose in the final seconds and Wilkerson came up with a steal. With that win, we clinched the Big Ten championship with three games still to play.

Our next game was two nights later, on Monday night at Illinois. We had beaten Illinois 73–57 earlier at Bloomington, but we were ahead at the half that game (36–34) only because Buckner made a basket at the buzzer. Gene Bartow, a very good coach, was in his first year at Illinois. He played his team in a two-three zone against us and jammed up the lane. We expected them to do it again and to counter it I felt we had to play our best shooter at the top of the key.

That's where I was going to play Scott May. Now, we're at Champaign without him.

The best shooter on our bench was the senior who usually was our first substitute, John Laskowski. At our Sunday afternoon practice at Champaign, I pulled Laskowski over to the top of the key and said, "The first time you get the ball, I want you to shoot. The second time you get the ball, I want you to shoot." He scored twenty-eight points and we won easily, 112–89. My idea of how to play against their zone had worked fine.

But the eighty-nine points Illinois scored was twenty-five more than we had been giving up. Sure, because we were scoring so quickly Illinois was bound to get more chances to score than the first game. But our defense just wasn't as good.

Playing Laskowski meant we had to make changes in our defense that wouldn't have been needed if we had just replaced May with the man who was a starter for us the next year, Tom Abernethy. Quinn Buckner and Bobby Wilkerson were the best pair of defensive guards I've ever seen in college basketball, but with Laskowski in the lineup we had to put Wilkerson on a forward, and that broke up the Buckner–Wilkerson combination. With Abernethy, we wouldn't have had to do that. It was my mistake, nobody else's, and I believe it cost us a chance to win the NCAA championship.

It wasn't just an automatic decision that I made at Champaign and then stopped thinking about. I wrestled with it every day for three weeks. When we started in the NCAA tournament against Texas–El Paso four games later, I sat in the locker room at the old Memorial Coliseum in Lexington just before the game still debating whether to start Laskowski or Abernethy. I stuck with Laskowski. We won that day, and we won our first regional tournament game over Oregon State that way. But our defense just wasn't good enough in the regional finals and the best team I've ever had was eliminated by Kentucky, 92–90. We'll never know, but I don't think it would have happened if I had kept Buckner and Wilkerson together.

There was a huge crowd at the Bloomington airport when our team came back from Dayton the afternoon of the loss. It was great of the Indiana fans to turn out like that, because they didn't feel any better than we did. I tried to tell them how much we appreciated their coming out, but the truth was we all just wanted to get away somewhere in private. That was a tough day.

I wasn't surprised when a letter came in from New York a few days later. The "father" of Chip Hilton still was quite a writer. Clair Bee's letter told me:

Take a deep breath. Get your bearings. Set your sights on even greater heights and start all over again. All a frustrated young man can expect to see when he looks back over his shoulder is a desolate cemetery where broken dreams lie buried deep in defeat. The dead past is not for youth.

In basketball's burying place, tall tombstones cast shadows on lesser grave markers and bear words that certify to the greatness of players, teams and

*coaches who have ground out national titles, undefeated seasons, and tourna-
ment championships. But only the old men can afford a time to look back to
dream of past deeds, to savor the sweetness of the great victories, or to review
once again the faded memory of defeat.*

*The young man, the leader, rebounds swiftly from adversity. He has been
strengthened by the very blow that cut him down. Now he knows the rough spots
that pit the roads and the quicksand that lies so innocently nearby. He knows
because he has fought his way up that path of agony—almost to the very top.*

*Then, suddenly, refreshed by the driving desire that has always inspired
young leaders to rush forward and upward, he grasps the new challenge with
eager hands and races for the starting line.*

He will be back.

The man was seventy-nine years old when he wrote that, and virtually blind.
He was seeing more clearly than I was at thirty-four. I wasn't at all sure we'd
ever be back, because we had lost with the best team I'd ever had.

And I knew I had put every effort into that season that I was capable of,
including some things that I had never done before and haven't done again . . .
yet. Some of the greatest people in basketball talked to that team, by taped
recordings.

I've always had outstanding people come in and talk to my teams during the
season. That goes back—as so many things do—to when I was a player at Ohio
State. Each year, Coach Taylor had Dr. Novice Fawcett, the president of Ohio
State University, talk to us, and I remember thinking as a player, "Boy, that's
neat—the president of the university talking to the basketball team."

So, right from the beginning of my Indiana years, I asked President John
Ryan to come in and talk to our kids each year. The first time he did it, he wore
a three-piece suit and talked to the kids like a university president would be
expected to. I had the feeling he was there speaking to them then just because I
had asked him to. Within a couple of years, though, he'd come in wearing a
sweater and open-collar shirt, and I could tell that he looked forward to doing
it. He got better and better at it, and I know the kids enjoyed it—they seemed
to react as I had when I was in college: impressed that the school president
would do that.

They particularly liked it when he would needle me—"Now, there are times
when I have to kind of sit on your coach. . . ." They loved that.

In the 1974–75 season, I expanded on that to get tapes from several people
in basketball whom I particularly respected. I had some other tapes that I had
collected over the years, and I played those tapes for them, too.

These were intelligent kids, and I thought they would react well to hearing people like Pete Newell, Red Auerbach, John Havlicek, and Clair Bee talking to them about what they had noticed while watching them play live or in a televised game.

Pete Newell took such an interest in them he was almost like an extra assistant coach. We played in a Christmas tournament in Honolulu that year, and Pete is almost a resident there. He watched us beat Florida, Ohio State, and Hawaii there to win the tournament. Then he put together a tape to run with each game film, and he included some other observations. The game-film comments were technical: "As Kelly was advancing toward him, Buckner wasn't in any kind of a retreat. As a result, Kelly went right by him. . . . Really an alert play by Benson. Very, very alert. . . . The communication that time was not good."

But we were right on the verge of opening the Big Ten season, and Pete did a great job of summarizing our position in a special tape:

> *You've met every challenge. You've had the close game, the overtime, the game that causes you to test yourself, your mettle as a team. You've had the game where you didn't play as well as you could. You still managed to win it. And the game I saw against Ohio State, you played the game of basketball just about as good as a team can play it, totally.*
>
> *Now there's no doubt in my mind that you have, within your grasp, the finest season that Indiana's ever had. . . .*

I could feel the chill that went through them when they heard that.

> *You can't be too dependent upon the coaches, game after game, to get you up. Sure, you'll get yourself up for the Purdues, but when the Iowas are down, you've got to make sure that you're up.*

Steve Green said the first time he and the team were gathered together to hear that particular tape,

> *I can remember the room up there at Michigan State . . . the ocean going in the background. . . .*
>
> *The thing we liked about the tapes was they were personal. They really only applied to us. It made us feel like an elite group, that here Red Auerbach is worrying about us, Pete Newell is worrying about us. Auerbach with the championships, Havlicek, Pete Newell—they'd all been through something. These people wanted us to win.*

Before we ended the regular season against Michigan State, Clair Bee told them by tape:

You're on the threshold of an undefeated season, which really is hard to get. Never mind what happens after that game. You've got to get this game. Very few teams playing the schedule you have played will ever be able to get an undefeated season, because they're few and far between. And when you get one, it's something you never forget.

And Red Auerbach:

Now, even though you've got a real good ball club, your reputation is not going to win ball games. You can take it from me. Get ready for the game mentally and physically. Study your opponent; look at the films, and be ready. Don't ever go into a ballgame and think you're going to win it just by showing up, because the other team could start out pretty good, and all of a sudden they'll get their confidence, everything they throw up will go in, and you'll find at times a comparatively weak team will upset you. That's happened to us this year, after winning the world title last year. About seven games in a row . . . we thought being world champions the other guys were gonna play dead. When that ball was on the floor, they were scratching and grabbing and diving for it, and we thought that ball had our name on it. Of course, it doesn't take long to straighten those things out, but they should never happen.

That was just one of many, many times Red Auerbach did something for me that I could hardly believe. I met him way back in 1962 when Havlicek was a rookie playing for him. The first time I talked with him was during the Holiday Festival at the Garden my first year as coach. Then in 1970, I saw him at the NIT—my team was in the tournament but wasn't playing that night. I had gone to the Garden because Tates Locke's Miami of Ohio team was playing. I ran into Red, and he said, "Let's go get something to eat afterward. I'll meet you in the press room." Miami lost a pretty tough game, and it took me a half-hour longer than normal to get to see Tates. After we talked, I hustled to the press room as fast as I could but I figured Red wouldn't have waited. There he was, sitting there reading a paper, waiting. I thought then, "Boy, for Red Auerbach to wait on a young guy coaching at Army . . ." That impressed me.

The weekend Scott May was hurt, Pete Newell sent a tape to us before we played Illinois.

*When you lose a player like Scott May a team is going to feel it a lot. How-
ever, one of the fortunate things about your wonderful, great team is that you all
are contributors. Each one of you has to take another cinch in your belt and
determine to give it a little more input. This is one of the beauties of a team.
There is that interdependence, and that strength that you get from this interdependence that the group is greater than the individual. . . .*

*Your main concentration should be on your defense now—just that much
more alert for loose balls, for interceptions, for screening out the other team, for
helping out a teammate. . . .*

*And you'll probably pick it up at the other end, too. Just like this last game—
Green comes up with the best game he's had in weeks. That's great. That's just
exactly what I'm talking about. He took the challenge and more than met it.
That's the kind of club you are, and why you've got the record you have, and
why you're going to go all the way.*

Green had been hit hard by flu about a month before, and it had taken him a
long time to get his strength back. We kept winning, but over a nine-game
stretch leading up to the Purdue game, he scored just sixty-three points. That
day at Purdue, after we lost May and every shot became big, he took fifteen
shots and hit thirteen. He scored twenty-nine points that day and averaged
twenty-six points a game from that game on.

Because I put so much into that 1974–75 season, and I knew those kids put
everything they had into it, and we all felt so much disappointment, I have
always respected more than anything I've ever seen in sports the toughness of
the kids who came back the next year and beat everybody.

I didn't make it easy for them. I challenged them to do just that.

We had a team meeting the day before practice started, and I told them their
objective was not to win the Big Ten or to win the NCAA, "the objective of this
team is to not lose a game, and you're capable of doing that. Nothing less than
that should be satisfactory to you and it will not be to me. The only way we will
lose is when we have ourselves to blame."

That year we weren't as dominating in our regular-season games as the
1974–75 team had been before losing May, but we couldn't have started the
season much better.

We preceded our schedule with an exhibition game in Indianapolis against
the Soviet Union national team, which included the Belov brothers and some
other players who had taken what I always will consider to be stolen gold

medals home from Munich, and were getting ready to defend their "championship" the next summer at Montreal. This was Scott May's first game back since full recovery from his arm fracture, and he was terrific—34 points, 13-for-15 shooting, as we whipped them pretty solidly, 94–78. The Soviet coach, Vladimir Kondrashin, was a man I enjoyed. I told his interpreter after the game, "Tell him he has a well-conditioned team, a very good team . . . and we wouldn't want to play him in Moscow." Kondrashin heard the interpretation, smiled and answered, through the interpreter, "How about Leningrad?" Years later I did spend some really enjoyable time with Kondrashin on his turf. While I was in Russia on a fishing trip, I was with him for two days.

We followed that 1975–76 game against the Russians by playing awfully well in our first two official games—84–64 over UCLA at St. Louis opening the season (May had thirty-three points), and 83–59 over Florida State at Market Square Arena in Indianapolis. Hugh Durham, who had taken Florida State to the NCAA championship game in 1972, is a good coach with a sense of humor. After that game in Indianapolis, he said, "I'm glad this isn't like baseball. I'd hate to play these guys in a three-game home stand."

I couldn't believe the letters I got from UCLA people, about pouring it on. From a place where it had seasons where its average winning margin was thirty? It was the first game at UCLA for Gene Bartow, who had gone there after one season at Illinois. He couldn't have been more complimentary to our team and our players, and he certainly didn't have any responsibility for those letters. Besides, he was getting worse ones from the same people. He left UCLA after two highly successful years and did a remarkable job of building a strong program from scratch at Alabama-Birmingham.

That opener with UCLA was one of the first major made-for-TV games—the first one set up to launch a season—and it started at 10:40, on a Saturday night.

Nobody has been a greater critic of late-night games than I have. I fought like hell against a TV arrangement our league once had—a "Big Monday" deal with ESPN that had us starting games after 9:30 our time. I raised enough hell that the presidents of our league in 1987 realized how ludicrous it was to be playing basketball that late on a school night and pressured the Big Ten commissioner into getting us switched to a better time slot on Tuesdays. It didn't really matter to ESPN. There's no shortage of other leagues or other teams willing to take any time the TV god offers.

Still, I was enthusiastic about taking that 1975–76 St. Louis game, because, first of all, it was a Saturday night, not a school night. But there was more involved.

The season before, I thought we had the best team in America. We were undefeated and unanimously ranked No. 1 when we lost May. I'll always believe that because of that injury, the best team in the country didn't get to play for the national championship, and I wanted to make that point clear. That match-up afforded us an opportunity to start the season playing the team that won that 1975 championship and had most of its team back: UCLA.

We played well and won big, and I thought it was a great opening to the college season.

Starting out the season as the first game on national television meant something then. They weren't televising games from Puerto Rico, Hawaii, Alaska, Anarctica, Celebese, the Marshall Islands, and Iwo Jima—from *everywhere*—the way they do now.

But we'd have played the game if there had been no television. Playing UCLA was the key for me, not TV.

After playing so well those first two games, we didn't reach that level again for a while. We scraped by Kentucky and Notre Dame, and the night before we played in the Indiana Classic in Bloomington, I told a tournament banquet audience, "My team needs an enema."

But we won. We were No. 1 in the polls when the season began and no one could get us out of there because we never lost. I guess there was a doubter or two, but in the coaches' poll no other team got a first-place vote until the middle of February. All year, in the two major polls combined there were only ten No. 1 votes we didn't get, which meant we got 99.9 percent of them. When I was a kid, a radio commercial said Ivory soap was "ninety-nine and forty-four one-hundredths percent pure." Hell, we were purer than Ivory soap.

But as a season like that is happening, it just isn't my nature to jump up and down and say, "Gee, you guys are doing great." During my year out of coaching, I did a commercial for Minute Maid in which I did things like that—things completely opposite of my personality. I had to practice that Minute Maid commercial for three days to get myself able to say inside a locker room, "Would anybody like some good treats?"

In the 1975–76 season, though, I got a good lesson in that kind of thing, and it came from Clair Bee. I brought him out to Bloomington to see us play Minnesota at Assembly Hall. We went the whole season in 1974–75 without ever being behind at the half. Then we led at halftime our first fifteen games the next year, forty-seven games in a row without ever going into halftime behind.

That streak ended when Minnesota led us 45–40 at the half at Minneapolis in our sixteenth game at Minneapolis. Then it started happening regularly. The day Coach Bee was there at Assembly Hall, Minnesota led us at halftime, 39–38.

Coach Bee had always told me he actually preferred to be a point or two behind at the half because he felt his players would listen to him better. I never quite bought that one. We played well the second half and beat Minnesota fairly comfortably (76–64). I told the press afterward that the first comment I had made to the team after the game was negative—how we didn't handle the press or something like that.

"Then," I said, "Coach Bee talked to the team for an hour, and the main thing he talked about was being positive.

"He gave these kids a hell of a pep talk. Boy, he was great. They knew who he was, but it was the first time they had met him. They really enjoyed it."

And so did I.

But I'd still rather be twenty points up at the half.

The last game of the regular season was special to me. It was Coach Taylor's last game as a coach. He had announced his retirement, and I wasn't very pleased with the way Ohio State had treated him in his last few years. I had gone over to Columbus during the week to be part of a little ceremony honoring him. Woody Hayes, a man I greatly respected, was there. I told those Columbus people, "When I came to Ohio State, I had just completed fourteen years of consecutive attendance at Sunday School. And after my three years of sitting on the bench with Coach Taylor, I added words to my vocabulary that have done nothing but keep me in one jam after another for the last eleven years."

I may have lied just a little.

Then on Saturday at Assembly Hall, we had a pre-game ceremony honoring him. We gave him a chair, with the Indiana seal. I told him our kids "know that most of what they're doing, you're responsible for. And I'll tell you one thing, they don't like all of it." Bloomington was an ironic place for Coach Taylor to go out, because in his early coaching days, he and Branch McCracken of Indiana were definitely not friends. With a grin, he referred to that during our pre-game ceremony, "There've been a few times over here when things weren't quite this nice."

And a fan yelled, "Just wait!"

Coach Taylor laughed along with everybody else and answered, "That's what we're stalling for. We don't *want* to play."

We won the game, 96–67. And that, as our last home game, was Senior Day for that great senior class. I don't use that word great very often, but it fits that group. The four teams Buckner, Tom Abernethy, and Jim Crews played on won one hundred eight games and lost twelve, and four Big Ten championships or co-championships. Scott May and Bobby Wilkerson were with them the last three years, and those teams won eighty-six games and lost six. No Big Ten team ever matched those records. The closest, for a three-year period, was the team Coach Taylor had at Ohio State with Jerry Lucas, John Havlicek, Mel Nowell, and the rest of us: seventy-eight wins, six losses, and three championships.

In introducing them that Senior Day, I told those Indiana fans, "Take a good look at these kids, because you're never going to see the likes of them again."

I think I called that one absolutely right.

On the Sunday after we had finished the regular season and were starting to prepare for the 1976 NCAA tournament, I talked to the team. They were 27–0, No. 1 in the country, and I just blistered them—about the hours they were keeping, one thing and another. I didn't let anybody else in the locker room but them and me—no assistant coaches, no managers, nobody. I wanted them to be absolutely sure I wasn't going to tolerate any outside interference. They had to go to class and they had to play, and that's all I wanted them to think about for the next three weeks. I didn't single out anybody or mention any names.

After I was done, I was out on the floor, leaning against the basket support, waiting for them to come out and get practice started. On their own, they stayed in the locker room and talked for ten minutes.

The first guy out was Scott May. Two-year All-American. Best player in the country.

He walked past me, dribbling a basketball. Then he turned around, looked at me, and said, "That was good, Coach. I think they got the message."

I couldn't help it. I laughed. That was one of the greatest things I ever heard a kid say, "I think *they* got the message."

He didn't think one thing I got on their ass about pertained to him. And he was right.

Our first tournament game was a rematch with the St. John's team we had played very well to beat in the Holiday Festival at Madison Square Garden in December. We won the second game a little easier, 90–70, and in the press conference afterward, Gordon White of the *New York Times* asked me, "Is your team better than a year ago?" I had a good time with Gordon over the years, so I tossed his question back at him, "You saw them. What do you think?"

"Well," he said, "they were sure as hell better than they were against Kentucky."

"Write that and quote yourself," I said. "You ought to put *something* of yourself in your story."

I felt the best team we played all year was Alabama in our opening game at the Midwest Regional at Baton Rouge. They had beaten the ACC champion, North Carolina, while we were beating St. John's in the opening round. Their coach, C. M. Newton, had done a great job of putting together an outstanding team.

We got ahead by fourteen points, but Alabama was good. They came back to go ahead by a point late in the game, the first time they had led. Scott May's jump shot with two minutes to go put us ahead again, 70–69, and there was a time-out.

Kent Benson was our center—big, strong, rugged kid. Alabama had one, too: Leon Douglas. They were the two best centers in the country; each had four fouls. And Douglas's team had the ball, down one point. During the time-out I made it a point to clarify exactly how I wanted us to play defense. I can do that. I said, "They're going to want to go to Douglas. Now, Bennie, *I don't want Douglas to get the ball*. In fact, Bennie, if Douglas so much as *touches* the ball this trip, just start running through that door down there because I'm going to run your ass all the way back to Bloomington."

I thought I made what I wanted done pretty clear.

Then I looked up after they went back onto the court and I saw Buckner talking to Benson, and Benson nodding yes. I'm thinking: *What the hell will be coming out of that conversation?* We won the game. In the locker room afterward, Buckner was bent over, head down, untying his shoelaces. I said, "Hey, Quinn, I saw you and Kent talking out there after the time-out. What were you saying?"

I knew what Buckner was thinking: *I've only got three more games to play. He's stuck with me now.* It was like I wasn't even there. He didn't look up, just went on working with his shoes.

"Quinn, I want to know what you told Bennie."

Not even a glance.

Now I was curious, and I am capable of being a little more insistent. But I knew I wasn't going to go without an answer, because Benson was sitting there bouncing up and down, almost putting his hand in the air. So I asked him, "What did Buckner say?"

Bennie was a junior. He *had* to tell me.

And he couldn't wait.

"Coach," he began, "you remember what you told me at the time-out about Douglas, and running back to Bloomington, and . . ."

"Sure, I remember. I want to know what Buckner said."

"Well, Quinn said, '*I* don't want to see Douglas get the ball, either, and if he does, we'll have your ass before he can get off the bench.'"

That's leadership from one and effort from the other, because Bennie didn't let Douglas get the ball.

Al McGuire had a great team that year. His Marquette team was No. 2 in the country when we beat them 65–56, at Baton Rouge two days after that Alabama game to advance to the finals at Philadelphia.

Many times when we've won a big game, I wasn't as happy as I could have been because I felt genuinely bad for the coach who had lost. I always felt that way when it was a guy I liked and respected a lot, and Al McGuire was one of those. He hadn't won an NCAA championship yet—he did the very next year, and I was thrilled for him. But I'm sure at the time he felt this team was the best shot he had at winning one, and he had to be crushed.

Al was a coach who did things very simply, but he controlled the games and controlled the players. He got some very talented players to play great basketball—outstanding defense, patient offense. I'm sure his assistant coaches, Hank Raymonds and Rick Majerus, gave him a lot of help, but those were his teams and they were good.

He had an understanding of what had to be done to win. He understood fully how well you had to play defensively.

I remember him telling me I had to get out of West Point. He was right about that, and he was right about a dozen other things he told me over the years. He was a brilliant guy in his own, New York way. In a press conference before our game at Baton Rouge, he told about being invited to speak to the Associated Press Sports Editors a year after I had spoken to them.

"They mentioned a figure they would pay," Al told the writers who were there that day, "so I had my secretary call Bob's secretary and find out how much he had got. Only there wasn't a record of it in the correspondence. So I told her to give them a figure of x dollars. I got a call a few days later from a guy in Chicago who said you guys don't pay that kind of money. I said, 'Why not?'

"You guys are amazing. Do you ask Frank Sinatra to sing for nothing? Do you ask the carpenters to come over and fix the stairs and say, 'See you later?'"

And the writers loved it. I don't say that as a complaint. I had a lot of fun at some of those tournament press conferences, too.

Twenty-four years later at Wisconsin, in the CBS telecast of the last regular-season game of what turned out to be my last year at Indiana, Al worked the game with Dick Enberg. It was obvious, seeing him that day, that the leukemia he had been battling for so long was winning. Dick told me later that, the night before the game, Al had cried and said he couldn't do it anymore. He had been scheduled to do some tournament games, but he pulled out. He hung on for several months before passing away. It was very hard for me to call him those last months. It was like Joe Cipriano, all over again.

One thing that honestly never concerned me that 1975–76 season was the pressure that was supposed to go with being unbeaten. Most of the time, when coaches say something about your team, there's an ulterior motive. I don't think that was the case with Al when he said and kept saying right up to the last game of the tournament that we would have been better off to have lost a game somewhere. I didn't agree then and I still don't. I just don't think players worry about that kind of thing. Or a lot of other things.

It's so much different as a coach. I remember when I was in college and our Ohio State teams were so dominant. We were playing Wisconsin my junior year and I said something to a couple of the Wisconsin players during warm-up. John Havlicek came running up to me and said, "What did you say to those guys?" I said, "You guys are just wasting your time here today."

I wouldn't even think of saying something like that as a coach. And the next year Wisconsin did beat us pretty good up at Madison.

As a player, you're not worried about anything. You just know, "We've got good players, a good coach—we're just better than anybody." As a coach I have never thought that way, more like: "There are a thousand ways we could lose this game. Don't let me screw this up."

Before that Marquette game, I was asked where a national championship fit into my coaching goals. I was as honest as I could be, "Sure, you have ambitions as a coach, but that is something you can't worry about or it can consume you. You have to sit back and realize that of the thousands and thousands of guys who have coached this game, only about twenty-two have coached NCAA champions."

In the Final Four at Philadelphia, we played the way I hoped and expected we would. But we did have a couple of unexpected hurdles to get over.

UCLA, which had gone 26–2 since losing to us in St. Louis, lost to us again, 65–51. Two things stood out: I started the game with Benson guarding UCLA's big forward, Richard Washington, and Benson picked up two fouls in about a minute. Tommy Abernethy took over the job and just shut Washington down, which was a big key to our winning. Another key was Bobby Wilkerson's rebounding—nineteen—from a guard. I've never had that or seen that, before or since. It was all the more impressive because he was a guard out-rebounding six starting front-court players who all went on to have NBA careers.

In the other semifinal game, Michigan had a fairly easy time with Rutgers, which also had come into the finals unbeaten. That set up the first championship game between two teams from the same conference.

We'd had two tough games with them in the conference season, and I loved Johnny Orr. The first time we played them that year was in January up at Ann Arbor. John stopped by our shooting practice after our kids had finished and left the court, and I could tell he knew he had a hell of a team—not big, but extremely quick. We joked around for a few minutes, and as he was leaving, I called out to him, "Hey, John, remember one thing: it isn't going to be a damned track meet." And we awoke the next morning to see an *Ann Arbor News* story breaking down the two teams and giving Michigan, because of speed and quickness, an edge at four of the five starting positions, all but Scott May's.

In Crisler Arena the next day, their crowd also thought they were going to get us. The place was pandemonium when their lineup was introduced. Our players were already back on the bench after their own introduction. You could see from the look on their faces and in their eyes—I remember Tom Abernethy's in particular—an almost amused expression, as if to say, "You people really think you're going to *beat* us?"

I wasn't so sure about my track meet remark when their quickest kid, Rickey Green, took the opening tip and blew right through us for a lay-up. The noise was overwhelming.

Three minutes later, the score was 16–2, Indiana.

They were good. They came back well, but we won, 80–74.

And the tendency that was evident in our team all year, to be much more vulnerable at home than on the road, was never more evident than when Michigan came into Assembly Hall in February for the return game. They had us all but beaten before Buckner, who hadn't been able to hit a basket all night, hit one in the last half-minute to get us within two, they missed a free-throw, and Jimmy Crews made a remarkable save to get the ball up on the board for Benson to put in the basket at the buzzer that got us into overtime. Wayne Radford had his best game as a sophomore in helping save us that day with sixteen points, and we finally won, 72–67.

Now we were playing them the third time, for the national championship.

I was genuinely happy to see Michigan there because of what if meant for Johnny Orr. He and I had a great week. After they had won their regional on Saturday, I called him at home early Sunday morning to congratulate him— early enough that the call woke him and his wife, Romey. She answered the phone and I told her, in not exactly my voice: "Mrs. Orr, this is the White House calling." She got John on right away, and I was sailing along, pretending to be President Ford, congratulating him for winning the regional and telling him how proud he had made "M" men all over the world. 1 went on too long. If I had just stuck with short sentences, I think I'd have had him. "President, hell," he said. "How could any dumb bastard from Ohio State get to be the president?"

That came out at the press conference on the Sunday before the finals, and that was one of those conferences where we both had some fun.

Somebody asked John if his team played over its head in winning its semifinal game over Rutgers, which had come in undefeated. "Nah," John said. "We may have played over our heads when we played at Indiana, but not against Rutgers. That game down at Indiana, we played everything—zone, man-to-man, sometimes both at once, we were so confused. But we had them confused, too. Knight asked me once, 'What in the hell are you playing?' I said, 'Damned if I know, but we're not changing.'

"Some guy asked me if Rickey Green's penetration is why we do so well against Indiana. *So well*? We only get beat four or five points. He's an Indianapolis writer and they think that's pretty good."

Somebody asked me about our national recruiting, which we really weren't doing very much then. I told him, "We never go after California kids. I was speaking to an alumni group out there and they were kinda on me about that. I just told them, 'Hey, if you guys think going back to Bloomington, Indiana, is such a good thing for a California kid, why don't all of *you* move back to Bloomington?' They haven't asked me back."

Years later, we got a lot of mileage out of a couple of California kids named Dean Garrett and Joe Hillman.

The question about me and pro coaching came up, as it often did. I told them it wouldn't happen because "I never think a player should be paid more than a coach, although I think there are some colleges where that happens."

The 1976 tournament was just the second since it had been opened up enough that two teams from one conference could be in the championship game together, and here we were—two teams from the Big Ten in the finals. Orr said a lot that Sunday about how this proved which conference was really the strongest, when most of the national attention all year had been centered on the ACC. I didn't get into that. Then.

When we were in the huddle, just before the game, I sent one of our managers over to tell TV colorman Billy Packer I needed to see him. Billy loves to tell the story. It was the first final game he had worked, and he was nervous. He says he took his headphones off and ran over to our huddle, thinking he was going to get a last-minute scoop. "Yes, Bob," he said. "What is it?"

"I just wondered, Billy . . .

"Where the hell *is* the ACC now?"

I wasn't cracking any jokes when, less than three minutes into the game, Wayman Britt of Michigan ran into Wilkerson on a fast-break. Bobby went down, his head snapped back and hit the floor, and when he didn't bounce right up, I knew he was hurt. He was knocked out, and they took him to a hospital to get checked out. He had a concussion, so there wasn't any question that our best defensive player and the guy who had nineteen rebounds two days before was through for the night.

Jimmy Crews filled in for Bobby and played well, but we were behind 35–29 at the half. I switched to Jimmy Wisman starting the second half, and he did a great job. But when I looked at the game films later, Jimmy Crews also had played better than I thought. We just missed a lot of pretty good shots.

May and Benson had great second halves—and so did Buckner. The game was tied 51–51 with ten minutes to go. That means our edge was 35–17 the last ten minutes, because we won 86–68.

That also means that during the most important ten minutes of the year, our kids played on offense at a 140-point pace. It was the absolute best way for that team to go out: playing at its best, under championship-game pressure, and winning convincingly.

The national championship that we had been after for two years was ours.

And what that team did that year, nobody has done since.

So was it the thrill of a lifetime to stand up there on the awards platform that March night in Philadelphia after we had completed the unbeaten season?

I'm not sure thrill is the right word.

Had we won the year before when for the first time I knew we had the best team in the country, it would have been an unbelievable thrill. That's the major reason from a basketball standpoint that I went to Indiana, to coach a team that could win the NCAA, and winning one in '75 would have meant that, step by step, in an orderly progression we had put together not just a champion but one of the all-time best championship teams.

Not winning it then, however, made it more of a relief than anything else when we won in '76. A lot of very good teams and coaches haven't won the ultimate championship, whether it was the World Series, Super Bowl, the NCAA tournament, or whatever. I didn't want that team, those kids, to go out without winning the NCAA. A regret I'll never shed is that those 1975 seniors—the first kids to join our brand-new program—didn't get to experience that championship feeling.

In all the elation going on around me and all that I felt, I did think of how this had to feel for the great friend I had in the other locker room, Johnny Orr. That was the one negative. A positive was the man on our bench who had just completed his first year as one of my assistants: Andy Andreas, the guy who got me started in coaching thirteen years before.

It was pretty late by the time all the postgame ceremonies and interviews were over. When I finally got a chance to talk to our kids, I of course told them how happy I was for them. I knew a big thing on their mind was how Bobby Wilkerson was doing. I relayed to them what the people at the hospital had told me—he seemed to be doing all right, and it would be best for them not to go out to visit him because he was resting and that was the best thing for him. I knew he wouldn't be able to go back with the team the next morning.

As he had in 1973 at St. Louis, John Havlicek had come in that afternoon just before our pre-game meal and talked to our players. He came into our locker room afterward to congratulate them. When I left the team at about midnight, John and I went to Temple University Hospital to see Bobby. He was so drowsy I didn't think he'd remember we were there, but a nurse told me the next morning how thrilled he was that John Havlicek had been out to see him.

From there, John and I went to a pasta place, and we just talked the rest of the night. He had to play in Buffalo the next night. Tates Locke was an assistant coach under Jack Ramsey at Buffalo then. Tates told me that at a time-out, John was walking off the floor and Tates asked him, "How late were you two up last night?"

John said, "I don't think we *ever* got to sleep. And I'm playing like it, too."

And Tates said, "Yeah, that's why I asked."

John scored about half his average that night and Buffalo won, but Boston already had clinched the division championship.

John had to travel to Buffalo by himself to play that night. He just did it. He'd never fully understand how much that still means to me, twenty-five years later. When someone is willing to go a little out of their way—or a lot out of their way—to do something for anyone, that's a great mark for that person in my eyes.

That was like Red Auerbach waiting a half-hour to go eat with the young Army coach.

In 1976 the Academy Awards presentation was on the same night as the NCAA championship game. I didn't see it live, of course, but during the Oscars show, the actress Isabel Johns was onstage with Elliott Gould presenting one of the major awards. She said, "And the winner is . . .

And Gould said quickly, "Indiana, 86–68."

I always wanted to meet him, because of that.

I finally did, several years later, and we talked about some of the roles he has played. I knew enough about a lot of them that he had to know I wasn't just pretending to be a fan of his.

I told him, "I know this was a relatively insignificant role in your career, but in *A Bridge Too Far,* you were a colonel in the engineers who just did things the way you thought they should be done, regardless of what the hell the army thought. You can imagine how that appealed to me."

He laughed and said that facet of the role "was exactly why I took it."

Years later, he called me just to let me know he was thinking about me and pulling for me after the mess at Indiana.

Two months after the NCAA championship game, Buckner, May, and Wilkerson went to the Olympic Trials in Raleigh, North Carolina.

Dean Smith has always told me he wanted all three of our guys on the Olympic team that he took to Montreal. The final selection left Bobby off. I wasn't involved with it at all, but I think—as Dean did—that it was a mistake.

Dean was successful in getting a lot of kids he was familiar with on the team, including four of his North Carolina kids and three more from the ACC. He did a great job with that team, and won the gold medal. May and Buckner were starters, and Buckner was the team captain.

That team was 7–0 at the Olympics, which meant Buckner and May that year led teams that went 39–0 and won the two biggest championships in amateur basketball. Only two other players in history ever did that, play on an unbeaten NCAA champion and an unbeaten Olympic champion in the same year—Bill Russell in 1956 and Walt Hazzard in 1964.

As long as we're sending pros to the Olympics, that list will never grow. But another one might.

When Boston won the 1984 NBA championship with Buckner on the team, he joined my old teammate, Jerry Lucas, as the only guys who played on teams that won state high school, NCAA, Olympic, and NBA championships. In 1992, as a player on the first professional team we sent to the Olympics, Magic Johnson joined that list. But it's a short one, and those are three pretty good names on it—and three guys strongly associated with winning.

At Indiana, I never went back to playing tapes for teams, the way I did in the 1974–75 season—to, I thought, great success. In 1975–76, the players were basically the same, so I didn't do it then and just never got back to it. I think that was probably a mistake. In my off-year, that's one of the things I decided I'd try to resume in my next coaching job.

I've always had people come in and talk to my teams. I wanted them to hear from successful people their thoughts on why they were successful and what it took to be successful.

Bob Skoronski was a former Indiana football player who was offensive captain of the Green Bay teams that won the first two Super Bowls. Bob, who was a highly successful businessman after his Packer days, was articulate, and his message to our kids was about life and competition. He didn't pretend to be an expert on basketball, but he was great at talking to them about dedication, effort, and what they could get out of it—what playing meant as far as life was concerned; what he thought he got out of playing for Vince Lombardi, because of the demands he made of his players, and what that enabled him to do later in his business career.

One of my smartest invitations was to Janos Starker, acclaimed worldwide as a cellist and a professor in Indiana's School of Music.

What would a man critics around the world have called "the king of cellists" have to say that young basketball players would benefit from? Here's what:

> I started playing the cello when I was six. At that time, I didn't choose it. My mother did. Eventually, three years later, I realized that, first of all, it was something that I loved. I realized that I couldn't go through a day without thinking, doing, making music. This is one of the basic principles that I state: that anyone who can go through a day without wanting to be with music or hear music or make music is not supposed to be a musician.
>
> I believe that to be valid for every single profession. If you can go through a

day without wanting it or thinking it or living with professionalism in the pro-fession that you are in, you are not supposed to be in it.

It wasn't important to me as a boy, nor did it ever become important to me, to be recognized as No. 1 or No. 2, because it is a nonsensical listing. Always, I tried to do the maximum with what nature gave me. What is necessary in my profession is no different from yours.

I forgot anything else that existed in the world. There was no music, no par-ents, no girlfriends, nothing but concentrating on the game.

This is what seems to be the problem, looking at all my students, in the study-ing process: to have the willpower, the ability to concentrate. When I go on stage, nothing exists but that piece of music that I'm playing or that objective which I set for myself.

Discipline means concentration, and concentration means discipline. Disci-pline means that you have a routine that you follow with total conviction of pri-ority. Is the priority to win alone, or to do the best one can do? We must have total conviction that we want to do it, not just when the chips are down but at all possible times. The practice is just as important as the moment when you are in front of everybody.

The only difference in our professions is that when the game is over, the score sort of unquestionably shows whether you succeeded or not. That's a little bit different for us.

But the self-respect is no different. Whether the audience cheers or not, it does not mean anything. If I know that I have done well, whether they liked it or not is not important. Did I do the best I could under the circumstances, with total concentration and dedication to the cause at the moment?

Discipline means to learn everything that helps us to the maximum perform-ance.

Where is the parallel, the musical parallel to basketball?

For a lifetime, we develop skills, so as to find the proper note. That's why you train for a lifetime, to find the basket.

As a cellist, when you are six years of age, eight, twelve, you have to practice three or four hours a day just to obtain the basic skills and the strength in your hand and your arms and muscles, because you do need considerable muscle power. We are hitting strings with the fingers sometimes at the speed of two thousand notes per minute.

There are people who can shoot successfully eight times out of ten in practice. To improve on the percentage, you must consciously know what part of the body functions how. This requires the thinking process. It doesn't mean just that you are following the instructions of the coach. Eventually you must use your own brain: Why does it work? Why is the coach right?

Until the individual discovers it for himself, it is never going to result in consistency.

The word consistency is the key. You have to do everything that we mean when we speak of professionalism. I'm not talking about being paid for something. The professional is the one who is consistent at a higher level than anybody else. And anybody else is called a dilettante. Dilettantes can sometimes succeed in doing things marvelously well. Sometimes. But they are not consistent.

I spent a lifetime trying to understand the underlying basic principles that make it possible for someone to use body, arms, and then the head. I find that the underlying principles are the same. When I watch you guys, sometimes I notice that artistry and grace are involved, and the fluency of motions that we are doing in music. How to improve it and to make it consistent is what we are all trying to get in every field. That's where brain process, analysis, and the total dedication, total priority for the game, in preparation as well as while it is in progress, and the discipline that is required.

That took at most ten minutes. Our players listened so intently there wasn't a conflicting sound during his talk. He was very tough as a teacher. He told our kids they were just like his students, who never had to worry about going to hell because with him they had hell on earth.

I think he was drawing some kind of parallel.

I'm supposed to be a guy perpetually at war with officials, and the truth is I've had a great relationship with a lot of them. Dozens.

And my all-time favorite was Charlie Fouty.

Charlie is from Terre Haute, Indiana, about an hour away from Bloomington. But before either of us ever got involved with the Big Ten and before either of us, I'm sure, had ever heard of the other, my Army team played Florida State and Charlie worked the game—with Ralph Stout, another very good official. Very early in the game, one of them called a three-second violation on my center, Mike Gyovai.

I got all over them right away: "What kind of call is that? This isn't a junior high school game."

Just after this happened, there was a time-out. Charlie came over and told me, "Now, Coach, here's the deal. We may have been wrong on that call, so I'll tell you what we'll do. We'll let your center stay in the lane just as much as he wants to from now on. We won't make the three-second call.

"But to be fair I've got to go down there (to the other team's huddle) and tell that big red-headed kid from Florida State he can do the same thing."

The big red-headed kid was Dave Cowens.

I said, "I believe we'll just leave it the way it is, Charlie."

He won me over that fast.

One of the guys he worked with in the Big Ten a lot, Art White, was a hell of an official, too. We played C. M. Newton's Alabama team in the finals of our 1977–78 Indiana Classic, with White and Fouty working the game. C. M. and I escorted the two of them to center court for the tip-off.

The next time we had them, Charlie walked over to me before the game and said, "Coach . . ."

I said, "What can I do for you, Charlie?"

He had one hand behind his back. He grabbed my coat, pulled that hand around and stuck something on my jacket. He waited a second for my reaction, but I damned sure wasn't going to look at whatever it was while he was standing there. He walked away, and I looked. It was a big button that said, "Smile. You might need a friend today."

When our 1975–76 team played UCLA at St. Louis opening the season, Charlie Fouty and Irv Brown were the officials. In that game, we pulled a little surprise—Indiana, the team the media experts tell you "never" presses, picked up full-court early in the game. Fine; we surprised UCLA. But we must have shocked Charlie and Irv, too. Buckner and Wilkerson jumped their guards when they were just trying to get the ball in-bounds to start up-court after we had scored. They were supposed to have five seconds to get it in-bounds or lose possession. I counted to about seven and Brown never did blow a whistle.

I was irritated but not hot. At a time-out right after that happened, I told Fouty: "What the hell is he doing? Go ask Brown if he can count to five? If he can't, tell him to come over here and I'll give him the numbers. That count had to go to eight."

Fouty went to Brown, then came back to me and said, "Irv said to tell you, 'What the hell do you expect? It's our first game of the year.'"

I said, "Go back and tell him it's our players' first game of the year, too, and they're doing a hell of a lot better job than he is.

"And every one of them can count to five."

Fouty was outstanding because he just worked the game. He didn't go through all the movements and gesticulations they do today—he controlled the game. He understood kids; he understood the emotions of coaches. He was just the best.

The Big Ten has had more than its share of excellent officials—conscientious guys who wanted to do a good job. I don't want to fall into the trap of listing names, because I'll certainly leave a few out. There were other guys I liked from around the country. John Nucatola was the supervisor of Eastern officials, and he took almost a fatherly attitude toward me that I really appreciated.

We lost a nationally televised first-round NIT game to Notre Dame one year—on St. Patrick's Day, with Jimmy Lennon and Art McNally as the officials.

We didn't lose because of the officials. They were two guys I would take in any game anywhere—Art McNally went on to become the National Football League's supervisor of officials.

But there *was* some irony in having two Irishmen do the Notre Dame game, on St. Patrick's Day.

Jimmy Lennon stayed with basketball, and I've maintained contact with him ever since. When I was at West Point, I knew that he prided himself in never having called a technical foul on a coach, and as far as I know he never did.

But I do know that at least once, he came close.

We were playing Temple in the Palestra, and Jimmy made a call I didn't care for—actually, he had made a few that night that I wasn't happy about. This time, I went down the floor after him and said something, but there was a time-out and I turned and went back to our bench before he could say anything back to me. I was in the huddle, talking to my team, when all of a sudden, there's Jimmy Lennon parting our players so he can stick his head into our huddle. He didn't even seem to care that he was interrupting the brilliant message I was delivering. He said, "You son-of-a-bitch, you *know* I've never called a technical on a coach, but you are god-damn testing my patience tonight!"

I liked and respected a lot of guys. But my favorite was Charlie Fouty.

And there's no question who's at the other end of that list: my least favorite. I have as little respect for Ted Valentine as any person I've ever known. I'll always feel he took an NCAA semifinal game away from us in 1992 at Minneapolis, making our kids pay when—I don't think there's any question about it—he used me to gain recognition for himself. Then, six years later, it cost me ten thousand dollars to tell the truth when I called the way he officiated in our

1998 Illinois game in Bloomington a travesty. And that's as much attention as I intend to give that guy.

If I could ever be accused of being hard on officials, it was when I was in West Point the first couple of years. Some of my "friends" in the New York press called me Bobby T. I don't think I got any more technical fouls than a lot of other guys, but I did get on officials hard.

Then I started noticing something when I studied game films. By habit, I would make a mental note of plays I had complained about. Then I would look at the film. Far more often than not, I was wrong and they were right. So I tried to get away from complaining about officiating so much to concentrate on the game.

Of many things that helped me in coaching, that was a big one. When I got out of the officiating business it made me a lot more productive coach. I've always told young coaches, "Coach, don't officiate."

I know some people, maybe most people, are going to read that and smirk, maybe laugh out loud. That's not my image. But my relationship with most officials is excellent. There are some exceptions, but not many. I've seen summaries that showed our team almost always was first in the Big Ten in fewest technical fouls—and never was last. I saw a ten-year study that showed Indiana (I and my players) had thirty-two technical fouls and our opponents fifty-three.

I think Big Ten officials in particular knew I was always in the forefront in trying to get officials' compensation in our league as high as—in most cases higher than—any other conference in the country.

Steve Welmer from the Big Ten and Larry Lembo from the East were good officials because they were big guys who had played college basketball and had an understanding of how the game is played, particularly inside. Obviously there have been good officials who weren't especially big or hadn't played at a high level—Ed Hightower, Tom Rucker, Rick Hartzell, and Sam Lickliter are examples from the Big Ten. The important thing is enough familiarity with the game to know what represents an unfair advantage—therefore, is a foul.

That official will know that if a defensive guy has his hands on a ball-handler's hip, he can't dribble in that direction. He knows what a hell of an advantage it is if a guy with the ball takes an extra step on the way to the bucket. He just knows why there are rules in the book against various things.

Once I told Gene Monje, a Big Ten official, "The guy is palming the ball. Every time he changes directions, he palms it." He looked at me and said, "That went out when you played." I said, "Then get it out of the rule book." The very next year, palming was declared a point of emphasis for national officiating. It still isn't called—certainly not by Monje.

I just don't think officiating is nearly as good today as it once was. I'm not sure there's an official today who wears a pair of pants that's the right size.

That is part of the problem—conditioning, and no one is in position to demand it.

Conferences used to be able to set standards. They say they can't now. Officials are defined as "independent contractors," which means they don't answer to anybody. It's not so much a matter of age as of conditioning. With all the physical exertion that's involved in the college game, including the travel, physical condition should be a term of employment.

And so should the number of games an official works.

There's no way a guy over thirty can just physically work six games a week well, and here we're talking about guys who are over forty and fifty. It's ridiculous that the NCAA doesn't step in and say the maximum number of games anybody can work in a week is three. That's one too many. Except for conference tournaments, teams play only two games a week, and that's with kids twenty years old in excellent condition, with substitutes available.

The conferences say they can't limit the officials' number of games—that "independent contractor" stuff. So, officials work in as many different leagues as they want—from all across the country, and all across the week's calendar—five, six, I'm sure some have done seven games in a week. And if one league doesn't like them, they don't give a damn. They just work in other leagues.

I don't understand why it wouldn't be permissible for the NCAA to adopt a weekly limit of games an official could work. I'm sure somebody would cry "monopoly," but the NCAA doesn't have a monopoly on basketball. Officials can work in the NBA, the NAIA, high schools, junior college—anywhere else they want to—if they don't like terms the NCAA sets down.

Another thing I've noticed and never even seen mentioned is the mental state of overworked officials going into different games. Officials are a lot like players: they've got a big game, Kentucky and Duke, and boy they're pumped up. The next night, they've got a game between two lesser teams—you can't tell me they're as ready and alert as they were for the Kentucky–Duke game. The second night they're just working for the paycheck.

I say that realizing that our games at Indiana were probably considered big, so more often than not we got the best officials when they were "up" for the game. But it's still something that comes into play when officials are allowed to book as many games for themselves as they want.

A lot of games are worked by tired officials.

• • •

One of the great myths in basketball is the "value" of a technical foul. It's a myth that is kind of self-sustaining. First, as TV coverage of the sport grew so big, the number of sideline experts grew, and they developed the idea that coaches deliberately get technical fouls to alter the way a game is being played, or officiated.

The more they said it, the more they convinced not just fans but young coaches coming along, and, you would have to believe, young officials. I say young officials, because they have to be young to see a televised game—the older ones are working somewhere every night.

I can tell you truthfully I've tried once to get a technical foul in all the years I've been in coaching.

And I didn't get it.

Red Strauthers, who officiated in the Big Ten when I was playing, was working the game when I tried and failed. He knew exactly what I was doing. He walked over to me and said, "The worse you get, the less likely I am to call a technical foul on you. I just want you to know that."

He handled it perfectly. What else could I do but shut up?

There have been times when I knew I was going to get a technical—I was really upset about something and I wanted to make a point. There's a fine line of difference there, and the point in the game has something to do with it. If you go back over my history of technical fouls, you'll find the majority have come after the game was decided. I want to prove a point: I'm upset with an official.

Now, I've gotten some when I was god-*damned* upset that I got them.

When you've coached long enough, you know what you can say and what you can't. There have been times when I thought I said more than I should have said without being nailed. I've been a little upset even those times—not with the official but with myself, for going too close to that line.

The two key words in understanding a coach–official relationship are intimidate and antagonize. I don't think a coach ever intimidates a good official. People say I do that. I say if I can intimidate an official, anybody can, because he's a bad official.

Antagonize? That's something else. I know I've said things to officials and gone back to the bench saying to myself, "I wish I had kept my mouth shut. All I've done is antagonize the guy."

But I think it is pure TV bullshit that a coach can get a technical foul and swing the game.

I'm not saying it isn't done—to try to get a game going in another direction. After he got on TV, Al McGuire openly admitted he did that.

I just don't agree—and never have felt—that it's a good idea.

NINE: *Return to the Top (1976–1984)*

*I judge too many situations by what I would do, forgetting that
not everybody is going to do what I do, or react the way I'd
react (which my wife Karen says is probably a real plus
for the whole world).*

The remark I made to the fans in Assembly Hall on Senior Day in 1976—
"Take a good look at these kids, because you're never going to see the likes
of them again"—was one I don't think many of those fans believed. I'm sure
most of them thought we could go out and get players like that and form teams
like that every year.

All these years later, they probably don't realize how close they were to at
least seeing things continue on an awfully high level for a good while.

The only starter we had back the year after our unbeaten championship
team was Kent Benson. We had some other good players—Wayne Radford by
then was a junior, and he had helped us win a lot of big games; Jimmy Wisman
was a junior, and he had been excellent in the national championship game.
And we had a good freshman class coming in, pretty much the players we had
picked out as the best in Indiana (Mike Woodson), Illinois (Glen Grunwald),
and Ohio (Butch Carter).

In that 1976–77 season we should also have had Jimmy Crews and Tommy
Abernethy, two very good players who had instead graduated. It's my fault we
didn't. I could have—and should have—red-shirted each of them for a year so
they'd have been around to take the leadership burden off Benson. Bennie was
a very good college basketball player in a great many ways, but leadership was
not something that came at all naturally to him and, in fact, actually detracted
from his own play.

Red-shirting is the term for holding an athlete out of competition for a year
to save the season of eligibility for future use. College athletes have five years to
get in four seasons. The original intent of the rule was to provide a full season
for an athlete who was injured early in a year and missed most of the season. In
football first and later basketball, it became a way to keep a player from, in

effect, wasting a season on the bench when he could be a valuable contributor to a team later—mutually advantageous, when it works out right, because every kid would prefer a season when he plays a lot to one spent mostly on the bench.

That description fits what I'm sure would have happened with and for Abernethy and Crews. I didn't even think of red-shirting them until they had graduated.

I could have held Abernethy out his sophomore year (1973–74) and Crews his junior year (1974–75). Both of those teams would have been all right without them, and those two would have been around to have great senior years on what then would have been a much stronger team. I've been ahead on a lot of things, planned red-shirting was one—eventually we pretty much introduced it to Big Ten basketball. But I started a couple of years later than I should have. I just didn't look into the future with Abernethy and Crews. They were two of the six most instrumental players in '76, and the depth, the leadership, and the intelligence of the '77 team would have been greatly increased with those two players.

Both were very smart players. Jimmy was especially good against a zone defense because he mastered a very simple thing, the pass fake. That made him deceptive on top of a zone, and he added to that by being a good shooter.

He handled his time at Indiana extremely well. He can look back on his career and feel he should have played more, with justification. He was a starter as a freshman on a Big Ten champion and Final Four team. As a sophomore, he still played a lot. His junior year—the one I think was an ideal red-shirt year for him—he didn't play as much as he had. Then his senior year he was invaluable as our sixth player. We actually played him some as a forward. I could substitute him for anybody in our lineup and we could go right on.

I used to think a lot about that missed red-shirt opportunity because Jimmy was around me every day for eight years. He came back to join our coaching staff in the 1977–78 season, and he did a great job for us until he went to Evansville as the head coach after the 1984–85 season. He has just been outstanding there.

A third person could have made a difference in 1976–77, and the year after.

Those could have been the junior and senior seasons for Larry Bird.

Instead, the 1976–77 season is when he first began to show the world what a truly great basketball player he was to become. He did that at Indiana State.

I first saw Larry play for Springs Valley High School, about sixty miles south of Bloomington. Physically he wasn't the Larry Bird everybody remembers. As a high school senior, he was about 6-foot-6 and 180 pounds.

But he had great hands and great vision. And an excellent high school coach who has won more than five hundred games, Jim Jones, was his coach for his first three seasons.

When I'm trying to evaluate a player as a prospect, I tend to compare him to players I've had. I compared Bird to Steve Green; I felt both came into college not real quick, with some excellent skills, and both knew how to play. At 6-foot-6 and 180, I couldn't envision Bird ever being what he became, but I thought he would be a damned good player for us. I saw him play three or four high school games, and we signed him in the spring of his senior year.

He came to school in the fall of 1974. Ordinarily, our kids would start getting together for pick-up games as soon as they got to campus in August. That August, Steve Green and Quinn Buckner, our two best leaders, weren't there. They were playing with the United States All-Star team that Norm Sloan was coaching—against the Russian National team on a tour across the country.

As hard as it is to imagine now, in those fall 1974 pick-up games among our players Bird would commonly get left out when they were picking teams.

Another problem he had that fall in his adjustment to college was my fault. I had him rooming with Jim Wisman, who was exceptionally sophisticated for a college freshman. Wisman was outgoing with a vibrant personality. Bird was withdrawn and quiet. Wisman dressed very well and had a closet full of clothes. Bird had almost nothing. It was a bad match-up. Long before we even started pre-season practice, Larry left. He hitchhiked home, and stayed.

I didn't handle that well. I just let him go. I had a lot of very good players who were happy to be where they were. We had a great team shaping up. I didn't envision Bird playing much for us until he was a junior. I saw a story several years later quoting Larry as saying if he had it to do all over again, he'd have gone back to Bloomington after he had gone home. He certainly would have been a great addition. But, as painful as it was in some ways for me and my program, I was genuinely happy that things worked out so well for him at Indiana State and I dropped him a note telling him that. I had indications back that he appreciated the note and carried it with him for a while.

The first inkling I had of what he was going to become came in the summer of 1975. John Ritter of our 1973 team told me he saw Larry play in an outdoor tournament in Lebanon and he was about 6-foot-9 and 220. By that time, he was set to go to Indiana State.

He would have been a truly remarkable player for us or anybody—a perfect fit for the way I wanted to play. And, if he grew that much that quickly, who knows how ready to fill a gap he might have been even as a freshman when a great team lost Scott May?

I was pleased for Bird later for the fine job he did as coach of the Indiana Pacers. He got good people around him, worked the team hard, got them into condition to the point where they had good stamina, had a lot of success—and then impressed me even more by the way he left. He got them to the NBA play-off finals, and his ego didn't demand that he stay in that spotlight. He just left. He probably realized it was going to be extremely hard to ever get back there again. I thought that was a great move—like a politician who knows his time has come and if he extends it one more election, he's probably going to get beat. Knowing when to quit is a rarity.

Bird took his team farther than the vast majority of coaches ever would have been able to take it. I'm sure the money they're making has a lot to do with it, but today's pros don't seem to listen to very many people. It was obvious the Pacers listened to Bird—how could anyone who watched the NBA in his years *not* listen to a guy who accomplished as much as Larry Bird? That's where I think the Pacers were smart in hiring him, and that's what I'm sure they're trying to recapture with Isiah Thomas.

Playing without Larry Bird, Jimmy Crews, and Tommy Abernethy, maybe I should be happy the 1976–77 team did as well as it did.

I wasn't, and players on it weren't. It was a long, hard year for everybody—including Benson, although he came out of it a consensus All-American for the second time, the Big Ten's Most Valuable Player, and the No. 1 pick in the NBA draft. But after all the success and fun of the years that had come before, it was a miserable year. We lost eleven games and four players.

The last of the four had just transferred out when Pete Newell, Bob Boyd, Wayne Embry, and I went to Hollywood Park for an afternoon of horse-racing. I'm no gambler. I'm not sure what we were doing, but we all took a horse for some combined bet. They sort of assigned me a horse—one that couldn't lose, a prohibitive favorite. He was out front for most of the race, then he started to fade—fifth, seventh, eighth. Embry slammed his program down and said, "Dammit, Bob, even your *horses* are quitting on you."

That's the kind of year it was.

That day, Pete Newell had spent the whole morning explaining what you look for in figuring out how to bet in a race. He gave me a four-hour lecture on

how coaches had an edge, because you have to take in all kinds of elements: track conditions, fitness of the horse, on and on and on.

Then we got to the track, and Pete did all his calculations and came up with Number 4 for the first race, the absolute "smart" pick. I went to the betting window with him. We were in line behind an extremely attractive young lady in halter top and shorts. She bet on Number 6, and when Pete followed her, he thrust his money out and said "Number 6."

All that calculating and evaluating was overridden by one good-looking woman in a halter top.

I went ahead and bet Number 4. Neither one won.

I had seen Wayne Embry score forty points for Miami against Xavier my senior year in high school, on a recruiting visit. As a college and pro player, he was big and strong, and he maximized his talent to be successful at both levels.

He also is one of the most genuinely caring people I've ever met. He was general manager of the Milwaukee Bucks when I got to know him well. He and Jerry Colangelo of the Suns saw our teams play a lot. Jerry, the baseball owner whose Arizona team won the 2001 World Series in just their fourth season, sat on our bench when we won a game at Michigan State in 1981. The two of them greatly helped our kids when they were seniors going into the NBA draft. They gave me straight information I could pass along about which team was going to take them, contracts, positioning.

I always felt that Wayne in particular really liked our players and rooted for them; he was just sincerely concerned about them, and, I knew, about me. I still get letters from him that mean the world to me.

And never, in any of them, does he ask me to go back to a race track with him.

In that 1976–77 season we got an exceptional freshman year out of Woodson, who scored more points in Big Ten play (three hundred ninety-six) than any other freshman ever. He wound up leading our team in scoring because Benson went down at Purdue with four games to go and had to have season-ending back surgery. That was the only time in my twenty-nine Indiana seasons that we didn't play in a postseason tournament.

Woodson and Radford, who as kids had lived in the same Indianapolis neighborhood although they eventually went to different high schools, gave us consistent two-man scoring the last two months of the 1977–78 season. We won our last eight regular-season games to get back to the NCAA tournament, and we went over twenty in wins again (21–8).

Each of those years, we had some big wins. Michigan, which closed the regular season ranked No. 1 in the country in 1976–77, came into Assembly Hall No. 2 and we won, 86–78. Then the next year, Notre Dame was No. 2 when we beat them at Assembly Hall, 78–77, on a free-throw by Radford with two seconds to go.

By 1978–79, Woodson was a junior and one of the best players in the Big Ten, Ray Tolbert was a sophomore, and Randy Wittman and Landon Turner were freshmen—that's four NBA-caliber kids. But that season started badly. We opened our season in the Alaska tournament and lost our first two games, the only time in my twenty-nine years at Indiana that happened. I had gone up there thinking we had a chance to be a pretty good team.

Two weeks after we returned home, that Alaska trip came back to hit me as hard as anything ever has in coaching.

I don't know how much it had been used before. I don't know how much losing those games had to do with it, or how much using it had to do with losing those games. But in Alaska, somebody got some marijuana and one night seven of our players sat around a room smoking it.

In some cases, at least according to them, that was the only time it ever happened. And there were some awfully good kids involved, some of the best kids I ever had. There's no player I've ever had that I liked or enjoyed more than Mike Woodson, and he was involved. That was very tough to handle.

Maybe the most difficult thing in that for me was personal. It was hard for me to believe that—as opposed to the whole drug situation as I was—I was a coach who had seven players involved in using marijuana.

I probably have a tougher time than most guys with that kind of thing because I never drank. I never had a beer when I was in college and high school. I never took a puff on a cigarette, ever. I'm so unalterably opposed to those things that it's hard for me to accept people in athletics smoking, drinking, or using drugs.

I judge too many situations by what I would do, forgetting that not everybody is going to do what I do, or react the way I'd react (which my wife Karen says is probably a real plus for the whole world).

But in this situation I knew I had to do some things. I dropped three players and put the others on probation—*my* probation, which started with a guarantee that there would be frequent testing and any repeat violation during their college years would bring automatic dismissal.

I had to make some hard decisions fast, but more than twenty years later, I don't second-guess the ones I made. I think I handled it the best way I could have. I told them if anybody lied to me, he was gone. And that's where the eliminating started.

I had known something was wrong within my team. We were 2–2 when we went to play at Georgetown. We lost that game, and on the flight home, I walked up and down the aisle in the middle of the airplane and told them something was going on and I wanted to know what it was. Searching for answers, I even asked something I had never asked a team—was there a black-white problem on the team? I got nowhere.

The Georgetown game was on a Wednesday. We beat Bradley at Indianapolis on Saturday. That weekend, the whole thing unraveled. A couple of players came to my house. I talked to others.

On Monday, I made and announced my decision: three players dismissed, seven others put on probation. It was headline news, and not just in Indiana.

Once it was done, we had to refocus quickly. We had a wounded team, and on Saturday Kentucky was coming to Assembly Hall. They had lost some players from the team that won the NCAA championship the year before, but they still were damned good—No. 6 in the polls. The Kentucky game wasn't even on my mind when I was making my decision, but it damned sure was shortly afterward.

We won in overtime, 68–67. Mike Woodson hit two free-throws with five seconds left in overtime to clinch it. I'll say now what I said immediately after the game, "As long as I've coached basketball, I've never been happier for a bunch of kids than I was after this game. This was a day for our players. This was a day they earned after all the heartaches and soul-searching of the week.

"It was absolutely fitting that Woodson hit those last two free throws. Very rarely have we ever tried to go to one guy the way we did with Woodson today. That puts a lot of pressure on the guy.

"But we just said we were going to go to Woodson, and that's what we did."

Woodson scored twenty-seven points and played forty-four minutes, and he drew thirteen fouls on Kentucky's inside players. He shot nineteen free-throws and wasn't shooting them very well until he had a chance to decide the game: our team one point up, Woodson shooting two free-throws, with five seconds left in overtime. Those two put us three points ahead, and we didn't have a three-point shot to worry about then, or a clock that would stop after a basket. They were out of time-outs, so we stood by, let them score, and let the clock run out without having to pass the ball in-bounds.

A quiet key to that game was Randy Wittman. It was just his sixth college game, but he held their All-America guard, Kyle Macy, to six points in regulation time, eleven altogether.

Our team wasn't over any hump. We struggled all the way up to the last game, when our record was 17–12 and we had a chance to salvage a spot in the NIT if we could win at Illinois.

The load went back on Woodson. He scored twenty-nine points—in the first half. He wound up with forty-eight, the most I've ever had a player score. He actually led Illinois for much of that game, and the guys Illinois used to try to slow him down, Eddie Johnson and Mark Smith, were excellent players, good athletes and taller than Mike by two or three inches. We won, 72–60, and got the NIT bid.

Our NIT opener was the first game I ever coached in Lubbock, Texas. Gerald Myers—the athletic director who is my boss now—had done a good job with his Texas Tech team. They were 19–10 and the campus and town were excited—I had never seen a community as keyed up for a game.

But we jumped out to a 15–2 lead, Woodson was still pretty warm, and his thirty points helped us win, 78–59.

Then we faced Alcorn State, which twenty years later stands as the last unbeaten major-college team not to get an NCAA tournament invitation. We won, but the score was just 73–69 at Assembly Hall. Davy Whitney had them well coached and they had a forward named Larry Smith who had a good and long career in the NBA. The NCAA selectors missed one there. (Dave Whitney later invited me to speak at their athletic banquet, and he brought his team to Bloomington again to play in our Indiana Classic.)

Beating Alcorn State made us one of the four NIT teams that went to New York. Winning the NIT gave me one of my greatest thrills in coaching, because that tournament had been such a big target for us, such a dream, when I was at West Point, and finally, in my thirteenth year as a head coach, it had happened. I was more victory-dazed that night than any of the three NCAA championship nights. I can remember walking around the floor saying almost in disbelief: "We've won the NIT. We've *won* the NIT." With that "we," I was including all our Army teams that had tried so hard to win it.

Winning was just part of the thrill. After we beat Purdue in the championship game (Jerry Sichting made a hell of a cut to get a buzzer shot that just missed beating us), I was able to bring Mrs. Joe Lapchick out onto the Madison Square Garden floor to be in on the trophy presentation. She had seen a few of those presentations in her lifetime—her husband's St. John's teams won the NIT four times. This night she had come to watch us, and I got her out there, "walking with the kings."

The 1979 NCAA champion was Michigan State, which beat Indiana State in the finals in the first of what was to be many Magic Johnson–Larry Bird meetings for a championship.

Our teams never played Larry, but Magic Johnson ranks way up there on any list of great players they ever met. I thought he was even better in the pros than in college because, though he scored well, he wasn't a really good shooter in college.

I'm not sure we ever beat Magic. The record book says we were 1–4 against Michigan State in his two years. I remember the four a lot better than the one. Their national championship team is the only one that ever beat us three times in one season. Like all really good teams, they were well put together and very well coached. Jud Heathcote had inherited some good players from Gus Ganakas and then added some to them and did a great job of getting them all to adapt to his style of play. Greg Kelser, an outstanding player, is an example of those inherited players. Magic, from Lansing, was the best of Jud's additions.

We "got" to play their championship team three times because we were both in the Far West Classic at Portland, Ore., and we made it to the finals. Michigan State beat Washington State in the semifinals, and we played Oregon in the second game that night. When our kids came out the locker room door to head out to the court, there was Magic with that great, enthusiastic grin, grabbing them, calling them by name, and genuinely urging them to make it an all–Big Ten final. We beat Oregon all right, but after Michigan State beat us 74–57 for the championship, I told Magic, "Damn. No wonder you were wanting us to get there."

Magic is the only player ever whose teams won a state high school championship, an NCAA championship, and an NBA championship in just over three calendar years—from March 1977 through June 1980.

What I thought he had more than anything else, or maybe anyone else, was personality. Like that old song, "Personality"—he had a great personality to play.

His senior year in high school, a former Army player of mine was living in the Lansing area. He went to see him play and told me, "They've got this kid up here but I don't think he can ever play."

So much for him as a talent scout.

A few weeks after we won the NIT I was back in basketball, running try-outs in Bloomington to pick the team that I coached that summer in the Pan American Games in San Juan, Puerto Rico. And we did play basketball there, no matter what anyone's read.

One thing that continually amazes me is the litany of my supposed crimes against humanity that is pulled out and run in newspapers every time I'm in the news.

Some of them are legitimate. I've certainly done my share of dumb things, some of which I'm genuinely sorry for (and some that, in my own perverse way, I still kind of enjoy).

But a lot of them are myths, which I'm using as a nice word for lies. And one of the biggest myths/lies is the line that comes up almost every time, "He punched a cop in Puerto Rico."

Let me tell you about that.

We were about a week into competition in San Juan when I had my U.S.A. team practicing at its scheduled time at an official site. We were close to finishing when the next team that was to use that gym floor, the Brazilian women's team, came into the gym.

My practices are quiet. That's my classroom, where I do my teaching. Nobody knew that better than the young coach who was on my staff there, Mike Krzyzewski, who probably has always run his own practices—at Army then and Duke now—the same way.

We had arrived by bus a little ahead of our practice time and been kept outside the gym until the team before us finished its work. I had no problem with that. I thought it was the right thing to do. The same policeman who kept us out brought the Brazil players in during the final minutes of our practice. They were in no way trying to cause a problem, but they were laughing and talking among themselves, pretty loudly. Mike went to them and the accompanying cop to ask for the same privacy we had given the previous team.

I kept running the practice, until I saw that Mike was getting upset with the cop. I went over to them, and in the process of making a belligerent point about his authority, the cop jabbed a finger toward my face. The finger hit me right in the eyeball. I can't say it was or wasn't accidental, but I do know it was damned painful. I ducked my head away from him and in the same reflex motion put out an open hand to push him back while I regained my vision.

That was my "punch." That got me convicted in a Puerto Rican court for assault. That branded me an "ugly American" in the eyes and words of many in the U.S. press corps, especially those who weren't even in San Juan.

Mike, in talking with a reporter after we were back home, one more time substantiated just how everything happened and added his genuine frustration at being listened to and then ignored by so many American reporters. "You know, we have a thing called the honor code at West Point," Mike said. "I went through school there under it, and I'm coaching there now with it. I'm telling you right now that (the policeman's version) was a lie."

From the day our team arrived in San Juan and put on a free clinic for kids there, I had been ripped regularly in the San Juan newspaper. After the gym incident, I was harassed at every game there and compelled to give depositions or appear in court more times than I can remember. Don Miller, the executive director of the U.S. Olympic Committee, was there, a damned good man who supported me in every way. But it was a difficult time.

And still I have some fond memories of that experience because we won the gold medal and some great kids under amazingly difficult conditions played awfully well.

I've always thought that team was better than it has ever been credited with being, in part because more attention was paid to the legal circus going on around me than to what those kids were doing on the court. However, twenty years later I saw something that made me realize someone *was* watching them play. Just before the most recent Pan American Games in 1999, *USA Basketball News,* a magazine put out quarterly by the USA Basketball organization in Colorado Springs, ran a ranking of all the teams that have represented the U.S. in men's basketball in past Pan American Games.

Ranked No. 1 was our 1979 team.

The accompanying story said the selection "would be hard to argue against. Averaging 100.8 points a game, the U.S. won all nine of its games, including a very impressive 113–94 victory over host Puerto Rico in the gold medal game."

That's a terrific compliment to those kids, because No. 2 was the 1959 U.S. team that had Oscar Robertson and Jerry West, and tied for fifth were the 1983 team with Michael Jordan and the 1963 team that included Willis Reed. All of those teams also were unbeaten and won the gold medal.

I've always thought that 1979 team was damned near as good as our 1984 Olympic team. I think it was capable of playing any team that ever represented the United States as an amateur team.

Michael Brooks, from LaSalle, was a hell of a player for us.

Before we ever went to San Juan, we played some exhibition games. We played one at Lexington, and the next day I called Brooks over to talk after practice. I let him have it pretty good—about how he was never going to be a player because he refused to work hard or play any defense at all. I went on for a while and finally said, "Just go shoot free-throws."

After several minutes, I saw him walking toward me.

He said, "Coach, I'm twenty-one years old. I've never had anyone talk to me like that."

I was thinking: *where is this headed*?

"And I just want to say thanks."

From there on, we couldn't have found a better player. In his senior year at LaSalle, he was the coaches' College Player of the Year. Because of a knee injury, he never had the NBA career he might have had, but he was awfully good for us.

That '79 Pan Am team also had Kevin McHale, Mike Woodson, and Isiah Thomas and a lot of other excellent players—Kyle Macy of Kentucky, Ronnie Lester of Iowa, Mike O'Koren of North Carolina, John Duren of Georgetown, our own Ray Tolbert, and a good, strong player who went on to play as a pro in football rather than basketball, Sam Clancy of Pitt. That team also included a very young Ralph Sampson, fresh out of high school, just like Isiah.

Macy, an Indiana kid (he played high school basketball at Peru), had played on an NCAA championship team at Kentucky in 1978. He was doing a great job for us until a Cuban player's sneak punch broke his jaw and we had to send him home for surgery before the medal round. Kyle had played at Purdue before going to Kentucky, and those were two of our biggest basketball rivals. I liked the kid, and one of the first things I did when we got home from San Juan was make a trip to Lexington to take him the gold medal he had earned.

Kyle's dad and mother were there when I gave Kyle his medal, and it was a nice, warm ending to what had been a reprehensible act. His father, Bob, had coached him at Peru, so I had met both him and Kyle's mother before that day of the medal presentation. Kyle is coaching at Morehead State now. He has a line he uses whenever he speaks at a luncheon or dinner, particularly in Indiana, about how he alienated all the IU fans in the state by going to Purdue, then alienated all the Purdue fans by leaving there for Kentucky, so there was no one left in his home state who wasn't mad at him.

There was at least one. I wasn't mad at him at all—more at myself. I didn't do as good a job of evaluating and recruiting as I should have done, and we didn't go after him. We also made a recruiting mistake that year with Jerry Sichting of Martinsville. Both Sichting and Macy played a lot as freshmen at Purdue. As good as each was, and as much better as they became, they probably wouldn't have played much that year for us. We had guards named Quinn Buckner, Bobby Wilkerson, and Jimmy Crews, with Jimmy Wisman a pretty good sophomore back-up. But any of the next three years, I'd have loved to have had Sichting and Macy around.

It was a shame we didn't have Macy for the championship game with Puerto Rico at San Juan. I don't think any U.S.A. team ever won a gold-medal game under more adverse and testing circumstances than those 1979 Pan Am kids.

First of all, the Puerto Rico team was very good. It came into the gold-medal game unbeaten (from the bracket opposite us; we also were unbeaten) and was seeded first, ahead of us. Pressure-packed does not begin to describe the atmosphere at the gold-medal game. We played in a building that had seating for 9,000 and there must have been more than 14,000 there.

We got up by fifteen points at the half and won by nineteen, but in the second half when Puerto Rico made a good run at us, the crowd noise was unbelievable.

Our kids responded with some great pressure plays, especially Woodson and Thomas. Because of foul trouble, Woodson played only twenty-four minutes but scored twenty-three points. Isiah never started a game down there, but in that championship game he had twenty-one points, five steals, and four assists, including a three-point play in the second half when the crowd was at its loudest and Puerto Rico was as close as it got, down by three. Thomas led our team in assists there, and Woodson led in points.

I thought at that point, going into his senior year, Mike Woodson was the best player in the country—and might even be the leading scorer in the country. In the Pan American Games he averaged eighteen points a game on just twelve shots a game.

I can't leave the subject of the Pan American Games without telling a story about my friend Joe Cipriano, the Nebraska coach.

Joe went along with us when, shortly after we made the final cut, I took the Pan American team to Italy for some preparation games. We left the hotel one night to play a game just outside of Venice. As we were pulling away from the hotel, Joe—who had apparently taken a nap and overslept—came running out of the hotel, stuffing his shirt in his pants as he ran. The bus driver was going to stop but I said, "Just keep going. He'll get there."

George Raveling was one of the other coaches I took with me. George and I had become friends when he was an assistant coach at Villanova and I was at West Point. George was a recruiting encyclopedia; nobody knew more about recruiting and where kids were going.

I used to go down to Philadelphia to watch the summer leagues, and I'd stay with George at night. He had newspapers from everywhere. I tried to contact every kid in the country who had at least made all-county, to ask about their interest in West Point.

That night in Italy, without me around, George talked to our kids in the locker room. He said, "Let me tell you guys something: when Coach Knight tells you what time to be on the bus, that's when he's leaving—whether you're there or not. The guy he left behind tonight, Coach Cipriano, is one of his closest friends.

"Now I want you to think about that—if you don't think he'd leave any of *you* behind."

In the fall of '79, ABC sent its top announcing crew—Chris Schenkel and Ara Parseghian—to Bloomington to do the Indiana–Nebraska football game. The day before the game, Chris, Ara, Bob Hammel, and I had about a two-hour lunch at the Holiday Inn. Every minute was splendid. The stories flowed— great, funny tales, most of them from Ara, who I'll always rank with the all-time greats of coaching. In many ways over the years, he also has been a dependable and thoughtful friend to me. But this day he was hilarious—we all hated for the lunch to end. A lunch remembered twenty-two years later was obviously pretty special.

Chris is from Indiana—Bippus, a town of three hundred in Hammel's home county, Huntington. He graduated from Purdue, and occasionally he reminds me of that. That's no problem, because he is such a genuinely good and nice man.

I think many of us in collegiate athletics forget what a gigantic role Chris and so many others in his profession have played in helping college sports became as nationally popular as they are. In basketball, particularly, Billy Packer and Dick Vitale have been great for the college game, because of how hard they work to prepare for every game they do. Vitale takes criticism for coming across like what he openly claims to be: a wacko. But the first thing that comes through when Dick does a basketball game is the passion he has for the game he genuinely loves, and how he wants it to be good for everyone who participates in it—the coaches, the players, and the fans. The guy has one of the great hearts I've ever come across.

I worked with Brent Musburger at a couple of Final Fours, and he's another I respect greatly for his approach to his job. In football, Chris and Keith Jackson were professionals I really admired and liked. In Keith's last year as ABC's No. 1 college announcer, he did a game in Bloomington. Indiana University gave him a carved wooden football as a tribute, and—it's no cliche—I did feel privileged to be the guy handing it to him at a half-time ceremony.

All of them I consider friends.

And No. 1 for me of all in that field is Curt Gowdy.

• • •

Finishing the 1978–79 season with a drive to the NIT championship put us back on a premier competitive level we had been having trouble reaching after our great teams in 1974–75 and 1975–76.

I thought we could be pretty good in 1979–80, with Mike Woodson, Ray Tolbert, Landon Turner, and Randy Wittman coming back, and Isiah Thomas and Steve Bouchie among the freshmen we were adding. Bouchie had been "Mr. Basketball" in Indiana, and he was a very good all-round player at 6-foot-8 and 220 pounds.

We were a lot better than "pretty good" when all those kids played together. In pre-season, that team buried the Russians, 78–50.

There was a world poll of amateur basketball teams that year, because of the upcoming Olympics. The Soviet National team had been No. 1, and after we beat them so bad, Indiana—not the United States but Indiana—became No. 1. I'm not a big believer in polls, and I didn't say anything about it at the time, but it was kind of neat: No. 1 in the *world* in amateur basketball. It probably was true of a lot of college teams over the years—I'd have taken our '75 and '76 teams up against any national team anywhere anytime. But I'm not sure any other college team ever had something actually declaring it the best in the world.

We *were* awfully good. We followed that Russian exhibition game with big wins over Miami of Ohio (80–52), Xavier (92–66), Texas–El Paso (75–43) and, in a game extremely well played by both teams, Georgetown (76–69). We were a solid No. 1 in the college polls.

Then, in fairly quick succession, we had injuries to Bouchie, Wittman, and Woodson. We dropped off fast.

Bouchie came back, but Wittman never played again that year.

Woodson was our medical miracle.

He had back surgery in December, for a herniated disc. It's a problem that, when it reached a point where surgery was needed, ended seasons for athletes up to that time. Arthroscopic surgery was just coming in, minimizing the muscle damage involved. In six weeks, Mike was as ready to play as he would get for a while, but doctors wanted to wait a seventh week so we did.

By then we were in deep trouble in the Big Ten race, but we were still alive. The Saturday before Mike returned, we took a pretty bad beating at Illinois, 89–68—on the same floor where Mike had scored his forty-eight points the year before. That dropped us to 7–5 in the Big Ten, with six games to go. The rest of the league had missed its chance to bury us. We were just a game out of first place, behind Ohio State and Purdue at 8–4.

The first game Woodson was cleared to play with us was on Valentine's Day at Iowa.

I had seen enough of Mike in practice to know he was ready to play very well. I started him. Our second possession, he worked off a screen, went up for a jump shot and hit it. A minute later, he hit another one; two minutes after that, another.

Mike had been like a big brother to Isiah Thomas from the Pan American Games on, a senior taking a freshman under his wing and guiding him in every way he could. We've won a lot of games over the years because we've had kids do things like that, and it requires genuine feeling at both ends—a sincere desire by the older guy to get a young player into position to make our team better, and a willingness by the younger player to accept and appreciate help being extended to him and to understand, listen, and learn. Isiah listened and learned very well, and no one could have been more appreciative. Four years later, when Isiah was named Most Valuable Player of the NBA All-Star Game, he was asked if that was his biggest basketball thrill. Now, this is a kid who by then had been named the Outstanding Player at the Final Four, for a championship team; been a first-team All-American; been the second player taken in the pro draft, the NBA Rookie of the Year, and an NBA All-Star starter from his first year on.

But his answer that night at the All-Star Game was, no, it wasn't his biggest thrill in basketball: "My biggest thrill was watching Mike Woodson come back from back surgery and hit his first three shots at Iowa."

I'm sure NBA writers had no idea what he was talking about, but that's the kind of inspiration Mike Woodson's return gave our team. He didn't just return; he played so well and so hard every game that he made us incomparably better. We won all six league games that we had him, including 76–73 over Ohio State in overtime on the last day of the season to win the Big Ten championship.

That Ohio State game was on Sunday afternoon on national TV and it was a great showcase for college basketball. The two of us went into the game tied for the lead at 12–5, so it was winner-take-all. It was a hell of a game, with outstanding players on both sides. Only thirteen players got into the game. Six of them became first-round NBA draft picks, three more played in the NBA, and a tenth, our Landon Turner, I believe would have been the first pick in the whole 1982 draft if not for the accident that ended his career in 1981.

To win that championship, Mike had given us everything he had. Through those last six games the kid averaged 40.2 minutes a game, more than the regulation forty minutes because of the Ohio State overtime. In that three-week stretch, he played tired at times; he had lost all of his conditioning during the seven weeks he was out. He couldn't come out of games without stiffening problems. So, game after game, he just gritted it out—and averaged twenty points a game. And we won.

The people in our conference noticed what he was doing for us. They voted him the Big Ten's MVP, and it was such an obvious choice the voting wasn't even close. But think about that: he played six of our eighteen league games. What other kid ever won a league MVP award in any sport at any level playing a third of the schedule? I think that's the greatest compliment ever given a Big Ten player.

When we got in the NCAA tournament, we beat Virginia Tech before losing to Purdue. Woodson was out of gas. But nobody who saw us in those closing Big Ten games will ever forget Mike Woodson's determination to give all he had and then find some more, for his team.

As gratifying as winning the 1980 Big Ten championship was, there was some frustration in that season, too. Without the injuries, I believe we were the best team in the country.

If I were going to put much stock in fate, I'd have thought even the extra things were lining up pretty well for us. Woodson, our captain and leader and best player, our version of "Chip Hilton," was from Indianapolis. For the first time, Indianapolis was the site of the NCAA Final Four that year. And the championship game was played in his hometown on March 24—Mike Woodson's birthday.

But the game that night was between Louisville and UCLA.

I can give you two other stories that will tell you how much I thought of Mike, and why.

He was a very good NBA player. One night with Kansas City he hit twenty-two field goals, in twenty-four shots—and he scored forty-eight points, just as he had at Illinois to get us in the 1979 NIT.

He lived in Kansas City in the off-season. One summer day I was flying west with an early-evening change of planes in Kansas City, so I made arrangements to have dinner at the airport with him while I was there. A flight was canceled, so I was backed up to where I would be going through Kansas City after midnight. I had Mary Ann Davis, my secretary, get in touch with Mike and tell him to forget meeting me because of the change.

When I got off the plane in Kansas City at about one o'clock in the morning, there was Mike. Yes, Mary Ann had called him. He still wanted to be there. I've said what kind of player Mike was; this tells you what kind of friend he became.

Not long after that, in December 1984, I was talking to Bob Hammel on the phone and asked if he was coming to practice that night. He said, no, he wasn't. "Michael is in town to play the Pacers tonight and I thought I'd go up and talk to him."

I said, "When are you leaving?"

"About five."

"Come out first. I might go with you."

He knew how I valued practice time. Michael or no Michael, we probably were playing pretty well or I wouldn't have thought about it. But I cut practice short that night and I was ready when he got there. We were on the road up to Indianapolis, a mile or two out of town, when I said something about Woodson and Bob got kind of a blank look.

"Uhhhh," he said. "The Michael who's playing against the Pacers tonight is Jordan, not Woodson."

I didn't say a word, for a mile—maybe a couple of miles. Then I said, "Okay. I'll go. And I'll enjoy it. Jordan's doing great (as a rookie, he had a string of forty-point games going, and continued it that night), and I'll like having a chance to talk to him.

"But, remember this: Michael—in this program—means Woodson."

Over the years there have been insinuations that somehow playing for me at Indiana was detrimental to a player's NBA career. Once I saw where an unidentified scout said he felt he had to be careful when evaluating players to take into consideration that a player coming out of Indiana had less of an undeveloped "up" side than most other players. "What you see is what you get," he said.

I considered that a compliment, not a criticism. We've always tried to make every player we've had as good as he could be at that time. But it still was an unfair tag to put on our kids, because maturity, experience, and the attitude associated with players from our Indiana program were bound to make them better as they added NBA experience.

Yes, Isiah Thomas is the only NBA All-Star we ever had at Indiana, but we had sixteen first-round draft picks who went on to excellent careers.

And—one NBA All-Star? I think that is the greatest kind of tribute to the kids we've had, for the accomplishments of our Indiana teams over the years. It took very good players and very good kids to do all that. And along the way they beat lots of All-Stars. What they accomplished is a tribute, too, to the style of play we developed over the years. I always thought we needed a certain type of kid to play the way we wanted to, but it wasn't necessary for us to have the best talent to win.

• • •

Six players from our 1979–80 team made a career out of the NBA. A seventh player on that 1980 team, Tony Brown, was in a big league of his own.

Tony came to us from Chicago the same year Isiah Thomas did. Tony's team at Chicago De La Salle ended Isiah's high school basketball career, eliminating his Westchester St. Joseph's team in the 1979 Illinois tournament.

Tony was a starter on a Big Ten championship team for us in 1983, but he was one of the relatively few players we've had who didn't graduate in the four years he was with us. Tony was certainly sharp enough to do it. He had more than enough hours to graduate, but he switched majors and was a few hours short of qualifying for a degree when he went off to play some pro ball in Europe.

A business contact there led to an opportunity that Tony developed into a terrific success story. He became a CEO, a multimillionaire, and then—as Isiah had done after leaving school early—he completed his degree work and graduated from Indiana.

When Isiah did it, he may have been the first major college player ever to leave two years early, achieve extreme success in his sport and financial wealth, and still go back to get a degree. Isiah was in the NBA playoffs with Detroit on his graduation day, so his justifiably proud mother came to the ceremony and accepted his diploma for him.

The circle involving those two Chicago kids came around a few years later when financially independent businessman Tony Brown completed his degree work and Isiah, a financially independent businessman himself and CEO of two thriving companies, came down to Bloomington to hand a diploma to his high school and college friend at half-time of one of our home games.

Within that tale of two young millionaire CEOs who grew up in the toughest parts of inner-city Chicago is the Indiana Basketball that I'm proudest of.

That 1980 team was one of three we had that I think would have won NCAA championships without key injuries.

Of course we'll never know, but I felt when they were healthy, our teams in '75 and '93 as well as the one in '80 were the best in the country—in 1975 before Scott May's broken arm in late February, in 1980 before the injuries to Mike Woodson and Randy Wittman, and in 1993 before Alan Henderson injured a knee in late February.

You could make a case for a couple of other seasons, particularly 1981–82. But that was a different situation. We never got to set up that 1981–82 team, because of Landon Turner's summertime accident. As it was, we were a good team but not competitive for the national championship that year. Landon would have made a big difference. It certainly would have been a team that somebody would have had to play pretty well to beat.

And, of course, in a different era Isiah Thomas would have been a junior on that team.

In between the what-might-have-been seasons of 1979–80 and 1981–82 came a national championship. Just as the 1976 team followed an outstanding season with a championship despite losing two good scorers, our '81 team made up for any leftover disappointment from 1980 by winning the NCAA championship despite the graduation of Mike Woodson.

When that team beat North Carolina at Philadelphia to win the 1981 championship, it achieved something that sounds negative: its 26–9 record was, at the time, the worst ever for a champion.

Don't ever downgrade that team because of its record. By championship night in Philadelphia, that team had become one of the few in college basketball history that could have stepped onto the court with our 1975 and 1976 teams and competed very well.

There'd have been a good match-up in the backcourt: Isiah Thomas and Randy Wittman against Quinn Buckner and Bobby Wilkerson. And Ray Tolbert and Landon Turner would have been a good counter to Scott May and Kent Benson, too. The fifth starter and the bench—no big edge either way. One team lost nine games, the other none. I have to always wonder what *I* did wrong in 1980–81. The answer quite possibly may be that the '76 team had a much greater focus throughout, and getting that is part of the coach's Job.

We had some bad losses in '81. Ray Tolbert missed a lob dunk that would have put us ahead late when we lost by two to Kentucky. Clemson beat us in Hawaii by one when Randy Wittman missed an open shot and Tolbert missed with a point-blank rebound. We came back from Hawaii 7–5, but we started off well in the Big Ten. I don't think we were ever out of first place.

The key to the national championship was that Landon Turner finally became the player that all of his physical assets equipped him to be. And when he did that, late in his junior year, we finally became the team we had the ability to be—the best in the country.

Landon had played some very good basketball in his first two years. As a freshman, he played a big part in the NIT championship game, holding Purdue's All-America center, Joe Barry Carroll, to fourteen points after Carroll had scored forty-two against Alabama in the semifinals. The next year was the same: Landon had some outstanding games, but some that weren't even close to what he should have been doing.

I tried everything with him. I've never bought the "Knight doghouse" idea—"so-and-so isn't starting because he's in Knight's doghouse." I've always had an ass-to-the-brain theory—when a player's ass gets put on the bench, a message goes straight from the ass to the brain saying, "Get me off of here."

Landon Turner is one person I give a little latitude on that whole "doghouse" theory. Landon made even me laugh last spring when I heard what he had told a rally of our fans, "I hear people talk about Coach Knight's doghouse. I'm the one who *built* that doghouse. I put it together layer by layer. I laid the foundation; I pounded the nails."

Nobody ever did a better job of converting it into a birdhouse, either.

We played at Northwestern in Landon's junior year. We won 93–56 and Landon was the last guy to get in the game for us. He played eighteen seconds. When I put him in, I happened to look up at the clock and told someone on our bench, "He's playing eighteen more seconds than he deserves to off the way he's been practicing."

A few weeks later we played Northwestern again, at Assembly Hall. I told him the night before the game, "Tomorrow we're going to announce that you're going pro. You've got a better chance to play in the NBA than you do for me."

I didn't play him at all the first half. We were twenty-five points ahead in the second half when I put him in. Right away he missed a blockout. Northwestern scored six straight points. I took him out. Then I thought, if I'm going to go ahead with this pro threat, I'd better let him show just how poorly he's playing.

I put him back in with six and a half minutes to go.

He just played great the rest of the game, and the year.

He played so well in that Northwestern game Steve Downing and I took him into a room after the game and talked with him for a good thirty minutes about how capable he was of playing that way every game. Steve was very good at helping kids, and he was great that night with Landon. He was something of a hero for Landon—both were centers from inner-city Indianapolis, and Landon wore Steve's No. 32.

After the Northwestern game and that talk, I began playing Landon more. He was playing pretty well, but I still didn't start him. We lost a game out at Iowa, but during the game I put him on Kevin Boyle, who was much smaller than Landon and a good, active player. Boyle played outside a lot of the time, where his size should have given him an edge, but Landon just went out there with him and played him hard. It was about the only thing I saw that night that I liked.

The next game I started him, and he never came out of the lineup again. With him starting, we won our last five games to win the Big Ten, and we won our next five games to win the NCAA tournament. Without any question, the key to that finish was Landon Turner.

He made the All–Final Four team, ahead of the College Player of the Year that season, Ralph Sampson. That was just the start. He was coming around in every way. I got reports back from his tutor on how well he was doing in a summer course. Then, on a Saturday morning in July, Landon was driving some kids to Kings Island amusement park outside Cincinnati when he lost control, his car hit a cement culvert, and this kid with such a great future came out of the accident paralyzed from the chest down. For life.

I thought he'd be the best player in the country that next year and go on to a long pro career.

Instead, he has made me as proud as any player I've ever had. No one I've ever known has faced extreme adversity and disappointment and handled it as well as Landon Turner.

A lot of people made me proud that summer. It was obvious Landon was going to be facing some big expenses just to live, paralyzed. All over Indiana people did things to raise money for him. We all pitched in, and we raised enough to give him a trust fund that took the financial pressure off him for the rest of his life.

There was never a moment in all that when I saw Landon bitter. He has the greatest parents in the world, Adell and Rita Turner, and they certainly had a lot to do with his attitude. But give Landon the credit. Right from the start, he went to work to make himself as mobile as he could. He helped other patients. That's the way he still is. He's a great motivational speaker. He's always upbeat.

And he still comes to our games. He was down for Senior Day in 1994. Before I brought the senior players to the microphone, just on the spur of the moment I asked all our former players who were in the audience to stand up. They were still standing, and the crowd was applauding, when I glanced over beside me and saw Landon in his mechanized wheelchair. I wanted to be sure he felt included, so in a tone I knew he'd appreciate, I said, "Landon! Why aren't you standing up?"

He looked at me with a great grin and said, "I am standing, Coach—in my heart."

That is the warmest feeling I've ever had on a basketball court.

• • •

There was one other moment like that for me, where Landon was involved. The spring of 1982 when he would have been a senior, I was with Red Auerbach and mentioned to him what a great thing it would be if after the Celtics had gone as far as they intended to in the draft, he would consider taking Landon Turner.

I never mentioned it again. But three weeks later when they had the draft and it was winding down, Red stood up and said, "The Boston Celtics take Landon Turner of Indiana."

Landon heard about it and immediately sent Red a wire, "Thanks a million. You made my day. When do I report?"

And, one more time in one more way, I knew why I admire the hell out of Red Auerbach.

On the court and off, that '81 championship team's leader, unquestionably, was Isiah Thomas. But, like all good teams, everyone had to join in a common interest in winning and playing as well as possible for a championship to happen.

Isiah was, like Michael Jordan, a great combination of toughness and intelligence. He may be the closest to Jordan of anybody I've been around in the peripheral qualities that enable you to win. John Havlicek, Willis Reed, Bill Russell (he may have been the best)—players like that had a toughness, an intelligence, an understanding. Forget the extraordinary ability. Isiah had the other ingredients in great quantity that enabled him to be a player you could win with.

Plus, he *really* wanted to win.

He scored thirty-nine points one day when we beat Michigan. He could come back the next night and score eleven points and be just as effective, it made no difference to him. He just took what was there.

He was a hell of a prospect in high school. He was extremely well coached (by Gene Pingatore at Westchester St. Joseph's in suburban Chicago, one of the best coaches at any level I've ever been around).

Tom Miller of our Indiana coaching staff had played for "Ping" in high school before becoming a very good player for us at Army. Tommy was on Isiah early.

Even in high school Isiah was solidly built and strong—he weighed 180 pounds. He was tough. And he had great physical skills.

And in Mary Thomas he had a great, great mom.

Very few kids and mothers have been as devoted as he was to her or she to him. She was a tremendous influence on his life, but he allowed her to be. He knew that his mother wanted what was best for him. His mother always was a big supporter of anything we did with him—and the best recruiter we had, until the NCAA passed a very poor rule that kept people like her from telling other parents what a coach or a basketball program or a school was truly like.

Isiah went out with an outstanding string of NCAA tournament games: five games, ninety-one points, forty-three assists, thirteen turnovers. I've never had a team play much better than that team did in its first NCAA game against Maryland, at Dayton. We got behind at the start, 8–0, and did not take a time-out. I've always felt it's best for a team to work its own way out of a stretch of poor play—if possible. I'm not sure any coach in history has "saved" more time-outs than I have, in the interest of making my team more self-reliant. But my thoughts on that are a little different in tournament play, and 8–0 was getting pretty close to bringing a halt from even me. This team responded in exactly the way all those untaken time-outs of the past were intended to develop. We won 99–64 over a pretty good team.

Everybody we had played well in doing that, but Isiah had nineteen points, fourteen assists, and no turnovers. Jimmy Lynam of St. Joseph's called it a "time capsule" game. Lefty Driesell, the Maryland coach, said, "If they'd been playing the 76ers today, they'd have beaten the 76ers."

We beat Alabama–Birmingham (which had upset Kentucky) and St. Joseph's (which had beaten No. 1–ranked DePaul) in the regional at Assembly Hall to get to the Final Four, then played an outstanding second half to pull away from LSU in the semifinals, 68–49.

In the championship game, Isiah got a pass to Wittman for a basket at the halftime buzzer that gave us a 27–26 lead over North Carolina. Then he opened the second half with two steals and breakaway lay-ups that Dean Smith called "the turning point" and I don't think I'd argue. But we got outstanding play from a lot of guys—including Jimmy Thomas, who came off the bench to be, I'll bet, the first nonstarter ever to make All–Final Four.

Isiah won the Outstanding Player Award. When we were walking off the floor after the game, I told Jimmy Crews, "That's the last we'll ever see of Isiah Thomas at Indiana."

A few days after the tournament, Isiah announced that he was going to do what Magic Johnson had done two years before: turn pro as a sophomore after being on two Big Ten champions and an NCAA champion. I think he did the absolute right thing, and I thought so then, too, because I knew Mary Thomas would take care of the only possible objection I would have and make sure he finished the work to get a degree.

Kids by the dozens are making the decision to go pro early now, and people always ask about each one, "Is he ready?" Very few are.

But for damned sure, Isiah Thomas was ready to play in the NBA.

When I got home from Philadelphia on Tuesday, I already had a special congratulatory note from Tim Cohane, a former *New York World-Telegram and Sun* sportswriter who later was sports editor for *Look* magazine. Tim came up with the nickname "Seven Blocks of Granite" that made a Fordham line legendary, and he later recommended a member of that line, Vince Lombardi, to Colonel Blaik, the Army coach who hired him as an assistant. Tim authored Blaik's autobiography, *You Have to Pay the Price.*

In 1969, when I was at Army, Tim told me in a telephone conversation about the poem he had written and run in his newspaper after Clair Bee's Long Island team had won the second NIT, in 1939. It went:

> *Sing a song of set shots on the Garden floor.*
> *Five are plenty Blackbirds to roll up the score.*
> *The tournament is over, the Birds can sing with glee.*
> *Now, isn't that a tasty dish to set before the Bee?*

He knew how much I thought of Coach Bee, so he read it to me thirty years after he had used it his column. And I liked it so well I memorized it from that phone conversation.

Then, when I got back home after the 1981 championship, waiting for me was a new version from Tim:

> *Sing a song of defense on the Spectrum floor.*
> *Five are plenty Hoosiers to hold down the score.*
> *The tournament is over and the Tars were put to flight.*
> *Now, isn't that a tasty dish to set before the Knight?*

The envelope's postmark showed it was sent before we even played the game Monday night. That was confidence.

The player voted MVP in the Big Ten in 1981 was not Landon Turner nor even Isiah Thomas: it was Ray Tolbert, who also was a first-round NBA draft pick that year.

Ray came out of Phil Buck's program at Anderson Madison Heights, which also gave us Bobby Wilkerson and—a few years later—Winston Morgan and Stew Robinson.

Tolbert was different from all the others. Like them, he had a great enthusiasm to play, but this was matched by his affinity for knee pads, elbow pads, and wrist bands—anything else he could put on.

I eliminated that in his freshman year. He came out to start practice and I sent him back to the locker room to get rid of all that crap.

The summer before that, I went to the Indiana–Kentucky All-Star game at Indianapolis. Tolbert had been named Indiana's "Mr. Basketball," but he wasn't playing like the best player in the state—and his pouting and histrionics on-court certainly weren't looking like what even by then had been identified as "an Indiana player."

Mike Woodson was standing near me, and somebody in the stands yelled to him, "*Woodson! Woodson!* Tolbert won't last two *weeks* with you guys."

Mike just looked up at the guy, and didn't particularly disagree.

Actually, the same thing could have been said of another recruit we had in that game, Steve Risley. Risley went on to be one of those kids every outstanding team has to have—very unselfish, able to make great contributions in games, and happy to do so.

Tolbert, with all those extras, also had great enthusiasm and a tremendous desire to please. In the 1981 NCAA championship game against North Carolina, I took him out and just ripped him, "You don't need to score another point. If you'll just get in there and play your ass off on defense and rebound, we'll win." He sat there nodding his head, went back in, and made a great contribution to our win.

At one thing, Tolbert was the best inside player I've ever had, or ever seen—playing the high post in a delay game. He'd make one quick move, a dribble, and it was a dunk. Plus, he could shoot free-throws, and he could pass. He made ours the most effective delay game I ever had or ever remember anybody having.

The other two starters, Randy Wittman and Ted Kitchel, were sophomores and roommates who we had back to lead our next two teams to damned good seasons.

Wittman was one of the best players that I've ever coached. For a while, he seemed reluctant to shoot much—people in the stands yelled at him about that, and I'll admit I got a little exasperated a few times, because he was such an excellent shooter.

By the time he was a senior, he was shooting a lot and scoring twenty-two points a game. Before that he had played with very good scorers—Woodson starting out, then Thomas and Tolbert—and he just had a tremendous approach to team play. He felt his role was something other than trying to be a scorer. He was the epitome of an outstanding player who didn't need to shoot a lot.

He played more minutes than any player ever at Indiana. His freshman year we used him to handle the ball and play defense, and for a freshman who hadn't handled the ball much in high school, he did it at this level of competition as well as anybody I've ever seen. A lot of times I see where people pick all-time Indiana teams or all-time Bob Knight teams, and Randy Wittman is seldom mentioned. But Wittman was a *great* player. There wasn't anything he couldn't or wouldn't do—he was big (6-foot-6), could play guard, could defend, could shoot the ball, was smart, and didn't make mistakes. He wasn't going to get you beat by something he did, but you were going to win with things that he did. And he was a great kid, too.

One of the best stretches I've ever seen a college player have came when Randy was leading us to the Big Ten championship in 1983. With two weeks to go, we lost Kitchel to a back injury and after leading all season fell back into a tie for the lead with three games to go, all against teams that were in the race. Wittman wouldn't let us lose.

And neither would our fans. All three games were at home; we beat Illinois, Purdue, and Ohio State, and we won the league by two games. Assembly Hall has never been more passionate than it was in its roaring support for those kids who offset the loss of an All–Big Ten player and won a championship. That was the only Big Ten championship we hung a banner for at Assembly Hall—and it hung there for eighteen years in recognition not of the team but of the crowd.

I've heard that banner is no longer up. Whoever took it down had no idea of the role heart plays in sports. Whoever took it down surely couldn't have been there those three nights when a crowd worked as hard as a battered team did roaring down the stretch to the 1983 championship.

And the symbol of that team was Randy Wittman, who was everything I wanted in a player.

Ted Kitchel was slow, he didn't jump real well, and he was a starter on a national champion, on two Big Ten champions, and twice first-team All–Big Ten.

He also was a very tough kid, very smart offensively—and one of the best shooters we ever had. The difference between him and his five-year roommate Wittman was that Wittman had the same approach and intensity on the defensive end as he did on the offensive end. Scott May and Calbert Cheaney were other scorers who were very good defenders. But a lot of our great offensive players just weren't—Mike Woodson, Steve Alford, and a kid I had much later, A. J. Guyton, kids I liked a lot and who gave us some terrific things but at times were real liabilities defensively. Kitchel was in that group.

He played at a small high school, Lewis Cass, near Logansport. He scored points, but he didn't become a great shooter until college. He was not a primary scorer on the 1981 national-championship team, although against Illinois he had that team's biggest game—forty points. It was the most efficient forty I've ever seen anyone score. He took thirteen shots and hit eleven, and he set a Big Ten record by going 18-for-18 on free-throws.

The Big Ten adopted an experimental rule permitting the three-point shot in the 1982–83 season. I was the only guy who voted against it, because I honestly didn't think it was good for basketball. Even when I voted no, I looked around the table and thought, "I've got the two best three-point shooters in the league in Wittman and Kitchel—maybe the two best in college basketball." In a press conference after that meeting, I kind of casually mentioned, "I have two of the three best three-point shooters in this league." Of course writers asked me who the third guy was, as if I had just forgotten to say. I told them, "Oh, I don't think I want to talk about another coach's players."

I never went beyond that. And that whole year, a kid or two on just about every other team in the league came into our game trying to show me they were my third guy.

In our nonconference schedule, we never took a three-point shot. Not that we needed it. We were 10–0 and No. 1 in the country going into Big Ten play.

In our second conference game, at Illinois, we put Kitchel and Wittman on the sides against their zone and they shot like hell. Kitchel's three-point percentage that year, .656, is still the best ever in the Big Ten, and Wittman wasn't bad at .444. All those coaches who were so in favor of the experiment voted it out the next year, over my vote for it. We didn't have to look at three-point shots again until it became a national rule in 1986–87.

Prior to Landon Turner's injury, we had signed one of our most interesting recruits: Uwe Blab—pronounced *oo-vay blop* although it sure looks like *oo-wee blab* to me (wasn't it Mark Twain who said "Foreigners always do spell better than they pronounce"?).

Uwe was the biggest player ever at Indiana: 7-foot-2, 250 pounds. He was also the greenest. He grew up in West Germany and came to the United States after his club team played some American kids visiting over there. He played two years of high school basketball under an excellent coach, Jim Maxedon, at Effingham, Illinois, and then signed with us.

I thought it would be great for him to have a red-shirt season, going against a player as good as Landon Turner every day in practice, then ease into college play and maybe be pretty decent by his fourth and fifth years with us.

He didn't get that opportunity. After Landon's injury, we had to use Uwe right away, even though he had so much to learn to even begin to catch up with American players.

He was a good kid. Basketball was not an easy game for him, because he wasn't blessed with good hands. But he just worked his ass off. He tried—you had to like him because of the effort he put into what he was doing.

And what a bright kid he was—the first Indiana basketball player to make Phi Beta Kappa in thirty-two years.

We won a lot of games with Uwe, without having a great team. His freshman year, 1981–82, Minnesota won .the Big Ten championship and had the All–Big Ten center, Randy Breuer, who was even taller than Uwe. We beat that team at Minneapolis because freshman Uwe outscored Breuer, 18–9, and outrebounded him, 8–5. Then the next year, we won the conference championship and usually started five seniors. Breuer led the league in scoring and was a first-round NBA pick. A big reason why we beat Minnesota twice was the way Blab neutralized Breuer.

Uwe was a junior the night we beat No. 1 North Carolina in the 1984 NCAA tournament. He scored sixteen points, three more than Michael Jordan. How many kids, whatever their background, can say they ever did that in a big game?

He just gave us an awful lot. And, he took a lot—from me, even after he had graduated.

He and his wife were living back in Germany when they had their first child. His wife told me about it by telegram, and I sent one back to her, "Congratulations. That's great. Now, please, don't under any circumstances let your husband hold that child over anything but a soft bed."

Good hands or not, he left Indiana as three things people commonly forget:

- A first-round NBA draft pick (who played in the league for four years).
- A first-team All–Big Ten selection (and Academic All-American, and Phi Beta Kappa).
- The No. 10 career scorer in IU history, with 1,357 points.

He's No. 20 now, but he's still on that career scoring list ahead of a lot of guys who are justifiably considered great Indiana players.

Like Tom Abernethy at Michigan in 1973, Uwe earned his scholarship.

Considering the way things ended for me at Indiana, I naturally look back at times when I had opportunities to leave and didn't. There were several, most of which I didn't consider because I was happy where I was and felt a two-way loyalty, between me and the people I worked for.

Joe Dean, the athletic director at Louisiana State for about as long as I was the coach at Indiana, was a man I liked a lot and talked with fairly frequently. One time when he had an opening, he called and asked me to fill out a contract with whatever it would take for them to get me, and he would sign it. I had other opportunities almost like that, and several chances to coach in the pros.

In 1976, when we won our first NCAA championship, Tom Cousins owned 80 percent of the Atlanta Hawks. He knew I was going to speak at Georgia's basketball banquet, and he called to ask me to come to Atlanta early and spend some time with him. I went, and he talked to me about coaching the Atlanta Hawks.

My Indiana salary in 1976 was about $30,000—maybe not quite that much. Tom went with me to the banquet and I rode back to Atlanta with him. When the day was over, I had convinced him I didn't want to coach in the NBA and he had offered me the job of president and general manager of the team, with a salary of $100,000, a $25,000 expense account, and 10 percent ownership of the team, with an opportunity to buy an additional ten percent.

I couldn't just brush that offer aside, so I called Red Auerbach to get an idea of just what that ownership part would mean in dollar value. He said the most recent price tag on a franchise was six million dollars, for the New Orleans Jazz to enter the NBA. "You can figure ten percent of that is what your offer at Atlanta would be worth," he told me. That's six hundred thousand dollars, with a chance to buy another 10 percent. Today, 20-percent ownership of a franchise might be worth—thirty million? I thought about it but felt I wanted to coach some more. I called Tom, thanked him, and let it go at that.

On that same trip, I spoke at basketball banquets at Florida and Stetson—three in three nights.

I flew from Atlanta to Gainesville, where the people who had invited me asked me what they could do for me during the daytime, ahead of the banquet. They suggested golf or fishing. I told them this time I didn't want to do either. I wanted them to introduce me to Roger Maris.

Joe Wittmer, a Florida professor whose brother Hank is one of my greatest Indiana hunting friends, set this up. Roger lived outside Gainesville, and Joe got me his address and told him I was coming. I drove out, and I knew I was at the right place when I saw the mailbox. The name on it was SIRAM—Maris spelled backward. Roger Maris loved his privacy.

He was up on the house roof, doing some repairs, when I drove up. He came down, we went inside and drank iced tea. I told him how I used to go down from West Point to see him play with the Yankees—how I loved to watch him play right field, how I talked to people who considered him one of the best base-runners in the game, especially first to third. I didn't mention home runs. I think he noticed that and appreciated it.

We talked for a few hours, until I had to leave. He was a quiet guy but he had some great stories. He still has the national high school one-game record for touchdowns on kickoff returns—four, set in 1951 when he was playing for Shanley High School in Fargo, North Dakota. I told him, "If you're running back all those kickoffs, your team must have had a hell of a defense." We hit it off great.

The next day, I was to drive to Deland, Florida, for the Stetson banquet. Roger came in to have breakfast with me in Gainesville. We talked and talked— finally, well after noon, I had to break it off and head for Deland.

Two years later, we played in the Gator Bowl tournament at Jacksonville, which isn't far from Gainesville. I was in the locker room before our first game, and Maris walked in. He had a big group with him from the Budweiser distributorship he owned, and I really got on him—he had bought tickets for everybody, when if he had just let me know I'd have gotten them for him. He finally gave in and let me leave tickets for him for the second night. I always wanted to get him to a game in Bloomington, but it never worked out. He was just fifty-one when he died of cancer in December 1985. They started a charity golf tournament in Fargo in his memory, and his wife Pat invited me to play in the first tournament and be the speaker at the banquet.

The summer of 1981 was a traumatic one for me—the closest I came in my Indiana years to walking away and doing something else. I had an attractive and lucrative option: shortly after we had won the NCAA championship that year, CBS offered me a job.

NBC had carried the NCAA tournament through the 1981 tourney we won at Philadelphia, but CBS had won the rights to future tournaments. CBS was just starting to set up its coverage. I was offered a $125,000 salary to be the analyst for telecasts of a schedule of games prior to the tournament and to have responsibility for putting other announcers and analysts together for the season and the tournament. I gave it some thought and told them I wasn't inter-ested—one thing I eventually wanted to do was coach the Olympic team and I knew I had to stay in coaching to do that.

This was early June. Landon Turner's accident happened in late July and I concentrated fully on that. At the beginning of September, I got a call from CBS asking me to come to New York to talk with them again. By the time that day was over, they had offered me $260,000 and guaranteed me they could set up another $100,000 in speaking agreements. I would guess my salary at Indi-ana then was about $50,000.

This was happening at the one time I wasn't very happy with Ralph Floyd. I found out about raises the football staff got for going to the Holiday Bowl, when nothing had been given to my coaches after we won our second national championship—this at Indiana, an obvious basketball school. Ralph treated me like a son, but he was a football man, from the South. I'm sure he didn't think twice about the logic of that situation. I was upset enough to think about leaving, and CBS gave me a legitimate chance.

Dick Stoner, a Cummins Engine Company executive from Columbus, Indi-ana, and chairman of the IU Board of Trustees, was a man with a very pleasant manner, and a soft, reassuring way of dealing with things like that—just a very concerned and very honest guy. He sat down with me one evening at home, we went over that whole issue, and in one night got it all straightened out. He became not only a close friend but a man I respected as much as anyone I met at Indiana.

If CBS had come to me originally with the offer it eventually made, the out-come might have been different. All the big increase did then was irritate me, because I had told them when we started talking that I didn't want to negotiate and hassle—tell me the highest you can go, and let me make a decision. Here they were in September doubling, almost tripling their original offer, and I felt if they could do it then, they could have done it before.

Not then, nor with Tom Cousins and Atlanta, nor at any other time when somebody approached me about a job and there was a financial offer, did I ever go to the Indiana administration and say, "Here's what I've been offered. You're going to have to match it." Never. I had invitations to write my own contract at some of the great schools around the country, including three in the Big Ten. Once we got things started at Indiana, I just never gave much thought to coaching anywhere else.

Our first 1984 NCAA tournament game figured to be against Auburn, with Charles Barkley and Chuck Person. We drew a first-round bye, with a second-round match-up against the winner of a game between Auburn and Richmond. Dick Tarrant of Richmond was a hell of a coach—four years later his Richmond team beat us in the NCAA. He beat Auburn in '84, then we beat Richmond, and we were matched with No. 1 North Carolina in the regional at the Omni in Atlanta.

We won the game, 72–68. North Carolina did the one thing in that game that they couldn't do: they tried to trap us. Steve Alford was a freshman and in that game he shot thirteen times and scored twenty-seven points.

Rarely did they trap us successfully in the games that we played against them. Even when they beat us in the 1979–80 and 1980–81 seasons, if they trapped us ten times, we scored nine.

But in that 1984 game, it wasn't like those two games—we didn't have Isiah Thomas and Randy Wittman, and I think North Carolina underestimated what the kids we did have could do in terms of handling the ball. And we had some breaks. Late in the game Marty Simmons got trapped, the ball was jarred loose, it bounced on the floor three times, and we got a lay-up.

It's not our offense that Indiana people remember from that game, though.

They remember it as the game that made Dan Dakich famous.

We had played twenty-nine games, up to the North Carolina game. Dakich, who later became an assistant coach for me and now is the head coach at Bowling Green, had started just five times. But he got the start against North Carolina and the defensive assignment against Jordan.

There were only two things I thought we could do with Jordan: take away the backcut and keep him off the backboard. Dakich was about 6-foot-5—not very quick but a tough kid. I thought he was the best we had to do both of those things.

We knew Dakich wasn't going to be able to overplay Michael and keep him from getting the ball. So we underplayed him—backed off him and pretty much gave him the jump shot, which wasn't nearly the weapon then that it became for him. He did two things that just killed you—he was great going to the bucket without the ball, and he was a very, very good offensive rebounder. But not that night.

We told Dakich in the hotel the night before the game that he was going to guard Jordan. He told the press later his reaction was, "I went back to my room and threw up."

But he did an outstanding job. Jordan scored thirteen points. We won the game. And, overnight, Dan Dakich—for a game in which he scored four points—was a national star.

As the years went by, and Jordan got better and better and better, Dakich's renown grew right with him until now you can find people who damned near think of him as the Defensive Player of the Century—a tossup, Danny or Bill Russell.

I've never blamed my Last Game–Next Game theory for our regional finals loss to Virginia after beating North Carolina.

I think it was fatigue.

We didn't get done playing North Carolina until about 11:30 on Thursday night and we had to play again at noon on Saturday. I can remember taking our team into a hotel room to talk to them about Virginia at about two o'clock in the morning on Friday—after they had showered, gone back to the hotel, and eaten.

That's terrible scheduling; that's ignorant scheduling; that's totally inconsiderate scheduling; but that's the way the NCAA tournament was run even that long ago and still is—at the whims of television, with no consideration for the kids involved.

And still we came within a play or two of beating Virginia, which was really almost as much to our kids' credit as beating North Carolina.

Virginia played a zone defense almost the entire game against us, and we were a step behind everything. We weren't sharp against it. Steve Alford got only seven shots.

Danny Dakich lost the ball in a circumstance where he hardly ever would lose the ball—a point ahead, about thirty seconds to go. He was a smart player who knew what to do. I think we were a better team than Virginia, which made it a great win that I don't want to minimize for Virginia, but I also think our kids deserved a chance to play the game a little better rested.

Their reward for a remarkable victory was an equally remarkable lack of consideration by the NCAA's tournament planners, who still do things pretty much the same illogical way in the regional tournaments today, based on whatever television wants.

TEN: *Coaching the Olympic Team, and Michael Jordan* (1984)

*I thought we'd win. I thought we should win. I believed we had
to win. And I'll never have a greater honor.*

After I met Pete Newell for the first time in 1969, our friendship developed over the years to near father-son. Somewhere in there, Pete made it clear to me that he wanted me to coach the Olympic team someday.

So did Henry Iba, another coach whom I revered and who, along with Pete, to me embodied Olympic basketball. Henry inspired me with a simple description of what made coaching an Olympic team special: "When you're coaching your college team, you represent your community and your state. But when you coach the Olympic team, you're representing your country." That was powerful to me.

Besides making the Olympic coaching job a special goal for me, I'm sure Pete and Henry were as responsible as anyone when that goal was realized at a committee vote in May 1982.

From the moment I got the appointment to coach the 1984 Olympic team right through to the gold-medal game at Los Angeles August 10, 1984, there wasn't a day that passed without some aspect or detail of planning for the Olympics coming up in my mind.

The Olympics is a no-choice situation for an American basketball coach. You've got to win. For me, it was like the NCAA in 1976. I was just relieved when it was over and we won.

I thought we'd win. I thought we *should* win. I believed we *had* to win.

And I'll never have a greater honor.

In the spring of 1984, we brought seventy-four very good players, almost all of them college kids, to Bloomington for the Trials. I also asked a lot of college coaches to come for the week and work with us.

C. M. Newton, Don Donoher, and George Raveling were my assistant coaches. And we had some NBA people there who helped us—Wayne Embry, Pete Newell, Jerry Colangelo, and Stu Inman.

We met every morning and every night to discuss players—who had played well, who hadn't, and who we should look at and keep.

It was a nice cooperative effort among guys who were all competing against each other during the regular season, but now they were working together to make that team the best it could be.

We cut the original group to thirty-two players, then to twenty, to sixteen, and, finally, to the twelve who played for us at Los Angeles.

We wrapped up the first phase of the Trials by cutting to thirty-two on Friday, then playing the thirty-two on four eight-man teams in doubleheaders Saturday and Sunday nights at Assembly Hall. Those nights were great for all kinds of reasons. Assembly Hall was filled, and for the first time I think the kids got an idea of how enthusiastic the support was going to be for them from fans just like these across the United States. It was primarily our Indiana fans, of course, and they reacted to everything Steve Alford did. But they reacted to every good play, whichever player made it. It was a great climax to an extraordinary week of basketball for all of us. I always loved those Assembly Hall fans, but I was never prouder of them than those two nights because kids from all across the nation first got to know what it was like to be cheered for not as a player from their school but as an American.

We met as a selection committee after the game Sunday night and Monday morning we announced the cut to twenty. We gave those twenty a seventeen-day break before bringing them back for the next round of practice and eliminations.

The first time we were together as the official twelve-man team, I talked to the players about what was going to be important to us in the '84 Olympics.

I said, "You guys have to have a faith in us, that we're going to prepare you. If you don't think you're the best-prepared for a basketball game you've ever been, I want you to tell me about it, because we have to do something to make sure that you are.

"And we have to have a feeling about you twelve that you're going to do what we want done. There has to be a rapport between coaches and players—a feeling for one another, a combined effort toward an eventual goal that on the night of August 10 each one of you will be standing on a platform, with the national anthem being played, and a gold medal around your neck.

"That's what this is all about.

"I've got some things to ask you. I want to find out some things about you. We've got a lot of things we have to do to win a gold medal."

Doug Blubaugh, the Indiana wrestling coach at the time, won the 161-pound freestyle wrestling gold medal in 1960 at Rome, and he let me get a picture taken of his gold medal. That first day we had our players together as a team, I gave each of them a three-by-five photograph of it to show them what an Olympic gold medal looks like. I told them "I want this picture in your pocket, whatever you have on, wherever you go, until the real thing is yours."

I gave them an eight-by-ten copy of the same picture. "I want this over your bed wherever you sleep between now and then."

The night before we went into Los Angeles, we were in San Diego and I had Alex Groza speak to our team. Alex was an Ohio kid who played on the Kentucky teams that won NCAA championships in '48 and '49. As a result of the '48 championship, five Kentucky kids were selected to play on our Olympic team that won the gold medal in London in 1948. Then after their 1949 NCAA championship those five became the nucleus of the Indianapolis Olympians NBA team and, uniquely in NBA history, actually were part of the team's ownership. That all blew up when Alex and a man who was to become a very good friend of mine, the great guard Ralph Beard, were among the former Kentucky players who were banned from all basketball for life as a result of the 1951 gambling scandals. Ralph maintains—and I believe him—he had nothing to do with shaving points or in any way working with gamblers. He said money routinely was being passed around the Kentucky locker room then and the gamblers' money didn't seem unusual. He asked me point-blank once, looking me eye-to-eye, "Do you think I could ever play basketball any way but all-out?" No, I don't.

In 1984, Alex was living in San Diego, and he and C. M. Newton had played together at Kentucky. C. M. said he was going to bring Alex to practice one day, and I asked him to see if Groza might bring his gold medal along.

Alex did, and he had made his into a necklace for his wife. I'm sure I'll never forget Alex passing that gold medal/necklace around among our players, and each kid looking at it, and each kid thinking about what he was going to do with his gold medal. I could see it in their faces: each kid held it, and was reluctant to pass it on the next kid, but finally did, until all twelve of them had held that gold medal.

When the last one gave it back to Alex, I said, "How many of you have a thought as to what you want to do with your gold medal, and who you want to give it to?"

Each kid kind of smiled, and every one of them raised his hand.

Whatever it was each had in mind, he got a chance to do it. Because they did win the gold medal.

The first time I ever heard about Michael Jordan was late in the summer of 1981, before I was named the 1984 Olympic coach. My son Tim was a "gopher" at the National Sports Festival in Syracuse, and when he came home from that, he sat down with me and went through all the players he had seen.

The first thing he said was that a kid North Carolina had recruited would be the best player in the country. And he told me about him.

Not long after that, I called Dean Smith about something and in the conversation said, "By the way, how good is this kid Jordan?"

"I think he can be a very good player," Dean said.

I told him what Tim said, and his answer was, "I hope Tim is right."

Several years later when our selection committee was giving a final look at players we were going to invite to the World Games Trials, a name came up of a player none of us had seen. As committee chairman, I mentioned that my son Tim—as a manager for Tom Davis at Stanford—had seen the kid and mentioned he would be worth taking a look at. I wasn't sure how that was going to go over to the other guys on the committee, but Dean stepped right in and said, "I know about Tim, and if he says we should look at him, I'm for it."

When he was playing on the Olympic team, one of the things I told Jordan was, "Don't ever give it a thought when I get on you about something, particularly when you think it's undeserved. It may very well be.

"But you're going to be the leader on this team, you're the best player, so I'll expect more from you and demand more from you. But I'll also probably at times get on you when you don't deserve it. I'm simply giving everybody else a message."

He understood that.

As far as his own play was concerned, if it ever slipped off at all, the strongest thing I ever had to say to him was, "Mike, you're better than that."

The guy was amazing. Whatever was necessary to do, he could do. He always had another gear.

He didn't play much more than half the time in Olympic games, but when he was on the bench, he rooted like hell for the guys who were playing.

I don't think there's ever been anything like him, in any team sport. The closest to him was probably Babe Ruth, and then Jim Brown. I'll still always contend that Bill Russell was the most valuable player ever to play basketball, because he won eleven championships in thirteen years.

But the best player was Jordan. To me, there's no contest.

As good as I thought Jordan was from watching him on tape and playing against him, my opinion of him just kept going up as I watched him every day in practice with the Olympic team.

One of those days I was sitting up in the stands with Stu Inman. I love Stu—he's a great friend, and he's been a big help to me over the years, in a lot of ways.

The draft was coming up in a few days, and Stu's Portland team had the second pick. Everybody knew the Houston Rockets were going to take Akeem Olajuwon of Houston with the first pick. With the second pick, Stu told me they were leaning toward taking Sam Bowie of Kentucky.

"Stu," I said, "you've *got* to take Jordan."

"Bob, we need a center."

"Well, play *him* at center. Nobody could guard him. He's the best player there is. You *have* to take him."

The kids were in Bloomington the day of the draft. Portland took Bowie. Chicago, which in truth was disappointed because it didn't get one of the two centers, settled for taking Jordan third.

Our objective was clearly the gold medal, and the experience of representing our country in the Olympic Games was the biggest memory I'm sure our players took away from that summer.

But I do think they had some other great memories—one, certainly, the pressure and yet the exhilaration of that week of Trials, all those excellent players together, competing for what then was a once-in-a-lifetime chance.

And I'm sure they also remember—as I certainly do—the summer of preparation that included a cross-country exhibition tour against NBA All-Stars who gave up summer vacation time to help us get ready, and fans at every place we played, waving flags, and letting us know we had a whole country behind us.

The pros were a terrific help. The NBA Players Association sponsored the teams that we played against, and we split the money from the games we played at big arenas across the country. We made over three million dollars for the Olympic effort with that basketball team.

In some of those nine games, we played against seven or eight players who had been in the NBA All-Star game. And guys like John Havlicek, Pat Riley,

Billy Cunningham, Kevin Loughery, Jimmy Lynam, Lennie Wilkens, Don Nelson, and Oscar Robertson coached.

We set it up so the pros had unlimited time-outs and nobody could foul out. Our team played exactly the way the Olympic games would be played—international time-out, all foul rules in effect.

I also asked the pro teams to do some things for us—play a little zone, press us, bang us around a little bit.

Our opening game was against a team of our former Indiana players at Assembly Hall. That was a great night for Indiana fans (they filled Assembly Hall, again), and a great one for me (thirty-five alumni players came back and seventeen played—including Tom and Dick Van Arsdale, who were then forty-one years old. Mike Woodson, Ray Tolbert, Kent Benson, Isiah Thomas, and Randy Wittman were the starters, and Quinn Buckner and Scott May, from the 1976 Olympic team, suited up and played. Buckner's Celtics team had won the NBA championship just eight days before he played on the team in Bloomington. He was the captain of Dean Smith's '76 Olympic team, and he told our '84 kids how he had felt eight years before.

> *I wanted to play on the Olympic team more than I wanted to play professional basketball. After being out of the country, having been to Eastern bloc countries, I really wanted to play in the Olympics. I know it sounds corny; people razz you about it. But there's nothing like representing America. When the opportunity's there, you've got to savor it. It is that special.*

The last eight exhibition games were against players supplied by Larry Fleisher and the players' association—at Providence, Minneapolis, Iowa City, Indianapolis (the Hoosier Dome game that drew 67,596, the biggest crowd ever to see a basketball game in the United States), Greensboro, Milwaukee, Phoenix, and San Diego.

John Havlicek was the NBA players' coach for the leadoff game in Providence. I told him, "Play some two-three zone against us. Give us a chance to work against that."

In the first three minutes, they were in zone one possession and I never saw it again.

He and I went out to eat afterward, and I said, "Where in the hell was the zone defense?"

He said, "Aw, at that first time-out, they told me they didn't want to play it anymore."

I said, "Damn. You're a *hell* of a coach. What if they had told you they didn't want to play at all?"

When we played the game in Indianapolis, Buckner was joined by three other players from that championship Celtics team—Larry Bird, Kevin McHale, and Robert Parish. A few nights before, we had a banquet in Indianapolis that brought in $150,000 for the Olympic fund. Oscar Robertson came back to his hometown for that one and told an Olympic story I hadn't heard. The night Pete Newell's 1960 team beat the Russians in Rome for the gold medal, Oscar said, "I had a little bet with Jerry West on who would get the Olympic basketball. I got it, and I've still got it."

The game was the first event in the new Hoosier Dome and it gave our kids a look at Bird, who had just won the NBA's Most Valuable Player award for the first time. At that point in his career, I'm sure even Jordan got a big kick out of going against him. Bird played twenty-six minutes and scored fourteen points; Michael that night played twenty-one minutes and scored twelve. Buckner, Isiah, Wittman, and Woodson were active NBA players from our program who played in the game.

What an unforgettably nice night that was—red, white, and blue all over that huge place and the fans warm and enthusiastic.

All nine exhibition games combined to make it a wonderful, patriotic send-off for our kids and the people who turned out. And the pros were unfailingly great. They played hard, and they worked to get us prepared to play. Several played in more than one game.

Isiah Thomas played in three. In Phoenix, he took the ball out in front of our bench and when he was looking away, I jumped onto the court and started guarding him. The look on his face when he looked back was priceless.

We won all eight games against the pros. The first four games I wasn't particularly playing to win. I changed lineups every five minutes and played everybody about the same amount of time. One of those games, in Minneapolis, we won by four points. The only other time they came close to beating us was in our last preparation game in San Diego, just before we went in to Los Angeles. We won that one by five points.

Gold medal night, when we were getting ready to go to the court to play Spain, I did as I always do—met with the team in the locker room to go over the final points I wanted to make.

I had put the things that were important to us defensively on one side of a blackboard, and the offensive things we were stressing were written on the other side of the board.

The players were already seated when I came in to talk to them. When I turned to face the board, I saw that right in the middle of it was a big yellow piece of paper off a legal pad. It said:

> Coach: Don't worry. We've put up with too much shit to lose now.

I still have that paper.

And I don't have any doubt about its author. By then, I knew what Michael Jordan's handwriting looked like.

I looked at that note, and everybody was watching. Michael had his head down, but he couldn't resist looking to see what I was going to do.

All I said was, "Okay, let's go play."

As we were walking out, I told Don Donoher and C. M. Newton, "This game is going to be over in five minutes." It was. We won, 96–65.

Donoher already had won a battle before we even went out to the court. Jordan, of all people, had forgotten his shoes. A cop took Don back to Olympic Village to get the shoes and bring them back.

We also had our uniforms screwed up. Six guys showed up with blue warm-up jackets and six with red. So we went out there with six of each; red, white, and blue all over the place—it looked like we had planned it.

As the championship game played out, I was sitting on the bench beside C. M. Newton (the initials are for Charles Martin and he was always Charles to me). I said, "Charles, look at the clock." He looked up at the scoreboard over the court and said, "That score is great, isn't it?" I said, "Naw, that's not what you're looking at the clock for. You and I have sixty-one seconds of international basketball left and then we're done with it."

Anyway, it was the end of international basketball for me. C. M., a great basketball coach, went on after the '84 Olympics to become for years the leading college representative in America's international basketball. And even he, as respected and influential as he rightfully was, couldn't keep it pure, once the NBA saw its marketing potential.

C. M. was involved in another of my favorite Olympic memories.

Wayman Tisdale, who played for Oklahoma against our 1983 Indiana team in the NCAA tournament at Evansville, was just a great kid to have around—a million-dollar smile, full of effort and enthusiasm. He wasn't used to my kind of criticism. He told an interviewer somewhere that when he got home from the Olympics, he was going to look up who he had always thought was the biggest, meanest guy in town, and give him a hug. And I'll bet he said it with a big, wide grin.

Wayman didn't always share my feeling about the importance of things like blocking out on rebounds, so in practice I was continually pointing out how much I wanted him to try doing things my way—pointing it out loudly, sometimes. In one of our games at Los Angeles, it happened again, and I wasn't happy. The blockout he missed led to a follow-in basket and a foul, three giveaway points, and while the teams were lining up for the free-throw, I shouted, "Wayman! Get over here!"

Everybody on our bench, probably everybody in the arena, knew Wayman was going to get an earful. But when he got there, he put one of his big bearlike arms around my shoulder, smiled down at me, and said, "Yeah, Coach?"

I just looked at him for a second, and finally said: "Wayman . . . you've got to block out." And I whacked him on the ass and sent him back out.

I turned around, sat down, and Newton whispered into my ear, "Just couldn't pull the trigger on ol' Wayman, could you."

Newton and I tried to work in as much tennis as we could, during our weeks in Bloomington. We were fairly even, until I ran into a stretch where I couldn't beat him at all.

One of those days, I hit a ball I knew was going to go out and threw my racquet in that direction. Very quickly and solemnly, C.M. declared, "The ball's out. The racquet's in."

When Andy Andreas was an assistant coach with me in the late '70s, he and I used to play as doubles partners. John Flynn of the Louisville paper watched us play and wrote that if we could have made all the line calls, as double partners we could have beaten Björn Borg and John McEnroe.

I'm sure it was a thrill for Don Donoher to be part of an Olympic gold-medal team, but he wasn't any happier about it than I was—for him. Of all the people I enjoyed and liked in coaching, nobody was ahead of Donoher.

I first saw one of his Dayton teams play when I was the freshman coach at West Point and I scouted them in the Kentucky tournament. He had big Henry Finkle, and the first thought I had of Don's coaching ability was what a great job he did using Finkle. I remember how hard I rooted for him when he had Donnie May and they played UCLA in the 1967 NCAA finals in Louisville. Seven years later in the West regional, they took one of the best UCLA teams into triple overtime.

I made sure I had Don with us all the way through the Olympic program, and during that period, I did more things with him than anybody. The two of us went to Paris in the summer of 1983 to scout the European Championships. We took a great side-trip. We went to Bastogne, where at an American low point during the Battle of the Bulge in World War II, the embattled U.S. general, Anthony McAuliffe, answered a German surrender demand with just one historic word—"Nuts!" The first thing we saw in Bastogne was an American tank in the middle of the town square. We walked up to the tank, turned around, and each of us at the same time saw a restaurant on the corner of the square. It had a red, white, and blue sign and it was called the Café McAuliffe. We looked at each other, didn't say a word, and walked straight to it.

From there, we drove across northern France into Normandy, where we spent a whole day walking the British beaches and the American beaches.

In France, we also went to the cathedral in Rheims, cool in the summer and warm in the winter because of how thick the walls were; with all the allied bombing, it was left standing intact. And it was at Rheims that Germany surrendered unconditionally in 1945.

I'm not sure which of us enjoyed all that history more.

During that trip and the whole Olympic experience, as we had as long as we knew each other, Don and I talked a lot about basketball, and how it should be played. In the years after he no longer coached, he came over to Bloomington many times. He was a tremendous asset on the Olympic team, and I've never had a better friend.

I've followed all those Olympic kids ever since that summer. We had a practice at Madison Square Garden when my Indiana team played in the Pre-Season NIT in December 1996. We came onto the court after the Knicks and Patrick Ewing finished their workout. Patrick was leaving the court when he saw me coming in from across the court. He came over to me with an unforgettable grin and grabbed me in a bear hug. We talked a few minutes, and he couldn't have been nicer. That was neat.

Every one of those Olympic kids played in the NBA, and many of them, like Patrick, went on to become great stars, some of them, like Patrick, sure Hall-of-Famers.

And I was tickled to see one of our guards, Leon Wood of Cal State–Fullerton, make it back to the NBA as an official after his playing days.

I'm not sure I want to admit helping to create a basketball official, but I may have. I was probably the first guy to put a rule book in his hands.

At one of our practices, I didn't think Leon—a great passer who had led the nation in assists—was aggressive enough going after a loose ball. I decided to put a little humor to work.

At our meeting the next morning, I gave Leon an international rule book and told him, "Leon, tonight when we have our meeting, I want you to show me the rule that the guy wearing number five doesn't have to chase loose balls."

Please, God, don't let that be what pointed him toward a life of officiating.

I've always been a huge, huge fan of Jerry West—I like the guy as a person, and I had a great respect for the way he went about playing. If there's one guy I would put with Jordan as a guy I loved to watch play basketball it would be Jerry West, because he played every facet of the game. He played defense, he rebounded, he was what I thought a basketball player should be.

In 1984, when he was the general manager of the Lakers, he was asked to compare his 1960 team and our 1984 team and he said, "You have to keep in mind, it's the same guy coaching both teams."

He talked about how close Pete Newell and I were, and how much we thought alike. I considered it a great compliment.

He went on to talk about their team—guys like Oscar Robertson and Jerry Lucas—and said, "They went on to be great players. Obviously, these guys haven't had a chance to do that." At that time, nobody knew how good Jordan was.

West talked about the two starting lineups, and the depth—indicating maybe his team had an edge in starters and we had an edge in depth. But all in all he felt a game between the two would have been great.

I agree with that—a *great* game.

I saw the 1960 Olympic team play an exhibition game in Canton, Ohio, against the Akron Goodyear AAU team. Joe Roberts, from our 1960 NCAA championship team, played with Akron.

I went to the Goodyear locker room afterward to see Joe, then to the Olympic team's locker room to talk to Lucas—and walked right in, with no problem.

Times certainly have changed for games like that. I bought my ticket to the game that night, with no problem, and the arena didn't hold six thousand.

Four years before that, the 1956 Olympic team with Bill Russell trained at Bunker Hill Air Force Base near Peru, Indiana. Bob Hammel was at the Huntington newspaper then, about forty miles away, and Bruce Drake, the Oklahoma coach who was running the team, was so eager to get his team some kind of competition before it left for Melbourne that Drake accepted a suggestion by Hammel and brought the team to Huntington to play some former area high school players and coaches in a gym that didn't hold quite four thousand. Bob still has a letter from an Olympic official thanking him for the event and the check that the game produced for the Olympic fund—after expenses, and a split with the local March of Dimes, about $167. For a game involving Bill Russell!

By contrast, I'd say our team netted three million dollars for the Olympic fund. We had the three games in Bloomington—fifty thousand people at ten dollars a ticket, all of it going to the Olympics. We had the dinner in Indianapolis that netted $150,000. We had the 67,000 crowd at the Hoosier Dome—the average ticket there was probably fifteen to twenty dollars, so that was nearly a million-dollar gate. Out of Indiana alone we had to net more than a million and a half, and the rest came from the eight-game tour. I did a lot of the organizing for all those things. I'm pretty good at that, and I think over the years, that's been proven. That's why in 1981 I had an inclusion in my contract that gave me total control of the basketball program, because I quite frankly didn't think I needed any help, nor did I want any interference. Indiana University made a lot of money from basketball.

The eight-game tour with the pros came out of an agreement between USA Basketball and the NBA Players Association—not the NBA itself, but the players' organization, which had Larry Fleisher as its attorney.

Brice Durbin, who represented the high schools in ABA/USA Basketball and was its president at that time, went with me to see Fleisher at his office in New York. I had known Larry through John Havlicek and I liked and respected him. I called him "The Mogul."

Brice and I had gone to the NBA offices in Manhattan, where we were supposed to meet Larry at ten o'clock. He didn't show up. I got him on the telephone and said, "Okay, Mogul, the mountain is coming to Mohammed." Brice and I got in a cab, went over to Larry's office, and in ten minutes we worked out the whole thing.

He hadn't gone to the NBA office because he was working a power play to get the NBA out of it. He wanted it between the Olympic basketball team and the players' association. That was fine with me. And it couldn't have worked out better.

The tour showed our kids how basketball fans everywhere were rooting for them. What came across to them was how happy they were to see the team, how hard they were rooting for us, and, "Let's bring the gold back to the United States!"

There was a concerted, across-the-board effort to root for and support that team. And the support started in the ABA/USA office, where the executive director, Bill Wall, and his assistants, Tom McGrath and Becky Roberts, couldn't have done a better job.

• • •

A lot was made out of the fact that the Russians weren't coming to Los Angeles, as a response to our 1980 boycott of the Moscow Games. President Jimmy Carter pretty much ordered an Olympic boycott in protest of the Soviet Union's invasion of Afghanistan. I thought the boycott was a real mistake. The greatest ambassadors for what America is all about are kids competing hard and fairly with kids from other countries. I think that was a tremendous error.

Right up to the 1984 Olympic deadline, I thought the Russians might come, and I was hoping they would. The United States and the Soviet Union hadn't met in an Olympic basketball game since 1972 in Munich. In 1976, Yugoslavia beat the Russians in a semifinal game so Dean Smith's team played Yugoslavia, not the Russians, for the gold. The next chance would have been in 1980 at Moscow, where Yugoslavia won the gold medal, the Soviets finished third, and we were absent. Now in 1984, another chance got away.

But I'll absolutely guarantee you the Soviet boycott didn't make one bit of difference in where the 1984 gold medal went.

In the two years after I was named coach I spent a lot of my summers traveling to Europe to see the international teams play. I had seen the Russians a lot. They were not the best team in Europe anymore. Spain's record in its last ten games with the Russians leading up to Los Angeles was 5–5. I had been a close friend of the Spanish coach, Antonio Diaz-Miguel, for nearly twenty years—I deeply respected him and I was very pleased when he went into the Basketball Hall of Fame. But I knew we could beat Spain soundly. At Los Angeles we beat them twice by more than thirty points, one of those times in the gold medal game.

The same thing would have happened if we had played the Russians. In 1984, they were slow. They couldn't guard anybody. It was going to be no different from our playing anybody else there.

Our closest game at Los Angeles was an eleven-point win over Germany. I saw that referred to as a dropoff in our play, because of the margin. It was nowhere close to an eleven-point game; we had them down by twenty-four, it was our last game before the medal round, and I rested some guys, most notably Jordan. Had we wanted to, we could have damned-near named the score against anybody we played.

From the time they came together as a team, those kids worked hard and had to sacrifice. It wasn't a pleasure cruise that they were on, getting ready for Los Angeles. I sure didn't want to lose the gold medal in basketball. I told our players, "We invented the damned game. Let's show them how it should be played." And, boy, they did.

Over the whole course of the games we played—the exhibition games and the games we played at Los Angeles out there—there were very few minutes when they weren't a great team.

Some outstanding people came to Bloomington or to Los Angeles to talk to the players. All did extremely well.

Bob Skoronski was one of the speakers, and I went through him to get Willie Davis to do it. In the Green Bay Packers' run of championships under Vince Lombardi, Willie was the defensive captain, and the offense's captain was Bob. Those two have remained close through the thirty-plus years since they were football teammates. Willie lives in Los Angeles, and he came out twice to talk to our team. The second was the day we played for the gold medal.

He didn't talk long, at most ten minutes, but he said, "You're going to play forty minutes tonight, and it will be forty minutes that you remember the rest of your life. This is not an ordinary game. This is not a game you will ever have trouble recalling. These forty minutes will stick with you forever, and you owe it to yourself to play the best forty minutes of basketball that you've ever played."

I thought that was a great approach. It would have made Vince Lombardi proud.

Johnny Bench was another great athlete who spent time with the team. He was retired then, and he came over from Cincinnati to Bloomington, then spent a week with us at San Diego. I knew what I was getting there. John had talked to my Indiana teams and always had our kids on the edge of their seats.

During our week at San Diego just before going to Los Angeles for the Games, we had a morning workout, and just before we went to lunch, John came out on the floor to talk to the team.

I introduced him as an example of defensive play—that he had played the most important field position in baseball better than anyone who had ever played it, and in being that good and working that hard at it, he was the cornerstone to the Reds' great years. And I said, "Without any reservation, I think this guy was the best ever at what he did."

It had been a tough morning, and I had been on them pretty hard. John said, "Remember what Coach said about my defense? Let me tell you another approach to defense. You just outscore that guy. If he scores twenty, the hell with him, you score thirty. That's defense."

They were all apprehensive, sneaking glances at me. He just kept going.

"Like you, Wayman. Don't worry about this defensive stuff. You're going to outscore guys. In fact, I'm going to bring in an offense tomorrow . . ."

I cut in, "Keep one thing in mind as you're listening to all this bullshit: Sometimes guys retire because of senility." And I just walked away.

But he carried the day. The kids loved it.

Bench is very smart. After a hard practice, he sensed that those guys needed something I wasn't going to give them. He stuck a needle in me and it worked great.

Bench had been an outstanding high school basketball player at Binger, Oklahoma, not too far from where Henry Iba was coaching at Oklahoma State. And Henry knew about him as a basketball player, but John signed in baseball right out of high school. He was the Reds' starting catcher when he was nineteen.

John told Henry, "Coach, I could have played for you."

"No, Coach," I said, "that son of a bitch would have shot too much."

That thought hadn't even occurred to Henry. "I'd have gotten that out of him in a hell of a hurry," he said.

Bench, Hank Egan, C. M. Newton, and I played golf one day at San Diego. I got to know Hank when he was coaching at the Air Force Academy. He's a hell of a basketball coach and right up there with Don Donoher, Bob Boyd, Joe Cipriano, Johnny Orr, Digger Phelps—people in coaching I was closest to. Hank was a good golfer. On the first tee, Bench unloaded on a drive—at least three hundred yards.

Hank said, "Man, you just knocked the hell out of that. That was a *great* drive."

Bench looked at him and said, "What the hell did you expect, Hank—popups? I hit damned near four hundred home runs."

John broke the major league record for home runs by a catcher, but he told me in high school and American Legion baseball he hit only eight or nine homers.

I'll give you my favorite Bench stat: in all of his major league postseason play, John stole more bases than were stolen against him.

I'm not sure even he knows that.

Red Auerbach came out and spent a day with us. He walked around and talked to the players. Then, just before he talked to them as a team, he reached in his pocket, pulled out a cigar, and lit it.

Theatrics at its best.

Red and Vince Lombardi—and I guess maybe Knute Rockne—had to be sports' all-time best motivators.

• • •

Bill Bradley—then a New Jersey senator and a national political figure—was at the Democratic national convention in San Francisco when we were at San Diego. He flew down and spent one whole day with the team—with no publicity at all. How many guys involved with politics would ever do that? People remember Bradley the basketball player as a great one for Princeton and the New York Knicks, but he was also an outstanding player for Henry Iba on the 1964 Olympic team. He talked to our kids about what they should get out of the Olympics beyond playing games.

I always liked Bradley. I had known him in kind of a peripheral way over the years and had always admired him. But his willingness to do that for these kids, particularly in the midst of the national convention—I thought that defined him as a person at least as much as any of his great accomplishments did.

My Army teams never played against Princeton and Bradley, but I certainly saw a lot of him and felt he was a great college player—a very effective professional player, but a truly great college player. He was not richly endowed athletically. He wasn't a great jumper, he didn't have blinding quickness—but he had gifts similar to Larry Bird: great hand-eye coordination, great hands. And he understood how to play the game as well as anyone ever.

Watching Bradley play in college was one of the reasons why, as long as I've coached, whenever I've had guys who could score, they've scored. And I've wanted the other guys on my teams to understand part of their job was to make that happen.

That applied to the Olympic team.

During a time-out at one of our pre-Olympics games with the pros, I asked our players, "Hey, what the hell does Jordan do to you guys in practice when you have to play him one-on-one? Somebody tell me what it's like."

One of them said, "Well, it's hard. It's tough. He tears us up."

"Then," I said, "do you think there's any chance we could see that he gets the ball a little bit tonight, because he's going to do the same thing to these guys that he does to you."

I know at least one guy heard me. Vern Fleming, who played at Georgia and then for a long time with the Indiana Pacers, told that story when I was at a Pacer practice in Indianapolis in 2001—seventeen years later.

As good and as fair as I thought the selection process was, there were, of course, disappointments. Big disappointments—Olympian. Some guys with very high dreams, including some who turned out to be outstanding NBA players, were dropped in the early cuts. And I knew how those kids felt.

I was keenly disappointed when I wasn't selected to coach the Olympic team in 1980, although I felt good about and for the man who was picked, Dave Gavitt.

The selection was made far enough ahead of the '80 Games that I was given the 1979 Pan American Games team as a sort of runner-up prize. I certainly felt honored with that. Any opportunity to take an American team into international competition is a tremendous honor.

Still, at the time I felt a personal disappointment about missing out on the Olympics.

The net effect was that, had I been selected in that boycott year, I would never have had the opportunity to coach in the Olympics. Gavitt coached a team that played a series of games with NBA All-Star teams—Isiah Thomas from our Indiana team was on it, and he played well. But it obviously wasn't like playing in the Olympics for a gold medal. I felt bad for Dave and Isiah— and additionally for Isiah in 1992 when, for whatever political reason, the best player his size ever to play the game was left off what was called the "Dream Team." There were a lot of great reasons to call it that, but it was one "Dream" short of what it should have been.

One of the players we cut in 1984 when we dropped from thirty-two to twenty was Karl Malone, who has been such a great NBA player he could look back now and be bitter or say he was robbed. The two of us never had any kind of contact after he left camp on the Sunday morning when we made the cut from thirty-two to twenty.

Then, after seventeen years, I heard from him, at a time when I deeply appreciated it. Of all the great telephone calls I got just after the things that happened to me at Indiana, none was nicer than one that came out of the blue from Karl.

He said he just wanted me to know that, while he didn't make the Olympic team, he felt that week at the Trials was where he learned what work ethic was all about and what it was going to take for him to play basketball at the highest level. Karl Malone, twice the Most Valuable Player in the NBA, sure Hall-of-Famer, was the opposite of bitter—very appreciative for getting the chance to be there.

John Stockton, Malone's teammate for so many years at Utah, certainly could have made the team. He had an excellent week at the Trials. As a college player, he was not a very good shooter. He was a tough kid, he moved the ball well, but as the Trials advanced it was clear we had more tough kids who moved the ball well than we did shooters, and with the zone defenses we knew we'd run into we strongly felt that we needed some. Steve Alford was the best shooter we had, and Chris Mullin and Sam Perkins were the two next-best.

We didn't feel at that point anyone was better with the ball than Leon Wood, who made the team. It was tight, picking among the guards. We kept Johnny Dawkins until the last cut, and one of the reasons beyond how well he played was that he was a good kid who had another year of eligibility left and we thought the experience would help him. Terry Porter, who had played for Dick Bennett at Wisconsin–Stevens Point, was another unheralded kid who had a great trials. Porter was very close to making the team, but he got sick and missed some time. For both Porter and Stockton, the Olympic trials was a perfect showcase and had a lot to do with their getting the opportunity for the pro careers they eventually enjoyed, because it gave them such a chance to be noticed and evaluated by professional scouts.

It's tough to tell any kid he's not going to make it. Every kid is hoping he has a chance. At least in the early eliminations, some kids see they're not going to make it. But when you cut to thirty-two, there are always some kids who think they should be in there. And when you keep twenty, then sixteen, then twelve—at each level, there are always some kids who were cut and thought they shouldn't have been. Some of them were very close. The one who was left out that I second-guess myself the most about was Tim McCormick of Michigan.

Another great pro player dropped at the same time as Stockton was Charles Barkley.

Nobody wanted Barkley on that team more than I did because I thought he would be very, very hard for people to play against. If anything, he was more of a hit than Michael Jordan with some of the people watching the opening days of the Trials.

When we weighed him in at the start of the Trials, he weighed 283 pounds. After a week, he had dropped to 274. He was among the twenty we picked to bring back in seventeen days for the next round of eliminations. I told him in those seventeen days, I wanted him to lose nine pounds, or half a pound a day, and get down to 265.

I was trying to do both of us a favor. He hadn't officially announced for the draft yet, but it was pretty well known that he was likely to do that and pass up his last year at Auburn. He did announce his decision, in fact, during those seventeen days, and—especially after his play in the Trials—he was sure to be one of the top draft picks. "You can't play in the NBA at any more than 250 pounds," I told him. "You just can't be quick enough. You're not going to be able to get off your feet with all that weight."

His career proved me right. He played most of his NBA years between 245 and 250, and of course he was a great player. And, weight that he put on in retirement was the main concern that came up when he and Michael Jordan were working toward a possible comeback the summer of 2001. Jordan came back, Barkley didn't, and I saw where Barkley said with all that work, "Michael got in shape, and I got tired."

In that seventeen-day period between practices with us in 1984, instead of losing nine pounds he gained eleven. I don't think he was excited about playing on the Olympic team. I think pro basketball was on his mind, not Olympic basketball—he was eager to sign and start making big money. (Rules then said our Olympic kids could be drafted and could even sign, but they couldn't draw any pay until after the games.) All I know is he certainly didn't seem broken-hearted when he was cut, maybe not as much so as I was. I love to have tough kids who can play on my team.

For the next eight years, stories kept coming out about how irritated he was about being cut in '84. I don't think that was all Barkley, by any means. I think the press kept that thing alive by regularly pushing him for an answer on why he didn't make the team—as if I were blind to how good he was and by cutting him had to be not just a bad guy, but a pretty dumb guy as well.

His attitude toward playing in the Olympics was altogether different in 1992 when they came up with the "Dream Team" concept and went to Barcelona with our first professional Olympic team. He wanted on that team, and he was justifiably proud to be part of it. And I was pleased that he started talking realistically then—that the way things went he shouldn't have made the '84 Olympic team. One of the people he discussed that with was C. M. Newton, and I'm sure he knew that C. M. and I were so close it inevitably would get back to me. But I also did see it other places and I appreciated it. I'm glad we didn't need him to get our gold in 1984, and I'm glad he got his later.

The search for story angles leads writers in all kinds of directions. They used to constantly ask Michael Jordan for the difference between Dean Smith and myself. He always had great answers. One time he said Dean Smith was the master of the four-corner offense and I was the master of the four-letter word.

But he would always say that we had the same end in what we were trying to do. Michael and I even discussed this, and I felt, as he did, that the press didn't care who he spoke negatively about—Dean or myself—just so it was one of us. They could then write about that, how Jordan was upset with Dean or upset with me. He was just far too smart to let that happen.

At Michael's first retirement celebration in Chicago, his friend Ahmad Rashad was the emcee. Dean and I were both on the stage, and Rashad asked a question about Michael's scoring average in college. I knew where he was headed with that. I had heard the line that I think originated with the press in the ACC area, "The only man alive who could hold Michael Jordan under twenty points a game is Dean Smith." I thought at the time the Rashad question may have been aimed at Dean, but I answered it, a little bit coldly, "There are a lot of NBA general managers who would love to have a player with Jordan's skills beyond scoring—rebounding, playing defense, passing the ball, running the floor—all of which he was taught to do extremely well at North Carolina."

It was being televised, and a commercial break came right after that. Dean and I left the stage to go sit down, and Rashad—who I don't think meant any harm—turned to Jordan and said, "I didn't mean to irritate Coach Knight." Jordan just said, "I told you not to ask that question."

Dean and I have been good friends for well over thirty years, and I have great respect for the basketball program he had at North Carolina. I think he always felt the same way about what we were doing. Players from the two teams have gotten along very well. They've been on Olympic teams together, Pan American teams together, and they have an understanding of what basketball at each of their schools has meant to them and a lot of other people.

I've said that Pete Newell wanted me to coach the Olympic team someday.

His coach at Loyola University of Los Angeles when he was playing in the '30s was Jimmy Needles, who was the first U.S. Olympic coach in 1936. Pete has told me several times that Needles was a great influence on Pete's own coaching.

Twenty-four years after Jimmy Needles, Pete Newell was the Olympic coach.

And twenty-four years after Pete Newell, I—influenced so much by Pete—was the coach.

The man I felt the best for in that whole 1984 Olympic experience was Henry Iba.

He was the only three-time U.S. Olympic basketball coach. He won with his 1964 and 1968 teams at Tokyo and Mexico City and should have won with his

1972 team at Munich. The handling of the final seconds of the '72 gold-medal game with the Soviet Union was just plain wrong, and a one-point victory for us turned into a one-point loss. It was the toughest loss of Coach Iba's career. I'm not sure anybody else could have handled it as well as he did.

That was his last time as the Olympic coach, but in 1984 he was with us the whole way.

He came to the Trials in Bloomington. Each time we brought the kids back, he was there. When we went on all the exhibition-game trips, he was with us. And when we went to Los Angeles, he was as much a part of our traveling party as I or anybody else. He celebrated his eightieth birthday with us at Los Angeles, during the Olympics.

Henry had been a golfer at one time, but he had given it up by 1984. Still, he went to the university course with us one afternoon and rode in a cart with Fred Taylor, and Don Donoher and I were in another. Henry rarely went anywhere without wearing a tie. I got all over him before we went out this time and all but ordered him to wear one of our Olympic golf shirts. Reluctantly he did, but I kept needling him—to the point that one time their cart went by us and, without looking back, Henry Iba raised his middle finger, just for me. Donoher erupted in laughter. "Don't you feel proud," he said. "The classiest man in history just gave you the finger."

Don Donoher belongs in any ranking of "the classiest men" in basketball. And Don's hometown, Dayton, Ohio, had two of my favorite sportswriters: Si Burick and Ritter Collett, both of them dead now. Si truly was one of the respected gentlemen of his profession—a close friend of another just like him, Fred Russell of Nashville, Tennessee. The times I spent with each of them, only a couple with Mr. Russell but many with Si, gave me a lifelong respect for them that was deep.

And Si gave me one of my best press conference memories from the Olympics at Los Angeles.

In 1968, Dancer's Image won the Kentucky Derby but a urine test after the race found some banned medication and the victory was given to the second-place horse, Forward Pass. When the final verdict came in, Si wrote a hilarious column—he interviewed the horse. The closing line from the dejected Dancer's Image was:

"Si, I just pissed it away."

At Los Angeles, in a press conference at the Main Press Center the day after the Opening Ceremonies, Si asked me if I had attended the ceremonies. I said no, I was glad that our players had been able to participate in the parade of athletes. "I had some things I had to do to get ready for our first game," I told him, "and I was able to see them and their emotions better on television than I would have if I were in the stands.

"And then, on the other hand, Si, maybe I just pissed it away."

He laughed harder than anybody, taking it for what he knew it was: a tribute sixteen years later to a great column. But there were a few others who ripped me, for humiliating an old man. I'll gladly take those rips for the feeling I know that one shared laugh gave Si, who passed away a few years ago.

Henry Iba and Clair Bee were great friends—I don't think the first name of Chip Hilton's coach, Henry Rockwell, was happenstance.

And, like Clair, Henry also liked to take an occasional drink—Walker's Deluxe for him. Once, after he had ordered, I heard him tell a waitress, "Now don't bring me one of those newspaper drinks." She said, "A what?"

"A newspaper drink," Henry said. "One so weak you could read a newspaper through it."

Before one of our exhibition games, I asked him to talk to our team. He said in his deep, gravelly voice, "Men, you know we didn't block out as well last night as we can. We didn't cut off lanes as well as we can. We've got to do those things tonight. We've just got to get out there and beat their ass."

The kids loved that. Here's this gray-haired man talking about beating somebody's ass. I can still see Alvin Robertson grinning and shaking his head, thinking, *Man, is that great—an eighty-year-old guy, that dedicated to winning.*

Alvin played at Arkansas and was a great defender, which was Henry's game. Alvin also was one tough kid. On gold-medal night, after the ceremony, Henry Iba, victimized at Munich, was the first man our team carried off the floor in triumph. And one of the shoulders Henry was riding on was Alvin Robertson's.

There were a lot of times that night when I felt tears welling up and I was genuinely close to letting them go—certainly when our kids were standing up there on the medal stand, wearing their gold medals, while the national anthem played and the American flag went up in their honor.

But not even then was I any closer to tears than when Henry Iba went bobbing off that court on the shoulders of one more generation of kids that he had touched.

Coaching the Olympic basketball team, where I had been preceded by Pete Newell and Henry Iba, would always have stood off by itself as a thrill and a highlight for me, but it will all the more so now because times have changed in Olympic basketball. We go there with pros now.

Even though that move killed the competitiveness of men's Olympic basketball, I don't think we'll ever go back to using college players as our Olympic team. But I would still prefer that we would.

We could. America decides how it picks its Olympic team. The rule saying we (and everybody else) can take pros doesn't mean we have to.

And I think one of the absurd myths that has built since the American team started including NBA players in 1992 is that a group of American college players couldn't possibly win a gold medal now.

I call that a myth, understanding that international basketball is getting better every year. I do that realizing that the all-pro team we sent into the 2000 Olympics had a two-point game with Lithuania and would have lost that game if a makable last-second three-point shot had gone in. And I do that realizing that more and more of our best players aren't sticking around in college basketball for three or four years anymore—and some aren't bothering to play in college at all.

But please don't tell me that these pro Olympians, especially since the honor and novelty of the "Dream Team" in 1992, have approached Olympic basketball competition with the hunger and raw determination, the enthusiasm, and the pride of wearing a United States uniform—the genuine Olympic thrill—that our kids had in Los Angeles, and that I'm sure college kids on our teams before had as well.

Yes, if we used college kids we would have to face the possibility that we could lose. The possibility of losing is what makes winning mean something.

And if I didn't think we *could* win, I of all people certainly wouldn't be arguing for it. I definitely think we could still win with our best college players, playing hard.

I know that we've lost something in college basketball without the Olympic Games out there as a realistic goal for kids. And what hurts college basketball hurts American basketball, including the NBA.

Going back to a college Olympic team is one step that might—in a rare case or two, maybe a few more than that—slow down the flood of players going to the pros so early. Giving college kids, with their effort and enthusiasm, the opportunity to represent the United States at that age holds open something uniquely special to them.

The NBA is shortsighted if it doesn't think college basketball is its major lifeline. Now, I would resent like hell any implication that major-college basketball should consider itself a feeder system for the pros. Even a pretty good college program may send one player to the NBA every five or ten years, although a few obviously send more. However, in all truly good college programs, in that same five- or ten-year period, every kid who played at that school should have benefited from a genuine college education. That's all we should be worrying about regarding the future of college basketball—not kids leaving high school to go to the pros, not kids leaving college early to go to the pros, but whether the kids who go to college to play ball, get an education, and maybe have a shot at the NBA are getting an honest chance to do all that. There's already been way too much compromising to get kids who have no interest in a college education in school so they can play a year or two. The more of those who go straight from high school to the NBA, the better off true college basketball will be. There will be plenty of talent. It's the NBA that is facing the looming problem from the wild-money situation they have allowed to happen.

It's a great time to be selling college and college basketball to kids capable of both, a lot better than it was several years ago when a federal judge ordered the University of Minnesota to take back a player who had flunked out, because the judge said that by being denied his chance to play college basketball the kid was being denied his only real access to a pro basketball future.

The situation today would be better yet if basketball players going to college for the right reasons had something like the Olympics as an extra incentive.

ELEVEN: *A Chair and a Championship* (1984–1989)

This (1987) team played the last five minutes of critical games
as well as I've ever seen a team play.

The lead-up to our 1976 NCAA championship was smooth. We started
toward it with our league championship and Final Four trip in 1973,
added the right players to fill out what we kept from that team, and continued
winning Big Ten championships until we went all the way with a mostly senior
team in '76. Our 1981 NCAA championship was preceded by a Big Ten championship season that might have been lots better without some key injuries.

By contrast, the drive to the 1987 NCAA championship came with very little advance indication and went over some bumpy roads.

I came out of the 1984 Olympics feeling pretty good about things. Our best
player, Steve Alford, played well there and had to have learned a lot from playing with the guys on that team. Steve was the only college freshman on the
Olympic team. I'm sure he was expecting a continuation of good times, especially after the way our 1983–84 season had built to a climax with the NCAA
regional win over North Carolina.

One thing Steve hadn't learned from his first season and the Olympic experience was just how much teams would turn up the pressure when going
against a guy who suddenly was one of the best-known players in college
basketball.

The message came quickly. In our third game his sophomore year, we played
at Notre Dame. David Rivers of Notre Dame was by far the best guard on the
floor that night. He scored twenty-three points. Pre-season All-American
Alford scored four—and got just six shots. Scott Hicks, whom Steve had played
with and against in high school, played Steve tough and scored fourteen points
himself. We were down 45–30 at halftime and lost, 74–63. That made us 1–2.
Louisville, which won the NCAA the next season, had beaten us pretty good in
the opener at Assembly Hall, 75–64.

The early messages seemed to sink in with both Steve and our team. He had twenty-four points and we beat Kentucky right after the Notre Dame game, 81–68. That started an eight-game winning streak, and during that stretch we played some very good basketball.

The eighth game in that streak was our Big Ten opener at Michigan. We knew Michigan was one of the teams that could win the league championship. But that night, Uwe Blab outscored the Michigan center, Roy Tarpley, 31–12, Alford had a strong game (nineteen points), and we beat them 87–62, at the time the worst defeat ever for Michigan at Crisler Arena.

By the time we played Michigan again in our final Big Ten game, they had won fifteen games in a row and clinched the league championship and our team and our All-American were struggling, unimaginably. So was his coach, because try as I might (and did), I couldn't find the right answers. Three nights after we had played so well at Michigan, we lost at Michigan State. We won a couple of games, then despite thirty-three points by Uwe we got beat at Ohio State, then at Purdue—and I was disgusted. I didn't think we had been getting the kind of effort we had to get. Our defense hadn't been worth a damn, and I wanted to see a team play defensively. So at Illinois I put Uwe with some guys who hadn't been playing much and got a hell of an effort. The other guys, including Alford, sat on the bench and watched. We got beat 52–41—fairly close, considering we hit only three of fifteen free-throws.

Benching Alford touched off a furor in Indiana, but that didn't bother me. We went back to our normal lineup and got beat four nights later at home, by Iowa. That was four losses in a row, we were 3–5 in the Big Ten, and it got worse. Along the way, I also had dropped Mike Giomi, our leading rebounder, because he wasn't going to class.

We won three games, then lost at home to Illinois—66–50, worse than when we used the freshmen at Champaign.

That was on a Thursday night. Saturday afternoon at Assembly Hall was "The Chair Toss."

By then, I was trying everything. I had always worn a sport coat and tie during games. That day, I decided the hell with that. I wore an Indiana golf shirt, white with thin red stripes. And very early in the game, when a play happened right in front of me that I thought was miscalled, I got a technical foul. When Steve Reid was at the free-throw line to shoot the technical for Purdue, I wheeled around, picked up a plastic chair, and sent it scooting across the court.

All these years later, I still can't understand the notoriety that brought. Also, the longevity of it. Rarely am I mentioned on national TV when a tape of The Chair Toss isn't played.

• • •

I was thrown out for it, as I should have been. It wasn't the smartest thing in the world to do. We played in the NIT that year, and at a press conference before the semifinals in New York, a writer asked me if I ever woke up the next morning regretting something I had done. I told him, "Oh, yeah. Sometimes I regret it when the chair is halfway across the floor."

But—hey! If I'd hit somebody with it, fire me. I deserve to be fired. But I made sure it didn't come close to anybody.

Ralph Floyd, our athletic director, came into the locker room after I had left the floor, and Ralph with his Southern accent said, "Dammit, Coach, if you had worn your coat you'd have thrown that instead of the chair."

All I could say was, "You're probably right, Ralph."

I had gotten tired of wearing a good dress shirt, tie, and coat. Who the hell were you fooling? When you got through a game, there wasn't a deodorant made that could have kept you from sweating through a good dress shirt into your coat. Five minutes into the game the tie isn't knotted anymore anyway. Look at my friend John Chaney of Temple. He wears a coat and a tie but he sure as hell isn't worrying about looking well dressed. Not that I'm knocking John; even at uniform-conscious West Point, I never coached with my tie knotted tightly.

As badly as it worked out for me that day, and as sick as I got of seeing that red-striped white golf shirt in TV playbacks, I never did go back to a coat and tie. I've worn a golf shirt and a sweater ever since.

But Ralph was right. I probably would have thrown the coat where I threw the chair, as a lot of coaches have. But how many coaches have kicked over chairs or water buckets or done something else ridiculous? I consider my link to infamy a pretty tame one.

In 1998, thirteen years after I threw the chair, I got an offer of a substantial amount of money—five figures—to allow a TV commercial playing on that theme.

The offer didn't require my going anywhere to do it. I didn't even have to be in it. I was offered that kind of money just so they could use my name. And my identifying symbol.

I was so troubled by that memory, so chagrined about that role in history, that it took me maybe ten or twelve seconds to say: *Sure. Go ahead.*

I just never, ever have understood why it's such a big deal.

It didn't help my team any. By then, Alford was into something he had probably never experienced—an awful shooting slump. He was 2-for-9 when we lost to Ohio State, 3-for-14 in the Illinois game, 3-for-12 against Purdue. For a six-game stretch, the best shooter I've ever had, the guy we set screens to get open, the most relentless player in pursuit of a shot that I've ever known, took sixty-three shots and hit seventeen—.270, for a career .533 shooter. We lost five of those games.

Our last game of the season was against that Michigan team. Suddenly, we played well again—and Steve hit eleven of sixteen shots. But we lost again, when Blab blocked a shot but Gary Grant picked up the deflection and scored just ahead of the buzzer to beat us, 73–71. That was our fifth straight loss in Assembly Hall. Unbelievable.

The first year that the NCAA tournament expanded to sixty-four teams (from forty-eight), we failed to make it. That's the last time we weren't invited. Instead, we went to the 1985 NIT, played well, and got to the final game before losing to UCLA and Reggie Miller.

People were telling me when that season ended that I needed a break and Alford needed a break—"post-Olympic burn-out" was the term someone invented. I thought our team needed just the opposite. I accepted an invitation for us to play in July in the Kirin Invitational Tournament in Japan. That was for seven games in ten days, taking us all over Japan to play in a round-robin tournament with national teams from Japan, the Soviet Union, and the Netherlands. Then I decided, if we're going that far, who says we have to come back the same way? So, we booked additional games—two in Canada before we left for Japan, three in China, three in Yugoslavia, and three in Finland—eighteen in all, spanning five weeks. We were 2–6 at one point, then won our last ten.

This was the summer after the 1984 Olympics that the Soviets had boycotted. They played us twice in Japan and beat us both times, and their excitement afterward—particularly the first time—was like they had beaten the U.S., not Indiana.

Now, that pissed me off, and not only me. Their second win over us was 91–71 in Kobe, and after the game somebody asked Steve Alford if he would have liked for the Russians to have played the Olympic team. *Would I!* Steve said. "We'd have killed them. There's no way those guys could have stopped Michael Jordan, Sam Perkins, Patrick Ewing, Wayman Tisdale, and the guys we had inside—not as careless as the Russians are."

I strongly agreed, and for one time in my life I was subtle about saying so. The tradition at international games is to exchange gifts before the game. Usually, they are trinkets or something not very expensive. Before our second game with them, I gave their coach, Vladimir Obuhov, a relatively expensive gift intended to carry a message: a pair of the brand new line of Air Jordan shoes. I just wanted to make sure they understood this was not the Olympic team, and the name on those shoes represented the vast difference.

Jordan wasn't yet the Jordan he was to become, but he was headed in that direction. I think Obuhov understood what I was doing.

Our traveling party included two truly special guests—eighty-seven-year-old Everett Dean and eighty-one-year-old Henry Iba.

Everett's 1942 Stanford team won the fourth NCAA tournament and Henry's 1945 and '46 Oklahoma A&M teams won the seventh and eighth.

Before going to Stanford, Everett coached at Indiana for fourteen years. Before that, he played at Indiana. In coaching, his colleagues called him "The Gentleman from Indiana." He had retired from coaching and returned to live in Indiana long before I arrived in Bloomington, but he adopted me as a part of a special family.

Everett Dean has almost as much of a claim to being considered the father of Indiana University basketball as George Washington has for our country. Everett in 1920 was Indiana's first basketball All-American; before that, Indiana's basketball record was pretty bad. In 1925, he coached the first IU basketball team that won a Big Ten title. He recruited Branch McCracken, who became an All-American and Hall-of-Famer, then a two-time national champion coach himself as Everett's successor. Everett had a role in Branch's 1940 NCAA championship. He brought in the players who—after he had left for Stanford—Branch coached to not just that championship but three great seasons.

Everett would have been the last to mention any of those things. If there ever is a Gentleman's Hall of Fame, he should be the first man inducted. As it is, he's in both the Basketball Hall of Fame and the College Baseball Hall of Fame. He coached Stanford to an NCAA championship in that sport, too.

He was an outstanding athlete with an extraordinarily astute mind that was geared to the fundamentals of the game. Indiana never had a better or more respected alumnus than Everett Dean, nor did I ever have a nicer friend.

Our round-the-world tour provided me with an unforgettable image in my mind of the athlete that Everett Dean was. We had just eaten lunch at our hotel, and we were about to cross a parking lot to get back to our rooms. It started to rain. Everett broke into a loping run across the lot and hopped over a little fence to get inside. I just looked at that in amazement—here was a guy nearly ninety years old who looked like, acted like, and ran like the great athlete he once obviously was.

Both Everett and Henry, and our athletic director, Ralph Floyd, had lost their wives the previous year. They were great people to have on the trip, and I believe the trip was great for them, too.

We did a lot of traveling, we saw some historic things (the Great Wall, the Ming Tombs, the Forbidden City, plus Hiroshima and Nagasaki), and we brought back a basketball team.

Henry Iba said it best. When everybody was answering questions about what impressed them most on the tour, Henry said, "The Great Wall was wonderful. But to me the greatest thing was the way this basketball team came around. Now listen here, these fellows made some improvement.

"That to me isn't the bottom line. It's the top line."

Part of it was that modern word "bonding." I think the eleven kids we took did come back closer than before.

And another part was factual. We had just graduated Uwe Blab, and we didn't have another big man ready to take over at center.

Daryl Thomas, just 6-foot-7, showed us on the eighteen-game trip that he could handle center, and in the next season he did. He gave our 1985–86 team an excellent season of play there, and the experience he picked up in playing against the other Big Ten centers that year was invaluable the next year when he became about as good a "playing coach" as I've ever had.

Between the end of the 1984–85 season and the start of 1985–86, I made one of my biggest mistakes: I agreed to open our Indiana basketball program, from the start of practice in fall 1985 to our last game, to John Feinstein of the *Washington Post,* for a book he would write.

I'm not sure I had met Feinstein before the 1984–85 season. When he asked me about doing a book, I told him money was not a factor—I didn't want anything from it or any involvement in the authorship or credits. But there were some things he had to agree to, and if he did I'd give him the access he needed. I said, "I don't want the word 'fuck' in that book. There's a lot of other things I'll say that you can go ahead and use without detracting from your ability to show how I approach things." When I got the book, I read the first six pages and I think the word was used sixteen times. I put it down, sick, and never read another word of the book.

The second thing I said was, my wife, Nancy, and I were having problems at that time that led to our eventual divorce and I did not want any of my personal life in that book. I have heard there was just one reference to that.

A third thing, and the most important thing to me, was that the book was to be about the team, not about me. We'd had a poor year in 1985 and I told him we'd be back, and he could see exactly how a good team could be built with kids who went to class. People were saying, as they have always said, "You can't build a championship team these days without cheating some." That's the story I wanted him to convey—that that cop-out isn't true. It can be done and we did it, consistently. That was the main reason I was willing to do an "inside" book—to take that argument away from the phonies who were cheating like hell.

He agreed to all three provisions.

The first several weeks of practice and into the season, I spent a lot of hours just sitting and talking with him, trying to fill him in on the whole picture of Indiana basketball. By early January, I was sick of the guy's arrogance, his know-it-all attitude—I wanted to call it off and send him home. But I never did go back on my word about giving him access to places I had never let anyone go—to our locker room during the week, before games, at halftime, and afterward, right up through the Cleveland State game that ended our season. He had incredible access to everything. And, with my full knowledge, he got unbelievable help from my assistant coaches, mainly Royce Waltman and Kohn Smith. Feinstein made a ton of money out of the thing and never once offered to endow a scholarship or do anything at all for Royce and Kohn, who were putting kids through college on assistant coaches' salaries. He didn't owe me a cent—I didn't want anything from him at all, I had made that plain. But when profits came in for him way beyond any possible expectations, he sure as hell could have done something on his own to help those guys.

When *Season on the Brink* came out in the fall of 1986 and became a best-seller, people wondered why I was so upset with Feinstein because they said there were a lot of good things in there. As I said, I never did read the book, other than those first six pages. All these years later I still haven't read it, so I'm pretty sure I never will. But good and bad things in it regarding me weren't involved in how I felt about it. Word means a lot to me. In my mind, I kept comparing how I had lived up to my word with how he had lived up to his.

I don't think you're ever more sorry or disappointed than when a marriage doesn't work out. My wife, Nancy, and I did get a divorce.

I blame myself for it far more than her because I spent so much time trying to develop a career in coaching, I was gone so much and so oriented to making a success out of coaching that there was an inevitable strain on our marriage. I look at our two sons now and know she did a really good job with them, probably far better than I. For as much as I was gone, she obviously did well with them.

I've very proud of Tim and Pat, and I think they know they have always been a big and important part of my life. I did try to do a lot of things with them, and every year we took family vacations. I took each of the boys with me on my basketball teams' road trips when I could. Tim went on more of them than Pat, and sat on the bench with our team from the time he was really young. I have a picture of Tim and Bill Parcells sitting at the end of our bench when Army played an NIT game at Madison Square Garden.

We went to a lot of baseball games. Tim in particular saw some great performances from the "Big Red Machine" at Cincinnati in the 1970s. The first locker just inside the clubhouse door was Pete Rose's, and beside his was Joe Morgan's. I loved to talk with those guys.

One day Pete said, "Isn't Tim playing baseball? Here, give him this glove. I won a Gold Glove with it." Actually, he won two, as the Reds' left fielder in 1969 and 1970.

I told him no, I couldn't do that. He said, "Take it," put it in my hands and headed out to the field. I meant it; I didn't think it was right to do that. So, I put it on a shelf in his locker and went out to watch the game.

The next time I was over for a game, I was talking to Joe Morgan in front of his locker and I felt a jolt from behind. Pete had come up and with his bat punched me in the back to emphasize his point as he said, "Dammit, I told you to take that glove for your son. Now, here." And the glove was back in my hands. I started to argue again, and Morgan interrupted.

"Bob, will you *please* take that glove? The next time he might *swing* that bat at you and hit *me*."

One thing my Dad pounded away at me when I was a kid growing up was "Never get involved with gambling in any way." And I never have. I've always been antigambling. But I think Pete Rose should be in the Hall of Fame, on his merits as a baseball player. That's what got everybody else into it. A lot of guys in the Hall of Fame have done things they wish they hadn't. If they're in there, Pete should be, too.

With Daryl Thomas as our forward-turned-center and Alford back to playing well at guard, we had a good season in 1985–86. The one time we didn't have Daryl was costly. We lost our Big Ten opener at home to Michigan, and in a short practice the next day, Thomas sprained an ankle. He sat out our Michigan State game, and we lost that, also. We were 0–2 in the conference, with two home games gone.

I was very proud of those kids. They outplayed everybody in the league the next fifteen games and went to the final game at Michigan tied for the lead. That stretch is when I think the 'round-the-world trip paid off, when players became a team and took on a toughness that as individuals they hadn't had. But as a team we still had some holes and Michigan, with by far the most talent in the Big Ten and playing on its Senior Day, buried us. Then we let our concentration slip enough that Cleveland State, much better than its seeding, beat us in our first NCAA tournament game.

The thing that never got out of my mind was that first Michigan State game. If we had won that, we'd have bounced back from our 1985 season with a co-championship.

Thomas was just filling in at center his junior season. We had a legitimate center on the way—from an unusual source, for us. For the first time, I had decided to check out the junior colleges to see if we could get the help that we weren't finding in the Indiana–Illinois–Ohio area we had thrived on for fifteen years. Dean Garrett, 6-foot-10, 222 pounds, came to us from San Francisco City College where he had played for a friend of mine, Brad Duggan—an outstanding coach who loved our program and was thrilled to send such a good kid and player to us. We also picked up a junior college guard—Keith Smart, raised in Baton Rouge, a two-year player at Garden City, Kansas, Junior College.

Garrett got all the early attention, because we obviously needed a big man. That let us play Thomas at forward, and now we had two good inside players. Ricky Calloway was the other forward, and with Smart and Alford at guard, we changed from a team that got its scoring from two guys, Alford and Thomas, to one with all five starters averaging in double figures.

It's natural that coming in people thought of Garrett giving us a scorer and a rebounder, and he did that. His presence in the lane defensively may have been the biggest help he gave us. He blocked some shots; he changed the trajectory of a lot of others. He was what Ray Tolbert and Landon Turner had been, something we obviously didn't have the year before.

Daryl Thomas was great for Garrett. He led him around like he had a leash on him and helped him in every way possible. Every game, particularly in the conference, Daryl would talk to Garrett about the center he was going to go up against, because Thomas had memories from the year before.

Smart also was an excellent addition. He and Garrett were two kids who came in and worked hard to do what we wanted them to do. We couldn't have asked any more.

When I first met Smart, I thought he was going to wear himself out with all the chains and rings he had on. But he is a very, very bright kid. When he came to visit us, he thought Indiana was what he wanted. And we had a great chance for him to step in and play.

Alford was extremely good with Smart—and with the team. He had a good sense of wanting to win, and trying to win, and I think—better than any of his three previous years—was really focused on doing just that.

We had good success right from the start. We lost an early game to C. M. Newton's team at Vanderbilt and we got beat in our sixth Big Ten game at Iowa—101–88, the first time any of my teams gave up a hundred points. That was to what may have been the best Big Ten talent we ever went up against. That Iowa team was 17–0 and No. 1 in the country after beating us, and every player on their roster—not in their five-man lineup but on their whole twelve-man roster—went on to play pro basketball. I thought after our game they might go all the way unbeaten. Two days later, they lost at home to Ohio State. Last Game, Next Game . . .

So, a few weeks later we were 23–2, leading the conference by a game and No. 2 in the country the next-last weekend of the regular season. We went on the road and, in a three-day period, lost to Purdue and Illinois. We had been in position to get a No. 1 NCAA seeding and play our first two rounds in the Hoosier Dome—a perfect route for us, I thought. Now, Purdue was a game ahead of us with a game left to play. On our "Senior Day," we came from ten points behind to beat a good Ohio State team, and later in the afternoon—as Northwestern had helped us against Minnesota in 1973—Michigan drilled Purdue at Ann Arbor to give us a share of the championship. It also gave us our No. 1 seeding back, and our tournament route through Indianapolis.

We beat Fairfield there—fifteen thousand people came out the day before the game for our shoot-around—then got behind Auburn early before coming back to beat them pretty soundly, 107–90.

Our next game, at Cincinnati, was the first time Mike Krzyzewski and I had teams play against each other. I went to Dallas for the NCAA finals the year before and wore a Duke button when they beat Kansas to get to the final game but lost a close game to Louisville. Mike had lost some key kids from that team but this team still was good. We beat Duke 88–82, but two days later we looked dead late in the regional championship game against LSU. We were down nine points with four and a half minutes to go when Ricky Calloway missed a dunk and the ball bounced out of bounds. At a time-out, I never mentioned the dunk—just that we still had time to win the game. Joe Hillman came off the bench to give us a lift, and Calloway—who was from Cincinnati—was in the right place to catch a missed shot by Daryl Thomas and lay it in for a 77–76 win.

About that time, Iowa was running away from No. 1-ranked UNLV in the other regional still undecided. They led by twenty; UNLV came back to win.

We were in the Final Four, matched against the No. 1 team in the country. And I was glad our opponent wasn't Iowa.

Every advance analysis of the game talked about Indiana controlling the tempo, slowing the "Runnin' Rebs" down, if possible.

That wasn't the way I thought we could win.

The more tape I watched, the more I thought Las Vegas was the best defensive team in the country—their strength was their defense, not their offense. I felt if we tried to hold the ball, all we were doing was playing into their defensive strength. The longer we held the ball, the more opportunities they had to knock it loose and take it away. I felt we wanted to come down, work hard, and get good shots but get them quickly. Our kids carried that out extremely well, and I think that made the difference in the game. It was a hard-played, back-and-forth game. We weren't as good defensively as they were, but we weren't bad. They shot thirty-five threes and made thirteen. We shot four and won, 97–93, which was an indication that you could run an offense and score a lot of points without shooting a bunch of threes. Alford led us with thirty-three points; he played a great offensive game. But that game was an example of the defensive liability Steve could be. Mark Wade was theoretically his match-up, but we didn't want him going out to cover Wade. He was supposed to back off him and front the post man, Armon Gilliam—to make it more difficult to get passes to him and allow Garrett to play behind Gilliam. I can't say that worked too well: Gilliam got enough passes to score thirty-two points on a day when they weren't exactly looking inside all the time—not with those thirty-five three-point shots. Their other guard, Freddie Banks, hit ten threes and scored thirty-eight points.

Syracuse already had won its spot in the finals by beating Providence. The first time I worried about the championship game was when I looked out on the floor with not a lot of time left in the UNLV game and saw that the players on both teams were damned near exhausted. The uniforms were sweat-soaked. They were just tired, after a hell of a basketball game. We led UNLV by fourteen points two different times in that game, and they came back to get close each time. In addition to playing very tough defense and rebounding very well, playing hard all the time was a trait of all teams Jerry Tarkanian turned out at UNLV.

To be as rested and as fresh as possible, we did almost nothing the next day in the way of physically preparing for the game. Even with that energy conservation, we were half a step short the whole ballgame. At least twice Syracuse could have knocked us out of the game, and we didn't let it happen. We won when Thomas dropped the ball off to Smart for the shot with five seconds to go that won the game, 74–73.

The brand-new three-point shot helped us win. Steve Alford hit seven of them (still a finals-game record), and the whole Syracuse team hit four. Ed Steitz, the rules committee man generally considered the father of the three-point shot, genuinely thought he was creating a better game with it. We differed totally on that, and Ed, who passed away a few years later, loved to remind me that in the first year of "his" rule, we won the national championship on it. He had a point. By the old scoring, they beat us 69–67. I thought an awful lot of Ed, and as much as I was against that rule, when I looked at the box score after the game, I just smiled and thought, "*Thanks, Ed.*"

Smart, not Alford, won the award the NCAA gives at the Final Four, the Outstanding Player Award. Without question, Steve was our MVP for the season, off the court as well as on, but since the final game almost always determines how that Outstanding Player Award goes, Smart was the right pick. He scored fifteen points in the last twelve minutes of the game. Now, a lot of people will find this difficult to imagine, but I actually cooperated in a ghost-written column during that 1987 tournament—just to help out a couple of newspaper friends, Billy Reed and John Flynn. In that column, I stressed how much more important Keith's total contribution was than just the one thing it was sure to be remembered for, the winning shot. In those closing twelve minutes, I said, "Keith Smart made as many big plays in critical situations as anybody I've ever seen."

Go back and look at the plays he made in basically the last quarter of that game—play after play after play; pass, shot, drive, even a very smart foul, all of that in a game decided by one point, a national-championship game.

Even The Shot wasn't a one-man play, although almost everything else is usually forgotten in the excitement over it. Joe Hillman had six assists and no turnovers in that game, and here he put the ball in the right place—away from Alford, who ran a good cut to the opposite side of the court, and got himself in great rebounding position when the shot did go up. Hillman's pass inside was to Thomas, who didn't do what nine kids out of ten would have done in a situation like that—take the shot, even though he was covered. He passed it to Smart for an open shot Keith would hit more often than not. What a hell of a team play. The pass by Daryl was one of the greatest pressure plays I've ever had a kid make.

• • •

This was a rare national-championship team that didn't have a No. 1 NBA draft choice, but they handled the ball well, they could shoot free-throws, and they just worked at winning. It was a team that had great perseverance. The team's seniors—Alford, Daryl Thomas, and Todd Meier—did a terrific job of keeping that team playing and focused and doing what it was capable of doing, just keeping everything going in the right direction.

I said all year I thought the team had enough basketball assets to be very good but I wasn't sure it was tough enough. At our banquet, I corrected myself:

> *I have never in any way meant to shortchange this team. I have talked from Day One about this team being very, very tough to play against, when we play well, offensively. I have said on given nights during this year that nobody in the country could have beaten us that night.*
>
> *What is greatness in a team? Greatness in 1976 was Buckner and Wilkerson not letting anybody come across mid-court. Greatness was May being a tremendous defensive player, and the second-best defensive forward on our team, Abernethy being the best. Greatness was Benson playing in the middle. That was a team that was almost impossible to beat, because of its toughness, its strength, its size.*
>
> *In 1981, there was a greatness to that team. Wittman was a tremendous all-round player. Isiah Thomas was as tough—with as much ability—as anybody who ever played his position in college basketball. Tolbert and Turner were the two best defensive forwards I've ever seen on one team. Kitchel was a tough, hard-nosed guy playing inside. That team over the year developed into a great basketball team.*
>
> *And there was a greatness to this team. It doesn't have the two greatest defensive guards or the two greatest defensive forwards. Its greatness was a lot more subtle.*
>
> *These seniors as freshmen gave us a great treat when they came within a step or two of going to the NCAA finals in Seattle, beating the No. 1 team in the country, North Carolina, along the way. It was an unexpected brush with greatness.*
>
> *They learned a lot about the real world the next year. They weren't as good as they thought they were, as many of you thought they were. They had to suffer through a season that was very, very tough on them. They had to wonder, "What happened?" I'm not sure they had the answers.*
>
> *And then we made the trip around the world and they began to get a little better and a little better. The 1985–86 season was for them almost a single mission to become a better basketball team, and they did. The problems of the past*

crept up in their last two games. I think they still felt there were questions they had to answer.

It was in that regard that I feel these three seniors have carved a considerable niche for themselves in Indiana basketball history.

The greatness in this team may be a greatness no other team has had, to the degree that this one did—almost a total resolve not to recognize or be a part of defeat. This team played the last five minutes of critical games as well as I've ever seen a team play.

Still, I spent a lot of time the next year wishing that somebody else had made that winning basket. I think that one basket detracted greatly from Smart's approach and work ethic his senior year. It was only natural. Smart taking The Shot may be the most reproduced picture in the history of college basketball.

You still see prints of that everywhere.

The next year, there were spurts and spots here and there, but he didn't play as consistently well as he was capable of playing. And this time he didn't have Steve around to help him.

Garrett was more consistent the next year than Smart was, and made plays at the end that won us three big late-season games over Purdue, Minnesota, and Wisconsin. But here, too, I didn't think Garrett was as good without Daryl Thomas as he was with him.

We were good enough to make it to the 1988 tournament, but that's the one where Dick Tarrant's Richmond team knocked us out in the first game.

The NCAA tournament has been a big part of my life, as a player and as a coach. But I've never agreed with the sixty-four-team format—actually, sixty-five now. There just aren't sixty-plus teams that should be in it. I've always argued for thirty-two.

Everybody makes such an issue about giving the small schools a chance. Yes, some have stepped in and won an impressive game. If the selection committee is doing a good enough job, qualified small-school (or low-regarded league) teams could still be in the tournament, as part of the thirty-two—e.g., Cleveland State, the team that as a fourteenth seed beat Indiana in 1986. That was nowhere near the upset it was made out to be, because that Cleveland State team deserved a much better seeding than fourteenth.

But the biggest majority of those "small schools" shouldn't be playing for the national championship. With them in the sixty-four, you end up with a hell of a lot more mismatches than you have good games. I'd pick the best thirty-two teams, period—irrespective of league or size. A pretty good majority of those thirty-two teams would have a chance to do something.

You'd play one game the first weekend, giving everybody a chance to rest a little bit after the season's over, to get ready for this one final five-game push.

You'd have sufficient rest time even if you finished your season on Sunday, as many teams do now because of the TV god. The difference between a thirty-two-team field and sixty-four is with sixty-four you have to get right back to work and play again on Thursday, or at best Friday.

We started 1988–89 with a lot of holes to fill. We obviously didn't fill them very fast, particularly on defense. We got to the semifinals of the Pre-Season NIT, but Syracuse beat us 102–78 the night before Thanksgiving and North Carolina beat us 106–92 the night after it. A week later at Indianapolis, Louisville beat us 101–79. I had gone all those years—almost twenty-three—with Iowa in '87 the only team that scored a hundred points against us. Here it happened three times in eleven days.

The year before, when things just weren't fitting together for us, I went to a "three-guard" lineup and we put a pretty good run together. I thought having Joe Hillman, a 6-foot-2 guy, at forward limited us, so we played with a more orthodox lineup the next year right through that Louisville game. Then I stopped worrying about limitations and went to the same three guards—Hillman with Jay Edwards and Lyndon Jones, two kids who had come in together after leading Marion to three straight Indiana high school championships, a tremendous run for those teams and their coach, Bill Green.

We lost at Notre Dame the first time we used three guards. Then we won thirteen games in a row, including our first six Big Ten games to shoot out ahead in the league. We lost at Illinois, then won eight more in a row to clinch at least a tie for the championship with three games left.

It was a hell of a run. Edwards hit a shot with two seconds to beat Purdue, 64–62. Then Michigan came into Assembly Hall and led us until Edwards got a long three-point shot away just ahead of the buzzer to win, 76–75. He hit another shot—from along the baseline, over the backboard, and shot clock, to tie our second game with Illinois with two seconds left. But Nick Anderson hit a long shot—at least thirty feet—at the buzzer to snatch it back, 73–70. We clinched the outright championship the next game at home, against Wisconsin.

We won our first two NCAA tournament games, but Seton Hall knocked us out in our first regional game at Denver. The Michigan team we had beaten twice and the Illinois team that had beaten both Michigan and us twice made it to the Final Four, where Michigan beat Illinois on a last-second rebound basket and went on to beat Seton Hall in overtime for the championship. In a year that started so poorly, we obviously worked our way back into the national-championship picture.

Immediately after the season, Edwards—who as a sophomore had made second-team All-America and was the media pick as Big Ten Player of the Year—announced he was leaving school to go into the NBA. He wound up playing in just four NBA games.

I always felt Edwards was unselfish. He had a great ability to score and shoot, but he also passed the ball, made some crucial defensive plays, came up with rebounds. But he had such a terrible approach to his personal life that it got in the way and eventually negated all his abilities.

He was made to play this game—his size, his abilities, his understanding of the game. His lack of self-discipline and lack of appreciation for the opportunities he had and what he had to do to take advantage of those opportunities prevented him from having a remarkable career. Emotionally he was in no way whatsoever capable of going into the NBA when he did. Even physically, he needed more time.

I always regretted the way things worked out for him. He was immature. He'd get out of one problem and into another. To me, the best testimony to what Edwards could have been was that Joe Hillman, an ultimate team player, thought he was a hell of a guy to play with.

I think Lyndon Jones was able to get a much better grip on himself and his future and what he had to do to be good. Lyndon completed work for his master's degree, and he has done very well since. He's where you try to get every kid who plays for you—beyond the fact that they were great high school basketball players, or very effective college players, or the recognition and adulation they had received, to where they overcome all that and live a successful life. Lyndon has done that.

The reason we were so successful in going against conventional thinking the two years we used three guards was how exceptionally efficient those teams were on offense. We had a high shooting percentage and scored a lot of points. That, and the fact that our third "guard," who actually played forward at 6-foot-2, was Joe Hillman.

Defensively, the only forward Hillman couldn't play was Nick Anderson of

Illinois. Joe fought the hell out of him, but Anderson—so much bigger and stronger—just wore him down.

Joe outplayed a 6-foot-8 All-American Glen Rice, and we won both games against that Michigan team that won the NCAA championship.

If Joe Hillman had been 6-foot-8, he'd have been one of the three or four best players we ever had at Indiana. He was damned good as he was. If you had five Joe Hillmans of various sizes, you wouldn't lose.

I once said something similar about an LPGA golfer, Dottie Pepper, and she came back, "Coach, if you had two of me *we* wouldn't lose." Dottie has been one of my favorites ever since.

Todd Jadlow was the third junior college player who made a big contribution to that '89 Big Ten championship for us. He had some big games—thirty-two points in a key win over Iowa, twenty-seven in a couple of other games. And Eric Anderson was the Big Ten Freshman of the Year for us at forward.

We also got a hell of a year from a kid only Dick Vitale, our Indiana fans, and I remember. Brian Sloan averaged just over two points a game, but he was vitally important.

No kid who has ever played gave himself up more entirely to the role that was designed for him. Brian Sloan is the best screener that I've ever coached. That wouldn't even register with a lot of people, but screening was the guts of our offense, the heart of it. And Brian was the best I've ever had because he developed a fixation for screening. He was relentless. Vitale, almost fifteen years later, still raves about him.

Brian epitomizes for me what you want in a kid—from the best player to the simplest role player. His whole objective was to win and do what he could to help his team win. He started just twelve games in four years, but his teams won ninety-five games. He's a doctor now, which was another one of his objectives. He was relentless about that, too. Would you expect anything less from Jerry Sloan's son?

It tickles me when I read or hear some expert say how simple we are to prepare for, because we have been doing the same things on offense and defense for twenty years. I suppose I should take that as a compliment. Another guy they said that about was Vince Lombardi.

But I'll guarantee you that the guy who says that about us, and most media people just like him, could in no way even begin to recognize what we're doing—let alone what we're doing that's new.

I experiment every day with what we do offensively—not defensively, but offensively. On angles, on who the screener is. There's a dynamic to our play offensively as well as defensively that just doesn't exist in most offensive and defensive basketball. We change daily. What we emphasize in our offense in this game may not even be involved in the next game, except in the very basic fundamentals of play.

It's obviously not unique to us, but how we go about playing against the next team, and our points of attack, can be all different.

As an example, let's say on our team we've got a pretty decent fifteen-foot shooter as a post-man, and we've had a number of those over the years. We're playing a team whose defensive post player is reluctant to go out and cover. We use our guy as a backscreener, so he screens, a guy cuts, and if he sets a good screen, the defender on the screener has to at least pay attention to the cut to the basket. That leaves the screener wide open at fifteen feet to shoot the ball.

Or, we might move our man out even farther than that. In his freshman year, 1994–95, Andrae Patterson hadn't made a three-point shot all year and had tried only a couple before we played up at Wisconsin in March, our twenty-ninth game. That year Wisconsin had Rashard Griffith, a huge guy, at center, and naturally, they preferred to keep him around the basket. In that game, Patterson backscreened, then stepped out for wide-open shots at the top of the key, and he made four threes. We won a close game (72–70).

I always felt you can beat average, mediocre teams in a lot of ways. You can only beat good teams with good, solid basketball. My whole concern with everything we do is how will it work against the best teams—not in most games against most teams but in the biggest games against the best teams. When Kentucky won the 1996 national championship, one of the reasons was that Rick Pitino, a damned good coach, called off the press. He used the press far less in the second half of the season than he did in the first half.

You can press and win games, but who ever won the national championship with a press except UCLA in 1964 and '65? And that was more of a false press, a delay action.

How many times did we lose to a team that used a press? Our record there is far, far better than most fans and media experts think.

Every morning during the season I run through the newspaper list of college basketball scores, to see how teams coached by guys who coached or played for me came out.

I also look for scores of some coaches outside the "family" that I've personally liked—most of them guys I thought just plain liked basketball. They'd coach it if nobody showed up, if they were never interviewed, if they were never on television—they just coached because they loved the game of basketball.

There's no better example than Don Haskins of Texas–El Paso, one of my all-time favorite people and a premier defensive coach.

Defense was why I always liked for my Indiana teams to play against Texas–El Paso in a pre-conference game.

Haskins never thought his offense was any good. He'd cry and complain about that.

Every once in a while he would have an especially good player—Jim Barnes, Dave Lattin, Tiny Archibald, Antonio Davis, and Tim Hardaway are a few who come quickly to mind. But for the most part he took average players and made them hard to play against because he was such a good teacher of defensive play. He won an NCAA championship the first year I coached, and he's in the Basketball Hall of Fame now, as he should be. I'm not sure there's any other coach who could have done at Texas–El Paso what Don Haskins did.

He was a perfect fit there. As it was for me in Bloomington, what he liked to do was right there, available to him—fishing, hunting, golf. He's a great golfer—beyond great, so good he's like the old-time hustlers. That's why I called him El Paso Ed—from Jackie Gleason's portrayal of Minnesota Fats in *The Hustler*. For years, I'd call and say, "Ed . . ." And he'd know who it was right away.

We took three of our Indiana teams down to El Paso to play, just because of how much I respected Don, and how much I knew our teams would learn from playing them. Those were special trips.

The first time, in December of the 1972–73 season, we were playing in his Sun Bowl Classic. The last time our team went down there, in December of the 1989–90 season, when we both came out of the locker rooms just before the game, I was wearing a cowboy hat and he was wearing a red sweater. We had a hell of a game—they had Antonio Davis and we had Calbert Cheaney as a freshman. We won, 69–66, the only time we beat them in three games there. (That's also the only time I ever went through with something like that entrance. I was going to spoof Bo Schembechler the first time we played at Ann Arbor after he quit football, but I let Ron Kramer, the great Michigan, Detroit Lions, and Green Bay Packers tight end, talk me out of it. And the first time we played at Penn State, their fans were waiting for me because when they were admitted to the Big Ten, I answered a question at an Evansville outing by saying I wasn't enthused about taking my team there because "Damn, it's a two-day camping trip to get there." So, that first time I took along a knapsack and a fatigue cap to wear when I came onto the court, but Joe Paterno talked me out of it. Then I came out, and a bunch of students had a simulated campfire and tent set up on the court, and they were all wearing camping gear. It would have been perfect.)

Don Haskins was a good friend of another guy I liked, Norm Ellenberger, who coached against Haskins at New Mexico and then—after being out of basketball—was an assistant to Haskins at UTEP before joining our staff at Indiana.

The three of us went on a four-day fishing trip together, up near Chama, New Mexico.

The first day, Haskins slipped on a rock and fell into the water. We fished him out, he dried himself off, and I said, "Are you all right?"

"Yeah," he said, "but I've still got twenty-six more games to play."

He loved to coach, loved to practice, and hated games.

But, boy, if you could score points against his team, your offense was pretty good.

Shoe money in college sports bothers some people. I'm one of them, because I don't understand—I've never understood—how a college team's wearing a certain shoe could possibly be worth the money that was thrown around, which raised my suspicions that other things were involved.

In terms of increasing national and international sales, I think Michael Jordan would have been worth a huge check. I just never thought any school was.

From Day One, I could never understand why schools didn't take over that process themselves. That's why in any contract I was involved with, I tried to determine how much of the check covered the value of appearances I made for the company, my endorsement of the product, and my wearing the product in appearances. Then I used the rest of the money in a lot of ways at Indiana. As an example, I always used some of it to add to the income of our coaching staff and others, including secretaries in my office and others on the support staff. Word about that got around. I was criticized by other head coaches for what I paid our nonrecruiting coaches, as if somehow I was getting an advantage over them. My answer always was: "Hey, you've got a shoe contract, too. Use it to do the same thing." I'm not aware of anyone who did.

That money went everywhere—to the IU Library (when Tom Ehrlich left as president he told an alumni group I had been responsible for five-million dollars in gifts to the library); to a fund I had set up to endow a chair for two great teachers and friends of mine, Bob Byrnes in history and Harry Pratter in law, and for a number of other university causes.

A Nike official told me one time during negotiations that the only two coaches he was aware of who gave shoe money back to their university were Bear Bryant and I. (My favorite Bear Bryant memory is a letter he sent me; all it said for a return address on the envelope was Bryant. No address, not even a city. Evidently, with a Tuscaloosa postmark, that was enough.)

I was slow about getting involved in that whole shoe-money process.

I grew up thinking Converse and college basketball were synonymous. We wore Chuck Taylor Converse All-Stars shoes at Ohio State—I think almost every college team did. My teams wore them at West Point, and I didn't have any question about wearing them when we began at Indiana.

In my early years at Indiana, a certain enlightenment about the shoe business came to me, somewhat unintentionally.

Joe Cipriano, who was coaching then at Nebraska, mentioned to me some extra things that Converse was giving Nebraska coaches—golf bags, over-the-shoulder bags, nickel-and-dime things in comparison with what was to come. He almost didn't believe me when I sounded surprised: "Don't tell me you aren't getting that stuff?"

We weren't. We weren't *buying* our shoes; Indiana spent almost nothing on equipment in all my years there. But other coaches were getting these bags and things—we were on TV almost every week, and we weren't getting a solitary thing from Converse.

A little while after that we started wearing *adidas* shoes. That's when the whole idea of a contract first came up. I asked other coaches what they were getting, and then I talked to Bill Claus, who had brought the *adidas* operation to America and retained the western regional operation, set up in San Jose. He had fourteen western states, and Indiana. I got $15,000 from them the first year, and for that I spoke at two or three clinics for them, our team wore their shoes, and we got shoes for the cheerleaders and the pom-pom girls, which was always a part of contracts that involved me.

At that time, *adidas* was the most popular shoe and the biggest name. Then Nike came into it and those two competed hard against each other, and the money reached levels I could never understand.

The Byrnes and Pratter endowments were personal projects for me. Of the many good friends I had on the faculty at Indiana, first and foremost were Bob Byrnes, a history professor, and Harry Pratter, a law professor. Both were accorded status as Distinguished Professors, and the fund established professional chairs in both their names.

By the time he was in his early thirties, Bob advanced to a position comparable to brigadier general in the Central Intelligence Agency. He worked through World War II in the Office of Strategic Services, the forerunner to the CIA, and he was well acquainted with Wild Bill Donovan, Allen Dulles, and all the people involved in America's clandestine operations during the war.

Harry, along with his sister when both were children, had walked out of Russia to Budapest, where they waited for six months to sail to America and settle with relatives in Buffalo. He grew up there, went to the University of Chicago, and became a law professor at Indiana—at one time acting dean of the IU School of Law. They were great advisers for me. I was always very proud that both were big supporters of what I tried to do with basketball at Indiana.

TWELVE: *A Couple of Near-Misses (1989–1994)*

All those kids together made a team that was fun to work with.

The state of Indiana has a worldwide reputation for its high school basketball. It's well deserved. Nowhere else do kids grow up in an atmosphere so supportive of the game. Hoosiers love the sport—and I don't mean just Indiana University–type Hoosiers around the state, though those obviously always were my favorites, but awfully close to all Indiana natives. That love of basketball has been the subject of magazine stories, and John R. Tunis books, and that great 1986 movie, *Hoosiers,* for which I really think writer Angelo Pizzo and director David Anspaugh owe me some dialogue rights, if there is such a thing. Angelo—Andy—is from Bloomington, and he and David were both IU students and big IU basketball fans. Andy even went on some road trips with us. When the movie came out in 1986, I don't think I was the only one who recognized some of my coaching lines in Gene Hackman's dialogue.

But, what the hell. I don't begrudge him that. *Hoosiers* was up for some Oscars, and the night the Academy Awards were given out in March 1987, we were playing Syracuse for the NCAA championship. Andy and Dave skipped the Oscars and stayed home to watch the telecast and root us home.

For that kind of loyalty, they're welcome to any of my lines they want.

For as many truly great players as the state has turned out over the years, Indiana actually went through some relative dry spells in basketball talent during our years. And of course that hurt us, because from the very start of our program—when Steve Green of Silver Creek, Steve Ahlfeld of Northfield, John Kamstra of Rossville, and John Laskowski of South Bend St. Joseph's were our first recruits—I had always made it plain that Indiana kids were a priority for me. From our second year on, we got just about every Indiana high school player we went after.

But there were some years, some stretches of years even, when I had to go outside the state. That's why, when we built our last national-championship caliber team in the early '90s, I particularly liked the fact that it was full of Indiana kids.

We had two good whacks at a national championship with those kids. In neither case—in 1992, when we lost to Duke in the NCAA semifinals at Minneapolis, or 1993, when we were ranked No. 1 in the country but lost to Kansas in the regional finals at St. Louis—do I think the kids fell short of a championship-deserving effort. And I think the INDIANA across their shirts did mean something special to them—and to those Hoosier-loving Hoosiers around the state.

We had a pretty good knack over the years for recruiting the nucleus of a championship team in one class and filling in around it with the years before or after.

The class we brought in in the fall of 1989 exemplified that. The best player in it was Calbert Cheaney, who wasn't a particularly celebrated player in high school because he broke a bone in his foot and missed the last half of his senior year—which included the state tournament and the Indiana–Kentucky All-Star games.

Calbert is what any coach wants in every kid he ever coaches. He didn't come across that way to me the first time I saw him play—in his junior year at Evansville Harrison. Harrison was supposed to be pretty good, and Jasper that year hadn't won many games. The night I was there, Jasper won easily and Calbert looked like anything but a Big Ten prospect, let alone a future record scorer and College Player of the Year. He couldn't have gotten three rebounds. And he shot about thirty-two times and made six. Calbert claims I'm off on those numbers, but I'm sure not very far off. I just remember that he was a very soft player that night.

I didn't think there was any way we could recruit him, and we didn't through the rest of that year. Then some guys on my staff, after seeing Cheaney play in the summer, told me, "You've got to go talk to him." So fortunately we got back into it—fortunately for him, I think, and certainly fortunately for us.

After he signed with us that November, he had an excellent senior year going until he hurt his foot. And somewhere along the line he developed a tremendous work ethic. Nobody we had in any year that he was there worked as hard as Calbert Cheaney.

He went from being a good high school player, not particularly oriented to the defensive end, to being a very adequate defensive player. And he was a great offensive player. He worked hard, he played inside, he played outside.

Calbert was a guy with a Jordanesque quality: when he wasn't playing well, all I had to say to him was, "Calbert, you're better than this." Some guys you just have to stay on all the time to get them to play, but with him, just, "Calbert, Calbert, you're too good to play like this." And that's all it took, though I would guess that a time or two I probably said a little bit more.

He led us in scoring all four of his years, and he wound up leading everybody who ever played in the Big Ten. His 2,613 career points set a Big Ten career record that still stands—nine years and a lot of good players later.

I realize that sometimes when kids know I'm in the stands—or, I'm sure, any coach from a college where a kid hopes to play—they tighten up and just don't play well. Just a couple of years ago, I kept hearing how good a guard from an Indiana high school was, but every time I went to see him play, he just wasn't good enough for me to go after. His coach, who liked our program, finally got word to me, "He's a lot better than you've seen. He just has trouble playing when you're there." The word I sent back was, "Hey, that's fine, but if he does come here, I plan to be at just about every game." He went elsewhere. Those things happen.

The same season that I went to Evansville to see Cheaney, I watched junior Pat Graham at Floyd Central, near Louisville. Pat was one of the best shooters the state has turned out for a long while, but that night he couldn't put anything in the basket. I read afterward that he said he wanted so much to do well with me there that after he missed his first shot, and his second, and his third, "the basket started looking like a teacup." There was never much doubt, though, that we were going to go after Pat. He was "Mr. Basketball" in Indiana the year those kids graduated. He helped us win a lot of games and was an outstanding player, in spite of injuries that forced him to miss the equivalent of an entire season of games.

In the same class we brought in Greg Graham, from Warren Central in Indianapolis.

He was a tremendous player for us. His defensive play, the things that he did for us—he and Damon Bailey were an extremely good pair of guards, my kind of guards. I don't want a "point guard" and a "shooting guard." I want both of them to be able to shoot, as we had with Isiah Thomas and Randy Wittman on the 1981 championship team. If neither one of them can shoot, then I want both of them to be tough, big rebounders who can play defense, as we had with Quinn Buckner and Bobby Wilkerson in 1975 and 1976.

That's my feeling at all five spots. I'm not caught up in the one, two, three, four, and five numbering thing for positions. I've never recruited that way. I want players. My last Indiana team was pretty good, and its guards, Mike Lewis and A. J. Guyton, were good offensive players, but, partly because of their size, they did not give us great defense. I tried to always adjust with what I had, but I didn't always have what I preferred. With Greg Graham and Damon Bailey, I had it, with depth behind them.

Greg was a good scorer but a mediocre shooter when he came to Indiana. He just worked and worked at the fundamentals of shooting, and it all paid off. His senior year, he became the first player ever to lead the Big Ten in both field-goal shooting (.587) and three-point shooting (.535), and I think he's still the only one to do that—because the best percentage shooter usually is not a good shooter at all, a big inside player whose longest shot is about five feet. Greg shot his .587 from all over the court and almost swept the whole shooting thing in the league that year; he was third in free-throw shooting (.837).

He built that free-throw percentage up when he drew twenty-eight free-throws and hit a Big Ten–record twenty-six against Purdue. His only other points that game came on two three-point baskets, which gave him maybe the oddest box-score line I ever saw: 2–26–32, for field goals–free-throws–total points.

I don't usually get excited about individual achievements, but the night when Calbert hit a three-point basket that gave him the Big Ten career record was special—for our fans and for me. It was a great kid achieving a great honor, and I departed from character—we stopped the game (with permission from the opposing coach, Ricky Byrdsong of Northwestern) to recognize it.

Greg Graham also did something extraordinary that year. In February 1993 we lost our biggest player, Alan Henderson, to a knee injury. Coaches often say that in times like that, somebody else has to step up. Greg that year showed that "stepping up" doesn't particularly mean replacing the injured player's strengths. Twenty-five points was the most Greg had ever scored in a game for us until the day we lost Henderson. From then through the end of the season, he averaged twenty-five points a game.

Greg was a first-round draft pick and he signed a great contract—six years for $7.2 million. But as a pro he was like Ray Tolbert: neither of them was ever as good in the NBA as he was at Indiana. I think that was because they got away from how they could play best. That big contract seemed to be it for Greg. He had reached his goal, which apparently wasn't to be a great pro player because he just never worked at it the way he worked at being an excellent player for us.

• • •

Todd Leary of Lawrence North was a last-minute pick-up in that class. After we lost in the 1989 regional tournament, Jay Edwards announced he was turning pro. We had seen Leary and liked him, but we hadn't even been recruiting him until Edwards left. The night he did, I called Leary because I thought now we needed a shooter—he wasn't as good a player as Edwards was, but he was that kind of shooter. He didn't hesitate; he accepted right away.

At Indiana, Leary did two things that nobody may ever match. In the NCAA Final Four, he hit three three-point baskets in twenty-six seconds to give us a last-minute chance against Duke. And, he set the Big Ten record that still stands for consecutive free-throws made, forty-six—which, as a part-time player, he spread over *four* seasons.

The fifth Indiana kid we had in that class actually came the year before and red-shirted. Matt Nover of Chesterton was a hard-working kid who turned out to fit perfectly into this team, which needed a guy to defend the post. The guy we were trying to get that year—the year before the Cheaney class—was Chris Mills, the kid whose recruiting package got Kentucky in deep trouble. We were being told we were going to get Mills—I think his brother wanted him to go to Indiana. We had already told Matt we weren't going to take him so he could be free to find another place, which probably would have been Wisconsin. But when we saw that we probably weren't going to get Mills, we got back in on Matt, he came to visit, and we got him.

Matt was a forward playing center, and he never worried about a differential in size. It was almost a comical physical sight when he lined up to guard Shaquille O'Neal, but he just worked like hell and our team won.

The non-Hoosier in the class was Chris Reynolds of Peoria, Illinois. Like Quinn Buckner, Chris had small hands. I don't think there's ever been a good shooter who hasn't had good-sized hands.

But Chris had unbelievable spirit, he was very smart, and he was an absolutely relentless defender. He had an innate sense of leadership; he could get other players not just to play right but to live right. He was a devoutly religious kid who had a great sense of who he was and what he wanted to be. We were going to red-shirt him his senior year—the way we wasted Jimmy Crews and how much he could have helped a young team the next year always stayed with me. Then we got beat by UCLA in our opening game at Springfield, Massachusetts, and we decided not to do that.

That was our nucleus, and in fall 1990 we added Damon Bailey. For the next three years, we were a very good basketball team.

· · ·

We all have things that we wish we could do over again. Archie Dees came into my office one day and told me about a player in a little rural junior high school called Shawswick, about twenty miles from Bloomington. AAU basketball was just beginning to grow, and this southern Indiana kid already had been the national MVP on three teams that had won national AAU age-group championships—starting when this kid, Damon Bailey, was in about the fourth grade.

Without putting the kind of thought into it that I should have—just wanting to let an Indiana kid know we were interested—I went down to see him play as an eighth-grader.

The first thing I remember seeing him do was, palm down, lift the ball out of a ball rack with one hand. In warm-ups, he took a twenty-foot jump shot and put it up just effortlessly. In the game, he took off a defensive rebound and, before coming down, hit a teammate near mid-court with an outlet pass. I looked at him and saw Jerry West. I went back for a second look and took some of my assistants along. My being interested in an eighth-grade player generated a lot of attention and got into national publications. Bailey, who hadn't played a high school game yet, was one magazine's pre-season national Freshman Player of the Year. TV crews covered his first high school practice, and his first game.

That just started what in my experience was unprecedented attention and pressure on a kid, and I had unintentionally contributed to it by watching him play as an eighth-grader. I always regretted having a role in that, because no high school kid ever had four years of dealing with the pressure and expectations that Damon Bailey did. People all over Indiana followed him, from his freshman year on. It was estimated that his Bedford North Lawrence team played before 800,000 people in his four years.

People from fifty miles away bought season tickets at Bedford, or season tickets at other places where he was going to play once—just so they could be sure to get in that night. We had an autograph and picture day after the 1991–92 season, and by far the longest line wasn't in front of Calbert Cheaney, but Damon. One couple in that line, from Zionsville, which is a lot closer to Lafayette than to Bloomington, sat their two children on Damon's lap to take a picture. Their son was named Damon and their daughter, Bailey.

When Michael Jordan went to North Carolina, few people knew who he was. But this kid it seemed like everybody in America knew his name before he ever played a high school game, as a fourteen-year-old freshman.

He played against such great expectations all through high school, and, amazingly, he met them.

He became the state's career scoring record-holder, breaking a record that had stood since the '50s; his teams, with a new combination around him each of his years, won ninety-nine games and lost nine and went to the state tournament's Final Four three of four years—at a school that had never been there before and hasn't since. Because of him, the state high school organization moved the Final Four his senior year to the Hoosier Dome and set a national high school attendance record with more than 41,000 people at the finals. Because of him, ESPN carried the game. Everything built to a story-book ending when he scored his team's last eleven points to bring it from behind and win the championship, then ran up into the crowd to hug his mother. That night in that arena was a plot Clair Bee would have envied for Chip Hilton.

Then all those wild public expectations came with him to Indiana.

On Bailey's Senior Day at Assembly Hall in 1994, I mentioned to the crowd all that had preceded college basketball for him.

"I want you to just stop for a moment . . . and think how hard it might be to be an eighteen-year-old kid named Damon Bailey.

"I don't think there's anybody in this building who has ever—as an eighteen-year-old or a forty-year-old—been in quite the position Damon Bailey was when he came to Indiana. Was he a combination of Jack Armstrong, Superman, King Kong, Magic Johnson, and Larry Bird? Was he a little of all these things, or was he an eighteen-year-old who wanted to come to Indiana and play basketball, and play for a coach who wanted him to be *all* those things, I guess, all the time?"

Nobody could have lived up to everything people expected from Damon, and that's a shame because he was a damned good player. He was tough, strong, and a very good athlete. After his senior year with us I said I was disappointed—and I meant disappointed with myself, that I just never got him to be as consistently good as I thought he could be. He played as well as he could a lot of times, but it was almost as if he had played so much by then and had been so acclaimed he just didn't have that burning feeling that demands, "Every time I go out there I want to be the best I can be."

But he had lived with that pressure for four years before we ever got him, and it never went away. That had to be a hell of a burden for a kid to carry.

He had all the extra things that go with being a truly great player—he was a good student, polite, well-spoken, very bright. As I look back, it's remarkable that we never, ever had a problem with him, and that he was as good as he was, with all that he had gone through.

I heard that an Indianapolis sportswriter described his college career as "mediocre." Second-team All-America, All–Big Ten, 1,741 career points for teams that won 108 games, the only Indiana player ever to play in eleven NCAA tournament wins. The only thing mediocre there was that moron's judgment.

Damon Bailey was one hell of a basketball player.

We won a Big Ten co-championship in 1991, the sophomore year for the Cheaney class and Bailey's freshman year. The next year, we added the final two pieces—Alan Henderson from Indianapolis Brebeuf and Brian Evans from Terre Haute South.

You deal with some unique characteristics in every kid you recruit. With Bailey, it was the expectations. With Henderson, it was the background.

He came from a very strict family: high income, wealthy, private school. He had every opportunity to be a spoiled kid without a great capacity to develop a work ethic. And he was never, ever the first problem in any way—just a great kid, the kind of student and the kind of kid you'd like to have every kid be. His parents obviously had an awful lot to do with that.

Alan was 6-foot-10 but not a great, flexible athlete, like Ray Tolbert or Landon Turner. He got a lot out of what he had, which included exceptional intelligence. He broke Walt Bellamy's career rebounding record at Indiana, which meant it had stood for thirty-four years. They keep inventing new stat categories and one of them lately was "double-doubles"—usually, double-figure totals in both points and rebound in one game. Ten of those is a lot in any season. In his four college years, even with the time he lost to a knee injury, Alan Henderson had fifty.

Brian Evans was the opposite of Bailey in expectations, much more like Cheaney—both Calbert and Brian had a chance to develop as players without anybody expecting them to be outstanding. We were able to red-shirt Brian his freshman year. The first year that he did play, he was a valuable back-up on our 1992–93 team. He had graduated in the same high school class with those hyped kids from Michigan's "Fab Five," but none of them I'm sure had ever heard of him until he came off the bench to score seventeen points and help us beat them, 93–92.

Evans became a very good player, a well-rounded player—he could rebound, he could pass, and he could score. His senior year, my twenty-fifth season at Indiana, he became my first player to lead the Big Ten in scoring. That in itself was kind of remarkable. All those Big Ten MVPs we'd had, the great scorers like Steve Downing, Scott May, Mike Woodson, Steve Alford, Calbert Cheaney, and Alan Henderson—each of them had someone in the league who scored more points. Until Evans in 1996. And he became my last Big Ten MVP.

All those kids together made a team that was fun to work with. For three years, 1990–91 through 1992–93, they kept us in the Top Five in the nation most of the time—thirty-eight times in forty-seven weeks, No. 1 much of the time. In our twenty-nine years, only the 1975 and '76 teams had a longer run at the top than that.

In '91, after we pulled out a share of the Big Ten title on the last day, we were 29–4 when Kansas beat us in the regional at Charlotte. They hit six three-point shots on us in the first seven minutes and just buried us before we could even get started—13–2, 23–4, as badly as I've ever had a good team outscored at the start of a game. In the middle of all that (16–4, about five minutes into the game), they stopped play to repair the playing floor. John Clougherty, a Southeastern Conference official who usually worked our Kentucky game, came over to tell me a screw had come loose in the center of the floor and the wood was raised up. I said, "No problem, John. Why don't we just call it a night and start over again tomorrow?"

That was the best suggestion I had all night. We got beat, 83–65.

The next year, we had a great year going but finished the regular season struggling. Then we put things together in the tournament and could have won the whole thing—maybe should have won it, the way our kids played before fouls broke them up against the Duke team that went on to win the championship. That year we got to the Final Four by beating UCLA in the West regional championship game at Albuquerque—the same UCLA team that had beaten us 87–72 in our season opener. The first game was at Springfield, Massachusetts, part of a Basketball Hall of Fame celebration commemorating the hundredth anniversary of basketball. Red Auerbach was there as the honorary chairman, and he spoke at a game-day luncheon with both teams present. The guy is amazing. He mentioned that day that he knew both Jim Harrick, the UCLA coach, and me, and he said, "I think Jim is lucky. Bobby's teams usually get better, every day, so if you catch them early you've got a better shot at it. I think if this game was played later on in the season, it would be a little tougher to beat Bobby." I'd never make a sweeping statement like that about our teams, but he was dead-on with the particular situation he mentioned. We won that second game, 106–79.

In 1992–93, that full group was together and No. 1 in the country when we lost Henderson to a knee injury. It happened in mid-February; we were in the final minutes of a short practice on a Friday afternoon, getting ready for a Sunday game with Purdue. There was no bump, no contact. Alan went up by himself to lay the ball in, and when he came down, he just crumpled.

I think we had absolutely the best team in the country. Without Henderson we were stuck just as we were without Scott May in 1975—we went on, we still had a very good team, but we had lost a key component. In this case, it was size. Alan at 6-foot-10 was our biggest player and our best rebounder. Without him Nover at 6-foot-8 and Evans at 6-foot-7 were our biggest players, and Evans was playing hurt—with a shoulder that kept popping out. We became more of a perimeter team with great outside shooting: both Grahams, Bailey, Cheaney, Evans, and Leary all were good three-point shooters. But Kansas, a very good team that had beaten us earlier in the season, was big enough to exploit the size difference and knocked us out one step short of the Final Four, the same point where the '75 team lost. Maybe Kansas would have beaten us anyway, but I don't think so. I don't think anyone would have.

In those three peak years, those kids won eighty-seven games, a Big Ten record. They deserved the one thing that got away: a national championship. We put up a banner in Assembly Hall for them, anyway. They were too good a team to forget.

When we were playing in the 1992 Final Four at Minneapolis, I picked up an article on the regional tournament in *Sports Illustrated*. That's a magazine I almost never read, but I thought there might be something in its regional stories I could use with our players.

What I saw was a paragraph about how, as Duke's coach, Mike Krzyzewski was trying to get out from under my shadow without making me mad.

Before leaving our hotel to go to the Metrodome for the game, I clipped that out and put it in an envelope along with a note I wrote. After the game, I gave the envelope to Tom Rogers—the good friend of mine who had been with me at West Point and now was on Mike's staff at Duke. I asked Tom to give it to Mike sometime over the weekend. I never heard back from Mike, which I'll admit kind of surprised me.

Probably over a year later, I wrote him once and then called and talked to him. That seemed to go all right. Then I asked him to check with someone on a rules thing and I never heard back from him.

I figured if it was his choice not to have a relationship with me, that was entirely up to him. I don't have any problem with it. If it's a matter of wanting to establish himself on his own, for what he has been as a coach, he certainly did that a long time ago.

Across the board, all things that go into college coaching considered, I've said several times that for the last ten years his program at Duke has been the best in the country, without any question.

Tom Butters, the Duke athletic director, genuinely didn't know Mike's name when he called me in 1980 to ask if I would have any interest in the Duke job. I was enjoying my time at Indiana then and there was no way I could even contemplate going someplace else. I told him I wouldn't have any interest in it, but he should talk to Mike, who was at West Point, and Bobby Weltlich, who was at Mississippi. Whoever he liked better, whoever he thought would do the best job, he should hire.

Weltlich wasn't interested in the job, and Mike obviously was. Things turned out well for both of them—great for both Mike and Butters, who liked what he saw and heard with Mike, and hired him.

Iowa State was also open at that time, and I actually thought that would be a better job for Mike, a Midwestern job—he was from Chicago. But he preferred Duke and he has done a hell of a job. When he took his team to the Final Four for the first time in 1986 at Dallas, and when he won his first NCAA championship at Indianapolis in 1991, I couldn't have been prouder of him, and I think he knew that.

Mike and I had always had a great relationship. With that note, I tried to point that out. I know I ended it by saying if they were to beat us, nobody would be rooting harder for Duke to win the championship. And it was true. I did root for him, when, after beating us, they beat Kansas to become the only team in the last twenty-five years to win two straight championships.

I was just as pleased for him when his 2000–01 team won him a third NCAA championship.

But nothing made me happier for him than the night in September 2001 when he was inducted into the Hall of Fame at Springfield. It was, of course, just a matter of time, an honor both deserved and inevitable considering the record he has and the championships his teams have won.

I was sincerely honored when he asked me to be part of the ceremonies, because no one who has played for me was ever closer to me than Mike, nor have I ever been more pleased by anyone's success.

I've always enjoyed going to movies. I enjoyed it, too, when in the latter part of the 1992–93 season, the movies kind of came to us.

Bill Friedkin, the director of *The French Connection,* among other films I had seen, went through Red Auerbach and called me about a film he was planning. It was called *Blue Chips,* and it involved a college basketball coach who was playing by the rules and not winning as much as he wanted because too many other guys weren't worrying about those rules.

Ron Shelton wrote the book that was the basis for the movie. Friedkin lined up Nick Nolte to be the coach, and Friedkin asked if he, Shelton, and Nolte could come to Bloomington during the season to observe how one college coach does things.

That was one of our best seasons, with a great group of kids. The three guys came and stayed for about two weeks, which included the night when Cheaney became the Big Ten's all-time leading scorer, and the 1993 "Senior Night" when Cheaney, Greg Graham, Nover, and Reynolds played their last game—before the emotional crowd we always had for one of those.

The thing I liked best about their visit was the way Nolte got along with our players. He spent two hours in the locker room with them one day—just talking with them about movies, and movie people. Our kids asked some excellent questions, which showed they were enjoying it, and Nolte was candid about people he had worked with or people the kids had seen, and how movies were made. He was just very good to have around.

When they left, Friedkin told me he wanted me to bring our four seniors to filming in California during the summer. At the time, he was selecting a cast. Shaquille O'Neal and Anfernee Hardaway were in line for two of the three player-actor roles, and the third one was open. After what they had observed in Bloomington, both Shelton and Friedkin thought Nover would be perfect for it.

I met with Bill in California after the season, and he told me as much as he felt Nover was the best choice for the role, he wanted to keep the four Indiana kids together. His reason: Nover, as an actor, playing against Indiana, "would destroy the Pirandellic quality" and the story's "similitude"— none of which I understood except that it had to mean that it wouldn't look right to people who knew college basketball to see Matt Nover playing against Indiana. As Friedkin tells the story: "Bob said, 'The hell with Pirandello and similitude. Take him.' I said again I didn't think it would be right, and Bob said, '*Take* him. I'm tired of him. I've coached him five years already. I don't want to look at him anymore. If you *don't* take him, I won't even use him.'

"I knew what he was doing. He saw the great opportunity this would be for Matt and wanted to make sure he got it."

He was right, of course. Nover may have been my wife Karen's all-time favorite player during our Indiana years, because he played so hard with so little recognition. I'm not sure she would have seen through what I was saying the way Bill did.

All I know is Nover got the role, made $75,000 for it, and in Friedkin's judgment did a great job. (The irony of it was here was a kid from our program playing a role where he was holding out for a $30,000 under-the-table payment before he would sign with Nolte's school. Friedkin told a newspaper interviewer that scene in the movie, where Nover got Nolte to cheat, was Matt's "toughest hurdle. He had to be something he wasn't. He did not like the guy he was playing, just as Gene Hackman didn't like the guy he was in *The French Connection.* Matt Nover does that scene as well as it can be done. Oh, we could get John Gielgud to do it, but I don't think John Gielgud could look like a top recruit. I'd rather have Matt Nover do that scene than John Gielgud.")

I'm pretty sure that's the only time Matt Nover and the great actor John Gielgud will ever be in the same sentence.

Besides Matt's role, we did get our other three seniors plus Joe Hillman, Keith Smart, Jamal Meeks, and Eric Anderson from our former teams to play for the Indiana team I coached. Friedkin made sure all those kids got paid, too, though not nearly as much as Nover. Bobby Hurley of Duke played with us, and several guys who still are in the NBA played on teams in the film—George Lynch, Allan Houston, Chris Mills, Rodney Rogers, Rex Walters, and Rick Fox. Bill Friedkin is a genuinely big basketball fan, and his idea was to make a basketball film with real players who were taught to be actors rather than actors taught in a few weeks to be basketball players.

Rather than shoot the basketball action in California with 6,000 extras filling a gym and reacting on cue, Friedkin's time in Bloomington convinced him his best bet for believable crowd shots was to fill a gym in Indiana with fans and let those Indiana basketball fans act as they always do when they're watching good basketball.

They picked as the filming site for the basketball scenes the high school gym at Frankfort—an extremely nice, typical Indiana gym, with a capacity of 5,500, in a town of 15,000. When we came to shoot the game, the place was packed. The climactic scene was Nolte's team against Indiana and before the filming started, Friedkin told the crowd: "I have a problem. I have to ask you to root against the Indiana Hoosiers." Frankfort is a lot closer to Purdue than it is to IU, so there were some people in there who didn't have a problem with that. But the big majority of others had to be given gold and blue stuff to wear over their usual red.

We were supposed to lose the game. Indiana, in the story that was revised

some after their visit to Bloomington, represented the right way to run a basketball program and by losing to illegal recruits presented Nolte with a tainted
"victory" that he ultimately couldn't take.

In the script we were to be ahead by a point with a few seconds left, and
Nolte's team would win with a last-second shot. I couldn't keep myself from
getting a little ornery. We had played a real game, hard and competitive in front
of that crowd, to give Friedkin all the realistic footage he wanted. The "Western" team we were playing had O'Neal (who had just finished his rookie year in
the NBA) and Hardaway (who that spring left Memphis State to go pro and
was the No. 3 pick in the draft). And, of course, they had Nover, who was our
starting center. But our kids actually did beat them. Except, that wasn't the way
it was scripted, so we had a time-out while they set things up for the first
shooting of the movie finish. In our time-out, I told our kids, "The hell with
that. We've beaten them all night anyway. Don't let them score."

We blocked their "game-winning" shot.

Friedkin wasn't amused. They had been filming all night, and they were
down to the end of their supply of film when they shot that scene. We all had to
wait around while they went back to their motel, got some more film, and shot
it again. This time they scored.

It was a great experience for all of us, and it was certainly great for Indiana
University. In addition to what he paid the players, Friedkin paid me $15,000,
which went to the IU Library Fund, and he had the world premiere of the
movie in Bloomington, which meant more income for the university—about
$350,000, altogether.

And Bill Friedkin personally endowed a basketball scholarship at Indiana, in
the names of Pete Newell and Red Auerbach. No one ever was a better friend to
Indiana basketball than Bill was.

While I'm discussing movies and generous good guys, let me mention again
the movie *Hoosiers,* which always ranks at the top or close when sports movies
are rated. I do it to bring up one of its biggest fans, who a few years ago said he
had watched it a hundred times and may be approaching two hundred by
now—George Steinbrenner. He's one man in sports who is bigger than life—
and a whole lot bigger than his critics, which he does have.

I'm an unabashed Steinbrenner fan who can never catch up for good things
done for me by him. I'm not alone. He has done so many things and affected
the lives of so many people nobody can keep track. On top of that, I'm not sure
anybody in sports today has a better understanding of winning—how to go
about it, and what's necessary to achieve it—than George does. In the latter

part of the twentieth century and the start of the twenty-first, who has put together a more dominant professional franchise than George has with the Yankees? And he has built World Series championship clubs three different times. I've always enjoyed learning about people who have been successful in sports and other walks of life, but I've never made a judgment on them unless I got to know them. The George Steinbrenner I know and like a lot above everything else is a damned good man who has done more for people than all those critics combined could dream about doing.

When we came back for the 1993–94 season, we realized, quickly, that we had lost a lot with that 1993 senior class. We got beat in our 1993–94 season opener at Butler in Indianapolis.

Seven days later, in Indianapolis again, we got a great game from almost everybody and an outstanding leadership effort from Bailey in beating Kentucky at the Hoosier Dome. Except for the opener, when the Butler kids just outplayed him and everybody else we had, Bailey was as consistently good in a stretch of games as I had ever seen him. He had twenty-nine points against both Kentucky and Washington State, thirty-two against Eastern Kentucky, thirty-six in an overtime loss at Kansas, then twenty-four, twenty-four, twenty-five, and twenty in consecutive games that we won.

That 1993–94 team led the nation in three-point shooting. Henderson came on the second half of the year to be one of the best inside players in the country. But injuries slowed Bailey down and it was not a team with great stamina. John Chaney had the two guys who have gone on to be outstanding NBA players, Eddie Jones and Aaron McKie, but we played well to beat that Temple team to reach the regional at Miami. There, Jim O'Brien had done an outstanding job with Boston College and they beat us in our first game.

At that point, we were the only team in the country that had been to four straight regionals. In my remaining Indiana years, we never got back to one. Things were starting to change within the university, in many ways, and within two years it would not be the same situation. Ralph Floyd had passed away in December 1990, and his eventual successor was not the man Ralph was and nowhere close to being as good an athletic director. This is the time—1994 or 1995—when I should have left.

But at the time, I was having as much fun coaching as I'd ever had in my life.

THIRTEEN: *Change of the Guard* (1994–2000)

*Our big problem in college basketball is not with the kids we
lose to the pros but the ones we pervert the process to admit . . .*

Our teams of the early '90s carried Indiana basketball to pretty spectacular heights, but even in the good times I could see signs of trouble ahead. I ignored them, instead of realizing that—like my last year at West Point—it was time to move on.

I did have some happy, emotional, and really memorable personal moments in the 1994–95 season. The team co-captains were Alan Henderson and my son, Pat. I have pictures of the hug Pat and I shared when he came off the floor after playing very well when we beat Iowa in the final home game of the year. That's one of those prized personal moments.

There were some great times in each of the follow-up years, but there were sour ones, too. Brian Evans did a great job with young kids around him in 1995–96. The freshmen on that team were what we had hoped would be the new nucleus to build around, but for different reasons it never worked out.

Our one real mistake in the group was recruiting Neil Reed. I can't even describe how much chaos not bringing him in would have avoided. We were finally able to eliminate him after his junior year. I told Reed, Andrae Patterson, and Richard Mandeville that they *should* leave, not that they had to. I allowed the team to vote on keeping any or all of the three. The vote was unanimously for Patterson and Mandeville to stay and 8–0–1 for Reed to leave. Reed transferred to Southern Mississippi, where coach James Green, who had him one season, told me he was the most disruptive player he ever had on a team.

In a relatively short period after that, we also had to drop Sherron Wilkerson, lost Steve Hart on grades, and Jason Collier, who had come in as one of those high-profile recruits, transferred. A year later, another of those, Luke Recker, transferred. I don't know whether anybody noticed that despite these things, we kept winning our twenty games a year, going to the NCAA tournament, and bringing in good prospects.

I was genuinely excited about the prospects shaping up for us after fall signings in 1999 of Jared Jeffries, an excellent prospect from Bloomington North, and A. J. Moye of Atlanta, another player I liked a lot. We made strides on the floor with our 1999–2000 team, too. When they played the Final Four games in Indianapolis, we had beaten three of the teams in it, and we weren't far from having gone 5–0 against those teams. We had also beaten Kentucky and Temple, and we had some good, experienced players coming back to go with our new players—plus George Leach, the freshman center who had to sit out a year through no fault of his own. Plans for how we could best fit those players together were always in my mind. I was caught up in that. I should have been smarter. But coaching was giving me some wonderful times.

The night before our 1994–95 game at Notre Dame, one of their law professors, G. Robert Blakey, went to dinner with us. He had been the chief counsel for Congressman Louis Stokes's House Select Committee on Assassinations, which had investigated the assassinations of President Kennedy and Martin Luther King, Jr.

Blakey collaborated on a book: *Fatal Hour: The Assassination of President Kennedy by Organized Crime—The Contract, The Killing, The Coverup.* Blakey was convinced it was a mob "hit," and he had impressive research backing him up. That was always my own suspicion; I never did buy the Warren Commission finding that Lee Harvey Oswald did it alone. Blakey's particular expertise was in organized crime legislation, including the 1970 "Rico" law that was part of the Organized Crime Control Act. That was a fascinating evening.

We had some great road-trip dinners. At Michigan, we usually got together with Ron Kramer and Tom Maentz, two '50s teammates who were among Michigan's all-time greatest football ends, and sometimes Bo Schembechler was able to join us. At Minneapolis, we went to the same Italian place, Vescio's, for about twenty straight years—Sid Hartman our host, a waitress named Mary Jane our virtual private hostess, Bud Grant a regular, and Paul Molitor and Tommy John among other outstanding players and great people who joined us at least once or twice. Sid loved to listen to those conversations on coaching between Bud and myself. The "conversation" mostly was my asking the questions and Bud answering. Sid sat there, quiet, for longer than I can ever remember him doing.

Sometimes we took our own interesting people along on those trips. Otis "Doc" Bowen, a small-town physician who was one of the state's most popular governors ever, was sitting on the bench with us at a road game once. At a time out, I got on the players pretty hard. I looked around afterward, saw him, and said, "I'm not sure you wanted to hear all that." We didn't have a bigger fan than "Doc." He said, "Don't worry about it. I felt the same way." He was Secretary of Health and Human Services under President Reagan, and he was our host when our 1987 national championship team went to the White House.

Michigan State was one of my favorite stops, because of Walter Adams. Walter grew up very poor in New York City and he became a brilliant, greatly respected economics professor at Michigan State and interim president of the school for a while, during the worst of all times to be a college president—the late 1960s. He had made it clear he was only bridging a gap, he would definitely be returning to the classroom, but 20,000 students and 950 faculty members signed a petition asking him to stay on.

He also was a devout basketball fan who had season tickets for him and his wife about four rows behind the opponents' bench. He had a New Yorker's tendency to needle people—like the opposing coach.

The first time I noticed it, he was on me for a whole game. I ignored it until the game was almost over, and we were well ahead. I turned around, looked at his wife, Pauline, and said, "Does he belong to you?" She, kind of sheepishly, nodded yes. I said, "Does he ever shut up?"

The next year, when we played there, I looked back in the stands, saw him, and waved for him to come down. He did. I reached in my pocket and pulled out some of the round, cellophane-wrapped peppermint candies I always carry and said, "Do me a favor tonight: chew on these instead of my ass."

The next year, I came out for the game and he was waiting with a gift for me—a green-and-white Michigan State T-shirt. I was still wearing a coat and tie then. I reciprocated by pulling off the tie I was wearing, blue with red IU's on it, and giving it to him.

A great friendship started. Every time we played up there after that, he went out to dinner with us the night before the game. Even after he had retired and moved out of state, he'd come back to Lansing for dinner and the game. He was one of the most fascinating people I ever met. He fought in World War II as an enlisted man and landed on Normandy, and he told great stories. The whole fieldhouse was aware of the pre-game ritual we had going: everything stopped while we exchanged gifts. Then we played the game. Walter passed away a couple of years ago. Both Michigan State and I lost someone special.

On a White Sox baseball telecast not long ago, Ken Harrelson said one of the strengths of Jerry Manuel as a manager is that he is "not afraid to lose a game."

That's an interesting thought, because so much of managing a baseball team or coaching a basketball or football team starts with eliminating or minimizing the ways you can lose.

That has always been a major tenet in my coaching philosophy: to win, you have to eliminate the reasons why you lose—sloppy ball-handling, poor defensive effort, lack of blockout, poor shot selection, a whole variety of things that you probably cannot totally eliminate but you can really cut down. There is going to be a bad shot taken, a missed blockout. Basketball is a game of errors. You try to reduce the number of errors to give your team the best chance to win.

But "not afraid to lose" means to me that you're willing to do what you think has to be done to win, even if it deviates from the norm—even if it puts you out on the limb for criticism because it deviates from what the consensus thinks has to be done. Our game with the UNLV in the NCAA semifinals in 1987 at New Orleans was an example, when we went against conventional thinking by running with them and outscoring them rather than attempting a delay game.

There is another element to that idea of not being afraid to lose. We've had a few games over the years where I made moves that made defeat more likely than victory—on that day, in that game, but for a purpose. Our 1985 game at Illinois, when I sat down Steve Alford and all the other regular starters except center Uwe Blab, exemplified that.

Why did I do that? I'm a teacher. I felt we weren't getting the defense and the effort we have to have, and if we had to lose a game to teach them what was important, in terms of their recognizing their responsibility and handling their responsibility, then that's what I was perfectly willing to do.

Two years later we were national champions. I don't know whether that afternoon at Champaign in 1985 had anything at all to do with that 1987 championship. But one of the keys to winning in '87 was that some kids who sat on the bench that day in '85 handled their responsibilities very, very well.

In 1989, we lost on the final day of the season at Iowa, and I angered some people that day, too, by sitting down four of my five starters.

This time was a little bit different from the message-sending day at Champaign. I wasn't really trying to teach anybody anything at Iowa.

It was a simple matter that earlier in the week we had clinched the outright Big Ten championship. I looked at the team that was about to go into NCAA tournament play and saw a lot of guys who were banged up and tired.

So, we rested Eric Anderson, Jay Edwards, Joe Hillman, and Todd Jadlow. Lyndon Jones was the only regular starter who played a lot in that game, and he didn't start.

We got beat pretty soundly that day at Iowa. But, in the process, we not only rested our starters but also gave our nonstarters a game's worth of experience.

I'm not sure how many of the people who ripped me for taking a loss at Iowa noticed the after-effects of that. We began NCAA tournament play the next weekend at Tucson against George Mason. We got into all kinds of foul trouble, but we beat George Mason—and then Texas–El Paso—because we got a lot of good play off the bench from these guys who had a chance to play at Iowa.

I wasn't afraid to lose when we played at Minnesota in 1994, either. And that was different from either of the other games.

This time, we were in the middle of a crucial stretch of our schedule. We won a pretty tough game at Northwestern (81–74) on a Thursday; now, we were at Minnesota on a Sunday, and just ahead on Tuesday night was a game with Illinois.

We got behind Minnesota by twenty points before the game even had a good start. They just pounded us. By half-time, they were leading, 56–24.

Long before halftime I thought, "All right, we can go all out, wear our guys out trying to keep the score reasonable, and then we'll be too tired to play Illinois. I can take a chance on losing this game and the next game, or I can do all I can to win the next game."

I picked the latter. I just told myself, "The hell with the Minnesota game. Let's make sure we're in the best shape possible to play Illinois." We got thoroughly drilled at Minnesota, 106–56, one of the worst defeats in the history of the school.

I caught it pretty good for that decision. I almost had to laugh at the idea of people criticizing me for not caring enough about winning, or for taking defeat too lightly. I'd question whether there was anyone out there who likes to win—or hates to lose—more than I do.

But I had a team with a stamina problem in the first place and a difficult scheduling stretch that complicated the stamina shortage.

Two nights later, Damon Bailey, who had played fourteen minutes at Minneapolis, played thirty-four minutes and scored twenty-two points; Pat Graham, who hadn't played at all against Minnesota, played thirty-five minutes and scored twenty-one points, and Alan Henderson, after playing six minutes at Minnesota, played thirty-six, scored twenty points, and led both teams with eleven rebounds.

And we had enough to win, barely—82–77.

So my conclusion is Ken Harrelson made a good point about the value of not being afraid to lose.

With a caveat: if it's for a purpose that can make future victory and championship chances better.

Speaking of the White Sox, I met Tony LaRussa when I was at a White Sox game in Chicago in the mid-1980s. Before the game, I ate lunch at the ballpark with Eddie Einhorn, one of their owners and a man I had known and liked for a long time because of his role as a pioneer in national telecasts of college basketball games.

As we talked, Eddie told me I should meet his manager. He took me right from there down on the field to meet Tony. I'll always be grateful to Eddie for that introduction, to a man who has become a very special friend.

I looked for chances to get together with Tony after that first meeting. I was speaking in Chicago at an alumni luncheon just before the start of one of our seasons. He happened to be in Chicago then, and he accepted my invitation to come to the luncheon—then got on the university plane with me and went to Fort Wayne, where our basketball team had come up from Bloomington to play a pre-season exhibition intrasquad game that night.

We made that Fort Wayne trip every year until the NCAA made one of its strange decisions and outlawed games like that. In so doing, they eliminated one of the nicest, healthiest things we ever were involved with. Fort Wayne was a great Indiana basketball town—even though it's way up in the northeast corner of the state, more than a hundred miles from Bloomington in southern Indiana. We would announce the date of that exhibition and the first morning tickets went on sale, they'd sell out their Coliseum—10,000 tickets.

People up there loved our kids and looked forward to that night all year long. Our players always came away from the experience understanding a little better just how many people around Indiana were rooting for them and wishing them the best. Half the money, after expenses, went to charities in Fort Wayne and half to our library fund. Nothing could have been a more positive promotion of college sports than that one quick annual visit.

Tony, I'm sure, remembers the warmth of that crowd, but the thing he talks about from the time he was there involved me. He tells how I stopped the scrimmage, set up something I wanted them to do on the fast-break—then in front of 10,000 people, turned, took a shot, made it . . .

And sat down.

I don't remember that, but I know if I did take a shot like that, and if I did make it, I damned sure would have sat right down.

I did know when to quit, sometimes.

• • •

Tony is a big animal rights advocate, very sincere about it. And I'm a lot more of one than I ever let him know. I have too much fun needling him about it to do that.

I was bird-hunting in Montana one fall and the group I was with had a pretty good day. Somebody took the whole harvest and laid it out on the ground for a group picture. I'm not big on that kind of thing, but once they were laid out, I couldn't resist taking advantage. Tony was with Oakland then, and I had brought along a bright green-and-yellow A's cap he had given me. I put on that cap, knelt right in the middle of the birds, and had a picture taken that I sent to him.

The day he got it he was on the phone. "*Big* man," he said. "*Big, big* man."

"Did the birds have guns, too? *Big* man."

He made "big" sound like it had two or three syllables.

Barry Weinberg, his trainer with the A's and now with the Cardinals, is an Indiana graduate—he helped some with our basketball team while he was getting his master's degree. A few years later I did the same thing wearing a Cardinals cap, sent the picture to Barry, and he taped it so firmly onto a blackboard at training camp that not even Tony could rip it off.

But one thing I know for absolute certain is he tried.

We were invited to play California in the first Pete Newell Classic at Oakland in December 1999. Tony lives in the Bay Area in the off-season and he came over to our team hotel to have breakfast the morning of our game. The day before, when we had our workout at the arena, I wasn't very happy with the way we were playing and just stopped the practice and left the floor. And the building. By myself.

A lot of times over the years I have walked back to the hotel after a game-day shooting practice and let the team ride the bus back without me. I've always enjoyed walking. However, this particular day I was not happy with what I had watched. I figured the walk would help me *and* my players.

I was born with a great sense of direction. I hadn't spent a whole lot of time in Oakland, and I knew we were a pretty good distance from the hotel, but I headed out toward where I thought the hotel was. I walked.

And I walked.

At breakfast the next morning, I told Tony where I crossed an interstate and the places I went through. I got to one point and he said:

"*What!?*

"You were *where?*"

I told him again, and he just shook his head.

"You walked through an area where when I was the manager out here it was an automatic fine for our players if they even *drove* through there.

"There's only one reason you got through there. Guys looked out at you walking along by yourself and thought, 'That son-of-a-bitch has to be crazy. No way I'm gonna mess around with him.'"

The truth is a guy driving along recognized me and stopped, backed up, and said, "Coach, where in the hell are you going?" I told him the name of our hotel and he said, "Get in here. I'll take you."

By then, I was glad to be picked up. I had already walked about eight miles and we had at least that far to go.

But my direction was right. I was headed right for the hotel.

One of the greatest thrills I've ever had as a fan was following Tony's Cardinals the 1998 season when Mark McGwire hit seventy home runs.

That could have been a tough year for me, as much as I liked Roger Maris. But no better guy than McGwire could have challenged that record and held up so well to the unimaginable pressures of that run he and Sammy Sosa had. I'm not sure there's ever been a nicer thing in sports than the Cardinals having the Maris kids there to watch and be part of the night when Mark broke Roger's record with his sixty-second home run.

McGwire became a personal friend for me during that run. He gave me the shoes he wore when he hit his fifty-first through fifty-fifth home runs.

The first time I met Mark was in April 1992, the week we played in the Final Four. I had committed myself to a speaking engagement in Phoenix the Monday of Final Four week. I could have worked out of it, but I thought it wouldn't be a bad time for the kids to take a one-day break. So I flew to Phoenix that Monday morning, and I got there with enough time before the speech to drop by the ballpark where Tony and the A's were having spring training.

The players weren't out yet. I was standing with Tony in the infield, talking, when all of a sudden I saw something whirring out in our general direction, then clattering onto the grass.

It was a chair.

And standing in the dugout, proud of himself for his choice of missiles and grinning widely, was McGwire.

We had a great talk that morning. In the seasons that followed, I was around Mark enough to know there has never been a professional athlete who was a finer person. I felt the same way about Roger Maris. How lucky could a guy be, to have known both of those guys and to have great personal memories of each?

I followed Tony's White Sox teams, and, after he left Chicago, his Oakland A's teams, then his St. Louis Cardinals teams. I've enjoyed them all, and I have special memories from each.

One from Chicago didn't really involve me or Tony. Carlton Fisk, the Hall of Fame catcher, was brought to Chicago from Boston when Tony was manager. It was one of the first major moves by Eddie Einhorn and Jerry Reinsdorf after they bought the White Sox in 1980, and Fisk was a big reason why Tony's 1983 White Sox team won the American League West by twenty games.

After Tony left Chicago and relocated in Oakland, I still followed some of his White Sox players. I loved Fisk for his sheer toughness—never more than in 1991 when Deion Sanders was breaking in with the Yankees and Fisk was in his closing years with the White Sox. Sanders hit a pop-up, tossed his bat away, and didn't even bother to run it out. Now, Fisk was playing *against* Sanders, but Fisk ripped into him—right out there on the field—for being a disgrace to the professionalism of baseball by not running out that pop-up.

I told a friend of mine who went to some Sox games and occasionally was in the clubhouse that if he ever got the opportunity I'd love for him to tell Fisk how much I admired that move. One day he did, and he said Fisk grinned, threw back his head and laughed, and said, "I'll bet he of all people really did like that." Later, Glenn Banks, a friend of mine from Elkhart, Indiana, set it up for me to meet Carlton and play a round of golf with him. It was as enjoyable an experience as I thought it would be.

I've always really liked baseball, and nothing was better for me as a fan and follower of baseball than Sparky Anderson's Cincinnati Reds teams of the 1970s.

Sparky was one of the best managers in baseball history and I was able to spend a lot of time talking to him about why he did certain things. He and his staff were great storytellers, and baseball has the best history that can be verbalized. He was fun to be around—energetic, enthusiastic. And you always knew where you stood. He let me do a lot of things in spring training, just as I do now with Tony LaRussa and the Cardinals. Sparky for me was a baseball fan's dream come true.

Sparky as a manager had a tremendous appreciation for players of his who went at things in a professional way and really worked at what they did. I think he genuinely felt privileged to be around the great players he had on those Reds teams. And at the very same time, I was feeling much the same way, for the kids I got to deal with at Indiana.

When Sparky left, John McNamara took his place. Once the Reds were playing an exhibition game. I was sitting with John in the dugout, and he called over Jerry Crawford, who was one of the umpires. John told him, "Crawford, I'm not going to say a word to you tonight. I've got a real expert to get on your ass." Jerry leaned over to look into the dugout, saw me, and said, "Oh, Jeezus."

Among today's players, Jim Thome of the Indians was as big a fan as our Indiana teams had. He was from Peoria, and he came over to Bloomington for games with his brother and their dad, who I've heard were almost legendary softball players over there. All I know is the Thomes were three big men who went out with us—and the Indians' general manager then, John Hart—for some pizza and a great evening of conversation after one game they came to at Assembly Hall.

Baseball is a kind of universal language, appealing to all kinds of people.

When we played in the NCAA tournament in Landover, Maryland, George Will, the political essayist and Cubs fan who has written a couple of books on baseball, went to dinner with us the night before our game. Baseball was the primary conversation, with a little bit of Washington politics thrown in. Then he came to the game the next night.

David Halberstam, a great journalist and historian who could fill a library with his outstanding books, is a big basketball and baseball fan. His basketball interest got the two of us together, and he knew me well enough that when he was writing *Summer of '49*, he called and said he needed to talk to Joe DiMaggio and Ted Williams and couldn't get in contact with either one. I told him I didn't know DiMaggio but I'd see what I could do with Williams. He told me later he set up a meeting at Ted's home, and when he knocked on Williams's door, he said Ted's first comment was, "Just keep in mind: you're here because that goddamned basketball coach said you're a good guy, so you'd better be." He spent a productive day with Williams and in the credits of his book said, "Robert Montgomery Knight was valuable serving as Ted Williams's press agent."

Dick Enberg, who has excelled as a football, basketball, and tennis announcer as well as baseball, is an Indiana graduate who got his start broadcasting basketball games there as a student. My last year at Indiana, the school honored him and I was happy to be there for the ceremony. Dick was the NBC announcer for our 1981 NCAA championship game, the last one he did before NBC lost the Final Four rights to CBS.

Several years ago, I sat with Dick and watched the Padres beat Tony LaRussa's A's in an exhibition game in Yuma, 3–0. The A's had a meeting the next morning at nine o'clock. I went, and after it I got on Tony about his offense. He flipped the lineup card at me, hit me in the chest, and said, "Okay, dammit, you make out the lineup."

I know he expected me to hand it back. But I said, "Sure! Give me a pen." The only condition was I had to use the names he gave me. I did.

So he and I were sitting in the dugout together, watching "my team" play, and in the second inning, a guy behind the dugout started to get on us. "God almighty, there's two guys in there—one's in basketball and doesn't know anything about it and the other one's in baseball and doesn't know anything about it." Tony said, "Don't turn around." The guy kept it up for an inning, and finally I couldn't resist taking a look.

It was Enberg, with that great voice of his disguised.

In the spring of 2000, the day of the NCAA basketball championship game, I was sitting in the Cardinals' dugout with Tony and Bill Parcells before they played an exhibition game with Cleveland. All of a sudden a baseball came bouncing in, bumping against my leg. I picked it up, and it had come from the Indians' dugout. Written on the ball was, "Tony: How could you possibly lose with a brain trust like that? Grover." That's the baseball nickname for Mike Hargrove, who was managing the Indians then. I wrote on the other side of the ball, "Mike: If Parcells could coach, the Jets would have been in the Super Bowl. And if I could, we'd be on TV tonight. Bob." I threw it back to him, and he picked it up, showed it to his coaches who were sitting with him, then put it in his pocket. I've heard he still has that ball.

Whenever the opportunity arises—and with me there never seems to be a shortage of opportunities—a newspaper story involving me almost always includes something that runs alongside called "A chronology of events involving Indiana basketball coach Bob Knight," maintained by the Associated Press.

Okay, let's play this game.

1975–76
Upset over two turnovers, Knight grabbed sophomore Jim Wisman by the jersey and jerked him into his seat.

It happened, and a picture of it ran across the country. It does look pretty mean. But there is a degree of humor to it. After we won the NCAA championship, we visited the White House. We were lined up on the steps to have a picture taken with President Ford, and the first thing he said when he came out was, "I want to meet Jimmy Wisman." We all laughed, and I said, "See, Jimmy, I told you I'd make you famous." In our home game with Michigan, we had worked hard on playing against the Michigan press. With the team we had, especially the guards, I didn't think there was any way we were going to lose the ball. Now, fairly late in the first half, we weren't shooting well and we weren't playing particularly well, and all of a sudden Jimmy was responsible for throwing the ball away twice against their press. I called a time-out, and as they were coming to the bench, I just reached out and grabbed the first kid I saw and sat him down, and it was Jimmy. Jimmy's comment at the time was, "I should have been wearing my tear-away jersey." When reporters called his mother to get her reaction, she said she didn't blame me—she would have grabbed him, too, if she could have. One of my hottest critics was Bob Collins, a sports columnist from the *Indianapolis Star* who eventually became one of my good friends. In my irritation with the whole newspaper world, I threatened to ban photographers from the Assembly Hall playing floor, and I got a quick letter from the president of the National Press Photographers Association:

> *Representing the more than five thousand press photographers across the nation, it is my task to call to your attention the first amendment guaranteeing a free press. In this light, I'm sure you understand our concern for the correctness of the right to cover, not only in text but also in photographs, such events of legitimate news particularly when they occur on publicly-supported grounds. The nature of such coverage is largely dictated by what takes place before our lenses, circumstances over which the subjects have more than passing control. We are sure you understand the position of responsible photojournalists, not only in Indiana, but across the entire nation in this regard. Finally, I feel compelled to say that were I in your shoes in Bloomington Saturday and had Jimmy Wisman turned over the ball twice in as many blinks of the eye, I would have jerked his godamned ass off the floor just as fast and told Bob Collins to stick it up his.*
>
> *Sincerely, Rich Clarkson*

I knew Clarkson well, and so did Jimmy; Rich and Bob Hammel had combined for a book on our program just the year before. Before that and ever since then,

I've always enjoyed a great friendship with a guy who is the absolute best in his field. This letter provided the perfect touch; he got his point across and got me to laugh about my own position in a silly situation. (The extra irony of it all came later, when Jimmy replaced Bobby Wilkerson in the NCAA championship game and played so well when we were pulling away in the second half of that game—against that same Michigan team. That game Jimmy made no turnovers.)

1979

Was charged, and later tried and convicted in absentia, for hitting a Puerto Rican policeman before practice at the Pan American Games. Knight was sentenced to six months in jail but Puerto Rico decided in 1987 to drop efforts to extradite him.

I discussed that one in Chapter 9.

1979–80

Playfully fired a blank shot at a reporter. A week later Knight and his wife took turns at the microphone and chided the Assembly Hall crowd for not cheering enough during a game against Northwestern.

It was a track starter's pistol that didn't accommodate real shells or blanks, and I don't remember if I fired it at him or up in the air. I did it entirely as a joke, with a guy I'd had some disagreements with, trying to inject a little humor and defuse the situation. It didn't, obviously. I'll plead guilty to questionable judgment and an unshared sense of humor. As for the courtside microphone, I used it a lot more times to shut down chants or boos or distracting waves by our fans, stuff that is openly encouraged in some arenas. I'd be surprised if I've used that microphone during games as many as five times, but whatever the number, the supportive but extremely positive decorum by Indiana fans at Assembly Hall was something I was proud of—proud for the fans themselves, who showed you don't have to be arrogant or demeaning to opponents to be passionately supportive of your team, and proud for whatever role my occasional bits of amplified advice played in creating that.

1980–81

Irritated Purdue fans and officials by bringing a donkey onto his TV show wearing a Boilermakers cap.

After our game at Purdue that year, Purdue complained to the Big Ten office about Isiah Thomas hitting Roosevelt Barnes, which happened after Barnes had taken a really cheap shot at Thomas. In the same game, Keith Edmonson of Purdue damned-near decapitated Randy Wittman with an elbow that easily could have broken his jaw. I showed those things and other incidents on the Sunday show. I had invited their athletic director and former basketball coach, George King, who seemed to be particularly incensed, to come on the show with me, and he turned it down—not exactly to my surprise. So, to have a Purdue representative, I came up with a donkey and a Purdue cap. The next week, Fred Taylor talked me out of having cheerleaders bring in a donkey dressed in red and white, or saying I had received a letter from the American Donkey Breeders Association saying what an insult it was to a donkey—the most noble of all beasts, who took pioneers across the Rockies to the West Coast—to be shown wearing a Purdue hat. Coach Taylor said, "You're ahead. Why go any further with it? Just let it go." He was right, of course, but I wish I hadn't asked him. It would have been great.

1980–81

In Philadelphia for the Final Four, Knight was involved in a hotel shoving match with an LSU fan, who said Knight stuffed him in a garbage can.

We stayed at a Cherry Hills, New Jersey, motel where about two hundred LSU fans also stayed. The morning of our semifinal game with LSU, wherever our kids went—to the team meal, to our meeting room—some of their fans were around hollering, "Tiger bait! Tiger bait!" We won the game, went back to the hotel, and I was walking through the bar there to get to the restaurant for dinner. A guy said, "Congratulations," and I kept walking and smiled and said over my shoulder, "Well, we really weren't Tiger bait after all, were we?" I took about two steps and the guy started screaming, "Knight's an asshole! Knight's an asshole!" I approached the man. Now, that was twenty years ago. At a press conference the next day, when it was all much fresher in my mind than now, my version of it all was, "I said, 'Would you like to say again what you just said?' He said, 'I gave you a compliment and you were very sarcastic and rude to me.' I said, 'No, I wasn't sarcastic and rude to you. I just threw back at you something our kids have been hearing all day long.' He said, 'Well, you're still an asshole.' I grabbed him, shoved him up against the wall, and turned and walked away." I remember a Philadelphia newspaper ran the story (that's where I read that the guy wound up in a garbage can) and the headline was KNIGHT TRADES SHOVES, INSULTS WITH LSU FAN. At the press conference, I said, "We didn't trade shoves. I did all the shoving. And we didn't trade insults. He did all the insulting." The press had mellower but more perceptive people then. We hadn't shot exactly great in beating LSU, and one writer, after my explanation, said, "After watching your team yesterday, I wonder: did the fan go cleanly into the garbage can, or did he rim out?" I told him, "I understand the bartender called goaltending and a charge."

1981–82
Ohio State guard Troy Taylor said Knight cursed him after he thought Taylor flagrantly fouled a player. Knight denied the charge and sent films of what happened to the Big Ten office and to Ohio State. Ohio State later supported Knight.

Taylor had undercut Jimmy Thomas, with a few seconds left in the game when we had an eight-point lead. Jimmy was lying on the floor, I walked out to check on him, and Taylor came over toward me. I said, "Get the hell away from here." That was my "cursing." And what Ohio State did took care of the rest.

1982–83
Critical of Big Ten officiating, Knight stood at mid-court cursing at Big Ten commissioner Wayne Duke, who was sitting in the press box. Two days later, Knight assailed the referees for the "worst officiating I have seen in twelve years."

Wayne was sitting in the press section, and I turned to say something to him about his officials. If there was any profanity at all, it certainly wasn't aimed at Wayne personally. I thought the world of him, and still do.

1984–85
Tossed a chair across the court during a game against Purdue. Knight was ejected and later apologized. He was suspended one game by the Big Ten.

Guilty, of course. I dealt with that in Chapter 11.

1985–86
Received a technical foul for shouting at the officials during a game against Illinois, then kicked a megaphone and chewed out the Indiana cheerleaders for disrupting a free-throw attempt by Steve Alford.

I have no idea what made that technical foul an "incident." As for the cheerleaders—they had gotten into a routine where they and the crowd chanted through Alford's free-throw routine: he'd dry his hands on the inside of his socks, he'd bounce the ball, then he'd shoot. When the cheerleaders and the crowd started calling out each of those steps, it did seem to bother him—and when Alford, probably the best free-throw shooter in the country, missed one just before halftime in a key game, it damned well did bother me. I always tried to keep things pretty good in Assembly Hall for visiting kids shooting a free-throw—no waving by fans behind the basket, no screaming, an atmosphere where it was up to the kid to make or miss the free-throw, without a bunch of artificial distractions. So I certainly didn't expect our people to be chanting something that would bother one of our kids up there shooting.

1986–87

Banged his fist on the scorer's table after being assessed a technical foul during an NCAA regional tournament game against LSU. The university was fined $10,000 by the NCAA and Knight received a reprimand.

That all started with the cheapest technical foul I ever received. A call was made involving Daryl Thomas, at the opposite end of the court from me and at such a bad angle that I didn't know whether the ball was going over to LSU because Thomas traveled or committed an offensive foul. I asked everyone on the bench, "What was the call?" Nobody saw a signal from an official. It was early in the first half, and a foul would have been his second—I'd have wanted to take him out right away. The call caused a TV time-out, so while play was stopped, I tried to get the attention of the official standing in mid-court in front of me so I could ask if a foul was called. I couldn't get his eye, so I stepped out to ask him what the call was, and he hit me with a technical foul. The tournament committee representatives were at a table behind our bench. I walked over to tell them the technical was ridiculous, and I banged my fist down on the table in front of them to emphasize my feelings. The receiver on a telephone jumped in the air, and the picture that came out of that wound up, I'll always believe, costing me $10,000 (in a fine levied after the tournament). I think the tournament committee had told officials, "Don't put up with this . . . or that . . ." That's fine, if I had come charging out, screaming or hollering, but when you have a question, where else are you going to get an answer?

1987–88

Refused to let his team finish an exhibition game against the Soviet Union after he was ejected for arguing with a referee. He was later reprimanded by the university.

We had a mixed crew of international and U.S. officials, and we were playing the game by NCAA rules—which, understandably, the Russians were unfamiliar with. Alexander Gomelsky, who was coaching the Russians that night, a couple of times came all the way to mid-court, out of the coaching box, obviously violating our rule. I just told the officials—a guy from Canada and Jim Burr, who did some Big Ten officiating—"Let him go. Don't worry about it."

Then at one point they had six guys on the court, during actual playing. It was unintentional, of course, but that's a violation in international ball, too. I stopped play and pointed it out. The officials hadn't noticed. Then it happened a second time. Then what ended the game was we were shooting a free-throw, and after the ball was handed to their shooter, one of the Russians walked across the lane. No call. Now, I stepped out to say, "This is getting ridiculous," and I got a technical for being out of the box, then a second one, which meant expulsion. Bill Wall from USA Basketball was traveling with the Russians. He was sitting near the end of the court. I walked to him to tell him to get the officials together and say, "There's no technical here—let's get this thing under control." I love Bill Wall. I've had a great relationship with him for more than thirty years. But that one time I did get upset with him, because he refused to get involved. Now, I didn't really end the game by taking my team off the floor. I was so mad I didn't leave the court when I was told to, and Burr said, as the rules give him the right to, "Okay, that's it. Game's over." And he signed the scorebook, closing it out. That's when the cameras saw me, not very pleased by any of this, wave to my players to leave because the game *was* over. You can say I caused it to end when it did, and be right, but I didn't pull my players off the court and quit. That's what's always said, and it's wrong. I will say we played the Soviets several times. I never cared for Gomelsky. Vladimir Kondrashin, who, ironically, was the coach when the 1972 Olympic gold medal was taken from Henry Iba's team, was a guy I really liked—he was a hell of a coach and a really good person (and, for the record, when he was the national coach, in a game against our team at Indianapolis, he disagreed with a foul call and pulled his team off the court, for a few minutes). Of all the coaches I met from foreign countries, Antonio Diaz-Miguel of Spain and Kondrashin were my favorites. I later spent time with him in Russia, when I was there on a fishing trip. He has since passed away. I wasn't very big on Burr for a while after that game because I thought he totally mishandled the situation, but I grew to think he was one of the best officials in our league. The only thing I remember about the guy from Canada was that after that six-men-on-the-court thing was allowed, I told him, "Why the hell don't you go home and officiate hockey? They *let* six guys play that game."

1988

In an NBC interview with Connie Chung, who asked how he handles stress, Knight replied, "I think that if rape is inevitable, relax and enjoy it." He explained he was talking about something beyond one's control, not the act of rape. The remark triggered protests and a march of about 300 people on the campus.

I was called by an NBC News executive who was an Indiana graduate, asking me to be part of a show on stress. I said right away that I'd rather not—"I coach basketball. That's not stress. What a brain surgeon or a heart surgeon does every day is stress. Feeding a family of four and getting laid off—that's stress. Not what I do." I went ahead with arrangements for the interview, thinking we had an understanding after my comment that basketball wouldn't be discussed. The taping was done the morning after we lost to Illinois at the buzzer, so I wasn't in the best of moods, but I went ahead with it. They set it up with Connie Chung and me sitting in folding chairs on the court at Assembly Hall. I was going to lunch afterward with Quinn Buckner, book author Joan Mellen, and Bob Hammel, so they were sitting on the sidelines waiting for us to finish. She kept persisting about coaching and officiating, as an illustration of stress, and I made a comment, "Why are we talking about basketball?" Finally, to try to shut her up relative to officiating, I said, "When rape is inevitable, you just relax and enjoy it." I knew immediately it was a dumb remark and I didn't even hesitate. I turned to the director and said, "And don't even think about using that in this show because somebody will run wild with that. We weren't *supposed* to talk about basketball; that's why I'm doing this. Now let's get back on with what you want and forget basketball."

Altogether, we must have talked for about an hour on tape and they used at most five minutes. Included—almost featured in the show—was that remark. They certainly had more than enough that was more pertinent to their stress theme. While we were taping, she said dozens of things that she and I both knew would never be on the show, including her describing her alma mater, Maryland, as a "shitty" school. This happened so far back in time that there were obscenities that actually weren't being allowed on TV then. In this case, at least as many, and I'd bet more, of those came from her than from me. That was the atmosphere in which that line came—talk freely here, don't worry, we'll edit it to what we need. Certainly, I made a mistake in saying it; if it had been done before an audience, I'd say they, as a news agency, had an obligation to use it. But under the circumstances—when so much was being said that obviously wouldn't be used, and they were imposing on me, not me on them— I was naive enough to think that asking them not to use that one thing would be enough. It's obvious that for her, at least, this was *modus operandi,* and once she had it she couldn't wait to exploit it.

Let me add this: Not long after that I read in a Lee Iacocca book how much he had disliked doing an interview with her. An incident with Newt Gingrich's mother which was similar to mine finally pretty much unveiled her to the public. She was light years away from the approach, the understanding, and the kind of intelligence that most women in television I've met and worked with, like Andrea Joyce, Andrea Kreamer, or Lesley Visser, brought to their job.

1990–91

Asked not to be nominated again to the Basketball Hall of Fame, calling the voters' rejection of him in 1987 a "slap in the face." He was elected and inducted into the Hall in 1991.

I saw somewhere that Bob Cousy said because of the Russian game, I couldn't be admitted. So I said, fine. If that's the way things are going to be, I don't want to be nominated. In saying that, I was just going by who already had been elected to the Hall of Fame, their credentials compared to mine. If it had been someone named Bill Smith instead of Bob Knight, the guy should have been elected to the Hall of Fame. I had always had a good relationship with the people at the Hall of Fame and done anything they had asked me to do; when Fred Taylor was inducted, they asked me to be the keynote speaker at the luncheon, and I was glad to do that; I had worked on their behalf; Curt Gowdy was involved in it as president for several years; I worked hard relative to Pete Newell going in the Hall of Fame, and nobody was more deserving than he was—nor was anybody happier to be there the night he went in than I was; and, as I mentioned, I brought Clair Bee to the ceremonies when he was inducted. I was "clean" enough to be asked to do all those things for the Hall of Fame but Cousy and that vote were saying I wasn't good enough to get in. I'm not a Cousy fan. He wrote a book with a sportswriter I like, Bob Ryan—called *The Celtic Mystique*. Now, why I would be in a book with that title escapes me, but there's a whole chapter in it about me. And the stuff involving me wasn't even accurate. I called Ryan and said, "This stuff did not happen." He said, "I took Cousy's word." I said, "You should have checked it. This is absolute bullshit." It had to do with a scrimmage when I was coaching at West Point and Cousy was coaching Boston College. Cousy's assistant, Jack Magee, called me about coming to West Point to play a scrimmage game. Eastern teams did that then (allowed by the NCAA if the scrimmage replaced a regular game in the schedule limit). Teams liked to come to West Point because we could put them up overnight and feed them and it didn't cost anything. Cousy had Jack call me two days before the scrimmage and say they wanted out of it. I just said, "We're counting on this scrimmage. We could have gotten anybody in the East to come. Why in the hell did you even contact us if you didn't want to scrimmage?" That's not the way I come out in Cousy's book.

1990–91

Publicly feuded with Illinois coach Lou Henson, who called him a "classic bully" who thrives on intimidation.

Henson and I went through a couple of years when we didn't get along very well, but I always had genuine respect for him as a coach. I think he had a couple of assistant coaches who went out of line with recruiting. But I felt he was a damned good coach and I enjoyed playing against his teams because they worked at playing against you, at both ends of the floor. I don't know that I've ever met a coach who genuinely likes basketball more than Henson does. He had enthusiasm—he coached like hell. He was up and down, he was on officials, I thought he really coached. There wasn't anything phony about his work along the sidelines, like there is with so many guys. And we wound up being good friends. I think Lou Henson was the most underrated coach that we played against, and I'm at a place now where we will be playing against him again, as the coach at New Mexico State.

1991–92

Barred a female reporter from the locker room, saying it was inappropriate for her to be in there and against university policy. All reporters were subsequently barred from the locker room.

We did close our locker room to the press and set it up for players to go to the press room for interviews. We did it the day after a woman reporter from the Associated Press made a national issue out of being barred from going into our locker room. Bob Hammel and I went to lunch to talk about it. I thought it was uncomfortable for players to have women in the locker room; Bob said as many good stories as he had gotten from talking to kids there after a game, it was unfair for men to be able to do that and not women. So he and I basically agreed the only fair thing to do was close the locker room to everybody and bring some players out to our regular press conference. That became the university policy, not just basketball—football had been operating the same way we did and switched after that. Bill Mallory was just like me—he felt opening the football locker room to everybody was uncomfortable for the players. Call us old-fashioned.

1991–92

Canceled the annual team banquet after a loss to Purdue cost Indiana a share of the Big Ten championship.

Yes, I sure as hell did—and not just for that one year, but for good. This was something I had been wanting to do for years and had just not done it. And when I did the players couldn't thank me enough.

1991–92

Playfully gave a mock whipping to Calbert Cheaney, a black player, during practice for the NCAA West regional. Several black leaders said they were offended. Knight denied any racial connotations. He noted the bull whip was given to him by the players, including Cheaney.

I don't think anyone from the NAACP who looked into the situation or knew me was offended. We had five black players on that ten-man team, and after the players had spent some time shopping in Albuquerque they presented me with a whip they had bought as a joking reference to what all had been said and written about how tough I was on them. They had my son Pat give it to me, and we all got a big kick out of it. I brought it out at our open practice at Albuquerque and pretended to use it on Calbert Cheaney and Pat Graham. The next day, during the UCLA game, Cheaney pretended to beat me over the butt with a towel. My relationship with black kids and how well I have seen them do beyond basketball are among my greatest pleasures. I'm proud, too, of how many very prominent black people said publicly during my era there that if they had a son who played basketball, Indiana was where they'd want him to go—Jimmy Brown, Bill Russell, Wilt Chamberlain, Jesse Jackson, and Harry Edwards, to name some.

1993–94

Was suspended for one game after a sideline tirade in a 101–82 victory over Notre Dame. Knight screamed at his son, Pat, and kicked his chair. When fans behind the Indiana bench booed, Knight turned and responded with an obscenity.

At least it does say "kicked his *chair.*" Pat's strength as a player was his passing. The game before, when we were beating Kentucky at Indianapolis, he had made a poor pass, through carelessness, and I got on him pretty good about it. This night we were beating Notre Dame by a pretty good score, but the score of the game has never meant a whole lot to me where carelessness was concerned. Pat had played well throughout the game but with about two minutes to go he made a careless pass, so I called a time-out. He sat down, and I kicked a leg of his chair, as I've probably done with damned near everybody who has ever played for me. *I* knew I didn't kick Pat. Obviously Pat knew, and in TV close-ups his facial expression never changed. Apparently some people sitting behind that area thought I had kicked him and reacted by yelling at me. I thought they should have known me better than that, and I let them know that. It was over in a few seconds. That was a Tuesday. On Wednesday, Bob Costas and an NBC crew came in to complete an interview, and he had a game tape that included a close-up of the kick. They set up a monitor on the first row of the bleachers, and we looked at the tape. Clearly, we all agreed, I kicked the chair, not Pat. We opened our Indiana Classic on the following Friday. Three days after the incident, three hours before game-time, I was informed by the athletic director that he was going to suspend me for that game for unsportsmanlike behavior. I asked him if he had ever asked Pat if he got kicked. He said no, he didn't have to. I sat out the game, but I knew then that things were different from what they had been under the four athletic directors for whom I had worked before at Indiana.

1993–94

Accidentally head-butted freshman Sherron Wilkerson during a time-out at Michigan State. After the next game, the Hoosiers' home finale against Wisconsin, Knight took the public address microphone and recited a profane verse directed at his critics.

Of all the charges here, this may be the most ludicrous. This happened at Michigan State, and in the press conference after the game, it wasn't even brought up—the story the people covering the game were interested in involved Alan Henderson, who had scored forty-one points for us, and Shawn Respert, who had scored forty for Michigan State, which won the game. ESPN made the "head butt" into a big issue on *Sports Center* that night and suddenly it was an "incident." Facts: The last few weeks of this season and into the NCAA tournament, I had a painful problem in my lower back. It came and went, but as people with back problems know when it hit it was excruciating. During games, I had to stand up for about one minute every two minutes because sitting brought it on—sitting or kneeling, the worst things there were for me then. I took Wilkerson out of the game, and as I knelt to talk to him, a shot of pain made me lurch forward and our heads accidentally bumped—a bump for both of us but a hell of a long way from a WWF-style head-butt. Then I told him what I wanted to, went back to my seat, and soon he was back in the game. The game played out without one bit of thought from anybody until ESPN came up with the "head-butt" angle that amazingly still lives. If there was an issue here, it involved how a network covers a basketball game, not how a coach treats a player. As for the Wisconsin game, my "profane" remark was a couplet that wound up with the words "kiss my ass." I wouldn't call that elegant, but profane seems a little strong, too.

1994–95

Was reprimanded and fined $30,000 by the NCAA for an outburst at a news conference during the NCAA tournament. Miffed that an NCAA media liaison erroneously said he would not attend the news conference, Knight lashed out at him.

Yes, I went too far. But (1) as well as press relations have been handled at most NCAA tournament levels, this one wasn't, and (2) I'll never buy the idea of fines for college coaches—suspensions, maybe, but not fines. Do you realize what an out-and-out criminal would have to do in society to be fined $30,000? We had just lost a tough game to Missouri. I've certainly been to enough tournaments to know the postgame routine. Our players went on as scheduled, and I was waiting for someone to come and get me to go on after them. Nobody came. I heard that the moderator, given wrong information by a student courier, told the media he understood I wouldn't be coming, then put Norm Stewart and the Missouri players on. When they were done, I left to go to the conference—thirty minutes after the game ended. I expected an introductory explanation of why I was late—through their error, not mine—but instead I heard something like, "I believe Coach Knight is finally here." That pissed me off, because now it looked like I came only because someone forced me to, which absolutely had not happened. I later heard the moderator was flustered but not trying to be a horse's ass, just to get a mishandled situation over as quickly as he could. Dave Cawood, who was there and whose job included press relations and press-conference procedures for the NCAA, knew what had happened and I think really tried to help me, but nobody on the tournament committee listened to him. Now, I understand: this is an incident that typifies my problems. There were a lot of times when I should have just shut up. There have been a lot of things I could have just accepted and gone on with. But that's tough, when somebody or something is wrong, or somebody is just totally inaccurate.

1997–98

Was fined $10,000 by the Big Ten for berating referee Ted Valentine, whose officiating Knight called "the greatest travesty" he had seen in his coaching career. Knight received three technical fouls and was ejected by Valentine during the second half of a loss to Illinois. Valentine was also penalized by the Big Ten.

I'll stand by my comment: the way that guy worked that game was "the greatest travesty" I've ever seen by an official. And the three technical fouls—the first was absurd, the second even the Big Ten said should not have been called, and, because it meant ejection, it led directly to the third. The officiating wasn't the only travesty in that whole issue.

1999

Investigated for possible battery after allegedly choking a man at a restaurant. The man reportedly confronted Knight as he was leaving, contending he heard Knight make a racist remark.

Please note the word "investigated" and the term "for possible," which is a hell of a long way from saying "guilty of" or even "charged with." No charges of any kind were filed because the prosecutor, after a ridiculously long investigation with daily press conferences and TV interviews, found the claim unjustified. That part isn't mentioned in the "incidents," nor the fact that I was with my wife and her two sisters, and people around us in the restaurant—seated much closer to our table than the guy making the charges—said as the people at my table did that nothing remotely racial was said by anybody. My explanations have a way of never being accepted in anything. Or those from anybody supporting me, like Sherron Wilkerson in the "head-butt" or Dave Cawood at Boise or Mike Krzyzewski at Puerto Rico, or the retired minister and his wife, who didn't know me or any of us but happened to sit at the next table at the Mexican restaurant and came forward on their own to say nothing remotely offensive was said.

The other items on the AP laundry list involve the charade played out at the university from March through September 2000. Bottom line: I have never stopped to figure out what's going to "play" the best in Peoria or anywhere else. I've just gone with my feelings. If I'm wrong about that, I'm wrong. I'm sure it would have been a hell of a lot smarter for me to have stopped and thought: what's going to create the fewest waves for me in what I say? I've just never done that. I keep going back to what Al McGuire said about the press, "It's a con job. You've got to be a con man in dealing with them."

I never was.

But Al, now—he was a master, and one of my favorite people.

As a coach, he did things very simply, but he controlled the games and controlled his players. He got some really talented players to play great basketball—outstanding defense, patient offense. I'm sure his assistants, Hank Raymonds and later Rick Majerus, gave him a lot of help, but his teams were good. He had an understanding of what had to be done to win. He fully understood how well you had to play defensively.

Al told me once I had to get out of West Point. He was never bashful about giving out advice. After he retired from coaching in 1977, when his team won the NCAA championship, Al worked a lot of our games as a TV analyst.

It happened that we played in his last TV game. It was the last regular-season game of my last year at Indiana, at Wisconsin. He was doing the game with Dick Enberg, who told me Al broke down in tears the night before that game at Madison and told him, "I can't do this anymore." He did our game, but that was it. You could see that day he was failing fast. He hung on but died several months later. As many times as I have, on request of their family or friends, made calls to people who were suffering and in many cases dying, I found it really hard to call Al over those months. It was just like the last few months of Joe Cipriano.

A lot of people think college basketball is in big trouble right now because kids are leaving college early to be pros—or jumping over the college game altogether to get to that NBA money.

I'm not against kids leaving college early to be pros. I spoke to a businessmen's group and during a questioning period, a guy suggested college basketball should have a rule requiring a kid who accepts a scholarship to stay a minimum of three years.

I told him, "There's no way you can require a kid to do that. This is free enterprise. You've got a certain skill; we can't tell you that you can only work east of the Mississippi River. That's essentially the kind of limitation you're suggesting in trying to deny some kids opportunities."

When it's the wrong move for a player to make, somebody has to convince the kid, "You're not ready"—whether the player's shortcoming is emotional or physical.

That's hard to sell to kids. Kids always think they're really good.

Bo Schembechler and I talked about that once. He was an assistant coach under Woody Hayes when I was a basketball player at Ohio State. I knew him then, and years later he said, "Do you remember when you came in to see me— you thought you should have been playing more than you were, and you were actually playing a lot. In fact, if you'll remember I told you that you were playing a hell of a lot more than you would have if I was coaching.

"You went away and felt a little bit better because I had you convinced you were playing a lot." And, in fact, I was.

He said, "That was like when I was at Miami. When I was a sophomore I thought I should have been the starting right tackle. And, dammit, I still think so today."

Well, kids think—always—that they're just a little bit better than they are. So a kid who's pretty good may think he's a lot better than he is.

Or maybe he can't understand, in a realistic way, the difference between his playing in college—or, much more extreme, high school—and what it's going to be like in the pros.

Those kids always get hurt by this tempting chance to climb to the top too swiftly, before they're ready.

We do one thing that's wrong right now. We let a kid announce for the pros, see where he's drafted, and if he doesn't like it he can come back to college.

I'd have a hell of a time coaching that kid. I would have to say to him, "You've got a decision to make. You're either going to go to the pros or you're not. You're pregnant or you're not; there isn't any halfway. If you decide to go, you're not coming back here." Because a team is involved. It's similar to a key injury. Immediately I, as a coach, start dealing with a new situation, talking with other kids on my team about their own roles now in a new situation, and with other kids who might be more interested in us as recruits. If you go out the door, you close the door, as far as your playing status is concerned.

That finality would deter some kids. Then a kid might say, "I'm not going to take a chance. I've got another year." It's tough for a kid today. Somebody gets hold of him—a family member, or maybe even somebody they don't even know—and convinces him, "This is your big chance," or, "The pros think . . . The pros think . . ." and he believes they actually *know*, in part because he wants to. But those people pushing him aren't the ones who might be blowing a lifetime, as a lot of poorly informed kids have done.

The person making the promise may be an agent, even a well-known one. The NCAA thinks college basketball has a big problem with agents right now, but it doesn't have to be as big as it is.

You eliminate agents by making representation for a professional contract part of the scholarship the kid gets for attending an institution. In our situation, I get three or four attorneys who are really willing to help our players, volunteer their services to any of our players who are capable of signing a contract, and it doesn't cost the kid anything to know the real pluses and minuses of going, with eligibility left.

You virtually eliminate agents by doing that. But the NCAA by 2050 will not come up with that as a solution.

Our big problem in college basketball is not with the kids we lose to the pros but the ones we pervert the process to admit—the ones who are in college only to become pros and take up a place that a genuine, degree-seeking student could have.

I've said for years the NBA should be financing minor leagues that would be open to those kids. The whole college basketball system suffers when kids make a charade of going to college and a coach and school add to the sham by calling them student-athletes. I said that when the NBA was a nickel-and-dime operation compared to the billions those people are pulling in and throwing around today. A whole minor league system could be financed by all the teams in the league putting up the money—combined—that any one of them is paying to a single player or two now. They would benefit and we in college basketball would benefit.

The NBA seems to be starting in that direction now, although I doubt if it's out of concern for anything but self-interest. Rather, it's probably the rising trend—and enormous cost to the NBA—of kids going pro straight out of high school. That may work for all the Kobe Bryants who come along—great athlete, lifetime background in the game, 1200 on the SAT.

Don't hold your breath until the next one of those surfaces.

Meanwhile, considerably less gifted and less ready players are putting the NBA in the baby-sitting business, team after team taking a raw talent and hoping he can be developed and matured into a good player.

I don't think an NBA-financed minor league, even with pretty good salaries, would hurt college basketball at all, not if college basketball accepts it as the challenge that it should. The college game has something worthwhile to sell, too: the opportunity to earn a college degree.

People who snicker at that don't belong in college basketball. If we don't believe that's a primary objective, why should a kid?

Minor leagues would leave the colleges for student-athletes. And there are lots more of those than there are NBA spots.

Take even a Kobe Bryant. There's no question he made the right decision for achieving maximum income in his basketball lifetime, probably even for his quick development as a basketball player.

But shouldn't there be more to it than that? Shouldn't a young player take a year or two, or four, and develop his intellect as well as his basketball skills?

We're failing in college basketball if a kid who leaves us at twenty-two isn't really well prepared to enter post-basketball life—whether that's after a career in the pros or without one.

That's a big part of what I have in mind when I talk about why I've stayed in coaching as long as I can. My game is educating kids.

Players today, even most fans today, aren't aware that one of the first rules adopted at the turn-of-the-century to govern college athletics made freshmen ineligible. Except for a couple of temporary waivers during wartime, that remained the case until 1972.

I thought changing it was a mistake then, even though we went to the Final Four with two freshman guards (Quinn Buckner and Jim Crews) the first year it applied. I still think it's a mistake, although I have probably started as many freshmen over the years as any coach has. To compete, on the floor and in recruiting, I have to work under the rules that are in effect. And I've always laughed at people who talk about how complicated the game we teach is. If a kid can play, he can play, and age doesn't really have a lot to do with that.

I'm not making a phony claim. In the twenty-eight years I've coached with freshman eligibility, I've had fifty-nine "true" freshmen—straight out of high school—start games, and twenty-five were what I would consider regulars. Four times at Indiana, our leading scorer for the season was a freshman. In the fifteen years that they've picked a Freshman of the Year in the Big Ten, our Indiana teams had four (Eric Anderson, Jay Edwards, Damon Bailey, and A. J. Guyton). That doesn't count Mike Woodson, the all-time leading freshman scorer in the Big Ten. He scored 396 points and averaged twenty-two points a game in league play in 1977, before they started naming a Freshman of the Year.

But I still think freshman eligibility is a mistake and has contributed enormously to some of today's biggest problems—proliferation of the tout sheets that put a rating on every kid in America, newspaper and talk shows' preoccupation with recruiting, the high transfer rate of recruited players, the intrusion of shoe companies into recruiting. Give a player a year out of the spotlight, to adjust from high school hype to college reality, and it would be amazing how many pressures would ease.

That doesn't even deal with the reason for the original rule against freshman play: anybody, athlete or not, is best served by having a year to adjust to college academic demands. The extra benefit of a year out is that we'd no longer have to deal with predictions of academic success or failure; the athlete would have a year to prove whether he or she truly is a qualified student-athlete.

I've never felt college was for everybody. I think it's long since time for the NBA, with all that wealth, to underwrite a developmental system for kids who can play basketball but feel they have to go to college for a year or two to gain entrance to the NBA. I hear people worry about the college game's future because so many players—maybe fifteen or twenty a year—are leaving college early. That's never been a worry of mine, and we lost one of the best early declarers ever when Isiah Thomas left with two seasons of eligibility to go. He was absolutely right in leaving then; he should have been able to leave then. And college basketball didn't miss a beat.

Isiah was doing fine as a student. In fact, he may be the only really high-salaried, ultra-successful athlete yet to leave school two years early and still stay with it academically and come out with a degree. He and his tough, demanding, proud, loving mother, Mary, probably deserve equal credit for that.

But Isiah was the exception in lots of ways. A high percentage of those kids leaving for the NBA early were failing academically when they made their decision—they were going to be missing from college basketball anyway. Those are the kids who were wasting college money and classroom space by being there in the first place. I have always favored far tighter academic requirements for college athletes than even the reformers in the NCAA have tried for, and a minor league underwritten by the NBA for kids who now are going to college only to play basketball.

Not letting freshmen play would help a lot, even without tightening requirements. You'd be playing freshman schedules. A lot of kids who were touted high school players would all of a sudden be unveiled as very average college players. Heads and egos would shrink, for both kids and parents. High school reputations would mean less. Talk shows and Internet chat rooms wouldn't essentially get more intelligent—damn, freshman eligibility isn't some sort of Lourdes—but they might not do quite so much damage to kids' heads. And, with that year of sitting out taking away the instant-turnaround possibility, those tout sheets would lose some popularity.

It would be worth the change if only the last part happened.

The credibility people give to national rankings of high school players absolutely baffles me.

To the best of my ability, I can't even imagine a coach, ever, who was capable of saying "This kid is the thirty-second–best or the thirty-fourth–best small forward in the country." I'm talking about a *coach*. I'm talking about a guy like me who has coached in college for thirty years: to rate this kid as the best prospect, or the twelfth-best prospect, or the eightieth-best prospect. That's impossible.

Most of these guys who rate kids have no concept of what it takes to put a team together.

But they give a ranking to each kid, and that sells newspapers or publications, and it's gospel. Meanwhile, nobody ever follows through and sees how often they were right, and how more often they were wrong.

Where, for example, do you suppose Larry Bird was ranked nationally as a high school player? Where was Calbert Cheaney ranked? Or Karl Malone?

So many things have happened that make it tough for a kid to keep everything in perspective as he advances in development as a person and a player—

the rating systems, the McDonald's All-Star games, the elevation of these kids at seventeen or eighteen years old to national status that a Jerry West or an Oscar Robertson didn't achieve until he had played three or four all-star years in the NBA. And when it did finally come to a West or a Robertson, he had earned it, rather than having it conferred on him by some moron with a pen.

The ratings silliness doesn't stop with individual players, of course. Every year you also see teams ranked for their incoming recruits, and just about every year someone has the greatest class ever put together—"What a great recruiting class!"

A great recruiting class is a class that, after having been there, has won a hell of a lot of games. It isn't a class that's coming in, it's a class that's going out.

We had a class that first year of freshman eligibility that was instrumental in a four-year record of 108–12, won or shared four straight Big Ten championships, had the only two unbeaten seasons since the Big Ten went to an eighteen-game conference schedule, went to the Final Four twice, and won a national championship with the last unbeaten season a college team has put together.

That's a great recruiting class. It's pure bullshit, ranking these kids before they ever play.

And I'll guarantee you: nobody is capable of doing it.

FOURTEEN: *A Long Year (2000–2001)*

Forget everything else and just coach. You have a contract that
protects you from interference with your basketball program.
And Indiana is the place you want to be.

Myles Brand arrived as Indiana University's new president in 1994. In the
fall of 1995, he invited Bob Hammel and me to dinner at his place. The
fourth person there was Christopher Simpson, who had been with Brand at the
University of Oregon and arrived at Indiana that year, as a speechwriter-
spokesman-adviser.

That night, Simpson was new to Hammel and pretty new to me. Before we
ever sat down to eat, the four of us talked. Right away, the conversation got to
football. What did we think of the job the Indiana football coach, Bill Mallory,
was doing? Was it time for a change? Each of us told them the same thing: he
was doing a great job, under uniquely difficult conditions—in a state that
didn't produce many Big Ten football players and split the ones it did have
between Indiana and Purdue, with Notre Dame and Michigan dipping in for
exceptional prospects. Outside Indiana, where high school coaches were great
allies for him, Mallory basically took second-choice recruits and regularly finished ahead of just about everybody in the league but Ohio State and Michigan. One year, 1987, his team beat both Ohio State and Michigan—the only
time in Indiana football history that ever happened.

I had watched Mallory long before he came to Indiana. I was particularly
impressed when he took Colorado to the Orange Bowl and then was fired two
years later after telling some big donors where to stick their money when they
started suggesting things he could do to compete better with Oklahoma and
Nebraska. I had to like a guy like that. He was out of football a year, then took
a job at Northern Illinois to get back in coaching again. He had been there
three years when the Indiana job opened in 1982, and—without ever having
met Mallory—I recommended to Ralph Floyd that he check him out. Ralph
had his preferred choice. He and Sam Wyche had been friends since Wyche was

a college player. Wyche had been an NFL quarterback, then risen in stature within the league as an assistant coach at Cincinnati and then as an assistant under Bill Walsh at San Francisco. Everyone knew he was "hot" among NFL assistants, likely to get a head coaching job soon. None had come when Ralph offered him the Indiana job. And Sam accepted.

I got along great with Sam. Anybody would; he's a hell of a guy. But he was a pro coach, not a college coach. He went 3–8 in his one season at Indiana, then got the offer he had been waiting for and—apologizing, I'm sure sincerely, to Ralph for leaving so soon—became the coach of the Cincinnati Bengals.

This time I asked Ralph if he would mind if I checked out Mallory myself. He didn't, so I called Bill at DeKalb, Illinois, where his fourth Northern Illinois team had just won the Mid-American Conference championship and a bowl game. Mallory has said since that he didn't believe the guy identifying himself was really Bob Knight, until we had talked a while. One of the things that convinced him was when he asked me, "Will Indiana support football, or is it just a basketball school?" I said yes, it would definitely support him. And his second question was, "What kind of talent do they have?"

My answer: "Not nearly enough."

He said he would be interested, Ralph followed up, and within a week Mallory was at Indiana, where he went 0–11 in his first year with the talent I had described. His third year, he put Indiana in a bowl game against Florida State, with Bobby Bowden—Indiana got beat, but played them well. That year and the next, he was Big Ten Coach of the Year. That bowl game was the beginning of an eight-year stretch with six bowl trips. He disciplined his teams. His kids went to class and graduated. I gave him every bit of backing I could with Indiana fans and I was proud I'd had something to do with getting him to Bloomington.

In 1993, he went to his sixth bowl. In 1994, they were bowl-eligible at 6–5, and Ralph would have had them in a bowl. The lawyer who had replaced Ralph couldn't come close to getting that done, because he didn't come close to matching Ralph's lifetime in athletics and the respect he had earned, or the contacts he had throughout college athletics, especially in the bowl community. Still, it was Mallory's seventh winning season at a school that had five in thirty-six years before he came. In '95, the season when Brand invited us to his house, Mallory's team had some crucial injuries and a couple of kids just didn't come through as well as he had expected. I'm a coach. A coach knows those things sometimes happen. Hammel and I went through all the things he had accomplished before the current year. I talked as a coach about how difficult it was in Indiana for football. Brand and Simpson obviously didn't want to hear it. They couldn't have been less impressed.

Bob and I left that night in the same car and we talked about that conversation. We had the same reaction—how could these two guys have any valid opinion whatsoever on the kind of job Mallory had done? It was evident to both of us that they had never played on a competitive sports team and were self-styled experts who knew nothing about athletics. I felt uncomfortable with them from that point on.

The next year, very early in the football season, I was invited to the same kind of dinner meeting with the two of them. I went, all set to discuss Mallory positively and all he had done as a football coach. Before I could even say a word, they told me he had already been fired and a committee was set up to find his replacement. Mallory didn't know it yet, of course. They fired him, publicly, with three games still left in the season. There wasn't anything said about the great job he had done for thirteen years. They said they were firing him to get somebody to take them to the next level.

Think of that: these people came in and fired—didn't just fire, in the process disgraced—a football coach who had the best run of successful teams Indiana has had in football in fifty years. Indiana has played in eight bowl games in 117 years; six of those came under Bill Mallory. And these people fired the guy.

I know that would not have happened with Ralph Floyd.

I know that would not have happened with John Ryan.

I know that would not have happened with Bill Orwig.

I know that would not have happened with Tom Ehrlich.

I knew I was dealing with people I couldn't trust.

And on September 10, 2000, the people who fired Bill Mallory fired me.

Coaching, kind of like the military, has a promotion system and has had it forever. In coaching, it usually involves moving. You win somewhere, you get an invitation to go to a better job. And if you win some more, you move up again.

Administrators talk a good game about graduation rates and keeping programs free of NCAA rules violations, but in most cases—Mallory's firing, for example—that's pure posturing. Coaches are hired or fired, promoted or dismissed, based on how many games and championships they have won and, to a great extent, how many tickets were sold.

My teams at Indiana won games and championships, before constant sellouts, and they added the two factors that most administrators really don't care about—a high graduation rate and no NCAA violations.

And I got fired.

The promotion system still worked.

I moved to a better job that—judging from the way I handled everything right up to my firing—my own stubbornness probably would have denied me, had I not been fired.

My dismissal forced me to look for a situation that I would really like, and where people would appreciate what I try to do. I found it at Texas Tech, where once again I have the opportunity to work with trustworthy and competent people.

And to enjoy coaching.

I tried my damnedest to keep my firing from happening. I accepted a no-win form of probation that every friend I had told me to reject and leave. I felt I could get by just by focusing on coaching and working with our basketball team. *Forget everything else and just coach. You have a contract that protects you from interference with your basketball program. And Indiana is the place you want to be.*

That's what I kept telling myself, so I can't blame anything but my own stubbornness for my being there to be fired in September 2000.

I hadn't changed. People had changed. When Ralph Floyd was athletic director at Indiana, I wasn't aware of one person in the athletic department who wasn't genuinely pulling for every coach and every Indiana team.

In just nine years, things deteriorated to the point that Assembly Hall, where all the coaches but Cam Cameron and his football staff have their offices, was split four or five ways.

The most hateful was the group around Ralph's successor, Clarence Doninger. Mary Ann Rohleder, who was a Doninger hire as an associate athletic director and had no prior allegiance to Indiana University at all, was the most vindictive person I've seen in an athletic department in thirty-five years. She told Steve Downing, one of my former players who was also an associate athletic director, that she'd do everything she could to get me fired, a year before it happened.

I liked bringing in people to talk to my basketball team. The key word there is that *I* brought them in. In early-season practice in the 1999–2000 season, I found out she had gone to the locker room and talked to my team that day about gambling. I left the playing floor, went to her office and told her, "You don't go in and talk to the basketball team on your own." And I left.

She told Downing, "I was just hoping he would slam my door or yell at me so I could write him up."

Instead of all the subterfuge that created so many problems for everybody there, I'll never understand why those people who wanted me out didn't just come to me initially and say, "We have a change of administration and the Board of Trustees, and we no longer want you as the basketball coach."

I would have left. I'm absolutely sincere in saying that, because I said it from Day One for me at Indiana.

Friends of mine who knew the situation my last few months at Indiana didn't want to see me stay. And yet I obviously thought enough of the job I had and the players who were there that I chose to try to make it work. It just didn't.

As disappointing as the whole thing was, it led to something far better for me.

That hasn't happened to anybody else involved in it.

My last year in Bloomington I was sick and tired of seeing my name and picture on the front page of the newspaper, or hearing news flashes about me at the start of telecasts. I was "news" for an odd variety of non-stories: because in Steve Alford's first year as the coach at Iowa, he and I didn't get around to shaking hands at the Big Ten press conference; because I went to a Mexican restaurant with my wife and her two sisters and I was accused of saying things I'd never even think, let alone say. The week of one of our biggest games, against Kentucky, I finally fired Ron Felling, a staff member I never should have hired and should have fired years before, with lots of justification.

Then, just as we were getting our team prepared for the NCAA tournament, Neil Reed, a player we had dropped from our team three years before, surfaced with charges that I had choked him at a practice his freshman year.

It bothered me, of course, that CNN put together a hatchet job timed for maximum press, just at the start of the NCAA tournament. It bothered me a whole lot more that nobody among the people in charge at Indiana had enough guts to tell CNN, the *Indianapolis Star,* and anyone else interested that in a collision of viewpoints, they were going to line up with the basketball coach who had been doing a pretty good job for twenty-nine years.

I genuinely had no memory of the practice or any incident involving Reed at all. At an IU baseball game, Felling told Downing that he had a tape of the practice. I immediately called a vice president, Terry Clapacs, to tell him I'd heard Felling had that tape and that Clapacs should involve the police if necessary but get it—and show it to Brand and the trustees. I *wanted* it shown. I knew it couldn't do anything but absolve me, because I knew I had never choked anyone. As far as I know, Clapacs made no real attempt to get the tape.

A few weeks later, CNN announced it had the practice tape—and again, I was glad. Let's see it. Brand sent a special university plane to Atlanta, carrying Simpson and a trustee (Fred Eichhorn). Another private, chartered plane picked up the trustees' chairman, John Walda, in Florida and delivered him to Atlanta. The costs went into the thousands of dollars, five thousand for Walda's flight alone, though there surely is no place in Florida where Walda couldn't have caught a regular flight to Atlanta at a tenth of the price of his charter. I had suggested that Downing, as an assistant athletic director and former player, could go along on the flight out of Bloomington and provide some expertise on what they were all seeing, at no additional cost at all. That was refused.

Reed had said in the interview that when I was choking him, I was so out of control my assistant coaches had to come up and pull me off. The practice tape—rarely shown at actual speed—showed that Reed and I, walking in opposite directions, met, were together for maybe two seconds, and walked on. The tape's detail in the critical area, my hand and Reed's chest, would make the Zapruder film look sharp and precise. What was shown was fuzzy and greatly magnified, and unexplainedly blurred in the central area: where my right hand contacted his chest—one hand, not two, which I assume chokers customarily use. Clearly, Reed walked away without reaching up to rub or at least touch his throat, any kind of reflex action that would indicate discomfort. There was no choke.

Just as obviously, the part about assistant coaches pulling me off was a lie. The only coach shown in that segment of the tape walks casually on in the direction he was going. And immediately the practice resumed, with Reed playing as before.

Reed also said I once threw Brand out of practice. Brand himself said that never happened.

So, after the tape was shown on TV, I thought: Okay, that's that. This bullshit is over. The tape absolutely shows the whole scenario Reed described was false.

But the witch hunt didn't end there. Instead, the trustees' two-man investigating committee, Walda and Eichhorn, announced the investigation was going to "broaden." I have since concluded that my antagonists in the administration and on the board of trustees were disappointed that what Reed said happened wasn't true. I think their cumulative mood went from "Oh, boy, we've got the tape now" to "That wasn't at all what it was supposed to be."

That is one more time when I am disappointed with myself, almost furious with myself, for not saying that's it—if it's not going to stop now, I'm leaving.

In the next few weeks, as part of this extended investigation, an amazing string of things surfaced, most of them on the front page of the *Indianapolis Star*. I was told I was part of the investigation and I should make no public comments, and every other person involved had been told the same. Most didn't have to comment themselves. Convenient leaks kept the *Star* full of charges, covering a period of more than twenty years. In 1976 I got into a hassle with Kit Klingelhoffer that was all my fault. He was the assistant sports information director at the time, and when his boss, Tom Miller, retired in 1982, Kit came to me asking my support for his promotion to Tom's job, which I gave. In the fall of my last season at Indiana, we lost Gregg Elkin, the sports information director in charge of basketball, to the Dallas Mavericks. My first choice as Gregg's replacement was Klingelhoffer himself. He decided not to take it, but I think all of those things that happened after 1976 describe our relationship.

I had been told not to talk, and I didn't, but the athletic director's secretary, Jeanette Hartgraves, went before the TV cameras to tell of how I called her a "f—ing bitch" once and another time threw a flower pot that hit a wall and shattered glass near her. In the first incident, I intervened after she had been involved in several disputes with my secretaries and I didn't call her anything, but I did say my secretaries were tired of her acting like a bitch with them— that they worked for me, not her, and if she had a problem with them to come to me and I'd take care of it. I did *not* use the other word.

As for the flower pot, that one I couldn't even recall. A friend of mine did. Phil Vukicevich, who had played and coached at the University of San Francisco and later was sales executive for *adidas,* called me after he saw that in a newspaper story. He said he was with me when I stopped by Ralph Floyd's office as Phil and I were headed out to lunch. He remembered me, irritated about an NCAA fine I had just heard about, swinging out back-handed and hitting a vase, which flew against a wall and did break—in an empty office. Phil said there was absolutely nobody in that outer office when it happened.

What bothered me most about the charge was the implication that I operated with a disrespect toward women in the department. Indiana had some great women in key positions who I not only admired and respected for their work but considered good friends—administrators Anita Aldrich, Marianne Mitchell, and Isabel Hutchison, for example, and basketball coach Maryalyce Jeremiah. Hartgraves' predecessor, Mary Jo Nichols, was a delight to deal with, a bright woman with a great sense of humor, loved by the whole department.

When Walda and Eichhorn got around to interviewing me for their "investigation," not one question came up asking my version of any incident except Reed. Walda asked some questions about that and took some notes. Eichhorn did neither. I saw nothing that justified his even being there. I remember Walda saying—seven times—how much pressure he was under. "You ought to try being the basketball coach," I told him.

When their finding came in, it was apparent that what I said or our players said didn't matter.

In the Reed case, players who had been on the team in '97 and attended the practice said there was no choke. Here was a kid who—after three years on our team—players voted 8–0–1 for eliminating from the team, and yet what he said meant more to the president of the university, his chief assistant, those trustees, and the athletic director than what all the rest of those kids said.

These same people just that year had been forced to abandon a project that would have built an expensive golf course in a questionable area of the campus, a course much more for show and high-level entertainment than for varsity team use, let alone student and faculty use. They showed a lot more interest in developing that elitist golf course than in improving the salaries of professors, or retaining any of the outstanding professors that they had inherited from past administrations but had lost to other schools in the last five years.

That is not a baseless charge. In this very time period, there was a widely perceived feeling of university decline. When two respected national academic rankings sharply lowered Indiana University's rank, the school's Alliance of Distinguished and Titled Rank Professors publicly asked for "an outside committee of outstanding scholars, administrators and citizens to study the state of IUB (Indiana University Bloomington) and recommend the necessary steps needed to restore its excellence and reputation." This president, with his once-great university crumbling around him, ignored that request and used me as cause for trashing his predecessors—under whom the higher rankings had been achieved.

Brand said presidents John Ryan and Tom Ehrlich let me run out of control. I got along with both of them well, particularly Ryan, whom I respect as much as anyone I've ever met. Ehrlich and I weren't as close as Ryan and I were and had our early moments of uneasiness, but I grew to like him and I think he felt the same way about me. He gave me a very nice thing when he left Indiana—a framed copy of a Disraeli quote that I had once mentioned to him, "Never complain, never explain." I first heard it from Bob Byrnes, the distinguished history professor who, right up to his death, had been a close friend of mine.

I misread Brand in May. He made his "zero tolerance" announcement on Monday, May 15. The previous Saturday night I had met with him. At that point I felt he was trying to work things out for me. He had met with the trustees earlier that day, and he gave me what he said were their demands. I told him how I felt. After we discussed things a while, he suggested a one-game suspension and a $10,000 fine and I agreed to go along with that. He said he was against fines, and we talked about other possibilities. I went away from that meeting thinking the guy was trying to do what was right.

He talked with the trustees again on Sunday, and when he and I talked that night, everything had changed. He was very antagonistic. Now the fine was $30,000 and the suspension was three games. I reminded him of what he and I had worked out the night before and said I didn't agree with either the fine or the suspension. He shouted back at me: "Then you're going to resign, *you're going to resign,* is that it?"

I said: "No, I'm not going to resign."

I never saw Brand again and haven't, to this day.

He announced the next day that I was staying, under his terms.

Even with the heavy, one-sided assault I had been taking in the Indianapolis media, I think most of Indiana felt relieved and happy that I was still the coach. That wasn't true of the national media. After Brand's announcement in May, he and the trustees were blasted as gutless. *Sports Illustrated* ran me on their cover with just one word: WHITEWASH. The story inside I'm told was every bit as objective as the headline.

I'm sure Brand and Simpson were shocked. Their whole style of operation courted the press, particularly the national press. It was like David Halberstam's book, *The Best and the Brightest,* where the Kennedy administration constantly checked polls to see how they should make decisions. It didn't start with me. I think they came in with an agenda that had absolutely nothing to do with the betterment of Indiana University—the betterment of Brand, period, using Indiana and eventually me as a stepping stone to . . . what? The Ivy League?

But here, just the opposite was happening. They weren't being hailed, they were being ripped by the national press. The *Indianapolis Star* wasn't pleased, either, but that was penny-ante stuff. The *Indianapolis Star* wasn't going to open any Ivy League doors. The last time the *Indianapolis Star* made national news was in the 1968 presidential campaign when Bobby Kennedy ran in the Indiana primary and, during an appearance in Indiana, an aide tried to convince him to commit an act of civil disobedience that would get him jailed and generate all kinds of national attention. Kennedy's response: "What! And put myself in a position where my only contact with the outside world was the *Indianapolis Star*?"

But *Sports Illustrated* was something altogether different. If I wasn't dead at Indiana before, I was the day that magazine cover hit Bloomington and was read by Brand and Simpson.

• • •

Throughout my summer of rising tension, I was entertained by some interesting backbiting among Brand's inner council. The last I heard directly from Brand was a call immediately after I was interviewed by Roy Firestone and Digger Phelps on ESPN. He said how well he thought that went and "Now it's all behind us. Let's go from here." Then he came out with a letter to the alumni that didn't sound like he had put anything behind at all, basically congratulating himself for how much better he had handled me than "the university" had in the past.

Simpson, who somewhere along the line had become a vice president, came to see me frequently. The feeling was general about him throughout the campus: nobody I've talked to trusted the guy. Knowing that, I was amused by his running back and forth between Brand and me.

Brand also set up Ed Williams, a retired vice president, to work back and forth between him and me. I wasn't bothered by that, because I had always gotten along well with Ed (who was the interim athletic director between Ralph Floyd's death and the hiring of Doninger). I just didn't understand the need for go-betweens. The good people I've known in administrative positions never have needed one.

From vice president Terry Clapacs, from Ed Williams, and from Simpson, from 1995 on I kept hearing: "Just be patient. Doninger will be out of there by the end of the year." Then it was "by next year." Then it will be "the day he turns sixty-five." That was four weeks after I was fired, and he still wasn't "out" for another nine months.

That's the way things were working in the upper circles of Indiana University athletics. Clapacs and Simpson were telling me how totally incompetent Doninger was, and that Brand wanted him out even more than I did. Clapacs would tell me what a jerk Simpson was, and Simpson would tell me what an asshole Clapacs was. Ed Williams told me the two of them despised each other, which I had pretty much figured out. And each of them told me, "Brand won't listen to anybody."

Meanwhile each of them—Clapacs and Simpson—was coming across as my loyal friend.

I believe there was at least a time when it was true with Clapacs, though Williams had warned me he would go "whichever way the wind blows," and "you can never count on him when the going gets tough." Simpson never in any way fooled me. The term I used for him almost from the start was "double agent."

With me, Simpson played the role of my inside, informative "pal" where the trustees and other parties in the whole mess were concerned—Brand definitely included. One day, my "buddy" Simpson would say, "I don't understand what Myles is doing now." Another day: "I don't understand [trustee] Jim Morris— he has changed." Another: "Walda, I'm telling you, Bob, he's the guy who wants you fired." He repeatedly told me Clapacs was my worst enemy. He told me how pissed off he was that Clapacs got a raise and he didn't.

There was double-talk everywhere. Morris told Cam Cameron, the Indiana football coach, that he talked to me several times about how he would like for me to conduct things, about things I had to do. That simply didn't happen. All I ever heard from Jim Morris was what a great job I had done for the university, how good I had been.

Both Morris and Pete Obremsky (a trustee who had played basketball at Indiana under Branch McCracken) had asked my help in getting them on the board of trustees. Once there, they had been the most frequent in asking me to do favors for them—signing things, calling people, or making speeches. Obremsky in particular used to show up at practices or games with bags full of items for me to sign. The point is he knew me well and seemed by his actions to endorse our program. Then, in the critical hours when he could have coun- tered spurious charges with his own personal knowledge and experiences, he recused himself because he had done some legal work for me.

Many times that summer of 2000, Simpson bitterly castigated Brand. Brand had publicly insulted the state commissioner of higher education over a plan to add community and junior colleges in Indiana, and Simpson said, "Myles got us in deep shit with that." Simpson told me of a conversation he had with Terry Hutchens, a sportswriter for the *Indianapolis Star,* in which Simpson ripped the *Star*'s editor for something. He didn't know Hutchens had a tape recorder going—I couldn't believe a guy who claimed to be so press-savvy was dumb enough not to suspect something like that. Hutchens turned the tape over to the editor, who apparently called Brand and raised hell, and Brand cut off Simpson's responsibilities as a liaison with the *Star.* That pissed Simpson off, although I'm not sure why. He kept getting his money and Brand just hired another six-figure flack to come in as his publicist. They were an amazingly free-spending group on their own behalf for an outfit that could find only two- percent raises for its best professors. And they could be tight when generosity was deserved. Three days after I was fired, I received a letter from Barrett J. Harrison, a man I didn't know. He reminded me that in 1998 Isiah Thomas was inducted into the Michigan Sports Hall of Fame, and Mr. Harrison had asked me to buy a congratulations ad in the induction ceremonies program. "Prior to coming to you," he said, "I had written to Clarence Doninger and talked to Kit Klingelhoffer and received a surprising negative response. When you were contacted, we got an immediate response, and a check. I'll never forget that." They couldn't find $1,000 for a tribute to a man who had done so much for Indiana University in so many ways as Isiah Thomas had.

The university had changed so much for me. Without Ralph Floyd, Bill Orwig, Bill Armstrong, Dick Stoner, John Ryan, Tom Ehrlich, George Pinnell, Danny Danielson, and other people with whom I had worked closely, it was just a much different situation.

After my lawyer, Russell Yates, advised me to avoid public appearances where I might wind up violating some interpretation of zero tolerance, I explained to Ed Williams I was going to have to cancel things I had always done on my own initiative in pre-season with alumni groups in Indianapolis, Bloomington, and Chicago. Williams relayed that to Brand and then told me Brand said he understood. That's the last I heard about that whole topic until it became a reason for firing me. For the same reason, I told Tony Mobley, dean of the school of physical education, that I would have to stop teaching the class that I'd taught for twenty-eight years—and enjoyed. Tony understood, and commented that he was sorry I had to do that because over the years he had received more positive feedback from that course than any they had.

But another of the trustees, Ray Richardson, after I was fired cited my dropping that class as an example of my insubordination—even though I was the last head basketball or football coach in the Big Ten to teach a class, and had been for years, and I wasn't even being paid for doing it. (In the summer of 2001, Richardson was the first of the trustees to come up for reelection; he lost, and it wasn't close.)

I feel strongly that the people who ultimately dismissed me were deceitful and duplicitous. Even at the end, I fulfilled the obligations of my contract; I told them exactly what I was going to do.

And Simpson always agreed: "I understand." "I wouldn't do that, either."

Every day it just got worse and worse with me.

I was sorry. As much as anything I was sorry that I was still there.

The months between May and September were at best for me an uneasy truce. People were speculating whether I could get through a season under Brand's vague "zero tolerance." I told Karen several times the season didn't concern me; I didn't know if I could get to October. Tension over the situation did nothing but build. Possibly from the beginning but certainly after they had been ripped by *Sports Illustrated* and some others, the people deciding my fate seemed sure

I wouldn't be coaching in 2000–01. Doninger said as much to both Tim Garl, the basketball trainer, and Steve Downing well before school started.

It was Simpson's idea to bring in some outstanding national writers for a press conference after Brand's "zero tolerance" announcement. The ones who came were giants—Dave Kindred, Hubert Mizell, Billy Reed, and Bill Gildea, writers with that kind of national stature, plus Ursula Reel, a young New York writer whom I had met for the first time that year, and two Bloomington reporters, Lynn Houser and Mike Leonard. I went along with the press conference but I did tell Simpson that all it would do was piss off everyone who wasn't invited. I was right, but even I was surprised by the nastiness of some of the criticism. Kindred has won every national sports writing award there is; he worked at the *Washington Post* with John Feinstein and was the closest thing to a mentor Feinstein had. Still, Feinstein ridiculed him and the whole group as "the sympathetic seven." Roy Firestone and Digger Phelps came in for an ESPN interview with me the same day and they were ripped nationally for being too soft. Gore Vidal was treated nicer in the national press for giving Timothy McVeigh an airing than were people who actually listened to me.

Feinstein's gall continues to amaze me. He and I had a lot of conversations during a four-month period in our lives fifteen years ago, and none at all since. Those made him such an expert on me that he still feels qualified to reshape what I say into what I *really* think, or to figure out what I'm *really* doing.

Just last summer I saw him quoted about me in a *Sporting News* interview. To the question, "Do you think it's important to him to break Dean Smith's record for wins?" he said: "Yes. Yes. And the more he denies it, the more it's obvious that it is. I think the reason he hung on for dear life at Indiana is because he wanted the record—and he really wanted it there. And the reason he's out in Lubbock, Texas, now is because he wants to break the record."

I wanted to say, Feinstein, you're into an area so far beyond your understanding that even I kind of pity you.

That area is coaching.

I continued to coach at Indiana for many reasons; a major one was how much I enjoyed the whole process of coaching. And that process starts with the kids involved: what I can do with them in basketball, what I can do to help shape their lives.

Because of that, I never could see a logical ending to my time at Indiana. When I began there at age thirty, I said to some people I wouldn't be there when I was forty. I certainly never thought I would be there twenty years, but when the number was twenty-nine, the longest for any basketball coach in the 100-year history of the Big Ten, I knew in my mind I would be there at least thirty-three years, because I felt that in recruiting 2000–01 freshmen like Jared Jeffries and A. J. Moye, and Andre Owens and Mike Roberts, and in bringing George Leach along through a red-shirt year that in effect made him a freshman that year, too, I had made a commitment to myself to see them all through their Indiana careers, and to see them graduate.

And I was thinking that when, as I expected, we would add Scott May's son, Sean, in 2002–03, that would commit me up to 2006. I presumed there would be others, too, by then but Sean I felt pretty sure of—and excited about.

That's thirty-five years. And not necessarily the end even then.

There were dozens of times in the years before when I was so torn up after a loss or so worn out as a season came to a close that I would have loved to step away from it all and quit—except for some kids who were there because they wanted to play for me, and I told them I wanted them to play for me.

Obviously, there has to be a time, but how do you decide which group of kids to—at least in this one way—walk out on?

This is why all the criticism from the press never was close to driving me out of coaching. Feinstein's pompous expertise on me has influenced a lot of people in his profession, and they in turn have affected thousands of people's opinions about me, because people are inclined to believe the written word.

So am I, like these from Theodore Roosevelt:

> It is not the critic who counts, not the one who points out how the strong man stumbled or how the doer of deeds might have done them better. The credit belongs to the man who is actually in the arena, whose face is marred with sweat and dust and blood; who strives valiantly; who errs and comes short again and again; who knows the great enthusiasms, the great devotions, and spends himself in a worthy cause; and who, if he fails, at least fails while daring greatly, so that his place shall never be with those cold and timid souls who know neither victory nor defeat.

And from Vince Lombardi:

> It's a reality of life that men are competitive and the most competitive games draw the most competitive men. . . . There is something in good men that really yearns for, needs, discipline and the harsh reality of head-to-head combat. I don't say these things because I believe in the "brute" nature of man or that men must be brutalized to be combative. I believe in God, and I believe in human decency. But I firmly believe that any man's finest hour—his greatest fulfillment

to all he holds dear—is that moment when he has worked his heart out in a
good cause and lies exhausted on the field of battle—victorious.

I love those images. I've had the privilege of watching kids I've coached do all those things.

Now, blend in there the opportunity I had as a coach to point kids toward a college degree and a lifetime of competing "fairly, squarely, decently, by the rules—but to win," in whatever career they choose, and you have the reason why not just I but lots of career coaches in both high school and college keep coaching when, as coaches, they have nothing left to prove. That—not a fragile record that even if I were to set it undoubtedly would move on to someone else before very long—is why I stayed at Indiana when everything in me said to tell Brand where to stick "zero tolerance" and walk away.

I love to coach, and I love its human involvements.

And if, when I do quit coaching, the record for major-college basketball wins is still in the hands of the man who has it now, I'll be very, very happy—for the life I've had, and for the achievements and accomplishments of a good and respected friend.

Bill Orwig, the athletic director who hired me, was a man of exceptional intelligence and class who knew how to get along with people and work with coaches. He had a great arrogance, in a positive way—he knew he was damned good at what he did.

I think more than anybody else in the school's history, Bill Orwig developed Indiana's athletic program into a major-league operation—facilities, teams, coaches. Sam Bell was a nationally respected track coach; Doc Counsilman was one of the greatest *coaches* of all time; John Pont took a team to the Rose Bowl; and Jerry Yeagley started the soccer program and built it from nothing into the best one going. The architect of all that, Bill Orwig, is in the college athletic directors' Hall of Fame.

Indiana spent several months looking for an athletic director when Bill Orwig retired, so I asked John Ryan if it would be all right if I called Paul Dietzel, who was Army's head football coach my first three years there: the two that I was an assistant coach and one as the head coach. Dr. Ryan said he'd be glad if I did.

Dietzel was the Ohio Valley Conference commissioner then. Indiana offered him the job, and he came. Ralph Floyd joined him, and with those two, the athletic department was run very well. Dietzel eliminated all the complimentary tickets Indiana was giving away. Though his career was in football (including coaching a national-championship team at LSU), he had a real understanding of the value of basketball at Indiana.

Ralph Floyd took the job when Dietzel left after three years to be LSU's athletic director.

Ralph was as country as Bill Orwig was sophisticated. Ralph was outgoing; Bill was reserved. But they were alike in the amazing number of people in intercollegiate athletics whom they knew and were respected by, people they could call and from whom get instant advice on which young coaches might be available, or get their football team into a bowl, or fill a schedule—all the doors that were open, from longtime friendships, to athletic directors who had coached and who knew athletics. The trend to turn athletics over to lawyers makes as much sense as putting old coaches on the Supreme Court.

Ralph was what an athletic director should be. The record of the athletic department under him—and its immediate nose-dive after him—is the best illustration of his effectiveness. Ralph was there when women's athletics began to take on prominence. No one fit the "good ol' boy" image better than Ralph, but when the Big Ten and NCAA began championship competition for women in 1982, Ralph was one of the most effective AD's in the country in making his women's program not just competitive but strong. He had a decade of Big Ten women's and men's competition, and five times in that decade, his combined Indiana program graded out first in the league in all-sports finishes—ahead of Michigan, Ohio State, the big-stadium, big-income programs and all the rest. The next ten years, Indiana's highest Big Ten all-sports finish was fourth—and that was in the first year after Ralph's death. After that first year, Indiana sank from consistent ranking with the top programs in the league to consistent finishes near the bottom—eighth, ninth, even tenth. The only personnel difference between the Indiana athletic department that was a model of success and one that had slipped so far was at the top, where replacing Ralph Floyd and women's director Isabel Hutchison with Doninger and Rohleder was like replacing Eisenhower and Bradley with Sergeant Bilko and Gomer Pyle.

How can an athletic director help or hurt an entire athletic program? One of the biggest improvements in athletics these days involves weight-training—once associated only with football, now crucial to the development of athletes in all sports, men and women. Football has a separate facility at Indiana, like most places. The weight room for all other sports is dirty, dark, and ridiculously under-equipped—way behind other major colleges. Doninger steadfastly refused to do anything about it. This was stubbornness that did nothing but hurt kids and programs. Athletes who were at Indiana suffered by comparison with what was available to the teams they played, and programs were hurt because recruits, who knew how important weight-training is, simply wrote off Indiana and went elsewhere. By contrast, Ralph Floyd was loved by all the coaches working under him because he always was at the front of the curve in giving all Indiana teams the best developmental facilities available.

It's a cop-out to call it a money problem. The women's basketball coach, Jim Izard, wanted some up-to-date TV facilities, and Doninger said no. I had an operating fund that was given to the university with stipulations that I had sole responsibility for using it, through the university. I told Izard I would pay for his equipment. Doninger refused to let it happen, even though it wouldn't have impacted his budget by a penny.

One of the dark days in my life was December 15, 1990, when just before I went out to coach our team against Bob Donewald's Western Michigan team at Assembly Hall, Kit Klingelhoffer opened the door to the room where I was sitting and told me, "Ralph just died." It was not a shock. He had been consumed by cancer and we all knew it was coming, but I certainly didn't expect to hear about it that way. It was all I could do to walk from the locker room to the court after that. And I didn't stay long. I drew two technical fouls and left, very early. It was one of the rare days in my life when I just didn't feel like coaching a basketball game, even against a good friend.

Ralph and president John Ryan were primarily involved in the contract we worked out in 1981 and that I worked under right to the end. It was put together and signed in an air of mutual trust. I wanted the control it gave me because I felt that I knew what was best for basketball all the way across the board. I was perfectly comfortable with the people in command then, but in the back of my mind was a comment I had read, attributed to Bear Bryant: "A coach must have an ironclad contract to protect him when an administrator has no guts."

I didn't want to have to argue about it or plead with somebody to be able to operate the basketball program the way I thought was best.

I'm the one who included in it a "noncompete" provision: that I would never voluntarily leave Indiana to coach somewhere else nearby—I could just as easily have said anyplace else, because that's how I felt at the time. It amazed me that, after firing me, the people running the university actually tried to use that clause in the contract against me, to keep me from taking a job at any other Big Ten school or any other college in Indiana or Kentucky.

We never had to test the legality of that. I don't think as a basketball coach I could be fired and at the same time told I couldn't work somewhere. After the university's interpretation of that clause surfaced, John Ryan told me: "That was something you put in there—I would have never done that. We had given you the authority to run basketball as you saw fit, and this was a voluntary pledge from you that in return you wanted to stay here and do the job."

I couldn't understand why the people who fired me wouldn't have *wanted* me to leave town for another job as soon as possible. The last thing I expected was an orchestrated attempt to keep me from getting *any* job. It took amazing chutzpah for a group of Big Ten presidents to put their signatures on an expensive, full-page *Chicago Tribune* ad backing Brand's action as a defense of academic integrity. The absolute last thing I would have expected anyone in education to blacken me with was any suggestion that I somehow damaged Indiana University's academic integrity. The president at the University of Minnesota, who presided over the most embarrassing academic perversion I've ever seen where basketball was involved, dared to make a public stand quite clearly targeting me. The coordinator of the *Tribune* ad project, Stanley Ikenberry, was in charge at Illinois when that school came the closest of any in the last forty years to getting kicked out by the Big Ten—for lack of institutional control. There wasn't a president or an ex-president who signed that ad who had a basketball program with an academic record close to ours or as clean as ours.

If presidents anywhere truly want to clean up academics, instead of posturing, they could do it with one simple rule that I proposed about twenty-five years ago: you tie the number of scholarships you can give to the number of graduates you have. A player graduates, you can replace him. A kid doesn't, you have to wait an established time to use that scholarship again. Very quickly coaches would be sincerely interested in bringing in kids who can and want to graduate, and all kinds of things detrimental to college athletics would be averted right at the start.

I, a coach, proposed that in the 1970s, and I have yet to find any presidents willing to go that far. It turns my stomach to see how sanctimonious they want to seem now, though they haven't yet given any hint of taking that one clear, simple step.

I challenge any presidents to come up with a rule like that, or as effective as that. Intead, they speak in groups and issue pious recommendations that won't ever be enacted and wouldn't work if they were. That to me is hypocrisy.

There are ways to judge a basketball program's administration. If a coach is winning games, his team is competitive, and people in large numbers are coming to see the team play, then the next requisite thing—at least in some cases, but not with all schools or all administrations—is adherence to NCAA rules.

We certainly had all those things and in addition had a graduation rate second to none in the country when I was fired.

The very week that I was fired, Simpson came to Assembly Hall and walked up the steps to sit in the stands with me while I was watching a two-hour workout for our team—four players at a time, for forty minutes, two-on-two. At the time, I was having a hell of a time getting a routine financial arrangement settled with Doninger. Todd Starowitz, who was the football sports information director, had stepped in after we lost Gregg Elkin to the Dallas Mavericks and handled the basketball SID job as well. When Starowitz took on the job, it was agreed—by Doninger, Starowitz, myself, and the athletic business manager, Fred Watkins—that he would be paid $10,000 for it. It was a very simple arrangement: Todd did the work, and we had agreed what he would be paid. After the season was over, Doninger just refused to pay him; Todd didn't get his money until more than a year later when I arranged for him to get it through private funds.

In September I was going through the same problem trying to get my new administrative assistant, Les Fertig, on the payroll, although I had hired him, as I had every right to do. Doninger was fighting that (Fertig has still never collected a cent, even though he had started on the job and actually taught a class before my firing).

That day at Assembly Hall I showed Simpson the form I was filling out to get the Starowitz payment taken care of, and another one for Fertig. I also told him I had picked out the four public appearances I would make, as stated in my contract—a talk to the students, an appearance I had always made in southern Indiana, and two in June at our golf outing. I had picked the three games I was going to sit out, as was ordered by Brand in May—the last two games of the regular season (Minnesota at home and at Purdue) and the first game of the Big Ten tournament. I explained I picked those because we had a young team and I thought I needed to be with them at the start. Simpson said, "I understand." I told him I was sick of going through things like this—that I was sincerely thinking about responding to some schools that had let me know they'd be interested if I ever wanted to move. I'll never forget Simpson's words, with Bob Hammel sitting in the stands with me and hearing them, too: "Take me with you."

That happened on a Tuesday. On Thursday, I was returning to Assembly Hall after lunch with Mike Davis, one of our assistant coaches. A student was coming out of the Assembly Hall lobby door as I was going in. He looked surprised when he saw me and said—I think not meaning to be rude—"Hey, Knight." As we passed through the door, I reached out and put my hand on his forearm as I said, "I'm Coach Knight or Mr. Knight to you. You should remember that the next time you're talking to an older person." Then both of us went on our way. I had absolutely no thought of an "incident" having occurred.

By that night, Simpson had heard from the kid's stepfather—a lawyer and a Bloomington talk-show host who had been my most vocal critic—and Simpson had alerted ESPN that a major story was breaking. By Friday morning, he had alerted newspapers. When I went into my office late that morning, the story was out that campus police were investigating. That was the first I heard of any of it. In all his calls, Simpson never got around to me—to tell me what was going on, or to ask my version.

I didn't think I had any choice. I'd had enough of being convicted in silence. I called a press conference for that afternoon, went over my version of what had happened, and Davis, who had been right behind me entering through the same door, fully backed me up in all that I said and demonstrated.

Even then I wasn't greatly concerned. How in the hell can an issue be made out of telling a kid to respect his elders? Even my national press critics were beginning to line up behind me on that.

My basketball team—a bunch of kids who were obviously affected, and upset—met Saturday morning to talk about what they could do in support. They went to the football game and in the press box talked to any reporters who wanted to question them. Larry Rink, our team doctor and one of my best friends, confronted Brand at the game and demanded that he talk to those kids before he made any decisions. Reluctantly, he did, and I was told Brand was shocked by how angry the kids were. He told them he was waiting for the police report and he wouldn't have a decision for seventy-two hours. He announced the firing less than twenty-four hours later, and he had said enough to Dr. Rink for him to feel the decision was made when Brand flatly lied to the team about waiting.

In his firing statement on Sunday, Brand said I showed "disrespect for our alumni" by not agreeing to speak at "previously scheduled" alumni functions. That's just wrong. None of those was scheduled when, in early June, I told Ann Carpenter, a truly wonderful and greatly underpaid employee of the Varsity Club, that I would not be making the alumni functions at Chicago and Indianapolis that I had originated years before because my attorney had told me I shouldn't make any appearances at all, given the potential for something happening that would violate the "zero tolerance" threat. I went against the attorney's none-at-all advice and picked out four, the number my contract obligated me to make.

Ed Williams told me that when he explained to Brand my reason for holding it to the four I had picked out, Brand said, "That's fine. I understand that." Then later that became insubordination, when against advice I was going to do what the contract said I should do.

I'm sure every year after that four-appearance minimum was put in I made at least twenty, or twenty-five, or thirty appearances for Indiana University. I put that minimum number in the contract so nobody could run me ragged— "You have to go to every Varsity Club outing," "You have to go to every alumni function." That's all that was. There never was a year when my appearances total was anywhere close to being as low as four.

And when the sanctions were removed, I had every intention of going back to what had been a normal schedule. A typical year for me was speaking at fundraisers or events benefiting the university at Fort Wayne, Evansville, Chicago, Indianapolis, Bloomington, and New Albany, the sites varying enough that at some time over the twenty-nine years I spoke in just about every community in Indiana. Anytime that I appeared for United Way, anytime I made a TV spot for Mothers Against Drunk Driving, anytime that I spoke somewhere just because someone had asked me to do it to raise funds, that was an appearance representing Indiana University and a positive reflection back on the university and the athletic department. No one in the athletic department ever did more for Indiana University in this regard than I did.

No year went by that I didn't do something for drug or alcohol awareness somewhere. I was involved with other things. Steve Downing coordinated a reading program we started in the Indianapolis inner-city schools several years ago. Kids who reached a certain level in reading were brought to Bloomington by bus to have dinner with our players—300 or 400 inner-city kids, many of them introduced to reading because of how they felt about our basketball program. I spoke in some Indianapolis schools to get it started and made TV spots every year afterward to keep it going, and Steve just did a terrific job of running it. The total number of kids involved by now would be incredible. And I would have stayed with that—lawyer's advice, zero tolerance, whatever.

In his firing statement, Brand also said I "verbally abused a high-ranking female university official in the presence of other persons." He referred to my asking university attorney Dottie Frapwell to leave my office, after for the fourth time she and I and my accountant had discussed a matter that should have been simple: how they were going to take from my pay the $30,000 they had fined me. When I felt that conversation was over, I—in a civil manner— told her I wanted to talk privately with my accountant.

For this hodge-podge, I was fired. In effect, Brand acknowledged that the incident with the student wasn't enough to cause even "zero tolerance" to kick in. "No one incident of the ones I have named may singly rise to the level for the removal of Coach Knight," he said. It was, rather, "this persistent and troubling pattern of behavior."

I believe the thing with the kid was just what the Reed tape had been—the people who wanted me out thought at first, here it is, the one big mistake they could use as the hands-down reason for firing me. When the tape strayed so far from what Reed claimed, and when the incident at Assembly Hall became a whole lot less confrontational and more a lesson in politeness, they reacted in September as they had in May. Minus the "smoking gun" they wanted, they filled in with their own smoke—"incidents," a "pattern." The tactics each time were exactly the same: they fired, they fell back, they went to Plan B—character assassination.

They did me a favor. They did what I couldn't bring myself to do.

They got me out of there.

While the firing was being announced by Brand at an afternoon press conference in Indianapolis, Karen was riding out to Presque Isle, Maine, in a private plane that picked me up there for the return to Bloomington. Almost immediately after the announcement, students in Bloomington had started demonstrating against Brand, the trustees, and their decision. Brand at different times described the campus reaction as an excuse some students used to get drunk and as an insurrection so frightening it forced him to move temporarily from his residence to Indianapolis. At no time did he face the students.

We landed Sunday night at Bloomington airport, where some TV mobile units were set up. My son Tim picked us up in a car and we went straight to Assembly Hall, where my team was waiting.

I talked to those kids and told them I was sorry because I had looked forward to coaching them. I don't think I ever faltered or hesitated in talking to them. It was an emotional meeting, of course, and there were some tears. But it wasn't a long meeting. I told them I was responsible for getting each one of them to Indiana, and I still felt that responsibility—if I could ever help them on anything, to feel free to call.

When that meeting ended, I met with my coaches and told them I had no idea what Indiana would do with their contracts, but if they wound up out of a job without a settlement, not to worry—I would pay their salaries out of my own pocket and take all of them with me whenever and wherever I got a new job.

By that time a crowd of students had formed in the Assembly Hall parking lot, and the situation was threatening to get out of control.

Police, in riot gear, had formed a line sealing off Assembly Hall and several thousand kids had moved right up to it. I walked out, and the kids reacted with loud cheers and yells. I went to the officer in charge and said I'd like to talk to them. He said I'd have to do it behind the wall of police. I told him, no, I wanted the police to back up—I would talk in front of them. He wasn't at all in favor of that, but he did set it up the way I wanted.

I didn't think the kids needed what was going to be a big confrontation with law and order. Those kids hadn't done anything. I think it's hard to find issues today that eighteen- to twenty-two-year-olds are passionate about. That part pleased me.

I told the kids to back up to the curb of the driveway in front of the building so I could have room to talk to them, and they did. They got so quiet I started talking without any kind of microphone. Somebody from the crowd came running up with a portable amplifier and I used it to thank them for all the support students had given our teams over the years, and to say a few other things—that the police were good guys who deserved to get home with their families, and that I wasn't going to make any kind of speech then but within a few days I would be speaking to them somewhere on campus. After that promise, I asked them to turn around and go back home.

And—I think to the cops' absolute amazement—they did. Very quietly. Very quickly. When those kids heard and saw me tell the police, "Back up, get behind me, I'll take care of this," I think they thought, "Here's a guy who is essentially for us—not one of us, but certainly for us." And I think they showed their appreciation by disbursing when I asked them to.

That was in the early hours of Monday morning. Wednesday afternoon, the student newspaper—*Indiana Daily Student*—arranged for an open appearance in a huge campus meadow beside the Student Union Building. There were no seats, just a platform, a microphone, and all that green space. There had to be fifteen thousand people there—packed together tightly, sitting in trees, on rooftops. It was televised live across the country.

I thought to myself as I was standing up there, *This administration and these trustees will never collectively have done anything in their span of time connected with Indiana University that will be rewarded with anything close to the appreciation these kids are showing me.* Sure I choked up, and so did Karen standing beside me. I thought what a shame it was to be fired by people who were totally out of touch with what those kids—the heart of the university—represented.

Again, the kids couldn't have been more orderly. I talked to them for about twenty minutes, thanked them, and left. So did they.

I read the affection of that turnout as an indication that they knew our players were always students, just like they were . . . that our players had to work like hell, we demanded a lot of them, but they also went to class, just like each of them did . . . and that they enjoyed going to basketball games, watching our kids play and rooting for them.

If that was my last view and my last memory of Indiana University, it was one that will stay in my mind as long as I live.

Four months after he fired me, Brand had the nerve to wangle an invitation to speak to the Washington Press Club, go there and talk about cutting back on athletic emphasis, then come home and pay his new athletic director almost double what the position had paid before. The same president limited full professors to two-percent increases at the time athletic department personnel were getting a three-and-a-half-percent increase and key figures in my firing—Clapacs and Frapwell for two—were getting twenty-five-percent raises, about forty thousand dollars each. I have a feeling he didn't mention any of those things in his Washington speech.

That speech followed the spin and P.R. nature of this entire episode. Brand and several of the trustees went through all of this thinking together on how best to present it, not what was best for the university to do but what would sound best for public relations and their press perception. I think they were shocked when *Sports Illustrated* in particular but also some others in the national press blasted them for not firing me in May. They couldn't wait for something that would get them better national press.

The symbol of justice is a scale. If Brand were to put on one side all those reasons for firing me, and on the other wide were all the things I had done for Indiana University, I think the scale would show how embarrassingly light his case was.

That scale has other applications. A common press shot at me is, "He doesn't think he's ever wrong." I know I've been wrong many times, dozens of times. We're talking about twenty-nine years. And I've acknowledged a temper problem that I have to work harder to corral.

Balance those off against the things I've done right. It's not even close.

I know the type of basketball program I told the Indiana committee I would give them in that interview at Houston in 1971, and I think I delivered fully on that, in all the ways that define a great college basketball program—ways that are wholly available to every college coach but accomplished by very few.

I am primarily responsible for my history with the press. At times my fun in feeding my own sense of humor with comments about the press probably irritated some good people in the press—people whose numbers I have too often understated in my blanket criticisms of the whole profession. I understand that, and some of those things if I had the power to do over I would do differently.

My first year at Indiana, I was on my own to set up my radio and TV contracts. I inherited or was required by contract to do a postgame radio show for what I considered then to be a pretty good amount of money.

Before the season even started, though, I mentioned what I was doing to my Ohio State coach, Fred Taylor, and he advised me not to do that postgame show.

His reason was: the press, newspaper guys.

"When you play at night, those guys are on pretty tight schedules," he told me. "They've done a lot for college basketball over the years. You owe it to them to get with them as soon as you can, before you do anything else but talk to your team."

So, after that first year, I never did have a postgame show. In deference to my coach. As a favor to newspaper guys.

I will say Coach Taylor was talking about a different type of reporter than we're seeing now—and not just in athletics. I have enough friends in the newspaper business that I've heard them talk among themselves about a "post-Watergate syndrome" in journalism—a tendency, since *Washington Post* reporters Bob Woodward and Carl Bernstein made names for themselves by bringing President Nixon down, to be skeptical and cynical toward any major figure. That's my press friends' judgment, not mine.

Repeatedly, polls taken in recent years have shown public respect for the media has been on a steady dive downward—lower than politicians now, lower than used-car salesmen, lower than just about any group that used to represent the ultimate in distrust.

And most of those people being polled haven't even dealt with the press personally.

I have. I think the polls are way too kind.

Some of the best people I've ever met are in the media. But so are some of the sorriest, and they're far more numerous than the others.

I got to musing about that one day last winter. I had seen enough brutal criticisms to make me wonder: Am I a bad guy? Do I get along with anybody? I thought through a number of questions I used to test myself:

How well do I get along with kids who have played for me?
How well do I get along with coaches who have coached for me?
How well do I get along with opposing coaches?
How well do I get along with high school coaches?

How well did I get along with IU fans?

How well have I gotten along—really—with basketball officials, referees?

With all of those groups, I'd say I have gotten along good to great. Who haven't I gotten along with?

The press.

If that's the only group I haven't gotten along with—bingo! I feel better than I would if it were any other group on the list.

Joe Namath once said, and I'll paraphrase it from an interview I happened to watch on television: "When I see in print something that's happened where I've been involved that's so totally different from what actually happened, how can I ever believe what's on the front page, either?"

President Ford told me, "If you think you have problems with the press people on the sports page, you should try dealing with the ones on the front page."

I'm not sure anybody who has had to deal with the press on a regular basis has much respect for the press per se. They all have writers they have respect for, but not the institution as a whole.

They see the right to criticize as a one-way street. The press can attack managers, coaches, players, teams—or presidents—but, boy, if any of those people who are under attack dare to fire back, the whole profession is offended.

You read the morning paper and a guy has just ripped you, just jumped all over you.

You run into that guy later that day, he has some more questions to ask, and . . .

You're not allowed to say *anything* about what you've just read?

And if you do, you're a bad guy?

Another thing I've noticed: criticism by the press almost never is *of* the press. There are exceptions—Bob Verdi, the *Chicago Tribune* columnist, Tom Cushman of *The San Diego Union-Tribune,* George Will, or someone of similar stature and character (which limits the available number considerably)—but otherwise you almost never see a writer say a contemporary is off-base or a fellow writer's attack on somebody was unfair.

One of my friends in the press is absolutely convinced there never was a "Deep Throat," that the mystery character was fabricated by Pulitzer Prize–winning reporters Woodward and Bernstein and probably editor Ben Bradlee to give journalistic credibility (if that isn't an oxymoron) to reports and leaks they were convinced were true but for which they needed a pinned-down source before they could, ethically(?), offer them as fact. The same guy feels Woodward used much the same kind of prove-me-wrong tactic in *Veil,* his book on William Casey and the CIA—attributing quotes to Casey he said came from private interviews with Casey on his deathbed, in a book written after Casey's death. But my newspaper friend hasn't written that, which proves only one thing: it obviously isn't Bob Verdi, Tom Cushman, or George Will.

I'm not saying the hesitation about sniping at fellow writers is absolute, because I've seen the opposite where I was involved—writers who strayed from the pack and heard me out, then paid for it with snide abuse. Guys in his profession, who should pay for the chance to shine Sid Hartman's shoes for all the stories he has dug up over the years, take shots at him regularly—because he gets along with people, me included. Consequently when he leaves a message asking for a telephone call, it gets returned—by me and a thousand other guys who aren't so quick to answer others. Sid Hartman could call Ted Williams, Roger Maris, Billy Martin, Casey Stengel, Bear Bryant, Lou Holtz, George Steinbrenner—anybody in sports, because he has a tremendous reputation for being fair, working hard, and, above all, being extremely honest. Sid's one of my all-time favorite people, not only as a writer but as a person, because of his integrity. Yet a guy like Sid is vilified by members of his own profession as being in someone's pocket, or he's soft on somebody, when it's simply a relationship he has developed out of honesty, and the guy criticizing him has built a reputation of being the opposite of a guy like Sid—one of the reporters who are quickest to complain about people who won't talk to them a second time.

I don't believe I've ever seen an occupation where there is more internal jealousy than in sports writing.

I've wondered how many guys who talk or write so knowingly ever played a team sport. I've always contended there's a huge segment of people who cover sports who don't like sports people—they don't like the salaries athletes or coaches get, they envy athletes the recognition they get and the aura around them, and they have ever since those were the guys getting girlfriends in high school.

They're an amazing group.

You should see some of the guys who call *me* fat.

You should see how some of these guys dress—and criticize *my* wearing apparel.

Writers are deceiving themselves if they think I'm the only one in sports who thinks of them as I do. I'm just the worst at hiding it, of which I'm kind of proud. But I pay for doing that.

There are occasional little triumphs within the annoyances. When the anti-Knights were firing their strongest barrage in the spring of 2000, one of my arch-critics was reduced to writing that he didn't want to hear how many kids I graduate, or how clean our program is, or how kids who played for me feel about me, or how well those kids have done in life, or how many games or championships we've won, or good things that I've done for people . . .

And my thought was:

Other than those things, what else is there?

He had pretty much covered the things I promised to try to do when I met with the Indiana search committee that March day in 1971 at Houston.

I think those things he was tired of hearing about added up to a hell of a good report card for my twenty-nine Indiana years.

To use some jargon of the day, I wasn't always reactive in my dealings with the press. Occasionally, I couldn't resist being a little bit proactive.

The classic was Ivan Renko.

Few things irritated me as much over the years as the rise of the self-proclaimed recruiting expert in newspapers around the country. A lot of fans are interested in recruiting news. Unquestionably, it sells newspapers—it even spawns whole magazines and periodicals and "services."

Never mind that what the fans read is frequently inaccurate, to use a kind word. Never mind that it puts public pressure on kids, when they and their parents are trying to make a quiet, serious decision. Never mind what extreme national recruiting attention does to kids' egos, their sense of self-worth.

Over the years I have taken an occasional shot at the sham that this whole evaluation process has become. In late January of the 1992–93 season, as my Sunday television show was ending, I dropped in an almost accidental news leak—"NCAA rules prevent me from speaking about specific recruits. I spoke at a clinic in Europe last July, attended by about four hundred coaches. I was given some information over there on a kid from Yugoslavia. When I got back from the Northwestern game, on my desk was an indication that this kid has committed to coming to Indiana. He's a six-foot-eight, two-hundred-and-thirty-pound kid that I think . . . anybody who follows the political situation of civil unrest in Yugoslavia can appreciate the fact that we'd just kinda like to leave it go at that. The kid's name is Ivan Renko. Let it suffice to say that we're very pleased to get this commitment."

The greatest fly ever tied never caught as many fish as I did with Ivan Renko.

The recruiting "experts" jumped at my bait. The waters exploded. Guru after guru commented. Some, to their credit, were honest—Bob Gibbons comes to mind. He and a few others—there are some good guys in the lot—said they had never heard of the guy but they would check. Others couldn't do that, couldn't let themselves seem to have been caught unprepared. Several said they knew about this Renko kid, had files on him, and they either agreed that he was an outstanding prospect or said how much I overrated him.

My favorites were the ones in the group who claimed to have actually seen Ivan Renko play and offered an instant, detailed evaluation of his skills and his future as a college player.

There was, of course, no Ivan Renko. I made up everything about him on the broadcast, and in a few follow-up comments that kept it all going. I wanted to make the point that so much of what people pay money to get from recruiting experts is sheer bullshit, and I think I—and they, in their reactions—did make that point. I figured it was kind of like the false D-day plans the Allied forces "allowed" to get into German hands.

It always amuses me when writers try to get into the intricacies of basketball—game tactics, strategy, and preparation.

I've thought as I stood at a press conference: How many people out there could come up and diagram the offense we used against a half-court press, or one that would have been better? The intricacies of the game are known to very, very, very few people in the press, just as there probably would be some writers out there who could diagram a sentence better than I could. But growingly few.

Sometimes I'd drop a comment or two at a press conference about things that hadn't happened at all, and that any reasonably knowledgeable writer would know hadn't happened. As an example, I might say "When we were in our zone . . ." and we hadn't been in one at all. I've usually tried to answer serious questions as fully as I can—not because of the writer or writers but because for information like that they are the fans' link to me, the coach.

In that checklist of people I do or don't get along with, high school coaches represent a group especially meaningful to me. Those are the people who come to clinics. Those are the people who judge my work and return their verdict by how much of it they incorporate into what they do. And within that group of coaches are a lot of people I admire greatly, most of all the one I'm married to.

I was headed toward one of my favorite southern Indiana bird-hunting areas not long ago when I went through the little town of Loogootee and saw a city limits sign that I loved: WELCOME TO LOOGOOTEE, HOME OF JACK BUTCHER, INDIANA'S ALL-TIME WINNINGEST BASKETBALL COACH.

Jack Butcher was born and raised in Loogootee, a town of about 1,600 people. Jack played basketball there, went off to Memphis State where he was an outstanding player and All-Tournament on a team that just missed winning the 1957 NIT, then came straight back to Loogootee and took the job that he has stayed in ever since. At Loogootee High School, he has won more games than any coach in Indiana history, about 800. In that state, where high school basketball is so big, that is a remarkable and significant achievement—No. 1, all-time.

And I read where Jack said that when I left Indiana, "the state high school coaches lost a great friend."

What a nice thing for a guy to say. What a nice thing from a guy whose opinion of me is a whole lot more important to me than all the guys who write about me and don't know me.

I have read frequently over the years that I demand discipline but have none myself. I think I've always had great discipline—the discipline that it requires to prepare a team to play every night, to forget about winning and get on to the next game, to spend six weeks on the road recruiting for West Point, to find the time to care about and do something about people who needed some support for any of various causes. That charge was always a point of irritation to me.

My discipline made me find the time not for press and TV interviews but for the common, ordinary people who care the most about how we were doing. Within Assembly Hall, for example, I liked virtually all the coaches and other athletic staff people who had offices there (*virtually* all—there were a few exceptions), but the people who made the department work were especially important to me—names like Clete Ellett, Myrna Moore, Wilma Southern, Olive Scamihorn, Donna George, Jay Sears, Tod Bruce (a special friend I fished and hunted with), Jimmy Butler, Dave Gentry, and many more, people whose names were never in the papers and were never on office doors but represented the heart and spirit of the place. When any of those people came up to me and said nice things, as they did, it meant more to me than they can ever know.

One of the great people at Indiana during my time there was Elizabeth "Buzz" Kurpius, who was one of the first people in American collegiate athletics to set up and direct an academic counseling program. I wish I could say I hired her, but former Indiana football coach Lee Corso got that done. Once I started working with Buzz, I developed the same respect and feeling for her that I had for Bill Orwig and Ralph Floyd. Her program became a national model, and on campus no one was more highly thought of or respected by athletes in sports. At her retirement recognition party, people and athletes came from all over, but neither Doninger nor Brand made it. The best administrator by far, chancellor Kenneth Gros Louis, carried the ball for all of them, somewhat courageously considering the vindictiveness in the air among that administration then.

When I first went to Indiana there were some wonderful characters who had been there forever. Red Grow was the equipment manager, Frank Anderson was the athletic business manager, Howard Brown—a great Indiana football player in the '40s under Bo McMillin—was an institution as an assistant football coach and a guy just devoted to the university, and Chris Dal Sasso was a former football captain and assistant coach who was in charge of scholarships.

Frank Anderson sent out one of the all-time great memoranda when he was hot about the high long-distance telephone bills he was seeing. He said: "It took Abraham Lincoln less than three minutes to deliver the Gettysburg Address. I have yet to meet anybody in this department who could possibly have something to say worth lasting longer than that."

Chris and Howard knew more about the history of Indiana University athletics than anybody did. I spent a lot of time with both of them trying to learn all I could.

I put Red Grow right beside Ralph Floyd and Bill Orwig as a person I enjoyed, liked, and had great respect for. He had been in Patton's army in World War II. Everybody enjoyed being around Red, and invariably when I'd run into an old Indiana letterman who had moved away from Bloomington, the person he would ask about was Red. I had a lot of good fishing trips with Red. I always tried to make him part of interesting trips we made, like Hawaii or the NCAA tournament. Red was the guy who first took me to Smitty's restaurant, which became my all-time favorite place to eat. Ralph and Jean Smith and Grandma took care of me at lunch almost every day for years. They were all just special friends.

Smitty's was a down-home place. No money was wasted on decor. Joe Kleine of our Olympic team reminded me just last fall of the time I told the team to get dressed up, I was taking them to a very nice restaurant and I didn't want them to be embarrassed. "We entered this little diner through the kitchen with everyone laughing at us," Joe said, "and we proceeded to have a great time with the bunch of locals there." That of course, was Smitty's.

I've always found a place like that. After Smitty's closed, I found Rosie's Diner in Hendricksville, a terrific place where a customer put up a classic sign that is still there: YOU'VE GOT TO BE TOUGH TO EAT HERE. I took my Indiana teams there a time or two every year, after I found it. I also started eating lunch in the deli of a supermarket. New Yorkers like David Halberstam or Dick Schaap would come into town and want to go to lunch—guys used to going to someplace expensive and elegant. With me they'd get Smitty's, Rosie's, or the Marsh grocery deli. They'd always want to pick up the tab, but that sometimes got complicated. Halberstam picked up the bill once, looked at it, and said, "I can't turn this in. They'd laugh at me." The two of us had eaten for something like $5.45.

But those places were perfect for me—cooks and employees and daily customers who kept me up on what was going on in their lives and otherwise left me and anyone with me pretty much alone, just part of their crowd. I've already found some of the same kind of places in Lubbock.

As we get started at Texas Tech, I'm very proud as a father to have my son Pat on my staff. I'm also very fortunate, because he does a great job recruiting and coaching. He'd be a good addition to any staff but particularly mine, because he doesn't stick with disappointments in players, games, or recruiting like I do. He is extremely good at saying, "Okay, let's just get on with it"—not looking back at what might have been or should have been.

Pat has given me some memorable moments as a player. One of the first came long before he was part of any team—and it was on our court at Assembly Hall.

When he was about ten, he was suited up and sneaking in some shots whenever he could while watching one of our practices. I got upset with one of the best players and kids I ever coached, Randy Wittman, because he wouldn't shoot and he wasn't as aggressive offensively as I wanted him to be.

In exasperation, I said, "Hell, Randy, *Pat* could guard you."

I couldn't let it drop at that.

"Get in here, Pat, and play Wittman."

And skinny little Pat ran out on the floor and lined up to take on All-American, NBA prospect Randy Wittman.

Now, Wittman just *refused* to shoot—he wasn't going to shoot under *any* circumstances. We worked for about ten minutes, and Wittman never took a shot. He was just burning—the only time I ever remember him being that mad.

I could understand that and accept that. I had set up a situation that was obviously embarrassing to him, so he had every right to stick it back in me—a little bit. It just told me Wittman was tough. I've always liked that in kids.

That phase of the practice ended, Pat walked off the floor, looked at me, grinned and said:

"Well . . . he didn't score."

When the time came, I wanted to give Pat the opportunity to play at Indiana, though I honestly didn't think he would come.

He did, and from a father's standpoint, I enjoyed seeing him every day.

From a basketball standpoint, he was a very average player with one outstanding quality—passing, understanding where people were. He was as good at that as anybody we've ever had, and he accepted his role.

But he never was as good a player as he could have been because of all the pressure that was on him. The way our own people would get on him was the only thing I ever really resented from our fans—so much so it almost caused me to leave. I don't think anybody understood the pressure he was under trying to play.

He made a lot of valuable contributions to our team, but I think if I had to do it over again I would have had him look harder at the schools that were recruiting him—go visit them, then out of that group pick the school he liked the best. If I thought it was a good place for him to go, we'd have sat down and debated back and forth between Indiana and that school, and, with the hindsight of knowing how things turned out for him as a player, I'd have encouraged him to go to the other school.

After he graduated, when I was trying to make a point about learning how to play, I used to ask players who they played with who understood the game best. Almost invariably those who had played with him would say Pat. That's one reason why he's a good coach now and he'll get better and better.

I have in a special place in my house a framed picture of the hug Pat and I exchanged when he came out for the last time on his "Senior Day" in 1995. I can't say how many more copies of it I have received from fans, along with notes that indicated that moment so special to me touched a lot of people. That day when I introduced Alan Henderson and Pat as the seniors who were being honored, I called Alan "one of the all-time great players that Indiana has had" and concluded: "I love Alan Henderson. He's one of my favorite players. Cheaney, Woodson, there are a ton of them. But . . . Patrick Knight is my all-time favorite Indiana player."

FIFTEEN: *Coaching Again*

I realize now that constantly trying to get back to a level that very few have ever reached weighs on you.

A winter without a team of my own wasn't all bad. Believe me, I didn't enjoy it, but there were moments. . . .

My wife Karen is a native Oklahoman, a graduate of Oklahoma University, able and willing to break into "Boomer Sooner" anytime anywhere, a passionate Oklahoma football fan. She's also a Hall of Fame basketball coach. She coached three of her Lomega High School teams to state championships in Oklahoma.

She does know basketball. I've joked about coming home after a tough game, wanting to just find a chair somewhere and sit down and think about something else, and she greets me with:

"I can't believe how many times we gave up the baseline tonight."

Or, "Can't you do *something* about the turnovers?"

And what I want to say to my darling Hall of Fame wife is:

"Aw, why don't you go bake a chocolate cake or something!"

She doesn't do that, of course, and I don't say that, of course. But I'm serious in saying that at games and even practices, she gives me another set of eyes looking at things from a different angle, with a good idea of what she's seeing.

The way things went in college football during our "off" year gave me a chance to be a big help to her, too. I came up with the ultimate Christmas present for her: tickets for both of us to the national championship game between Oklahoma and Florida State at Miami.

She has enough little girl in her that she doesn't want to know her Christmas present in advance. The game was on January 3, and one day in December, she told me she had something she wanted us to do that day—had to be that day, had to be January 3. She told me what it was—I honestly don't remember—and here's where the conversation went from there, starting with my response:

"I can't do it."

"Well, why can't you?"

"I just can't."

"Why not?"

"I don't want to."

"I do all the things *you* want to do. Why can't you do what *I* want to do?"

"I just can't."

"That's not fair."

I finally figured out the direction we were headed wasn't good, so I said:

"Okay, I'll tell you why I can't—because your Christmas present is I'm taking you to the Oklahoma–Florida State national championship game that night."

It stopped her cold. But not for long. After thinking about it for maybe ten seconds or so, she said:

"You shouldn't have told me that."

When we got around to talking about the football game, I told her: "You know Oklahoma doesn't have any chance of beating Florida State." She didn't argue. Then.

I'll say this: she is as good at figuring out things in sports as anybody I've ever been around. The day before the game, she told me at lunch: "I think Oklahoma is going to win tomorrow."

"Now whatever would give you that idea?"

Naturally, she told me.

She went over Oklahoma's schedule, in detail, and picked out some significant scores from bowl games already played.

For example: Oklahoma beat Texas badly, 63–14, and in the Holiday Bowl Texas was barely edged out by Oregon, 35–30.

In the November game that was built up as the game of the year, Oklahoma outscored Nebraska 31–0 after Nebraska had gone ahead 14–0. Then Nebraska just buried Northwestern, 66–17, in the Alamo Bowl.

Oklahoma beat Kansas State twice. Then Kansas State whipped Tennessee, 35–21, in the Cotton Bowl.

Her point was how much more difficult Oklahoma's schedule had been than Florida State's, and how exceptionally well it had handled that schedule. She was honestly convinced that Oklahoma would win the game—convinced not as a fan but as an informed analyst of the game.

Now, she didn't convince *me*—I was like everybody else going into the game, firmly convinced that Florida State would win.

Which made me all the more impressed—and silent—as I sat there with her and watched Oklahoma dominate the game and win, 13–2.

Even with that, even with her silent, smug, sideways glances as the game's outcome was in the process of becoming obvious, I did enjoy the evening. There was an electricity in the air. This game was for the national championship! I had had teams in games like that. I felt as good, as excited, that night as I had felt when we were playing.

We got there early, and we sat in the stands waiting for the kick-off. Our seats happened to be on an aisle, and occasionally people walking past recognized me and stopped to say something nice, or asked for an autograph. Several stopped to get a picture taken with me.

A woman a few years older than me was sitting in the row just below us, directly in front of me. We had talked a little before anybody had stopped, just small talk about the weather, the game coming up, normal things.

As the pre-game moments went on, she obviously noticed that several of those people seemed to know me. When nobody was in the aisle, she turned around and said, "Who *are* you?"

I told her I used to teach and coach.

"Did you ever play football?"

Yes, I said, I did play high school football.

"Where?"

Before that conversation could go any farther, a few more people came by and stopped, then a few more. When there was another break she turned around with a big, knowing smile and said, "Okay, I heard someone call you by name, so I *know* who you are. You're Coach Knight.

"Now, tell me . . .

"What did you *coach*?"

I answered the woman's question, but I didn't go into the detail that I could have. I didn't mention that what I coached was the best game there is—that I was sixty years old and I had coached it for thirty-eight of those years.

And I missed it.

What I missed most was spending every idle moment with ideas going through my mind of what I could try tomorrow with the kids or the team I had, and then seeing how those ideas worked.

As long as I was coaching, I always kept a notepad next to the bed, in case I thought of something during the night that I wanted to write down, so I wouldn't forget it.

Lots of nights I'd wake up and think of things I wanted to check on the next day. I'd get up and write them down. Then I'd fool around with the idea on paper the next day.

Or, if I had been watching tapes just before going to bed, I'd take a minute before lying down to list on that notepad things I wanted to check out in the morning, things that had flashed through my mind and I didn't want to lose.

That year out of coaching, I was still keeping a notepad beside the bed, in case I decided to go back into coaching. When you've enjoyed something as much as I've enjoyed basketball, it's hard to let it go.

Actually, I was enjoying those weeks a lot more than I would have expected. I was able to keep busy, in a lot of ways, and enjoyed that.

One of my first pleasant diversions was a hunting trip in Spain in early November.

Rick Rechter, a Bloomington businessman, was the key to my making the trip. Rick was one of the first people I met when I went to Bloomington, and for twenty-nine years, I had no better friend.

He headed the Midwest's biggest construction company, and he was the first guy I went to about getting summer jobs for our players. It wasn't an immediate sale. He hadn't been very happy with some Indiana athletes who previously had worked for his company, and he told me so. I told him, "If you'll give these guys a chance, they'll do it or they'll answer to me." Steve Green, my first recruit at Indiana, was the first of our guys that Rick hired. I couldn't have picked a better trailblazer, just as I couldn't have picked a better first recruit—a great kid, smart, raised in a terrific family, always represented the school and our basketball program well. After employing Steve that first summer, Rick's company hired our guys for as long as I was there.

Rick had gone to Spain on this same hunting trip two years ago. He had such a great time then that he called me as soon as he got home and said, "The next time we go, you're going with us."

We hunted together several times over the years, and we talked a lot about hunting other times. He knew I liked wing-shooting—birds. Sometime in the summer or fall of 1999, he called me and said they had set up their next trip for November 2000.

November meant we would have started practice, but even knowing that, I wanted to go—partly because I knew how much Rick wanted me to go. So my mind went to work on how I could do both: coach my team and hunt in Spain. I finally told Rick I'd try to set up our mandatory day off from practice (NCAA rules require at least one day off for players each week) so I could catch a flight to New York, fly all night to Madrid, hunt with them for a day or a day and a half (on the team's off-day), and get back to Bloomington without having to miss a practice.

It turned out I didn't have a team to coach in November 2000. One of the first calls I got when I was fired came from Rick, who didn't waste any time with sorrow or sympathy. He cut through all that and said, "The hell with these people. You can go hunting now."

I took him up on it.

Steve Chancellor, who had done very well in the coal business in Indiana, set up the trip and most of the people on it were friends of his who were enjoyable and interesting to be around.

Two men in the group were former president George Bush and retired General Norman Schwarzkopf. In Spain, we hunted with King Juan Carlos, who was waiting there to meet us and be our host for two days.

I knew President Bush, primarily through golf outings where we had met and talked—and a couple of times played together. I had been at West Point when General Schwarzkopf was an instructor there. I had met him then but didn't know him well.

The only real evidence I had that he knew anything about me came from a *Washington Post* article someone sent me. During Desert Storm, in January 1991 when the American troops were shredding Iraq's elite unit, the Republican Guard, a *Post* reporter named Rick Atkinson said General Schwarzkopf called the commander of the attacking corps, Lieutenant General Fred Franks, with a message: "Keep pressing, keep pressing. We want the Bobby Knight press." Now, in pure basketball terms, we rarely "pressed," but with our best teams I always said our defense was offense without the ball. It wasn't a matter of feeling flattered; I felt honored that our teams' style of attack was used as a description of what the commanding officer of that swift and great victory wanted.

I knew from other things I had heard and read about him I would enjoy being around him on the trip, and that's the way it worked out.

Obviously, there were times on the flight and while we were in Spain when we had chances to just sit and talk. When our plane stopped in Reykjavik, Iceland, to refuel on the way over, the general and I sat together in a lounge for about an hour. During that conversation, I said, "I'm curious about something: What one thought stood out most in your mind when you were given the command of Desert Storm?"

He didn't even hesitate. "You can appreciate this," he said. "I *wasn't* going over there to lose."

Yes, I did appreciate it, and I understood exactly what he was saying. I've always said winning is basically eliminating why you lose. You can make all kinds of great plays and still get beat, if you didn't eliminate the ways you could lose. If you go into a game with your mind made up, "I'm *not* going into this game to lose," you're better able to focus on the reasons why you can win and eliminate the reasons why you could lose.

So I loved that answer. He was just good to be around.

And I knew I would enjoy President Bush.

One night, our whole party was entertained by a family of five—three older men who played instruments and two young girls who danced. The girls, who looked like twins, were sisters, twenty-three and nineteen. This was not fla-menco—click-click, heels, smack the floor, really noisy. This was much more subtle. The girls danced with their hands, more Hawaiian than my idea of fla-menco, and the music was pleasant.

As part of their performance, one of the girls asked for a volunteer from our group to get up and dance with her. But nobody in our whole group wanted to get up and dance. I think everybody was thinking, *They're all going to make fun of me. I'm going to look foolish up there with people as good as these girls are.*

I should say *almost* everybody was intimidated. The general and I were sit-ting beside each other, and when the girl making the invitations turned toward him, he jumped up right away.

I thought that was a tremendous gesture, after so many in our group had turned the poor girl down. I had made up my mind that if they came to me, I would do it—as poor a dancer as I am.

The general danced for a minute or two—you don't even touch each other, you just kind of dance. When he was done, he came over and got me. And when I was done, I went over to President Bush.

He had declined the first time. This time I put my hand on his back and kind of lifted him off the chair, and I was thinking: *What the hell am I doing? This man was the president of the United States.* But I whispered in his ear, "These people will love this. It will be a great treat for them." And it was, because he made himself part of the fun. I'm sure that's something those girls will remember for a lifetime: they danced with an American president. I'll remem-ber it, too. Watching the Spanish people react to those two famous Americans' involving themselves in their culture was an unforgettable experience.

I don't know whether the trip's timing was better for me or for President Bush.

The group of fifteen people boarded a chartered plane in Evansville late on the afternoon of November 9. We were supposed to pick up President Bush at

10:30 that night, after he and other former presidents gathered for an observation of the 200th anniversary of the White House.

This was 10:30 on the Thursday night that came two days after the 2000 presidential election. Washington and the whole country were just in the early days of trying to figure out where that election stood, and nobody cared more about it than the former president whose son, George W., was agonizingly close to being elected. If all had gone well, Mr. Bush would have been out of the country before midnight. But all didn't go well. We were stuck on that runway in Evansville for six hours and didn't get into Washington until early the next morning.

President Bush certainly would have been forgiven for declining to go. But at 6:30 the next morning, when our flight departed for what became a seventeen-hour trip to Spain, he was aboard.

He is one of the great, down-to-earth people I've ever been around, much like President Ford. Obviously people onboard asked him about the election, and he said what he thought. He was very, very proud of his son and how he was handling everything. And, I think, he was happy to be getting away from all the chaos.

That's not altogether a guess. When I got back, someone sent me a clipping from a publication called *Texas Weekly*. In a group of quoted comments about the election was this item:

> *Former President George Bush [Sr.], who went hunting after the elections to escape: 'This is on everybody's mind all around the world, but I have just stayed out of it. One reason I was glad to be in Spain with such calm figures as Bobby Knight shooting redleg partridge was because I wanted to calm down and not be in the crossfire and not have an opinion or write an op-ed piece or comment about some chattering on the television.*

I enjoyed it, too, Mr. President.

The bird hunting there was not like it is here, where you might walk with a dog, the dog flushes the birds, and you shoot them on the rise.

There, we hunted in drives. Men would drive the birds toward the shooters, and we shot from stands. The first drive we had, I was about thirty yards to the left of King Juan Carlos, with no shooter in between us. The position was significant, I learned.

The king was accompanied by quite an entourage, including security people. Just as the drive was getting started, about a half-mile away, before the birds started to fly, a guy walked over to me and said, politely and pleasantly but very emphatically, "Coach, you must remember: the king is to your right."

I'm not sure whether he was saying that I was to be careful so much as, "Coach, let the king shoot *all* the birds to your right."

It didn't matter which. I made damned sure I didn't shoot that way. The king killed a hell of a lot of birds that came between us. I don't mean to minimize that. I have never seen a better shot than the king.

He was also one of the most gracious people I've ever met, and the Spanish people plainly liked him. He's more a ceremonial head of government than political, but he obviously has done an awful lot for his country.

We went to Avila, northwest of Madrid, spent the night there, and then went out and shot clay pigeons. We operated out of stations, and President Bush and I were at the same station. He had a painful hip problem; not long after our trip he had replacement surgery. We had to do quite a bit of walking to get to our hunting stations, but he gutted it out.

The group also went boar hunting that day. I just like to shoot birds. I went with them, kind of spotting for Rick. He shot four.

After three days of hunting, President Bush and General Schwarzkopf left our group to go to England and do some pheasant hunting.

As long as I was in Bloomington I had a plaque on my office wall with a quote from General George S. Patton:

> *You have to be single-minded, drive only for one thing on which you have decided. . . . And if it looks as if you might be getting there, all kinds of people, including some you thought were your loyal friends, will suddenly show up doing their hypocritical God damndest to trip you, blacken you, and break your spirit.*

One of the things I found out during that September and October was that only a few people understand the meaning of the word friend, and those people are special. An awful lot more have no idea of what the word entails.

I was a basketball coach without a team. I was fired, and you don't just "deal" with something like a firing, if you're the one fired. You relive it, and relive it. And every time you do, some new memory comes back that colors things a little, or takes on a brand-new meaning, in retrospect—after the fact.

There's a great line in *The Rubaiyat of Omar Khayyam*: "Your calculations, people say, have led the world to better reckoning. Nay, 'tis but the striking from the calendar of unborn tomorrow and dead yesterday."

I tried hard to put aside my dead yesterday and plan for my unborn tomorrow, when for the first time in my professional life I had a lot of time on my hands.

I've always felt time should be used well—and thinking is a great way to use it. All those years in coaching, I spent countless hours thinking about, working on, deciding what improvements could be made, how our team could be better, or I could get more out of a kid, or something that would enable us to be a better basketball team.

And the other great use of time, I feel, is doing something you and your family enjoy. Prior to our trip to Spain, I took a couple of fishing trips to Wyoming and Montana. Some longtime friends became invaluable for me, men like Tom Swanson of Minot, North Dakota, whom I met years ago through Sid Hartman, and Mike Pamplone of Merrillville, Indiana, who has hunted and fished with me and has a great place to hunt pheasants in northern Indiana. I was doing things I enjoyed doing, and yet I could still think about basketball, which I also enjoyed doing. I thought about games we had lost and what I might have done to give us a better chance of winning—what I might do in the future with our offense and our defense, if I were to get back into coaching.

I made some adjustments that helped occupy my time and my mind. I had reached a point about five years ago where I all but quit accepting off-season speaking invitations for meetings or conventions. You can make a lot of money doing those things, which naturally made it tempting. But I had reached an income level where it meant more to me to use that time fishing than it did using some of it up to make more money.

So, each year I figured out what it was going to cost me to make the summer fishing trips I wanted to make, then booked enough speaking engagements to cover that cost.

Almost immediately after my firing, International Management Group started talking to me about doing some things. Sandy Montag, who worked with John Madden and Lou Holtz, came out to Bloomington with Mark Reiter, who is IMG's vice president in charge of literary projects. Sandy asked me if I would be interested in some speaking appearances they might be able to line up. I was reluctant at first, but the more I thought about it, the more I realized that now that I had the time to do it, speaking to groups was not only something to occupy my time but something I was pretty good at and could enjoy.

• • •

Just before Christmas, Karen and I went to Phoenix, where a friend, Eric Carlson, loaned us his home for as long as we wanted to stay.

Superstition Mountain—about twenty-five miles east of downtown Phoenix—is one of the greatest golf courses I've ever played. It's thirty-six holes, designed by Jack Nicklaus, and the director of golf operations there is Jeff Steury, a longtime friend of mine. Jeff is an excellent player and an outstanding teacher. I had met him years before at the Elk Horn course in Sun Valley, Idaho, where I was playing in a charity tournament in memory of Danny Thompson, a 1970s major league baseball player who died of leukemia. I went to that tournament several times. Harmon Killebrew, the great home run hitter who was from Idaho, was one of the tournament sponsors.

Both as a player and as a teacher, Jeff was like a Bloomington friend of mine, Sam Carmichael. Jeff and his two daughters made our stay in Phoenix enjoyable. He is a great sports fan, which made for a lot of good conversations.

The first day we got there last winter, Jeff and I went out to play. After that, he worked with me on my golf game and helped me a great deal. I got to playing the best golf I ever played in my life, because I had a lot of time to spend on it with Jeff's help.

I had spent much of the last thirty years around Sam Carmichael, a one-time touring pro who coached both the Indiana women's and men's golf teams to Big Ten championships. Sam was one of the best teachers of anything that I've ever seen. I spent hundreds of hours with him on the practice tee, and every time he'd show me something new I'd get on him about holding the good things back. He always had an answer: "I can't give you everything at once. You're not capable of handling it all."

In Bloomington, I also became friends with Ted Bishop, when he was the pro at a course in Linton, west of Bloomington. I could never begin to thank them or tell them how much I appreciated all of the enjoyable hours I spent with the two of them on the golf course with my swing that once in a while led me to less than pleasant feelings about the game.

I went to only three college basketball games all year. While we were at Phoenix, I saw Arizona State play twice. Then we came back to the Midwest and I had three speeches to make in a week—in Columbus, Detroit, and Greenville, South Carolina. In that period, I was able to spend a few days in Akron, Ohio, with my son Pat, who had been picked up as an assistant by Dan Hipsher, the coach at Akron. I knew Dan when he was an assistant for Don Donoher at Dayton. He went from there to Wittenberg and Stetson, where he did very well. He had no obligation whatsoever to go out of his way, but when the opportunity arose for him to hire a coach, he called Pat. That was something a lot of people in coaching who I had helped along the way didn't do.

I watched Akron beat Bowling Green, coached by one of my former players and assistant coaches, Dan Dakich, who has done well there.

Karen and I also spent some of the winter in Florida, thanks to another friend. For several years I had been doing advertising work for Charlie Royal and Tom Martin, who own several automobile agencies in Bloomington and southern Indiana. Both came forward to do anything they could after I was fired. Tom gave us his house in Naples to use. We were there for a few weeks, and Tom's dad, Jim, was a great resident-host for us.

And, in Florida, I got together, for the first time in a while, with Don Canham, who as the athletic director at Michigan had the most profound effect on intercollegiate athletics of any man of his era, with the sole exception of Walter Byers.

Don had been an NCAA champion high jumper at Michigan, then track coach there. He went to Germany and obtained films of Jesse Owens at the 1936 Olympics, and he made them into the first teaching film in any sport. That eventually became standard procedure in all sports, and Canham, in on the ground floor, developed a multimillion-dollar business. We became friends during our overlapping years in the Big Ten. He was a perfect man for me to talk to about my future—what he thought I should do relative to going back into coaching, where he thought I should or shouldn't go. It was an evening that was both beneficial and enjoyable for me.

Karen and I also spent two days in Florida at the home of Jim and Pat Host. Jim, founder and president of Host Communications in Lexington, Kentucky, got in touch with me as soon as things happened in Bloomington. He has been active in college athletics publications and communications for thirty years. He has produced and directed radio coverage of the NCAA basketball finals for years. I was the color man on his first Final Four broadcast in 1979, doing the games with Cawood Ledford. Like Canham, Jim was a great person for me to talk to about my coaching future.

A speech I made took us to Honolulu. We stayed there for a week and got in a lot of golf.

One day there, Karen and I were playing golf at Mauna Loa, a great course on the island of Hawaii. We didn't get started playing until late in the afternoon, and I started out paying more attention to helping her than I was paying to my own game—just piling up a lot of great husband points. I was saying, "Watch your feet . . . hit another ball . . . take your club back . . ." And she was doing pretty well. She was a good athlete in high school and college. She was an outstanding coach herself, and she takes coaching very well.

I wasn't keeping score, but I figured up when we finished the front nine that I had shot forty. I birdied the fourteenth hole and thought to myself: *I'm even par on the back side, so for fourteen holes I'm four over par. I could par out and shoot seventy-six. Or, if I don't, I can still break eighty.*

Breaking eighty is always my goal, and when I succeed, it's a great day.

As we left the fourteenth green, I looked at the sun, and I could see it was going down fast—which meant if both Karen and I continued to play, we wouldn't be able to finish eighteen holes and I'd have no chance to break eighty.

I said, "Okay, Karen, get in the cart. You're done playing today."

All my husband points went out the window right there.

Not really. She was tired of instructional golf, anyway, and nowhere close to as score-conscious as I suddenly was. So she rode and I played alone. On sixteen, I hit my second shot into a sand trap, then hit a good shot out of the sand and made a five-foot putt to save that par. In almost darkness, I parred the last hole and I had my seventy-six. Oh, it was a great par, too. I hit a bad second shot, so I had to hit a wedge as my third shot on a par-four hole, and I made about a twelve-foot putt to save the par. Filling out that card after eighteen, I felt like I had been out there in a one-man tournament and I had handled the pressure of coming through those closing holes with the lead—which for me was the chance to shoot under eighty. That was a *really* happy day.

And then I took Karen to a restaurant of *her* choice.

Over the years, golf has given me a lot of happy days—and a few unhappy ones. I'm a little too free with my temper at times. Once I was playing with Lou Watson at the IU golf course. I missed a putt and sent the putter flying into the sky. . . .

Toward the sky, actually. Before it got there, a tree got in the way, caught it and kept it, in its highest limbs. I didn't care. I didn't make the first effort to get it down, I just finished the round and went home.

That night, I woke up during the night and started thinking about it. I got up, dressed, slipped out to the course and—still before the sun came up—climbed the tree to get my club. It was a pretty tricky climb, but I was so close to it I already was feeling happy that I had pulled it off, when I heard voices approaching the green. Women's voices.

The first foursome of an early-morning women's golf group was coming to my green.

It's hard to look invisible in a tree, especially at my size, but I tried. I prayed that none of them would look up. None of that group did, but before I could get down, another foursome from their group was there. Then another. None looked.

Finally, there was enough of a break that I dropped down and went home. I never did retrieve that putter.

I have always hoped that none of them went home and told their husband over dinner, "You'll never guess where I saw our basketball coach today. . . ."

I had some of those happy times and met some great people at an annual charity golf event at Dayton, Ohio, called "Bogey Busters." The host was a guy with a heart of gold, Cy Laughter—pronounced *law*-ter. At the suggestion of Don Donoher, he included me on the invitation list almost from my first year at Indiana.

Because of Cy, I got to play with President Ford once, and that's where I first met and played golf with President Bush, when he was vice president. Over the years, I played with Melvin Laird right after he was secretary of defense, and with Charlie Pride, Ohio governor Jim Rhodes, Jack Vessy, Paul Brown, Ara Parseghian, Johnny Bench, Dick Anderson, and Bud Wilkinson. Cy always lined me up to play with guys he knew I'd be interested in.

One thing these golf events are not is politically bi-partisan. They are so overloaded with Republicans it's like a party caucus. When my former assistant Bobby Weltlich was coaching at Mississippi they had an annual golf outing I enjoyed going to. It was run by Bouncer Robinson, the head of an insurance company in Jackson, and it was in honor of the great Ole Miss football coach, Johnny Vaught. They always referred to me as the token Yankee. That's how I looked at the few Democrats I met at golf outings. Congressmen Tip O'Neill, Dan Rostenkowski, and Marty Russo were just about it. I found all three interesting to talk with, and Russo became a close friend.

The "Bogey Busters" tournament was in June, and in August, President Ford hosted a tournament in Colorado.

There's nobody I've been more impressed with as a human being than Gerald Ford. I've always felt his contribution to the country was underappreciated. He supplied a calm, confident leadership desperately needed by America to get through the crisis of Watergate and Nixon's resignation. His pardon of Nixon probably cost him the 1976 election, but I think it not only was the right thing to do but a politically courageous thing, too. I'm sure he knew he would lose lots more than he would gain by it, but it headed off a lot of court hassling that might still be going on. He handled everything during his unexpected tenure just exactly the way we in athletics hope our kids will later carry out tough assignments: as a team player, putting the team first. I have a feeling a generation or so from now, history will accord him the respect I think he's due, for being a great healer.

And, one other thing with Gerald Ford: for all the ridicule the press heaped on him about his golf and athletic skill, he's one of the most accomplished former athletes ever to be in politics, let alone the White House. He was, after all, a football MVP at Michigan. I think that all fits together—that by his conduct, not his ideology or anything else, he was a presidential MVP, too.

I'd also say that, having played a lot of golf with him, I'd take him in a match over any writer I've ever seen play golf.

After we beat his alma mater for the 1976 championship he invited our team to the White House. It certainly wasn't just a routine visit. He put everything aside and enjoyed the time with our kids. We were in places most tours don't include. He had his daughter Susan take the whole team up and show them the family quarters. I've got a picture of my son Tim sitting in the chair in the Oval Office.

After we had been there quite a while, one of his aides came up to me and said, "Coach, I know you'll understand this: We've got to get these kids out of here. He'll stay with them all day long, because he loves this. But we're so far behind schedule already we'll never catch up."

Jack Nicklaus was at Ohio State when I was, one year ahead of me. Two other future tour golfers, Tom Weiskopf and Ed Sneed, also were there during my years. Ohio State had some pretty good golf teams.

I didn't know Nicklaus then. Several years later I met him when we were both on the MacGregor Sporting Goods staff and spoke at one of their outings.

Not long after that, I was playing in the Ford tournament and Nicklaus was there. I was on the practice-putting green and Jack, walking by, said just loud enough for me to hear it, "*Your* temperament is sure ideally suited for *this* game."

The one round I played with him out there, we talked a lot about fishing. On the ninth hole, I had about a four-foot putt for a birdie. Up to then, I hadn't done much for our team. I hit the ball out of bounds a couple of times. I was a little bit tight playing with Jack Nicklaus.

But I made the birdie putt, and as I picked the ball out of the cup I was expecting to hear the usual "Nice birdie," or something complimentary.

Instead, I glanced over to my partners and two of them, Nicklaus and Marty Russo, were laughing.

In the spirit of things I said, "What the hell are you two guys laughing about? I'm getting tired of carrying you."

"Before you putted," Marty said, "Jack said that was a straight putt and the only way you could miss would be if you moved your head to the left when you putted."

"And," Jack cut in, "you jerked your head farther to the left and still made that putt than anybody I've ever seen."

Then we all laughed.

But from that moment on, I've never stood over a putt that I didn't remember what he said. I *always* think: Keep your head still . . . keep your head still. . . .

Later that day, on the fourteenth hole, the pro in each group hit his tee shot from about thirty yards behind us amateurs. Jack hit a five-wood and pushed it to the right. I hit as good a drive as I've ever hit in my life. Because of where he hit from, the club he used, and the way he hit the ball, the drive-of-my-life left me a little closer to the hole than he was—so he was hitting next. I walked over to watch him hit, and his second shot wasn't great, either—an eight-iron he hit fat to about twenty yards short of the green.

I walked back to my bag, and when I was reaching in to get a club, I heard Jack from just behind me say, "Bob, what club are you going to hit?" I had my club in my hand, and I told him, "A six-iron." He nodded and said, "That's the perfect club for you."

That little scene to me defined Jack Nicklaus as a person. Jack had hit a bad shot and followed me fifty or sixty yards across the fairway to see if he could help *me*. I've played with guys who aren't nearly as good as he is who would have been thinking of themselves, not somebody else, after a bad shot.

There's one other thing about playing a round of golf with a great player. Yes, you're nervous, but there's a good chance that at some time during the day you'll hit a shot as well as you can hit it—like that drive of mine that day. I'll tell you this: it's a hell of a thrill when Jack Nicklaus, Tom Watson, J.C. Snead, Larry Ziegler, or any one of those tour pros says to a player like me:

"Boy, that's a damned good shot!"

I was lucky enough to play golf with Byron Nelson once. Of course I remember it, but I was complimented beyond belief that he did. He included me in his autobiography among the people he had most enjoyed playing with on a golf course. Compliments couldn't come from a better person.

We got to talking about great competitors and the first name he brought up was Ben Hogan. He told me about the time Claude Harmon was playing a practice round with Hogan at Augusta, and Hogan birdied the twelfth hole, a par-three. As they were walking off the green to go to the thirteenth tee, Hogan remarked to Harmon, "You know, I think that's the first time I've ever birdied that hole."

Harmon had just made a hole-in-one.

Hogan never acknowledged it.

Whether that was part of the Hogan mystique that he was able to create or whether he was just genuinely so locked into his own concentration that he was oblivious to what Harmon did, Byron wasn't sure, years later.

Besides allowing me to play with President Ford and Jack Nicklaus, the Ford tournament people at other times let me meet and play with a number of tour pros, including a couple of Indiana natives—Billy Kratzert of Fort Wayne and Jim Gallagher of Marion, two excellent people from outstanding golf families, all of whom were great Indiana basketball fans.

I enjoyed all of those acquaintances golf gave me, but one—Bruce Devlin—did something that particularly impressed me.

I had just been named as the 1984 U.S. Olympic coach when he and I played together at the Ford tournament in 1983. Some people involved with the tournament asked me to do a gag thing for a film they would show at the tournament banquet. I was to hit a ball in the water, hit another ball in the water, throw my club in the water, hit another ball in the water, then just pick the whole bag up and throw it in the water.

I would have done it. I would have done just about anything those people asked me—that's how much I respected President Ford. Before I did, though, Bruce came over and said, "Bob, I don't think you should do that. You don't know where that film is going to go. If they just showed it at the dinner tomorrow night, it would be fine. But if it gets out of here, you have no idea where it could show up, and you're coaching the Olympic team."

Since that day, I have never seen Bruce Devlin that that memory doesn't cross my mind. He didn't have to step up and do that, but he cared. I root like hell for guys like that.

In 1984, because of my Olympic coaching duties, I had to skip the Ford tournament. Wayne Rogers, one of the stars of M*A*S*H, was the emcee at the banquet. He mentioned people who couldn't be there, and when he got to me he said I was "in Los Angeles, working like hell to win the gold medal and keep us out of World War III at the same time." The next guy up was Bob Hope, and he said, "Wayne, those of us who know Coach Knight agree with how hard he's working to win the gold medal, but he doesn't give a damn whether or not it takes World War III to do it."

I met Bob Hope in Bloomington; he was a good friend of one of my close friends, Bill Armstrong, the head of the Indiana University Foundation. Not even knowing about the Ford tournament comment, I sent him some shirts after we got back from the Olympics and—thinking of all those generous, morale-boosting trips he made over the years to entertain American troops— told him what I strongly felt: "I don't know if anyone sent you anything from the Olympics, but I don't think anybody is more deserving of wearing something representative of the United States than you are."

Three or four months later, I got a handwritten letter from him. He said he had found the shirts and a sweater when he was cleaning out his office and didn't know how they got there. He was very nice about receiving them and said, "I haven't heard anything about you lately. Maybe you should go out and throw a table."

Linton, Indiana, was the home town of Phil Harris, and when Ted Bishop was the golf pro there, Ted started an annual celebrity tournament in Phil's honor. Phil and his wife, Alice Faye, annually came back to be the hosts right up to Phil's death, and the tournament drew an awful lot of sports people to a small Indiana town.

One of the guys I met there was the great former Yankees first baseman, Moose Skowron—a Purdue graduate, a Purdue Hall-of-Famer, and a great Indiana basketball fan when I was there. Nobody gave his heart any more to us than Moose.

He also came to Bloomington for our Players' Golf Outing each June—he and Hank Bauer, two great players who I'd always remind that I had hated them, as a young Indians fan in Orrville.

Once, speaking at our golf outing, Moose said, "I played for a guy, Casey Stengel, who was on my ass all the time—just demanded, rode me all the time, because, I figured out later, he knew I could be a pretty good player. And, you know, I've got seven World Series rings because of that."

Moose said he was hitting in batting practice one day and Ted Williams was watching him from the dugout. Williams got on first base early in the game, and when Moose was holding him on base, Ted quietly told him to quit pulling the ball all the time. That day he hit two home runs to right center to beat the Red Sox. When Moose walked into the Yankee clubhouse, there was a message pinned on his locker: "Call Ted Williams immediately." He called, and Williams told him, "Dammit, Moose, whatever you do, don't tell these writers here that I told you to quit pulling the ball."

Another time, in batting practice Ted asked to see Moose's bat. He gave it to him, Ted swung it a few times and said, "Moose, could I have this for a little bit? I'd like to work on it." Moose said, "Sure." What a compliment, Ted Williams asks you for one of your bats!

The first two times up, Williams homered. The second time, when Ted dropped his bat and started to run, Yogi Berra looked down at the bat, picked it up, and saw that the name and signature on it was "Bill Skowron."

While Williams was rounding the bases, Berra took the bat over to Casey. When the Yankees came in from the field, Casey got all over Moose: "You dumb son-of-a-bitch, don't you understand if you're going to give Williams a bat, you give it to him when we're *leaving*, not when we show up."

I believe so strongly in some of the premises of my approach to coaching basketball that—as I have always hoped they will be for the kids I have coached—I find them valuable and applicable in my own real life.

For example: my Last Game-Next Game theory. As a fired basketball coach, it was as hard for me to put that behind me and focus on the future as it has been for all those players and teams over the years to put the Last Game they played behind them and start thinking immediately about the Next Game.

After my life changed so abruptly, there were times when I thought back over my last several months at Indiana and tried, without success, to make some sense of it all. I had unbelievable help from friends. I heard every day from grassroots people. The letters and e-mails I got from basic, earnest Indiana basketball fans must have approached ten thousand. These were wonderful, tender, caring messages from people who shared every emotion I myself had, and I appreciated them all.

Every day, from the time my firing was announced, I heard something supportive from people in all walks of life—many I had met, several I hadn't. Two great college football coaches publicly offered support. Joe Paterno of Penn State said if what he saw me do on the tape was a firing offense, he could have been fired two hundred times. Bobby Bowden of Florida State said he wished his grandson could play for me.

I had Dick Vermeil speak to our team one time when he was in Bloomington to do a football game. He was excellent on the theme, "Don't Complicate Winning." That became a sign in our locker room. After he went back into coaching at St. Louis and his team won the 2000 Super Bowl, I'm sure all our kids who heard him on that visit were as happy as I was for him. I wrote him a letter then, and after all that happened at Indiana he sent me a great letter of encouragement.

I met Dan Rather when he did a *60 Minutes* segment with me. He went through a third party to ask how "my good friend Bob Knight" was doing and then sent me a note. Bill Walsh took the time to hunt me down on the road and give me some awfully nice encouragement.

Expressions of backing at a time like that from people like those who had nothing to gain for themselves meant more to me than I can say. I had tears in my eyes when the fairly lengthy conversation with Bill Walsh ended, that's how much I appreciated it.

And then—imagine growing up with Ted Williams as your hero, then to have the absolute joy of getting to know him as a person; to have shared invaluable time with him at the sport so special to us both, fishing; to have traveled and talked with him, and in the process of doing both added real reasons to turn that boyhood hero into a lifetime hero—then to read a clipping from the *New York Post*:

> *Ted Williams feels Indiana University has mistreated Bob Knight and says he never has met a man he would "put in the same league" as him. . . .*
>
> *"I really was hesitant to even call him because I know he was up to his eyeballs with problems of his own.*
>
> *"But I admire him as much as any man I ever met. Oh, boy, is he a great guy. I know it's killing him with all this (stuff) that's going on."*

You can bet when I read that, it was another time I had tears in my eyes. This wasn't a friend saying something to me, to console me; this was a friend, a great friend, talking to someone else about me.

That 1991 fishing trip with him to Russia will always be one of my greatest memories. When we got to our fishing camp and before we ever went out to fish, Ted had me show him my equipment. You can test a rod's strength by putting the tip up against the ceiling and bending it. I can still see him—he put my rods up there, and he said, "*Damn*, Coach, these are pretty good rods you have here. These are *damned* good. You're going to be okay with these rods.

"Let me see your reels."

I had never fished for big fish, and we were going to be fishing for Atlantic salmon. A small one was eight or nine pounds. We caught some up to twenty-four or twenty-five pounds. He thinks it's the most powerful fish in the world, and just relentless about getting away once hooked—strong as hell, head as big as my fist, the head shaking violently, side-to-side, trying to get rid of the fly in its mouth.

I had with me in Russia reels I had used out west to catch trout that probably didn't weigh more than three pounds. I put my reels on the table, he looked at them, and he said, "This is the greatest collection of chickenshit junk I've ever seen. How the hell are you going to fish with *this* stuff?"

Normally when I'm stream-fishing, I wade upstream. You have to read the water; you learn that fish get in certain kinds of water more than other kinds. You have to put the fly on that spot and let it drift over to where you think the fish are. Reading the water is just like reading the defense in basketball. The thrill is in reading the water correctly and having the fish take the fly, just as when your players read the defense correctly and score a basket.

You fish for Atlantic salmon downstream, not upstream. The fish lie on the edge of the current lines next to the swift water, when they're resting. And you can only get them when they're resting. You cast out directly across the water, perpendicular to the flow of the water. The farther you can cast the better, and you let the line swing so it comes right down even with you. Now, your line is straight out from you, going right down with the current. Then you bring it back in and then cast again. And maybe move a step on every cast. That's the way you work your way down a hole—a pool, they call them.

The first day we went out, nobody caught a fish because we didn't have enough time to get to good water. We fished close to camp. However, I felt pretty good at supper when Ted looked across the table and said, "Coach, I was watching you all day. You're going to be okay. You cast pretty damned good—I was surprised you have as much talent as you do.

"But, you've got too goddamned much wrist in it. You've got to cut the wrist down a little bit."

He would always give me something to think about.

The third day I hooked a fish that Jerry McKinnis swore took me two football fields down the river. Later, I was fishing by myself with our Russian guide, Sasha. I caught two fish about seven to nine pounds and hooked a third one I thought was about the same size. I was working it toward the bank when it took off, and I had my thumb next to the handle on the reel. The fish went so fast it broke the reel handle and damned near broke my thumb. The fish got out in the current, and Sasha, who didn't speak or understand much English but understood what was involved in fishing as well as anybody I've been around, took off with me running down the bank over rocks and logs. We were running and jumping over what would have been a hell of a course for an Olympic hurdler like Harrison Dillard or Edwin Moses, let alone a guy like me.

At one time the fish had taken all of my line and 150 yards of backing off the reel—I was down to the knot on the reel. Despite the language barrier, I was able to show Sasha what I needed and get him to break off little tree limbs and sharpen them with his knife, so I could stick them in my reel and wind it back. In that makeshift way we got the fish all the way back to where Sasha could go out and get it, but before he could grasp it tightly, it slipped away from him. We never did get a picture of it.

I'm not sure which I hated more, losing the fish or having to tell Ted about my reel. He gave it to me pretty good: "I *told* you those reels you brought with you were chickenshit." He rescued me with some of his own.

Ted had a bad knee that made it tough for him to get around. The wading was hard. You're always on the fringe of pretty rapid water or fairly deep water. He went down three or four times, slipped, and fell in. But nothing ever stopped him.

I sat and watched him a lot. He's a tremendous caster, with great timing, great vision, strong, extremely well coordinated—he was just damned good. And he stays at it. He studies fishing like a doctor studies physiology. He had that unforgettable left-handed baseball swing, but he threw right-handed and he cast right-handed.

In the evenings, we had some great times, and we didn't always talk about baseball. Boy, he loves the marines. So I said things like: "The *marines*? Did you guys do anything other than pose for pictures?"

And he came back: "You were in the *army*? I'll bet you were in the Boy Scouts, too."

To get to one place, I was walking through a woods and we had floated Ted downriver on a raft. From the bank I started singing "From the halls of Montezuma . . ." He came to attention, on the raft.

In spite of what I said to Ted, I've always had a tremendous respect for the United States Marine Corps. The thing that always impressed me was how proud every marine I've ever met was about the organization. That certainly included Ted.

He tied his own flies—he had thousands for Atlantic salmon. He wrote a book called *Fishing for the Big Three*—Atlantic salmon, tarpon, and bone fishing. He probably is as knowledgeable about those three species as anybody who has ever fished. A better authority on that than I am is Curt Gowdy, who broadcast Red Sox games in Ted's years and later introduced outdoor life to television with *American Sportsman*. Curt thinks Ted is as good as anybody who ever used a flyrod.

So the guy who was the greatest hitter who ever lived also might be the greatest fly-fisherman who ever lived—and the greatest possible tutor. He was never satisfied. He wasn't satisfied with himself, and he wasn't satisfied with me. I went in not knowing anything about that kind of fishing. I learned a lot of things. I learned immediately to take better reels with me.

We had some great times away from the fishing, too. I got us on a tour of the Winter Palace in St. Petersburg, which included the Hermitage, one of the world's major museums. He enjoyed that. But that was tiring even for me—looking at paintings that were worth four million dollars and I couldn't understand why.

We rode in the St. Petersburg subway—a hell of a thing. You walk in off the street and see high, domed ceilings, with chandeliers—just beautiful, like inside a palace. The escalator in the Atlanta airport is steep, but I'll bet it isn't a fifth as long as the escalators in this subway. I could hardly see the end of it.

I did a lot of walking through St. Petersburg. I saw a kid walking toward me wearing a shirt that said on the front, INDIANA 1987 NATIONAL CHAMPIONS. I thought maybe he was an American, but he wasn't, nor was he a long-distance fan. He was a Russian who had traded shirts with a friend and had no idea what that American stuff on the front said or meant.

Ted didn't go along when a group of us went into the little town of Umba. The stores were almost barren—no chicken, a little bit of fish, almost nothing the people could buy. They told us the average yearly salary of a school-teacher is three hundred and fifty rubles—eleven dollars, at thirty-two rubles to a dollar.

In a grocery store, I made one purchase—a two-pronged fork, just a plastic handle and a piece of steel, to handle meat on a grill. I paid three rubles for it, a cent and a half. And it was a mistake. After we had left the store, others in my group saw what I had bought and went rushing back in. Now it was "Five of those . . ."

And Russian people were just standing around, unable to buy anything, watching Americans quickly spend more money than they would make in a month.

When Karen and I were driving to Phoenix just before Christmas, I checked in by car phone with Sandy Montag of IMG as soon as we hit the road in the morning, near Gallup, New Mexico. John Madden, the best football analyst on TV and before that a great coach with the Oakland Raiders, also is involved with IMG. Sandy told me, "You'll probably go past Madden. He's driving to Indianapolis this weekend."

We had just hung up when I saw this gaudily painted bus coming toward us. I told Karen, "This has to be John Madden right here." When the bus got even with us I saw I was right; it was marked as Sandy had said it would be, "Outback Cruiser"—for the steakhouse chain that features John in its TV commercials. I called Sandy back and he worked out a phone connection that put me through to Madden on the bus.

John and I talked for about fifteen or twenty minutes. Sandy later told me Madden discussed that conversation that day on the daily sports report he gives on one of the radio networks.

I don't know what he said there, but I remember something he said in our conversation that I very much appreciated: "You've got to be back in coaching. Basketball needs you. Sports needs you. You're the last of a dying breed."

The truth is, with each message came a new reason for disbelief: if people like that feel so strongly about me or what we've been able to do with Indiana basketball over these years, why am I out of a job?

I knew I needed to refocus my mind to what could happen rather than what had happened. And I actually got better at that by simply thinking about what I wanted most in the future for myself and my family. A key was developing my Detour Theory—I was on a one year detour, not the end of my professional road.

In the hours leading up to midnight Friday, October 14, when colleges all across the country were getting ready for their first basketball practice, the thought ran across my mind: *For the first time in thirty-seven years, I'm not getting ready to start a season coaching a basketball team.*

I couldn't say then with any certainty that I would be coaching again the next year. Or that I would want to.

I had friend after friend assure me, "It will happen," but my unspoken, inward reaction always was: They don't *know* that. They can't.

You try to deal with it as lightly as possible, as I did when I was a guest on *Larry King Live* in late September.

It happened that I was the guest on a Wednesday, sandwiched between appearances by the two major presidential candidates, George W. Bush and Al Gore. When Larry mentioned the week's lineup and asked how I felt about my spot, I couldn't resist mentioning our common thread:

"We're just three guys looking for a job."

I thoroughly enjoyed that appearance. Larry King is a very good interviewer because when he has interesting guests with things to talk about or current situations to explain, he allows them to, so the list of people available to him never seems to shrink. He doesn't interview a guest for his own purposes, he does it for his audience. The consistent quality of guests, and return guests, proves he has built and maintained a reputation for honesty and integrity—so no one hesitates to go on with him. I'd put Charlie Rose and Roy Firestone in that same category—hosts who are far more interested in what the guest has to say than in using the guest to promote themselves.

I also must admit I got a smile when the King show's ratings came in that week; the rating for the night I was on was even with Vice President Gore's and just below Governor Bush's.

I hope that night, and that quick little quip about job-seeking, sent a message of indomitability out to all people dealing with dismissal. It's not pleasant but you have no choice but to go on, head up, believing in yourself, looking for a chance to show what a mistake somebody made—and that somebody wasn't you.

Of course, in my situation, I have already said that I did make a mistake—by staying around when I should have been smart enough to leave.

Even more than just staying on, I made long-range plans involving Bloomington.

I had known from the start that my years at West Point were preparatory, not permanent. It was a great place to coach, I appreciated the opportunity I was given there but, as General Koster had told me to do in our conversation thirty years ago, I knew I would go somewhere else as soon as the right place came along.

Indiana was that right place.

I've mentioned before how all the things I like to do—fishing, bird-hunting, playing golf—were right there for me. Anytime I read or hear that someone is burned out on work, my reaction is that there but for the grace of hunting, fishing, and golf go I. I don't think you can survive an intense occupation without diversions that you love, things that take you away from work or get your mind on other things—or, in a relaxed atmosphere, allow you to continue thinking about your job and what all is necessary with it.

Having the right people to share those diversions with you is important, too, and I had those.

I've spent more time with Jack Brannon than with any other person I've ever known. Jack was just great company. He had played both baseball and basketball for Tony Hinkle at Butler, and he was a fine high school coach for several years before he got out of it and remained in teaching. Another golfing-hunting-fishing friend of mine, Tod Bruce, got Jack and me together for the first time for a hunting trip. I showed up a few minutes late, and Jack said, "Hell, I thought you'd be on Lombardi time—ten minutes early."

I consider Jack the best hunter and fisherman I've ever been around. Johnny Bench may have his own opinion about the hunting part.

Jack, Johnny, and I were quail hunting in southern Indiana once with Bill Wedeking, our host. John and I were on one side of a ditch and Jack and Bill were on the other, when a bird went up. Jack shot, and some of his shot peppered John in the neck and ear. He went down.

I was right there, and when I knew he was all right, I told him, "I was thinking that if you were dead, I'd always remember you for the two home runs you hit in the last game against the Yankees in the '76 World Series."

But what I said first was, "John—are you okay?"

"Oh, yeah," he said, staying flat on the ground. "Is Jack done shooting?"

Later that day, we went into a new area and Bill said, "They found a body around here last year."

Immediately Bench said, "Anybody know where Jack was that day?"

An Indianapolis outdoor writer, Bill Scifres, introduced me to Dick Lambert, who operates a canoe rental on the Blue River, about an hour and a half south of Bloomington. Over thirty years, Dick and I must have spent 400 days on that river, fishing for goggle-eye and smallmouth bass. Dick was great as a companion and a fisherman, but he was either not very good or *very* good with the canoe, because he always had us fishing with my back to where I thought I should be fishing—fishing where we had been rather than where we were going.

He was a lousy food chairman, too. The first time we went fishing he said he'd take care of lunch. The main course was a Spam sandwich, which told me he had never been in the army. I ate it, but I told him, "I hope we'll have a lot of these trips in the future, but I'll take care of lunch from now on."

For providing me with a release from the pressures of coaching, Jack and Dick were the best. And it didn't make any difference to either one that I happened to be the basketball coach at Indiana. They just knew I liked to hunt and fish.

The people in the Bloomington community treated me great—nobody better than Charlie Deckard, a hard-working, unpretentious man whose religious beliefs wouldn't let him attend our games but truly was what many people sincerely claimed to be: our No. 1 fan. I called on him for a lot of things, at all hours of the day and night, and he never said no. He was most representative of the courtesies, the friendship, the genuine support, and the kindness extended to me by people in the community. A lot of them, unlike Charlie, were people I didn't even know. I just really liked what I had at Indiana.

I bought a farm on the southwest edge of Bloomington, where Karen and I were going to build a home. She was already planning for that, sort of a dream house.

I even thought beyond my coaching years, however far off that would be. I had a spot picked out in the stands at Assembly Hall, way up high, with quick access to get away. I'd sit there with Karen and maybe a friend or two and enjoy the games. And I'd probably try to beat the crowd out. I do that when I'm a spectator at anything.

In the back of my mind I always knew who I'd like to see down there in my seat, as the Indiana coach.

Jimmy Crews.

What he has done at Evansville tells me he would have done a great job at Indiana, and beyond that, I think he would have continued to do the things we had done that were important to us and I think set Indiana basketball apart from most other places.

I had all these plans and when everything inside me was screaming at me to move on, I kept thinking: *Do I really want to start over again somewhere else?*

And the answer was no, I don't.

That was the wrong answer then.

But it was also right in its own way, because the main thing about it was that I didn't want to quit, I wanted to coach. And that never changed.

When the call came from Texas Tech athletic director Gerald Myers, I realized I was lucky. There *was* a "right" place for me to "start over again."

For thirty years, I've known and respected Gerald Myers, as a coach and as a person. He had an outstanding twenty-year tenure as the coach at Tech. He served several years on the board of directors of the National Association of Basketball Coaches and was its president for a year. His teams were always tough to play against. And he has excelled as an athletic director, with both the men's and women's program, and with the facilities. I have already found that working for him is just like working for Ray Murphy, Bill Orwig, and Ralph Floyd.

Another person I'm enjoying working with at Texas Tech is Marsha Sharp, the women's basketball coach whose accomplishments include an NCAA championship. When I first met and talked to Karen, I was struck by not just how much she knew about basketball but how much she could see in what she watched. Some people just have that ability—Pete Newell has it, Andy Andreas had it, and Karen has it. And the first time I met Marsha, I was impressed in the same way with her. She has built the same kind of program, in terms of how the fans relate to it and the respect they have for it, that we had at Indiana—and that I hope we can have with the men's team. I know this: Marsha added an enthusiastic fan in Karen. In the weeks leading up to the start of the basketball season, I wasn't sure which one Karen was more excited about seeing—my team or Marsha's.

Gerald and I spent the summer and fall going all over Texas to talk to alumni groups and raise a lot of money for the Texas Tech athletic department and the library. A lot of the times we were with Marsha, although she didn't happen to be at the fundraiser when our outgoing chancellor, John Montford, mentioned that the interim chancellor, David Smith, and I are both from Ohio, and one thing we needed to do was learn to speak Texan.

When it was my turn, I said, "John, I've already learned one Texas word, and I love it—sumbitch. I spent all my life saying that with four syllables. It's a lot quicker with two."

I'm a grandfather now, and a typical one—I love being around that kid. And one of the greatest things about getting started down here is that my son Tim and his wife, Darcie, have also moved to Lubbock with Brady, who's two.

Tim and Darcie are really into child psychology. They're "time-out" people. Brady does something, and they say "No, now don't do that," and he does it again, and they say the same thing, and after a while one of them says, "Okay, Braden, I'm going to count to three and you'd better quit that or we're going to have to have a time-out. Now, I mean it, Braden. I'm starting: Onnnnnnnnnnnnnnnnne, twooooooooooo—I'm counting, Braden, you'd better stop—Onnnnnnnnnnnnnnnnne, twooooooooooo . . ."

Naturally, he doesn't stop whatever he's doing that brought all this on in the first place, because "time-out" just makes him go sit down in a chair till he feels like getting up.

That's where my new Texas word could come in handy. I can skip all the counting and say, "You little sumbitch, you sit in that chair till I *tell* you to get up."

I'm having a good time adapting to other Texas ways, too.

I've always been a great fan of western novels. One of the earliest things I remember was reading how Wild Bill Hickok got shot in Deadwood with his back to the door instead of the wall. I've always felt anytime a coach goes any-where in public he'd better sit in a corner with his back to the wall, so he can see where the trouble is coming from.

I'm like a bird dog on point. I can smell guys coming who might be trouble. I just want to see 'em coming.

One day last fall I was in the Dallas airport leaning against a wall. Two guys started walking toward me. From across the lobby, I knew they were coming right at me. And I was checking them out.

In the Midwest, I grew up seeing all these rhinestone cowboys—guys whose Levi's were designer jeans, too tight for them, guys who could hardly walk without stumbling in cowboy boots that had never seen a cow. Down here, there's no mistaking the real thing, and these two guys were genuine—in their seventies, it's in the summer, they're wearing straw hats, plaid shirts, worn Levi's, and worn cowboy boots. One of them says, "Hey, Coach, me and Charlie are big A&M fans, and we wanna know how long it's gonna take you to straighten things out at Tech."

I looked at him a second and said, "November. I didn't come down here to get my ass beat."

He hit his buddy on the back and said: "Charlie, what'd I *tell* you? The *hell* with A&M. We're Tech fans from now on."

What I hadn't noticed about my Indiana years was something that was miss-ing: the significance and satisfaction of beating somebody you weren't sup-posed to beat. That happened a lot at Army, rarely at Indiana, because of how fast things happened for us there. My fourth and fifth years at Indiana were so outstanding that in many ways they were almost a climax to a career. From there on, I realize now we were just trying to match that 63–1 stretch.

We never did.

Neither did anybody else.

We had two other teams that went all the way to the top, and still it wasn't like '75 and '76. We had spent twenty-five years fighting ghosts. And we didn't just *win* at Indiana. We won better over a long period of time than anybody ever had, at Indiana or in the Big Ten.

We won our three NCAA championships with three entirely different teams. Only UCLA in the John Wooden years did that.

So, should you quit because you reach the top? Maybe you should.

Ed Jucker did at Cincinnati, where his teams were very tough defensively and conservative on offense. Then he came back—at two different levels. He had two years in the late '60s as coach of the Cincinnati Royals. Then he coached at Rollins College where he really enjoyed it, and his teams were among the Division II leaders in scoring.

I'm sure my own college coach, Fred Taylor, felt a lot of the same things I did. He won the NCAA tournament faster than I did—in his second year as a coach, at thirty-three years old—and he had great teams for two years after that. He won a lot of Big Ten championships and went back to the Final Four, but I don't think he ever got back to a team like his second one or a player like Jerry Lucas.

Pete Newell always used to tell me you shouldn't stay any place very long.

I realize now that constantly trying to get back to a level that very few have ever reached weighs on you. You can shrug off the criticism you hear, "the game has passed him by," but I don't think you can help but feel your own internal pressure. There's such a tension—you're more irritated by things that don't go right and less satisfied when they do.

The contrast is the way I feel at Texas Tech—a sense of so many things we can do, not fighting to do something that just might be an impossibility.

Maybe what surprised me most in those months without basketball was that the void wasn't as big as I thought it would be. The most important person in my life is my wife Karen. She was there every day. We spent day after day together and talked about a lot of things, both in the past and in the future.

A great friend, David Israel, made the comment to me that life is a lot like driving a car. When you look in the rear view mirror, you don't see very much. But there's a hell of a panorama through the windshield. You're a lot better off and you see a lot more things looking ahead rather than looking back.

The rear view mirror greatly restricts life.

Thanks to all those supportive people but most of all Karen, I came out of that winter a windshield guy.

During the first part of April, I spent the last few days of the spring training season with Tony LaRussa and the Cardinals in Florida.

It was a bittersweet time for me because I watched the beginning of the seasonlong struggle that Mark McGwire would have in trying to come back from injuries that would eventually force one of the two or three greatest home run hitters of all time to retire from baseball at the end of the season.

Mark had come to epitomize for me what an athlete, a great player with tremendous resources because of his ability, should and could do for people through what he had accomplished. I have never seen an athlete of that magnitude who displayed a greater concern for people than Mark McGwire did.

A couple of days after I had been fired in September, I was in St. Louis for a

series between the Cardinals and Cubs. The first night I was there, I was standing in the dugout when McGwire walked down the steps, picked me up, which
isn't an easy thing to do, hugged me, and simply said, "Are you okay?"

On about the last day of spring training, Tony took me to a dinner following
a charity golf outing, in which a lot of baseball people participated. We were
walking up the drive to the clubhouse and the first person we saw stepping out
of a car was Stan Musial. He looked at Tony and said, "Tony, we gotta get some
more hits than we're getting," and then turned to me and said, "Coach, when in
the hell are you gonna go back to work?" At this point, I wasn't sure that I was
ever going to. There had been several people talking to me about the eventual
possibility of a particular job and would I be interested in talking to them
about it. I always said that if a decision was made to change coaches, and they
were interested in me after that had been done, just to give me a call.

Several days later, a call like that came from Gerald Myers, who was a friend
of thirty years and was now the athletic director at Texas Tech. Gerald had been
a very good player at Texas Tech, the head coach there for twenty years, and I
considered him to be one of the best coaches in my era in coaching. He had
virtually worked for and dedicated most of his adult life to the university. He
asked me if I would be interested in talking to him about the coaching job at
Tech. By this time, I had decided that if I did get back into coaching, it would
be simply because of the people that I would be working with and for, rather
than the location, the recruiting, the facilities, or anything else. Karen had met
Gerald along the way and liked him very much. When I told her that he had
called me, her first comment was, "Well, I'll tell you one thing: There's no place
in America where they will better understand or appreciate you than in West
Texas."

When I've spoken at dinners or to groups after coming to Lubbock, I've
used Karen's line and have always said, "I hope that all of you folks will take this
as a compliment, because she was talking about work ethic, integrity, and the
honesty that has existed through generations here in this part of the country."

After Gerald's call about the Texas Tech coaching job, I spent two days with
him and president David Schmidly. Through those two days, I kept comparing
Gerald and Dr. Schmidly to Bill Orwig and John Ryan, the athletic director and
president who hired me at Indiana. They passed that very tough comparison
test, so I knew I'd enjoy working for them .

At the press conference announcing me as coach, more than 8,000 people
came into the arena. Later, some media people scoffed that I had "orchestrated" it, because some of them were resoundingly booed over questions they
asked. It couldn't have been less orchestrated; these were students and basket-

ball fans I was meeting for the first time. A lot of people in the media can't look at themselves and say "Maybe I'm wrong," but they can always tell what's wrong with someone else.

The tremendous reception from the people of the university and Lubbock meant a great deal to both Karen and myself. Not everyone was happy about my coming. About fifty professors signed a petition against my hiring. I had never met or talked with any of the fifty. I hope they know me better now that I have raised more than $80,000 for the library that I'm sure will be of some help to students in classes those professors teach. And I hope some of those professors will be doing some research because of money that I will continue to raise for the university and library as long as I'm at Tech.

Gerald Myers and his wife, Carol, two great people, couldn't have done more to make our start at Lubbock enjoyable. Working with Gerald on a daily basis has been a satisfying and welcome return to a great work atmosphere. Dr. Schmidly and his wife Janet, along with so many people in the university and the community, made us feel very much at home in Lubbock. I've had so many invitations to go hunting and fishing I'll never be able to take advantage of all of them. We have a great airport here and it's easy to get in and out wherever we are going to or coming from. Karen immediately got involved in building a home, and loved it. And the arena that we will play in is the best basketball facility on any college campus in the country. The great coaching staff Gerald has put together includes, in addition to Marsha Sharp, baseball coach Larry Hays. Both have great followings; in 2000–01 their teams ranked in the top three or four teams in the country in attendance. They, and the entire Tech athletic staff, were tremendously helpful to me in getting started. Letters came in from basketball coaches across the state, welcoming us as a part of Texas basketball. Boy, I appreciated that. Through all those years in Indiana, nothing meant more to me than the feeling high school coaches had toward what we were doing with our team and our willingness to share it all with whoever was interested.

Both of my sons, Tim and Pat, are with us in Lubbock. Pat works on our staff, and I was particularly pleased when Tim was hired by Gerald and Dr. Schmidly to work on projects for the athletic department. I've always needled Tim about his Stanford education, but he knows how proud I was when he was accepted there, and when he graduated with a major in economics.

Tim came to Lubbock with me to help get things organized and off to a good start. After a couple of weeks, both Gerald and Dr. Schmidly asked if I'd object to their offering Tim a job. Object? It pleased me greatly. Tim obviously had impressed them up to then, and he went on to do a great job in setting up a West Texas television network for Tech coaches' shows in football and baseball as well as men's and women's basketball. The same network in our first year televised both men's and women's games that weren't part of our conference television package. All the things we had a part in increased the athletic department's income more than four million dollars. Tim had a big role in that.

My fondness for western history and Louis L'Amour novels made me feel that Karen and I, Pat and his fiancée, Amanda Shaw, Tim and his wife, Darcie, and their son Braden, were like the Earps going to Tombstone.

It's not just the pleasure of having my whole family here. Two of the best people I've ever known joined us in Lubbock. Mary Ann Davis, my secretary for twenty-four years at Indiana and one of the most efficient and competent people I've ever known, is on the job again and quickly made a great impression on everyone around her. I had just two secretaries in my twenty-nine years there, Linda Stines and Mary Ann, and both were great.

In 2001 when Indiana finally picked a new athletic director, Steve Downing should have been in line—to serve then, or at least some time. But he wasn't, simply because he liked me. Neither Steve nor former Indiana football player Harold Mauro, the good man who had been number two in the department under both Ralph Floyd and Doninger, was even considered when the job was filled. Then, after I was already here, Texas Tech had an opening for an associate athletic director. Steve came down, was interviewed, and he made such an impression on Gerald and Dr. Schmidly that they hired him on the spot. In just six weeks, he proved to be such a tremendous addition to the university here and its athletic program that he received his first promotion.

Mary Ann, though she was as good a secretary as there was on campus, after I was gone was banished to a virtual closet, with no responsibilities—just because of her ties with me. I'm sure Indiana hoped both she and Steve would quit. They did, as Indiana's loss and Tech's gain.

In the summer we hired Randy Farley as sports information director for basketball and academic counselor for our players. Randy and his wife Cindy have been friends of mine for more than twenty-five years—longer with Cindy, whom I knew as a little girl, because she was the daughter of one of my coaching mentors, Clair Bee. Cindy teaches English in an honors program, and Randy has proven to be outstanding at what he is doing relative to academics and dealing with the press.

There are reasons why I and all the rest of us Earps feel at home.

And so I'm coaching again.

I've never felt my job was to win basketball games—rather, that the essence of my job as a coach was to do everything I could to give my players the background necessary to succeed in life. I want them later in life to feel that no course they took at Indiana University—or at the Military Academy, or now at Texas Tech—was more valuable to whatever success they had than what they absorbed from playing basketball for me.

I've never expected anyone, including those players, to agree with all that I do. But to the absolute best of my ability, I've tried to provide them with a work ethic, and ability to excel at crucial times, and a determination to be as good as they could be at whatever they do.

Not every kid over the years has liked my approach, and with some kids certainly I have made mistakes, just as some selfish kids made their own mistake in coming to a program where it just didn't work for a player to be more concerned about himself than his team. However, over the years I've received enough letters to fill a room from former players, parents of former players, students that I have had in my class, people I haven't even met that have been affected very positively by things we've tried to do through basketball—letters that thanked me for one thing or another that the writer felt that I had done or said that improved the life of their son or daughter, or a friend, or the letter-writers themselves. Those notes, those people's genuine appreciation and thanks, were the only payback needed. Those players who used up their eligibility playing for me are the judges who mean the most to me. Inevitably, when I ask them questions, I only strengthen my resolve to be the best source I can be for what it takes for them to succeed in life. Mistakes? Sure I've made my share, more than my share. It's not because I haven't tried to get advice and coaching wisdom from some great people, and a lot of them. I doubt if anyone in coaching ever has sought out the opinions of more people than I have—demanding, successful, caring people. First and foremost among those may be Bo Schembechler and Pete Newell.

I've never been afraid to make a mistake, or to put myself out on a limb in trying to help a kid. I've sometimes known what I was doing would not be acceptable to a lot of people, or would seem harsh. But even in my mistakes, I've never done anything I didn't honestly feel was in the best interest of the team or the player involved. I look at my former players' high rate of career success and wonder: if I were to change my approach to conform to someone else's standards, would I shortchange a future player?

I admire former Georgetown coach John Thompson, because the stand he has always taken is what's best for kids—not what's best for the NCAA, or what looks the best, or what reads the best, or what will go over best with the media, but just simply what was best for the kids involved. While doing that great service for all those kids, he also was being one of the most demanding coaches in basketball. With all that personal respect I felt for him, imagine what it meant to me when, on a radio show after my firing, he said what athletics needed was more of me, more of people like me, not fewer.

About the same time, my name for some reason came up on Regis Philbin's television show while he was interviewing Sarah Ferguson, the former Duchess of York. Something was mentioned about certain events that supposedly showed my temper, and Ms. Ferguson said, "That's not temper; he has a great passion for what he is doing." I've never met her, I have no idea how, with her background and where she is from, she even knew who I was, but I hope some day I can personally thank her. Yes, or course I do have a temper, but many times what people read as anger was my being extremely passionate toward helping kids become the best they can be at whatever they're going to do. I want them—always—to be able to think back to a practice, a game, a halftime, a post-game moment when they need a little extra resolve, a little extra determination, a little extra effort. When they have to get something done personally, or for their son or daughter, I hope they can call upon what they learned at some particular moment to get it done.

Basketball has enabled me to do things I, as a kid, never even dreamed about being able to do, and it has been responsible for so many friends I have made. The experience at Indiana taught me that not everyone you think is a friend is a friend, and it also taught me that no one could possibly have more good friends in more walks of life than I've had. When I think about who those people are, and what they mean to their professions, I know that they, like me, don't confer friendship easily. I appreciate them more than they can know. Basketball gave me an opportunity to know these people, but I think I also had something to do with those friendships. I believe each, in their own way, says how something I did or stood for caused them to become my friend. If what Grantland Rice wrote is true, "When the one great scorer comes to mark against your name, it matters not that you won or lost, but how you played the game," I think I've reached this point in my life in pretty good shape. If there is just one spot left and the "great scorer" has made a choice between me and a lot of my critics, I like my chances. I think caring for and being honest with people is a pretty meaningful way to "play the game."

Frequently in interviews since coming to Tech, the interviewer has asked if I have changed. Yes, I have. Every experience anyone has changes that person to some degree. But basic change? No.

Gerald Myers answered that same question: "Maybe it's the environment around Bob that has changed. Maybe that's why Bob seems more relaxed, and more content than he has been for several years."

Obviously, I'm very grateful for all that has happened in my life because of an association with a game that Dave Knight started me playing when I was in the sixth grade at Walnut Street School in Orrville, Ohio. Nothing could have provided me with more pleasure, more enjoyment, or more satisfaction than my association with basketball, the greatest game of all. As my longtime friend Mickey Corcoran says, "There's no game like baskets."

But, where I have been most fortunate is something I had nothing to do with. It occurred the moment I was born, to great parents, in America. I, like most of you, inherited qualities of perseverance, of determination, of competitiveness, of just an all-out desire against all odds to succeed, things that have been a part of our country since the Pilgrims crossed the Atlantic in three boats that were not much bigger or more stable than rowboats. Our forefathers who fought for the right to guarantee us the freedoms that we enjoy today; those people who, through storms and famine, spread our America from the Atlantic to the Pacific; all of those men and women who fought to abolish slavery, to defeat Nazism, and to make sure we would always have the right to use whatever abilities we had to the fullest extent of their potential, have given us the opportunity to use those abilities in a way available nowhere else in the world.

The eight greatest words ever put together in the English language: *America, America, God shed His grace on thee . . .*

A part of that grace is a responsibility I believe each of us has: to make sure we provide those who follow us with the same opportunities you and I were given by those who preceded us. That's uppermost among all that I've tried to do as a coach—I and thousands of other coaches and teachers that kids across this country have been fortunate enough to have at some point in their lives.

EPILOGUE

For the most part, things felt familiar when I walked through the entrance out onto the playing floor at a few minutes after seven on November 16, 2001. It was opening night for my first Texas Tech basketball team. I was nervous; I'm always nervous the day of any game, because I see all the ways we could get beat in the game about to be played. There was one difference in this entrance: after wearing red sweaters for about five hundred straight games, I was in Texas Tech black. And it felt very good.

During my career in coaching, I've had five different jobs. I remember what my thoughts were going into each of the five—and each was different. When I went to Cuyahoga Falls High School to be an assistant to Harold Andreas, I wanted to see if I would like coaching. Teaching was part of that job—four classes of Problems of Democracy, a required course for seniors, and two study halls. I enjoyed the teaching, but I didn't think I would want to stay with that.

No coach could have had a better start than being with Andy. He was one of the best coaches I've ever been around. He not only guided his assistant coaches, but also allowed them to do some things on their own—which included making mistakes. He always brought mine to my attention, and I grew a little as a coach each time. The experience with Andy at Cuyahoga Falls convinced me that, at that time, I really would like to coach basketball.

After that season with Andy, the opportunity came along to go to West Point. It meant I had to join the army, but I didn't hesitate. I thought it would be a unique experience, and it was. I would have always been glad I did that, even if going to West Point had not worked out for me in basketball as it did.

When I started working there for Tates Locke, I wasn't sure if I would enjoy being away from home. I had lived in Ohio for twenty-three years, always pretty close to Orrville and the friends I had there. Now I was going to a place where I didn't know anybody. I thought that would be interesting.

Coaching basketball in college was what I wanted to do because in most cases classroom teaching was not part of the job. I picked up a lifelong friend in Tates, whom I found to be an outstanding coach although he wasn't much older than I was when I joined him. He helped me answer another question by letting me become involved with recruiting, another thing I had to see if I would enjoy. I thought that alone would determine whether I would want to try to stay in college coaching after West Point.

My third job came two years later when I moved up to head coach at Army. My thoughts starting that phase of my coaching life were: Can I do this? Can I organize a team, the practices, a coaching staff—all the things that go along with being a head coach? And there was one other big question: Can I put together a team that can win?

I've always felt that as a basketball coach I had two ultimate objectives. One was to provide my players with the best background possible toward success in their future lives. I wanted to be the best teacher each one of them felt they'd had anywhere in their educational experience. The second objective was to win games. I've never been ashamed that winning was always important to me—and not only to me. I also considered it extremely important that our players learned how to win and all that went into it.

The next step was leaving West Point. I wanted to make sure I used West Point as a stepping stone to a situation where I could coach a team that could compete for a national championship. Several coaching opportunities came along in the six years I was Army's coach, and one or two may have ultimately been as good as Indiana. I'm not at all sure about that.

When I went to Indiana, I had new questions: Will the way I teach basketball work against the best players and the best coaches in the country? I knew we were going to find that out against the teams that we played against there. It eventually became a question at Indiana of whether we stay on top year after year? Our run of Big Ten championships answered that particular question for me.

The fifth job in my coaching career is the one I have now at Texas Tech. When I first talked to athletic director Gerald Myers and university president David Schmidly about their interest in my coming to Texas Tech, I wasn't even sure I *wanted* to go back into coaching. I had reached the point where I enjoyed a lot of things and I knew I wouldn't have to go back into coaching just to have something to do, or to make a good living. The more I thought about it, the more I felt—really, I somehow knew—that I would enjoy working with the two of them.

The only questions that remained were: Would we be able to recruit in an area that was not around metropolitan cities? Could we bring into Tech enough kids good enough for us to compete against the schools we had to play? We would be taking over a basketball situation very similar to the one we inherited at Indiana, except Indiana was located in a heavily populated part of the country. Recruiting at Indiana figured to be much easier than at Tech.

But I underestimated some important things. I found the campus at Tech beautiful and spacious, easy to get around in. I have yet to meet a student or graduate, male or female, who didn't thoroughly enjoy attending the university. And Tech offers a much broader curriculum than Indiana does.

Both Karen and I thought Lubbock would be a place where we would enjoy living. From day one, there was never any doubt about that. It's an easy city to get around in because of an extremely well planned street and highway system. Our basketball office is just fifteen minutes from the airport. We can easily park and board our flight by arriving twenty to thirty minutes prior to departure. Our home is completely across town from my basketball office. I get there every day in about fifteen minutes.

The weather in west Texas is much better than anywhere I have lived. There's an average of 330 days of sunshine a year. The community gives great support to the student body and to the university in all respects. It's a great college town—in part because of its size, two hundred thousand people—that allows Lubbock to provide leisure time or recreation opportunities that smaller college towns just can't.

All of those things go together to make recruiting pretty easy, in the final analysis. As of December 2002, we'd had eighteen kids visit our campus in three recruiting years. Fifteen had signed with us.

You want to get off to a good start in any season. Certainly, in a new situation, I was hoping to do that. I'm not sure our start could have been any better. There was some emotion to it for me because an awful lot of my longtime friends came to Lubbock to help us get started. We opened our season on a Friday night, and those great people from all over the country started arriving early in the week. Mary Ann Davis, my secretary at Indiana for more than twenty years, was back with me at Tech by then. She knew the names and handled the traffic as efficiently as she always had, getting people picked up at the airport, having hotel rooms ready, and working out ticket arrangements. I have no idea what the total number was, but it had to be up in the hundreds—from every direction. Many of them came from Indiana, a long way from Lubbock.

When I took the job in late March, there were just four pre-conference games scheduled for the season coming up. At Indiana, we had our non-conference schedule pretty much filled three years ahead, and a lot of other schools are like that. Here in April we had six holes to fill. We ended up getting eight games. We were able to get the extra two because of Russ Potts, a long-time friend I had met when he was athletic director at SMU. He's in the Virginia legislature now, and his occupation is promoting football and basketball games for television. Almost immediately after I arrived at Texas Tech, he called to tell me he could get us an NCAA schedule-limit exemption. It had been granted to the Colonial Conference, of which William & Mary was a member. With the exemption, he was able to set up a four-team, two-night tournament at our place, bringing in San Diego State and Northern Iowa as well as William & Mary—all of us free to play two games that went into our won-lost record but counted as just one game against our schedule limit. It was a great way to start.

The night before will always remain unforgettable for me. I invited the people who had arrived early to go to dinner together. That's really all I meant for it to be, but it became much more. When we were done eating and about to break up, I asked each person to stand up and identify himself. One by one, guys stood up, introduced themselves, and most added a few words. Some brought laughs. Some, I admit, brought tears. More than forty people were there. Knowing each one of them, knowing how long each relationship went back, made it a special night I'll never forget.

The longest of those relationships was with John Havlicek. We had been good friends since we were freshmen at Ohio State. It really pleased me—pleased but in no way surprised me—that John came. He had come to help so many times at big points of my career.

Bob Leach came. He was the head of the Olympic medical operation in Los Angeles in 1984. He and I used to play tennis in the morning out there. He was a nationally ranked senior tennis player—very good. One morning I beat him—in a game, understand, not a set. I said, "Now, did I actually do that or did you just kinda let it happen?" He gave me a big grin and said, "We'll never know, will we?"

He came with John, all the way from Massachusetts.

John Ryan, the Indiana president when I was hired and for the next seventeen years, was there. Fuzzy Zoeller, who has won both the Masters and U.S. Open, came down. General Richie Cardillo, the oldest friend I had from West Point, was there. So was Mike Gyovai, still the toughest player I ever had. From Indiana, my first recruit, dentist Steve Green, and Tom Abernethy from our 1976 championship team were there.

One moment I'll never forget was a little talk by Abe Lemons. Abe was in the last year of his life and I'm sure he knew it. He was in the throes of Parkinson's disease, and he handled it as well as anyone could—his voice very weak but his humor as wonderful as always. No one I've ever heard had a greater combination of humor and intelligence than Abe. To the public, I think his humor often overshadowed his coaching abilities, though he was national co-coach of the year in 1981. He had a great grasp of what was important and what wasn't important in basketball. He had one of the smartest minds I've ever been around, period, and certainly that includes basketball. I think he was greatly underrated as a coach.

I shouldn't have started mentioning names, because I can't mention all of them and I appreciated every one as much as the others. But that first weekend—the whole weekend, the dinner the night before we opened, the tournament with the two bonus games Russ Potts got us, the way we played winning those two games—was a hell of a way to get a season started. Not to mention, a new program.

My number-one priority upon taking the job was putting a staff together. My first addition to the staff was my younger son Pat, who had played for us at Indiana; he and Jimmy Crews were the two best passers I coached. Pat went on after graduating to work in three different basketball positions: with the Phoenix Suns, where he worked with Dick Van Arsdale; as an assistant coach for Hartford in the CBA, then as the head coach for the team at Appleton, Wisconsin, in the IBA, which was a step below the CBA. Pat then came to work for two years on our Indiana staff. He was instrumental in putting our team together, including all of those players who were added to the team after he got there and went to the 2002 NCAA finals.

My next addition was Bobby Beyers, who spent two years as the head coach at Siena and worked under Kevin O'Neill at Northwestern. Kevin is a coach I really respect for both his intensity and his coaching ability. He gave Bobby his highest recommendation, and everything he said about him has proved to be absolutely true.

When we added Chris Beard, we picked up a man who had past experience as a recruiter at North Texas State and had been involved in junior college basketball for two years in Kansas and Oklahoma. His knowledge has been invaluable in all the recruiting we've done since his first day on the job.

We brought in Les Fertig, who worked at both West Point and Ohio State. At Ohio State, he was under Randy Ayers, another Big Ten coach I thought a lot of. Pat got to know Les when Pat coached at Columbus. Les became our operations manager; he's in charge of everything that takes place in our office regarding recruiting records and schedules.

Our last addition to our staff was Bubba Jennings, who had been one of the two or three best players ever at Texas Tech. He played for Gerald Myers at Tech and scored more than 1,700 points—he's still number five on Tech's career scoring list. He won a couple of state championships as a high school coach in New Mexico. Bubba is in charge of our video operations and he has done an excellent job. We use game tapes of our opponents extensively to prepare for each upcoming game. We also use tapes of our practices to show our players what they are doing and what they aren't doing. As a coach, I've always subscribed to the theory that a picture is worth a lot of words.

I also felt all season that there was another guy on our coaching staff, athletic director Gerald Myers. Never have I worked with a guy who was such a great friend and so valuable in his ability to help us with our team. Here is a guy who knows basketball every bit as well as I do. I could talk to him after a game or a practice, and show things to him, and call on his experience and knowledge for his opinion in any situation that might arise.

I inherited a Tech trainer Jon Murray who does an excellent job. I also inherited Leslie Hartline as a basketball secretary, teamed with Mary Ann Davis. I could have looked for six months and never found better people than Jon and Leslie.

I knew what I wanted in the coaching staff we were forming, but there was some luck involved in so quickly putting together a cohesive staff. Coaches on a staff really have to be alert to help in all situations in practice, but particularly in the situation we were in that first fall. On a new team, you're all unfamiliar with the players, so each of you looks to see which kids react the quickest to what you're trying to do—who absorbs it best. You're looking for players who can be your leaders.

I've never expected our coaches to be primarily recruiters, or to work just with big men, or to work with guards, or to coach defense. I've wanted my coaches to be able to do everything and be proficient in all areas, just as I've never used a numerical system as a designation for players, 1-2-3-4-5—1 and 2 for guards, 3 and 4 for forwards, and 5 for center. What we recruit, at the very least, is a kid who can play more than one position, preferably three—a 1-2-3, say, or a 3-4-5. The ideal player for me would be a 5-4-3-2-1, encompassing all positions.

We had to work fast as recruiters to get a team filled out. Working fast didn't mean just taking anybody we could get. We wanted good kids who would fit together. However you want to grade the kids we got, they were outstanding.

We were very, very lucky—and we worked damned hard to put ourselves in position to be lucky.

I've always felt that in anything I do I want to set objectives or goals—for either myself or the team. If I'm hunting or fishing, I tell myself, "Okay, I'm going to try to shoot a dozen quail today," or "I'm going to try to catch fifteen fish today," and see if I'm able to reach those goals. With a team, it hasn't ever really been winning a set number of games, because we're trying to win every game we play. Instead, it's to compete for the conference championship, or the national championship, or getting into the NCAA tournament, or the NIT. I've always tried to set team goals that would be realistic and require a lot of effective play to reach.

When we've been mathematically eliminated from a particular goal I might have set—for example, a conference championship—I immediately replace that with another goal, like getting into the NCAA tournament or, if that's not a possibility, getting into the NIT. If that isn't possible, it may be winning our last three games, or our last game. I always want them to think there's something out there that's important beyond simply winning a game.

Sometimes you can set a goal that you realize later was too difficult for a particular team to reach. The opposite is also true: you give them a goal that when reached, you see you hadn't set it high enough. I blame myself for how we played in the 2002 NCAA tournament, because I had set a goal of getting into the tournament, rather than getting there *and* playing well. But even if you do sometimes make a mistake in the goals you establish, I remain a firm believer that players must see reasons why we need to play hard and play well every time we play.

Midway through the preseason practice period, I told our team that our objective was to play in the NCAA tournament. I want our kids to be able to have experiences as college basketball players that kids playing at most other schools just don't have. I always liked several lines from General George Patton to his troops on June 5, 1944, the day before D-Day. My favorite was included in the movie *Patton:*

> *You may be thankful that twenty years from now when you are sitting by the fireplace with your grandson on your knee, and he asks you what you did in the great World War II, you won't have to cough, shift him to the other knee and say: "Well, your Grandaddy shoveled shit in Louisiana." No, sir, you can look him straight in the eye and say, "Son, your Grandaddy rode with the great Third Army and a son of a god-damned bitch named Georgie Patton."*

• • •

I want our players to be able to tell their grandsons that they did things most other college players didn't do—they won championships, they played for championships.

For three years in the early '80s, a nationally televised college seniors' all-star game was played in Cedar Rapids, Iowa — Big Ten seniors against players from all over the country. Al McGuire, Billy Packer, myself, Dick Enberg (for two years), and Curt Gowdy (the third year) were involved.

In 1983, the master of ceremonies at a luncheon the day of the game mentioned that we won the Big Ten that year but lost twice to Iowa. A few minutes later, I brought our two players in the game, Randy Wittman and Jimmy Thomas, up to the podium and asked them some questions:

"Does either of you remember how many times your teams beat Notre Dame?"

Both said, "No."

"How about Ohio State?"

"No."

I said, "Don't you remember anything like that?"

"No," Jimmy said. "But during our time at Indiana we won the NCAA championship."

"Yeah," Randy said, "and we won three Big Ten championships."

"And," Jimmy said, "when Randy was a freshman Indiana won the NIT."

I said, "How can you guys remember all that and not how many times we beat specific teams?"

Randy had a great answer: "Because at Indiana we're taught to win championships."

I really enjoyed that scene. It demonstrated what I was saying: Our kids on those teams were able to think back over things they had accomplished and championship teams they had played on. The vast, vast majority of college players can't.

Our first Texas Tech team didn't have great leadership, and it was understandable. They were all individually concentrating on what they were being taught to do, trying to make sure that they themselves were getting things done the way they were supposed to do them—or, I'm sure it was in their mind, doing things in the way that would enable them to play the most. And that's fine. The end result we want is to see our teaching absorbed and incorporated in our play—as part of how we go about playing the game. But that approach is not conducive to great leadership within the team. I entered our second year sure that what we would see better leadership from within the team. And right from the beginning we did.

The most prominent player we had back that first year was Andy Ellis, a 6'10" center, a three-year starter who had once scored thirty points in a game as a sophomore. I was familiar with that game. It came against my Indiana team when we were given the really nice honor of coming down to play Texas Tech in the first game in its new arena on November 19, 1999. I had a sophomore center I was pretty high on, too. Andy outscored Kirk Haston that night, thirty to two. He was the big reason why we had all we could handle before winning, 68–60. A little more than a year later, Haston was a first-round NBA draft choice. That night when United Spirit Arena was dedicated, he was thoroughly outplayed. But Haston, a great kid, went on a continual drive up from there and Andy, another great kid, had some injury problems. The next thirteen games, he averaged a little less than sixteen points a game. In Tech's fourteenth game, at Nebraska, he blocked a shot and dislocated his shoulder. He never made it back that year, playing just three conference games. His scoring average as a junior dropped to 14.2, his rebounding average from 8.9 to 6.3. All I knew was he had looked damned good—or we had made him look damned good—the only time I saw him play. I was really looking forward to having Andy on our first Tech team. It turned out I enjoyed it as much as I thought I would. He worked extremely hard and was just a tremendous player for us. I'd love to have had him four years. He was a good scorer and a good shooter, both—a player who could take on the individual responsibility of trying to learn our system, but being a leader while doing so. He was our most accurate three-point shooter — .511, twenty-four for forty-seven. I'd never had a 6'10" center shoot over 50 percent on threes. You don't usually want your 6'10" guys playing that far out on the floor, but in our case it gave both Andre Emmett and Kasib Powell room to post up, and they're very good at it.

From the first time I ever saw our kids play, I was impressed with Emmett. He played part-time as a freshman, averaging about seven points a game and starting only once. I saw him on film in games from that first season, but once he was on the basketball court with us, I could see that—the way we play—he could be very good. He has great baseline skills. He's every bit as good there as Calbert Cheaney was, and Calbert was the College Player of the Year for us at Indiana.

The other players we had coming back were two seniors who hadn't played very much, Chris Cassidy (5'11") and Jesus Arena (6'4"), and three sophomores, Emmett, plus 6'4" Mikey Marshall, who had started nineteen games as a freshman, and 6'0" Marcus Shropshire, who had started eight. All of them, including Ellis and Emmett, were Texas kids. I liked that. Our seven other play-ers had played for seven different coaches the year before, so starting the season our team as a whole was coming from eight different systems, trying to learn a ninth.

We recruited the other seven, starting as soon as my hiring had been com-pleted with an unforgettable introduction before the students and fans at the arena March 23. Our first signed recruit turned out to be the smallest player on our team: Will Chavis, 5'10". He had played two years at Panola Junior College in Texas, but he was from Philadelphia. In high school, he was the other guard on a team with Lynn Greer, the high-scoring guard John Chaney had at Tem-ple. Will was the perfect first recruit for us. He's an excellent student, planning to go to medical school the next year, just as my first recruit at Indiana, Steve Green, eventually became a dentist.

We knew we had to find some kids who could play right away, so we talked to everybody we could in the junior colleges. We thought we had an outstand-ing big man coming in. Ermal Kuqo signed with us. He was 6'10", about 250 pounds, and he had all the skills to be an outstanding player, with a real chance to be an NBA player. We thought he would fit right in with Andy Ellis to give us an extremely strong front-court. But he was an Albanian, like many foreign players facing an NCAA eligibility question. I know Kuqo really wanted to play here, but back home his family was in severe financial problems. Because of his family and the eligibility uncertainty, he signed to play in the Slovenian profes-sional league, which made him permanently ineligible to play here. I thought that was a tremendous setback. As well as our season went, I think we could have played with anybody in the country if we had kept Kuqo. But it didn't hurt us as much as I thought it would. I didn't realize what we were going to wind up with because that last scholarship suddenly was open. We got Kasib Powell, a 6'7" New Jersey kid who had averaged 18.7 as a sophomore on a good team at Butler County Community College in Kansas. He played there for Dennis Helms, who was both an excellent and a demanding coach. Kasib played a lot in the post for Dennis, and he was effective there for us, too. But he also did some other things. In our fifth game of the year, we were playing UTEP at our place. In the second half, they were playing a zone defense and at a time-out, I said, "Kasib, have you ever played on the point against a zone?"

"No."

I said, "Get on the point and see what you can do—handle the ball, get it to people, penetrate."

He was a natural. *Very* good. That night he had nineteen points and five assists, with just one turnover. From then on, he was always our point man against a zone. He wound up leading our team in assists for the season. He needs to work on his shooting, but he penetrates well, he sees well, and he gets the ball to people well. He's a combination player I really like, in that he can play outside and inside. He's an excellent post player. He developed to a point where I think he could be a draft choice in the NBA this year. And we were able to get him only because we lost a good player and that scholarship became available.

We also picked up Pawel Storozynski, a strong 6'8" Polish kid who played two years at Dodge City Community College in Kansas and helped fill the opening left when we lost Kuqo; Nick Valdez, a 6'7" Colorado kid who played at Northeastern Junior College in Colorado, and a couple of high school guards—Nathan Doudney, from Rockwall, Texas, and Ronald Ross, from just across the state line in Hobbs, New Mexico. Both Doudney and Ross played a lot and started some games.

Doudney, an excellent shooter, had signed with Tulsa and coach Buzz Peterson, a former North Carolina player. When Peterson left to take the job at Tennessee and we came to Texas Tech, Nathan wanted out of the letter so he could come here. I told him we were out of scholarships and he'd have to pay his own way the first year, but he came. And Ronald Ross came the same way—as a walk-on until a scholarship was available. We were really lucky to get kids like those two under the circumstances.

Where a recruit goes is often determined by people close to him, people who have a real interest in the player and respect for what you're doing and can help show the kid that this particular situation would be the very best for him. In getting Storozynski, for example, we were helped tremendously by Casey Malek, who grew up in Indiana, coached at Dodge City, and was athletic director there. He's a longtime friend. The same applies to Jerry Mullen, who was the junior college coach for a player we had at Indiana, Todd Jadlow. Jerry has his own business now, a national scouting service evaluating junior college players. He helped us get started well in recruiting junior colleges out here.

So here I was, in a position I hadn't been in for thirty years—starting all over, from scratch, to build a basketball team. I loved the challenge of that—trying to use the things I had found to work well over the years I had coached—seeing how players begin to understand what we were trying to do.

From the first day we were able to work out with our first group of kids on the basketball floor in September, I was looking for what we had, not what we didn't have. Too many people—in all walks of life, not just coaching—get caught up with shortcomings in what's available to them and don't notice and take advantage of what they do have. As coaches in those early days, that's what we were looking for: What do we have and where can we go from there? Let's see where we think what we have can take us.

We watched our kids play a little bit and as I observed things, I was wondering: What things that we've always done with teams can we do with this group? How much of our offensive play can they absorb and handle—what parts of it are best suited to these kids? What can we do defensively? We wanted to play defense as we had always played it, but I had to consider: maybe we can and maybe we can't.

Actually, we practiced very similarly to the way we always have, in what we did, the length of practice, and what we tried to teach. Pete Newell feels one of the most important tenets of teaching is repetition. We just repeat, repeat, repeat. Once we got started, that's what we did with this team. In basketball— in anything you do—there are basic, fundamental things that you have to learn to do, so as a coach you work on those things with individuals and put them all together into team play. I've always coached that way, and that's what we did with these kids. After just a couple of days of looking at our players on the court, I told Gerald Myers I thought we could get to the NCAA tournament. That might not qualify as the smartest thing any new coach ever did. Texas Tech—not this team, not most of these players, but Texas Tech—had gone 9–19 each the last two years. I don't think Gerald was so convinced that he went right out and set the dates aside. I meant it, though. And that's what I told our players—that our objective was to play in the NCAA tournament. I told them one other thing at the same time: I would never give them an objective I didn't think was realistic.

Some teams elect captains. My teams don't. I've always said the players decide everything that I don't care about. People who hear me say that take it to be humorous, but it's fact. There are a lot of things that are important to the players and unimportant to me. For example: we're going to practice once on a weekend; would they prefer Saturday or Sunday? Say they choose Saturday; then I let them decide the time we'll start practice, because I really don't care. After a home game, where do they want to eat? On a road trip, I leave it up to them whether, as a team, they want to go to a movie the night before a game. But we don't vote on substitutions, or how long somebody is going to play, or who's going to start the game, or who's going to be playing at the end of a game. Or, on who's going to be team captain. The captain is going to be the one I want. For example, the captain that first year was Andy Ellis. This year it's Kasib Powell. I hope Andre Emmett will mature in such a way that he will be the captain next year.

• • •

The two-night tournament was with William & Mary, San Diego State, and Northern Iowa. We had a chance to see after the first game how quickly we could get ready to play a different team the next night. We beat William & Mary, 75–55, and then came back the next night to play Steve Fisher's San Diego State team, which a few months later made the NCAA tournament. We played well right from the beginning against San Diego State. The halftime score was 50–33. We prepared for them with just a little work that morning. We won 81–71, and I saw from our team's play what I had hoped to see: things were being absorbed and executed.

Our first road game was at SMU. That was a hometown game for Emmett, which can make a player nervous. If it had any effect on Andre, it wasn't bad. He had his first thirty-point game as a college player and we won, 78–75.

It was the first exposure our players had to something that we're still working on trying to get them to anticipate and react positively to: the intensity that comes from a very large, loud crowd combined with a team that considers beating us high on their own list of objectives. We'll get everyone's best shot, so we have to respond with ours. We have not always done that and consequently we have lost some games I don't think we should have lost. In the SMU arena that night, there was a sign directed at me. I don't really remember the wording, but I remember where it was—over the entrance to the court, at the end of the bench. I thought at the beginning of the game, "If we win, I'll walk over and tear that sign down."

We won, and I did walk over and look up at the sign. It was a little bit higher than I thought. I'm not sure that on the best jumping day of my life I could have reached it. I did some quick rethinking and decided to just walk right on—there was no way I was going to jump up and miss it in front of all *those* people.

Now we were 3–0 and feeling pretty good about ourselves. We were at home again for our fourth game, playing Sam Houston State, and all my old theories about "Last Game, Next Game" and kids categorizing opponents returned. So did another one about the importance of how you end the first half.

I've always believed if you have things going in the right direction in a game, you have to keep them going that way. We were up nineteen points just before the half and they got a three-point play at the buzzer. Oh, boy—that *always* bothers me, to have to walk off the floor when you've just made a bad play or when you've lost part of the lead you've worked to get. Everything I had felt before was reinforced that night. They played very well in the second half and certainly deserved to win—as they did, 69–65. You can bet those three points we gave up ending the first half came up in my mind after that game. Fortunately for us, the Sam Houston State loss came on Saturday and we had another game on Monday. We played very well in that one and beat UTEP, 81–56. That was a big point in the pre-conference season for us. We learned that in three days we could lose when we weren't really focused on the game, and we could get back to where we should be quickly if we did play poorly in a game.

Among the coaches who helped us out when we were searching around to fill our schedule back in the spring was Lou Henson, who had retired after his years at Illinois. He had been talked out of retirement to coach again at his alma mater, New Mexico State, which he had taken to the Final Four in 1970 (just as he later did in 1989 at Illinois). I doubt if it took much persuading. Lou has always struck me as maybe the biggest true basketball fan of all the coaches I've met. I love the game, but not in the way he does—to the point of watching every game he can on TV, after he's spent all the hours of tape—watching practices and opponents—that coaching demands.

We started what I hope will be a continuing series with New Mexico State by going to their place, a very nice arena at Las Cruces. I liked and respected Lou so much that I did something I don't do very often: I spoke at a New Mexico State boosters' luncheon on the day of the game. It began with maybe the longest prayer I've ever heard, by a Baptist minister from Las Cruces. It finally ended and we sat down and ate, then it was my time to talk. I asked: "How many of you here are Baptists?" Almost everybody in the room put up a hand.

"Well, then, let me ask you a question.

"At events like this with an invocation—do you ever get to eat hot food?"

The minister was a good guy. He laughed as hard as the rest of them did.

I kept on the Baptist theme for a while. I told them, "Now, undoubtedly there will be some bad calls tonight, and you'll stand up and boo those officials—for calls *against* you.

"Don't forget, some bad calls inevitably will be against us. I ask you to do me a favor. In good Christian charity, just once or twice when you see a call against us that you know is really bad, stand up and boo those guys for us."

In the prayer, the minister had mentioned talking to the Lord. This was still in November, our war against terrorism in just its third month. So I turned to the minister to say, "By the way, when you talk to the Lord tonight, could you ask Him: 'Please make sure you help us find that son of a bitch in Afghanistan.'"

By then, he had become pretty fired up and he jumped up and said, "Let's *all* pray tonight that He helps us find that, uh, guy in Afghanistan."

That night we had a hell of a game. Unlike the SMU game, this time on the road we had to come from behind—we were six points down with not much time left, but we tied it up to get into overtime and then won, 81–80. In that game and at SMU, I thought both teams played pretty well, so it meant something to me that we were able to come out of those games with wins.

We had to play our first seven games without Pawel Storozynski, because of an NCAA ruling that I thought was ridiculous.

He was one of several kids from across the country who had to sit out some games because the NCAA ruled that back home they had played in games with some professional players—the rule that helped make up Kuqo's mind upon whether to join us at Tech or go home to Albania and play professionally. The Storozynski suspension (and others like it) didn't say that those kids had received money to play, but that they had played in games or leagues that had one or more pros.

The Storozynski case was pending all through our pre-season practices. Naturally that was disruptive. Here's a kid who should be a pretty good player and we didn't know if he would be allowed to play. He could practice with the others, but maybe he wouldn't ever be allowed to play in games. We were into the season before the NCAA handed its ruling down.

There were rulings like Pawel's being made all over the country, at the last minute before the season began. The NCAA rulings were consistent only in that they were ill-considered, ignoring the fact that the only chance kids in foreign countries had to develop their own game was to play against the best competition they could find. Let me suggest a very simple rule to handle all these foreign players attending U.S. colleges: if a kid reaches his nineteenth birthday before he enrolls at an American school, he has to sit out a year before he can play. Then, what you're saying is anything that happens until he's about the age of an American kid graduating from high school in essence doesn't count. That would eliminate all the decisions the NCAA wrestles with now: Is this player a pro? Is that league pro? They have no idea.

In Storozynski's case, I doubt if he ever played in front of more than thirty people. He certainly didn't get as much out of it as an American kid who plays on a traveling AAU team in the summer and gets a closetful of clothing, expense money, the shoe companies get involved, all kinds of things—an American kid who plays all over the country, his way paid for him, before he ever gets to college. The rule I suggest is just far too logical and far too simple for the NCAA to ever adopt. Instead, they have people making decisions who have never played and never coached. Situations like this one are why I think coaches almost across the board have a lack of respect for the NCAA's concept of fairness and how they arrive at their rules.

We finished our pre-conference season 11–1, and it was a pretty positive thing for us. Before the season, I thought to myself that we were capable of winning every pre-conference game, but that's different from feeling we actually would win all twelve. I didn't think we would do that. I thought if we could be 9–3 going into conference play that would be pretty good. We beat that by two games and the game we lost (to Sam Houston State) we had control of and let get away.

Our pre-conference record included 3–0 on the road. I've never paid much attention to whether we were playing at home or on the road. Coach Taylor told me he thought a mistake all coaches get trapped with is thinking, *If we can just win one out of two on the road* . . . . I've always thought you just try to win as many as you can on the road, and over the years with that approach that came from him we won a pretty high percentage of road games—and a much higher percentage than any other Big Ten teams on the road during my years in that conference.

But when you're just getting things started in a new program, I think your team feels more comfortable playing at home. So it was great for us that we were able to schedule both Wyoming and Minnesota at home that first year. It turned out that both Wyoming and San Diego State made it to the NCAA tournament and Minnesota had a good season. Now this second year—with guys back for us who have been through a season—those teams all became excellent tests for us on the road.

So, at 11–1 and about to play our first Big Twelve Conference game, I still was wondering a lot: Are we competitive? Do we have an established lineup with enough depth?

There were times at Indiana when we reached this point in the season that I thought we were going to be hard to beat in the conference race—a few times when I thought it would be difficult for anyone *but* us to win the championship. Most times when I felt that way, I turned out to be right. We won eleven championships or cochampionships in twenty-nine years, about 40 percent. Actually, I think it should be thirteen, and more than 40 percent. In the '90s, we were second to Purdue one year, and the NCAA later ordered Purdue to forfeit several games, many in the league, for using an ineligible player. In 1992 we finished second to Ohio State when a game ordered forfeited to us by Michigan would have boosted us into a tie. The Big Ten, in a late-1990s revision of its own long-standing policy, somehow decided it wouldn't apply for-feiture of games to the standings in a championship race, which seems idiotic to me. You don't forfeit games and keep championships. Won-lost standings determine who is the champion. Only in a conference with the commissioner and the presidents that the Big Ten has would a team required by the NCAA to forfeit games have those forfeitures overlooked where championships are con-cerned. So, as the standings dictated by NCAA rulings stand, our Indiana teams finished first thirteen out of twenty-nine times, about 45 percent of the time.

But just as I knew some years that we were in position to do well when the conference season started, there also were times when I thought going into the Big Ten season it was going to be very tough for us to compete for those cham-pionships. My situation in January 2002 was different. I had no idea what to expect in the Big Twelve. I knew the competition would be very good. This league in basketball has far and away the best coaching in the country—*really* good coaches. And the talent is good, a combination of high school kids and junior college kids.

Because of the population in the Big Ten states and the fact that the Big Ten schools had the first opportunities to recruit any of those kids, I always felt the talent in that league was extremely good. Everybody had good players. I think the same thing is true in the Big Twelve, but in this league every team, includ-ing ours, is augmented more by junior college players than in a league that is in a very highly populated area, like the Big Ten or Atlantic Coast Conference.

Just as was the case in the Big Ten, every place we played in the Big Twelve was on campus, and we didn't see anything but very big crowds. At Texas A&M, I think it was one of the two or three largest crowds they'd ever had. More than ten thousand came out at Colorado. We won, 97–79, and I was pleased about that because one of those ten thousand spectators was Colonel Ray Murphy, the Army athletic director who gave me my first head coaching job. He's living in retirement now at Colorado Springs. When it got around before the game how he and I were connected, he was interviewed by several press people. One of them asked him how I had changed. He said, "I hired him in 1965 because of what I thought he could do with our basketball team and because of his intensity. I've watched his teams through the years, and I'm here to tell you that his intensity has never changed. And I wouldn't want it to."

At Oklahoma State, we led by fifteen points in the second half and got beat at the buzzer. I hated that, of course, but something happened to me that night that I really appreciated. About an hour before the game, the Oklahoma State coach, Eddie Sutton, came to the room where I was passing the time by reading a book. We've known each other for more than thirty years, and he said, "Come with me. I want to show you something." We went out into the halls that go all the way around Gallagher-Iba Arena, and he took me to a display they had created in Henry Iba's honor. What he wanted me to see was one picture in it—of Coach Iba and me. I was honored, of course, to be in there like that, but it meant all the more to me that Eddie took the time to make sure I saw it. It didn't make the defeat feel any better, but I'll always remember what Sutton did, because he knew we both shared deep admiration for the coach Eddie had played for, Henry Iba.

We finished 10–6 in the conference and played three of those games very poorly—at Oklahoma, Texas, and Kansas. But we also beat Oklahoma and Oklahoma State on back-to-back Saturdays, when each was ranked number six in the country at the time. Winning those games was nice, but after our kids had been patted on the back around campus for ten days, we just never got turned around in time to play at Nebraska. We lost, 80–69, and we were outplayed from the start. A really good team handles big wins better than that. Not that Nebraska couldn't have beaten us, but we were outplayed right from the beginning until a little stretch at the end where we tried to get back in it.

At home, where we were helped a lot by big and enthusiastic crowds, we lost just one conference game—74–71 to Texas in overtime. We lost to a good team, but we knew we had done a lot to beat ourselves. The other seven league games at home we won by pretty good margins.

Included in the home wins were back-to-back games late in the season against Missouri and Texas A&M. Storozynski's mother, Brazenna, came over from where the family lives in France to see us play those games. After one practice, while Pawel and the rest of the players were showering and getting dressed, his mother went out on the court and did some shooting. At one point, I think she hit fourteen straight three-point shots. Somewhere in there we learned she was considered one of the five best woman players in Polish basketball history. She made all of us believers.

She was there for our first Senior Day game, a last-home-game tradition we started in 1973 at Indiana. This one had a special touch. Tom Rucker, who officiated in both the Big Twelve and Big Ten and at every level of the NCAA tournament, had worked his first Big Ten game at Indiana, against Iowa. Charlie Fouty was his officiating partner that night and Charlie brought him over in pregame to introduce us to each other. By no means did Tom and I agree on every call he made over the years, but I always considered him one of the best men in college basketball. I told him a few years ago I hoped we could get him for his last regular-season game, and I was happy that it worked that way. We introduced him to the crowd before our Texas A&M game, and I sent him a painted-up basketball commemorating the occasion.

Before that ball ever got to him, I received a letter:

> As I approach the final days of my thirty-year career, three men stand out who helped to make opportunities happen for me.
>
> First, Herman Rohrig, who gave a young Black official from Detroit the chance to work in a great collegiate conference like the Big Ten.
>
> Secondly, Charlie Fouty, who was a wonderful mentor for three years. Bob, I would never have made it without Charlie's help.
>
> Finally, Bob Knight, who demanded that you give your best effort all the time, and was never concerned about "who was right, but what was right."
>
> As a young official in 1972, I realized the tremendous responsibility I had to carry, both on and off the court. I always believed that my job was to protect the integrity of the game.
>
> As I leave the game at the end of this season, I know I leave a friend in you, but, most important, I leave with a tremendous respect for you. When you decide to leave the coaching sidelines, I hope I can be there to extend my hand and say, "Job well done." Best of luck to you and your family always.
>
> —Tom Rucker

The letter meant a lot to me, and so did the company he put me in. Charlie Fouty was always my favorite official. And I loved Herman Rohrig, who had been an outstanding football player at Nebraska and in the NFL. He was in charge of officials in both football and basketball when I came into the league, and he did an excellent job.

My first year in the Big Twelve gave me a much better feeling toward the commissioner, Kevin Weiberg. He had been assistant commissioner for several years in the Big Ten and I hadn't thought too highly of him. After I came here, he and I sat down and talked at some length. Afterward, I think both of us had a far better understanding of each other. I came to feel that my previous negative feelings and lack of respect were not so much toward him as toward the commissioner, Jim Delany. Kevin has been very good for the Big Twelve.

I also grew to think a lot of Kim Anderson, the Big Twelve director of basketball operations, and I was pleased to see that after the basketball season he got back into coaching at Central Missouri. He was replaced in his Big Twelve position by John Underwood, who was an assistant on Dave Bliss's staff for eleven years.

One guy in the Big Ten office that I truly respected was Richie Falk, the former Northwestern coach who has done a great job as the supervisor of officials. Kim and John are a great deal like him and, in fact, I'm sure learned a lot from him.

As much as I thought of Herman Rohrig, I've always felt a guy who had coached had the best background for being in charge of officiating. I don't think it's coincidental that the three guys I've mentioned—Richie Falk, Kim Anderson, and John Underwood—are all former coaches, rather than former officials.

We were 21–7 going into the Big Twelve Tournament at Kansas City. I thought that was good enough to assure us a spot in the NCAA tournament, but I always lean toward pessimism. I figured we'd better play well at Kansas City to be sure we were in.

We had ended the regular season by pulling away to a pretty solid 74–53 win over Texas A&M. That's the team that, by the way the seedings were set up, we played in our first conference tournament game. We had beaten them just 72–70 in the regular-season game at A&M.

They played better than we did in the first half and went to halftime leading us by two. We played very well starting the second half and opened a nine-point lead in the first seven or eight minutes. Then during a time-out, circumstances changed. I noticed a little flurry of activity across the court from me while the game was going. An official working the game, Rick Hartzell—the athletic director at Northern Iowa and an excellent official who Bob Hammel and I both know because he also works the Big Ten—came over to me not knowing Bob was involved and said:

"We have a man on press row who I think had a heart attack and they're getting some emergency help in there. I think we should stop the game for a few minutes. Okay?"

"Certainly," I told him. "I don't think there's any question."

And while he was asking me, another official was getting the same answer from Mel Watkins, the A&M coach.

I was standing with my team, thinking about what we had to do to keep things going, when my son Pat came up.

"Dad," he said, "I think it's Mr. Hammel."

I looked over and realized it was right in the area where I had seen Bob sitting. I went across the court with my heart in my mouth and saw that Pat was right—it was Bob. He was on the floor, unconscious. One of our team doctors—Jim Burke, an orthopedic surgeon—was one of the first people in there helping. Bob had passed out and had convulsions. The only thing I could think to do to help was to make sure they knew he was a diabetic. It was a scary sight, the worst I've ever felt on a basketball court.

Even Jim Burke told Bob several months later, "When I came up there, I thought you were dead." He was turning blue. They cut his sweater and shirt open to work on him. I told him later—much later—that when I saw that, I was thinking to myself, *The sun hasn't touched that stomach since he was eight years old.* I think that was probably right, but I really wasn't thinking anything funny then.

The Big Twelve people couldn't have been better. After emergency treatment at courtside, they got Bob out of there and on the way to St. Luke's Hospital, one of the best in America. Kim Anderson lined up a police car to take me to the hospital as soon as the game ended.

My first instinct was to leave the game and go to the hospital right away. But I realized I owed it to our kids to be there with them for the rest of the game. And all I could do at the hospital was get in the way. At one time we got the lead to twelve, then it started to slip away. It got down to three before we played well enough to win, 80–71.

I skipped all the usual post-game obligations and went straight to the hospital. He was still unconscious when I got there. He was unconscious for almost four hours. Several times during that period, the hospital doctor handling him would ask questions to see if he was regaining consciousness: "Do you know what day this is?" "Do you know where you are?" The answers he gave weren't very close.

I was talking to the doctor near Bob when he apparently heard and recognized my voice. He turned in my direction with his eyes now open, saw me, and said, "How'd the game come out? You did win, didn't you? You were about eight points ahead the last I remember."

I laughed and said, "Yeah, we won. And that's the first sensible thing you've said yet."

He said later he didn't know whether I meant the first sensible thing then, or ever. He regained rationality quickly after that. By then, we were to the stage where we could both joke. I told him that when the doctor asked him, "Do you know where you are?" and he didn't, I told the doctor, "Aw, don't worry about that. I've been with him on the road dozens of times when he had no idea where he was."

A few minutes later I told him, "We were playing really well when you fell off your chair, and then we damned near lost. We're playing Oklahoma State tomorrow. If you come, get yourself a big-enough chair that your fat ass doesn't fall off." And he came back: "Hey, I had you eight-up when I left. If you can't handle a lead like that, what good are you?" The truth was I was beginning to wonder that myself when the lead was getting away. And I knew there was absolutely no chance that he would be at our Oklahoma State game.

Bob was released from the hospital while we were playing that game. His wife Julie, his daughter Jane, and his brother Bill came to Kansas City Friday morning, took him back to our hotel for that night, and then drove him back to Bloomington on Saturday. At St. Luke's Hospital in Kansas City the day he was there and at hospitals in Indianapolis and Bloomington the next few months, they ran all sorts of tests on him and found no reason for the sudden attack, and no lasting damage from it. It has been written off as a random attack unlikely to happen again. The one time it did, it scared the hell out of me.

Bob did point out one "good" thing about the incident. Because the tournament game was on national TV, Bob's game-stopping problem wound up making just about every major newspaper in the country the next morning. It was on *SportsCenter* and all the other TV sports news shows the night it happened. Every time the incident was mentioned—on national TV or in print—his link with me and our book, three weeks from its national release, was mentioned. We figured there were guys in silk suits in Madison Avenue PR companies wondering how these rubes from the Midwest thought up such a great way to promote a book.

Shortly after Bob got home, a note came in from College Station, Texas. Mel Watkins, the A&M coach, and a guy I've always liked, told Bob he hoped he had recovered well and added a P.S.: "By the way, thanks. I think the timing of it all helped us a lot more than it did Tech."

That was a great note from a good and thoughtful guy.

Our team played exceptionally well in our second conference tournament game and beat Oklahoma State, 73–51. We were two even teams who had split during the year. We got off to a good start and won.

Then we just didn't have anything left for the next game, against Kansas in the semifinals on Saturday. They beat us 90–50, and I told the players afterward I discount that game. We were not physically strong enough to play three games in three days, a requirement that I think is one of many negatives about a conference tournament.

We went into the tournament 21–7 and came out 23–8, pretty sure we were going to be in the NCAA tournament. I don't think our players really thought we would get there until we had won about eighteen or nineteen games. Yes, I had told them at the beginning of the year that I expected that of them. But to be coming off two 9–19 seasons and all of a sudden be told they were going to play in the NCAA tournament—I saw a lot of question in their eyes that day.

We were paired in the tournament against what I knew was a good, well-coached team, Southern Illinois. But I felt very good about how we had progressed and thought, *All right, we have a chance to win some games.*

Except for the very beginning of the game and the end, Southern Illinois completely outplayed us. It was like our players, happy and a little bit relieved to get into the tournament, said, "We made it." It was the Nebraska game all over again. In both of those games, we were beaten by teams that certainly had a chance to beat us, but we also had a chance to beat them. We just didn't play as well as either of them did.

The beginnings of my life as the basketball coach at Texas Tech coincided with my life as a bestselling author. I was more at home with the coaching part of that, but pleasantly surprised with the reaction that people had to this book. We were eliminated from the tournament on March 15 and a little more than a week later the book was released. I went on a fast-track promotion of it from the first day on through the next month, mixing in some recruiting, of course.

We opened the tour with an interesting event—a signing at a Barnes & Noble store on Fifth Avenue in New York, right across from St. Patrick's Cathedral. That first swing took us to bookstores in New York, Washington, Atlanta, San Francisco, Los Angeles, and Chicago. There were TV and radio appearances each place, too — in New York alone with Bob Costas, Larry King, Charlie Rose, Regis Philbin, Mike Francesa, and Mike Adams, and I'm sure I've forgotten some. I had been on with Costas and King before and looked forward to being with each of them again. As a TV viewer, I've always liked the way Charlie Rose works, and I couldn't have been more impressed when it was my turn to be interviewed by him.

When the book-selling tour reached Los Angeles, I had a great experience with Jay Leno. When we were in their waiting room, Leno walked in the door, didn't say a word to me, and went right to Karen with a dozen roses. He told her how pleased he was that she would come to the show. Then he turned to me and said, "Oh, yeah, Coach, we're glad to have you, too." Then when I came on stage during the show, I carried a chair out with me. That wasn't scripted. His widened eyes showed he wasn't expecting that at all, but he loved it. I enjoyed being on his show as much as I did anything on the tour.

Another one like that came in Washington. I was on with Tim Russert, a fascinating and likable guy, obviously a genuine sports fan and obviously very bright. I also had an interesting interview there by Gordon Liddy. I don't think he's particularly sports-oriented, but he's a quiet, intelligent man who had put a good deal of research into the book and was able to talk about it knowledgeably. Also in Washington I did an hour-long interview with Oliver North, one of the most enthusiastic men I've ever met. North is a real sports fan. He brought up his time at the Naval Academy, remembering games our Army teams played against Navy—played against and won, I couldn't resist reminding him.

I didn't line up the sales and promotion trip; our book publisher, St. Martin's, did—it's part of their business and for the most part things worked out very well. I followed orders and used the transportation provided for me at all stops. The day we began the tour in New York, I was told the agreement was that the interview with Costas would be aired first, and that was fine for me because Costas has been a friend of mine for several years. The opening TV appearances were booked in between bookstore signings. I know New York traffic. I thought the bookings that first day were too tightly bunched, and it worked out that way. We were due for a filming with a guy I had never heard of, Bill O'Reilly, and got so tied up in traffic it was obvious there was no way we could make the scheduled time. My traveling partners made a call from the car to tell O'Reilly we were coming, but we would be late. Our understanding was that he had agreed to tape this show, and he would play his interview the next day. O'Reilly, though, was irate when we couldn't make the taping time and said he had been promoting it all day—to be run that night. Then he went on the show without me and ripped me as "not a man of his word." I have no idea how the discrepancy happened between the people who lined up that appearance for me and O'Reilly's translation of the agreement, but I do know I and the St. Martin's people were making every effort to get there. To me it was one more example of how loose with the facts some "big" media people can be.

On another swing that took me to Louisville and four Indiana points, I met a lot of great people and signed a whole bunch of books. I made several appearances in Lubbock and other Texas cities during those opening weeks of the sales campaign. I'm guessing that I signed twenty-five thousand books, a high percentage of those for people who stood in line for two or three hours, some up to five. The very first week it was possible, the book was number two on the *New York Times* bestseller list. I'll be honest, I wish we could have been number one, but we stayed in the top five for a month and in the top twenty-five for almost two months.

The signings are a blur in my memory now, they were so hectic. Bob was with me at Atlanta the night before the Final Four semifinals. That signing, of course, was lined up several weeks before the tournament began, and it happened that Indiana was one of the Final Four teams. That whole week, I was ripped coast-to-coast for not calling those kids on the team that I had recruited and coached to congratulate them and wish them well—criticized by the same people who, if I had done that, would have ripped me for not being able to stay out of the spotlight. One of my nationally aired critics was Jim Nantz, the CBS announcer, who worked the Final Four games with Billy Packer. In a note, I let Nantz know in not very nice words what a cheap shot I thought that was. Of course I was happy for those kids. They closed their year with a great tournament run. But if I were coaching a team that has made the Final Four, I damned sure wouldn't want a former coach making contacts the week of the finals. I don't think I'm the only coach who would feel that way.

The weekend after the Final Four, from Friday night through Sunday night, Bob and I were at bookstores in Louisville, suburban Indianapolis, downtown Indianapolis, Terre Haute, and Bloomington. We signed more than six thousand books that weekend alone.

Not everybody in the lines knew Bob, who had been out of sports writing for six years. Most did, but not the guy in Louisville who watched me sign his book, then saw Bob take it from me and start to sign his name. In a loud, irritated voice, the man asked a store employee who was helping us: "Who the hell is he?" Another in Indianapolis watched our procedure and—in the splitsecond it took for me to slide the book over to Bob—leaped onto the table with his arms wrapped around the book like a lineman recovering a fumble, looked up at Bob, and said: "No offense." Bob's Kansas City problem had been just a few weeks before this, and most of the people who came through the line knew about it. They'd say versions of "And how are *you* feeling?" Everywhere but Terre Haute. Maybe three out of twelve hundred or so said something to him there. So in Bloomington that night when the first person through the line asked him how he was doing, I couldn't resist. "Why, thank you for asking," I said. "There were only a few people in Terre Haute who had never even heard of the son of a bitch." Actually, it came out more like "sumbitch." My Texas language lessons already were being put to use.

My wife Karen's prediction that I would feel right at home quickly in West Texas couldn't have been more accurate. After my first full year at Lubbock, I knew I couldn't have found a better situation. But there are some differences from what I was used to in Ohio and Indiana. Hunting, for example. It's great, but it's different. I didn't do much turkey hunting before, but that's a big thing in West Texas. One of my first days out I was with a friend who showed me right where he wanted me to be—sitting in a little pine tree—and then walked away to another pine tree. A few minutes later, he was back with me. I asked what happened, and he said:

"I decided I'd rather sit with you than that four-foot rattlesnake over there."

He said it a lot more calmly than I answered: "The *hell* with the turkeys. Let's shoot that rattlesnake."

"Naw," he said. "That'll scare the turkeys."

"We can find turkeys somewhere *else*. First let's shoot the rattlesnake."

We never did find that snake, but we have killed three or four when we were hunting quail. From the turkey hunting I had done in southern Indiana, I knew the whole key to success is calling them into shooting range. I had never done that. I usually went back there with Barry Hadabaugh, a great turkey hunter from Salem, Indiana. I'd listen to him, watch him, and pay attention, but he did all the calling. He did give me a calling box, and—when I was riding in a car, or off by myself somewhere—I practiced on it on my own.

One day in Texas we were hunting about a hundred and thirty miles east of Lubbock on a ranch owned by a friend of mine. We hunted all day. We called turkeys, and they responded, but they never came close to us. The call is meant to trick tom turkeys into thinking it's from a female, luring them out of their nesting place at the height of the breeding season. The gobblers called back, but the two guys doing the calling, David Gregory and Ted Flowers, obviously didn't seem like sexy enough hens to get them to leave the hens they were with and come our way.

In Texas when you're turkey hunting, you do a lot of crawling—and you do it carefully and slowly, looking out for the same thing that was in that pine-tree area, a rattlesnake. Ted and David are excellent callers, but this time they were striking out with the toms they were calling. Since they weren't getting any results and I figured we had nothing to lose, I whispered, "Let me try." They gave me a box, I screeched with it, and we heard a really interested "gobble-gobble-gobble." Right away. Ted and David almost had cardiacs at my beginner's luck, and I was damned excited, too.

The response was from a tom about a hundred and fifty yards away, in the same ditch we were in. He was probably nestled in with at least two hens. To attract him to us, we had to be sexier than those hens. I screeched again and got another enthusiastic response. We kept crawling—now we and the tom are about seventy yards apart. One of the guys whispered, "Coach, that turkey's going to come flying over that hill in just a second. You take the gun and I'll call."

He called. Once, twice, a third time. Nothing happened. Keeping the gun I reached back in kind of a smart-ass way, he gave me the box, and I called. Right away—"Gobble! Gobble! Gobble!" Then louder: *"Gobble! Gobble! Gobble!"*

Ted was in front of me and he whispered: "Coach! There's another turkey coming from over here." He didn't hear it, he saw it. I looked where he was pointing and saw three turkeys coming, all gobblers. They walked down in a depression where we couldn't see them. I screeched and they gobbled. I picked up my twelve-gauge gun, and when the first turkey came over a rise about thirty-five yards away, I fired. Ted jumped up to go get it and he yelled, "Son of a bitch, Coach, you got all three of them."

I never did that in Indiana.

This is a fantastic state for someone who likes the outdoors. We start dove hunting the first of September, then quail season starts in November and goes to the end of February. Pheasant season comes in the first three weeks of December and then, around the first of April, turkey season starts. And there's some good bass fishing, mostly over in East Texas. But ranches around Lubbock have a lot of ponds where there are bass. You can go down on the gulf and saltwater fish, for redfish or trout. All the things I like to do outdoors are plentiful, most within two-and-a-half hours. And it's not just great for me. Karen has become an avid fly-fisher, and she's getting pretty good. I really enjoy her company.

My first few weeks as Tech's coach included a whirlwind tour of Texas with Gerald Myers to introduce me—and get me introduced—to Tech alumni groups all over the state, and of course to do some recruiting. We had outstanding turnouts at big cities where you could expect big turnouts—Dallas and Houston—but at smaller towns, too. We were on the go almost every night, somewhere. One swing we went sixteen hundred miles and never came close to a bordering state. We just had a great reception all across Texas, and we raised a lot of money for the university. One of our goals is to raise enough in donations to endow all thirteen men's basketball scholarships, and we're more than a third there. At Indiana, we raised enough to endow the scholarships doubly, with some money left over—plus more than $5 million for the library and at the minimum $50 million all told for the school, counting all facets of increased basketball revenue during my twenty-nine years. Despite all that, I had to sue to try to get those people to even meet their contractual agreements with me. But that's another story, and another university, and I'm very happy I'm where I am.

• • •

Shortly after I was announced as Tech coach, Gerald Myers, president Schmidly and chancellor John Montforth took me to Austin to meet the governor and to be introduced to the state legislature. Out of that came a picture that hangs prominently in my office area. It's of a cannon and a lone star, with lettering that says, "Come and Take It." There's a story, of course.

After I had spoken briefly to the legislature, a photographer told me, "Several staff people and legislators would like to have a picture taken with you. I've got a spot out in the hallway to do it."

So we went out and took the pictures, right in front of this picture. I looked at it, and saw the cannon and the words "Come and Take It" on what looked like burlap. I asked the photographer who had carefully set us up there, "What's this all about?"

"That's a famous incident in Texas history," he said. "They had captured a cannon from Santa Ana's army, and Santa Ana sent a message that he wanted the cannon back. The captain in charge sent a message back: 'Come and take it.'"

"I thought this was a perfectly appropriate place for you to be."

I felt complimented. A friend of mine in Dallas, Jim Sowell, framed for me the artwork that hangs proudly in my office.

Last June, I went to California to play a part in an Adam Sandler movie, *Anger Management*. When I got the invitation to do it and I saw that title, how could I turn it down? In the film, Sandler looks around the office and sees me sitting in a chair. "Coach Knight!" he said. "What are *you* doing here? Do you have a problem with anger?"

"Oh, no," I said. "I'm here for a Sexaholics Anonymous class."

"Coach, you're in the wrong room," Sandler said. "I think yours is down the hall." And I left.

We filmed it several times with me responding to him with something like "Oh, thanks — I appreciate your helping me," and leaving. The fourth or fifth time, I got bored and decided to spice things up a little. I didn't warn Adam but this time when he approached me I had a book in my hand. When he redirected me, I slammed the book down in front of his feet and shouted, "The *hell* with this. I'm going home." His expression when I slammed the book on the floor was priceless. I hope that's the version they use.

Jack Nicholson and John McEnroe also were in the film. This happened in June, and the sixth game of the NBA championship series between the Kings and Lakers was to be played that night in Los Angeles. Everyone knows what a big Lakers fan Nicholson is, and I'd also read that he enjoys finding interesting places to eat. When we were talking during the film-shooting that afternoon, I couldn't resist jerking his chain a little. "I understand you like to go to good restaurants," I told him. "I've found a great place out in the Valley and I'd like to take you to dinner there tonight." At first he didn't realize I was kidding. He said very seriously, "Coach . . . I'm sorry . . . . I'd like to but I can't. I'm going to the Lakers game tonight."

I was, too. But we did talk—about why he likes basketball so much, how he played it as a kid. He knew a lot about what was going on in college basketball as well as the NBA. It was a memorable experience, because I'm a great admirer of Nicholson's acting ability. I thoroughly enjoyed the time spent with him. And I really liked Adam Sandler.

I've had a good time being involved in several things like that. I did a parody on my temper for Glad bags and enjoyed it, just as in the past I had a good time with one for Minute Maid. Those were fun. Somebody in the press ripped me for daring to capitalize on my reputation for a fiery temper. I thought that was funny. Since people like that guy were the ones who "helped" me build up that reputation, I was surprised he didn't ask for a percentage of my pay.

Steve Alford, who did such a great leadership job on our 1987 NCAA championship team at Indiana, came to Lubbock for a few days last summer, and I really enjoyed spending a couple of days with him. We just talked about basketball—we studied some tapes of his team and then I showed him what we try to do with ours. I think he also enjoyed the time. When he came into the Big Ten as the coach at Iowa in the 1999–2000 season, I thought he did an excellent job. The first time we played was at Assembly Hall. It was a game I thought we should win, but he had his team so well prepared that winning or losing came down to a three-point shot from the corner that didn't go in for Steve's team.

After that, things got all messed up for him there. He told me about problems he had with Luke Recker, who transferred from Indiana to Arizona and then to Iowa. I kidded him a little. "If you'd have given me a phone call," I said, " I could have saved you a lot of trouble."

In late summer 2002, I was in the hospital for a few days. I had stomach pains that I thought were coming from a kidney stone. I had two great doctors with me that evening—Jim Burke and Mike Robertson, both of them team doctors. They said I had an obstruction in my small intestine and wanted to do the operation right away. I asked them, "Could you just observe it for a couple of days?" One of them said, "Oh, yeah, we can observe it for a couple of days. And *then* we'll operate— and you'll be a hell of a lot sicker than you are right now." So I said, "Let's go."

That was about 11 A.M.; at 12 they were operating. I think I came out of it about 4 P.M. At 6 o'clock the next morning I was walking. The surgeon, Dave Mangold, told me the quicker I could walk, the quicker I could get out of the hospital. I walked, but I didn't get out as soon as I would have liked. Karen was like an angel from heaven. She slept on a couch in my room. I'd wake up at 2 o'clock in the morning—I couldn't sleep because of a drainage tube in my throat. So we'd go walking until I'd get tired, and then I'd try to sleep some more. She was there every night. Carol Myers (Gerald's wife) came by during the day, and Pat's wife, Amanda, also came in and walked me. I was still attached to the IV machine; they'd push it and we'd go motoring up and down the hallway. I knew why I wasn't getting out. After the surgery, the nurses kept coming in and asking, "Have you passed gas yet?" By Wednesday morning, I hadn't passed anything, from any direction. Thursday, I passed a little bit of gas. That morning, Karen and I stopped to see one of the nurses who had been particularly nice to me. While we were standing there, I let out a huge fart, and we all three cheered. In all my life, I never thought I'd get applause for one of those.

An experience like that time in the hospital makes a person appreciate better what other people with far greater physical problems and far more pain have to endure. It taught me other sympathies, too. For the next several weeks when I spoke to groups that included a lot of women, I said, "After going through abdominal surgery and everything that occurred after that, no male on the planet is more empathetic to women's pains during pregnancies and other female problems than I am."

I got letters from all over the country from people I knew—and many I didn't—when Ted Williams passed away July 5. Of course it was a profoundly sad time, but it was probably the best thing that could have happened. He had no real quality of life left. He couldn't have enjoyed life as it existed for him those last months. Most of the time, he was unaware of what was going on. It was a blessing.

And I was very disappointed at what took place within his family, regarding how he should be buried. All I know is I felt blessed and fortunate to have known him as a friend.

The year 2002 was a difficult one for me. I have mentioned the passing of Abe Lemons. One of my best friends back in Bloomington, law professor Harry Pratter, died. So did a close friend of mine from coaching, Al LoBalbo. I also lost the man I never called anything but "Coach"—Fred Taylor. He died January 6, and for him, too, the last months were such that his passing was a blessing.

Few people knew Coach Taylor was a talented artist. His daughter Nikki, who I'm very fond of, gave me a painting he had done of two fisherman in a boat. She had gone through some paintings he had up in an attic, and she told me she thought this one was perfect for me. I saw why as soon as I looked at the picture. It's amazing how much the silhouettes of the two fishermen look like Coach and me. Then, the sister of an Ohio high school basketball coach I know—Frank Kahle of Toledo Central Catholic—bought at an auction a winter farm scene that Coach had painted. She bought it with the idea of giving it to me. Frank came all the way down from Toledo to see our 2002–03 team practice for one day—and to give me that picture. I appreciated that whole thing more than I could tell Frank or his sister. It and the other painting are precious possessions for me.

The Basketball Hall of Fame in Springfield, Massachusetts, carries in its Web site a comment I once made: "No one in the long history and tradition of the Big Ten Conference has given to college basketball what Fred Taylor has in terms of expertise and integrity. His Ohio State teams of the early 1960s are rated among the best ever to play the game and his approach to basketball changed the concept throughout the entire conference and propelled it into a position of national power never before enjoyed."

I'll stand by that.

And now it's time for Season Two.

It began with a disappointment for me. Just before our first game, Dr. Schmidly, the man who hired me, announced he was leaving to become the president at Oklahoma State. As much as I hated to see him go, I thought it was a good move for a great friend. At Oklahoma State, he is the president and chief executive officer, reporting only to the board of trustees. That was a situation he really felt good about moving into. Some things here he didn't like and had a difficult time dealing with. I told him from my experience at Indiana, you can never circumvent or overcome things like that. If you're in a position where you don't feel comfortable, the thing to do is move on, rather than fight things you can't change.

I'm sure Texas Tech will find an excellent replacement, but the personal effect for me was that we were losing a man who was a strong, effective supporter of our basketball team, a man who felt a part of our team and—if he was in town—not only came to the game but always dropped into the locker room afterward to talk about it with me, as John Ryan used to do at Indiana.

From the start, Dr. Schmidly and I had a great relationship that allowed kidding back and forth. He and Gerald Myers were in Florida with me at spring training time in 2001. I was down there to see Tony LaRussa and the Cardinals, and it turned out that Dr. Schmidly as a boy was a big fan of Stan Musial. Tony took David and me out for dinner one night, and just as we were about to enter the place, Musial drove up. The Cardinals had been having trouble scoring some runs that spring and Musial rolled down his window and yelled, "Tony, when the hell are we going to get some hits?" He saw me and added, "Coach, when are you going to get a job?" Then he got out, came over to us, and I introduced him to Dr. Schmidly. After that I always told Dr. Schmidly he wasn't completely sold on hiring me until he saw I was a friend of Stan Musial. I hadn't even signed my first Tech contract when that happened.

The recruiting for our second year went well. We needed a center after losing Andy Ellis, and we brought in Robert Tomaszek, who is 6'9", 240 pounds. It was not at all hard to make Tomaszek a Red Raider. The first time Pat talked to him, he said if he had a chance to come here and play for us, he wanted to do it. He's a strong kid who surprised us with a very good shooting touch. Like every kid I've ever recruited, he has to learn to play hard every second of every minute he's in a game. I think he will.

The other four kids we recruited for 2002–03 are all from Texas, which I liked. Josh Washington is an outstanding athlete from Lubbock, a 6'4" all-state football player as well as an all-state basketball player. He has a good work ethic. We have a lot of experience back on this year's team, which likely will cut his playing time as a freshman, but I think his future is very bright. John Ofeagbu, a 6'8" freshman from San Antonio, is just learning to play basketball. He has all kinds of potential, because he wants to be a player, and he works hard every day.

We red-shirted two other freshmen: Tanner Ogden, 6'7", from Seminole, and LucQuento White, 6'1", from Midland. As it did at Indiana, I think red-shirting will pay off for us with these two kids. I think they'll be very good additions to our team next year.

We're pleased that our first full year of recruiting went so well. It included an early commitment from 6'4" guard Drew Coffman, who is also from Midland. He committed to us during his junior year and signed with us in November of his senior year, the first player to do that for us here. He may be the best guard in the state this year. Another real plus in the early part of this year was a commitment from one of the state's best sophomores.

We have two junior college players signed for next year: Mike Travis, from San Francisco City College, and Devonne Giles, from Seward County in Liberal, Kansas. Travis is from the same school that gave us Dean Garrett, the center on our 1987 national championship team at Indiana. Dean came to us through the urging of Brad Duggan, one of the truly unique people I have met in his absolute, unwavering loyalty to friends. He coached Dean for a year and then became athletic director and head of physical education at San Francisco City College. He's still in those positions, and he was instrumental in Mike Travis's developing an interest in Texas Tech. I think his addition to our team will pay great dividends for him and us, as certainly happened with Dean Garrett. He's a work-ethic player—a rebounder and a defender. Scoring isn't as vital a thing to him as it is to some kids. The idea of being a scorer sometimes makes it difficult for a kid to be a good basketball player. He's so wound up with scoring that the rest of the game just slides by him. Giles is another kid from New Jersey, like Kasib Powell. I think Giles will be an outstanding player for us.

Our overall situation with Tech basketball has improved to where I think we can look ahead to having a good talent pool for the next four seasons, with kids we know will be here and those I think we'll have a good chance to add over those years.

What we had as we began the 2002–03 season were players who had played for us and played pretty well—guys who had to understand that just because they were a year older didn't mean they were going to be any better. I certainly felt they could be better. Who could know then what our record would turn out to be, but I thought we would have a better team.

Our goal going into the 2002–03 season was to be considerably better in two areas: our defensive play and our play in the last five minutes. That last thing alone, our play in the last five minutes, could have meant at least two more conference wins for us. That would have been the difference between 10–6 and 12–4—a big difference.

The most disappointing thing to me is when we just don't play hard enough to win — losing to a team that had a better sense of purpose and better intensity. We started off our second season at Tech with some very good efforts, but the slipoff happened again at Wyoming in our sixth game. We'll continue to work like hell to eliminate it, but I'm not sure any coach can. It's fighting a human tendency that sure isn't confined to Texas Tech. Until we can develop an absolute consistency game where game after game we're playing as well as we can play, we're going to have things happen to us that just shouldn't happen.

Between our tournament loss and the start of the book tour, I spent four days with Tony LaRussa at the Cardinals' spring training camp. For a couple of the days I was there they were having trouble scoring runs, but it was obvious with the lineup and pitching staff they were putting together that they were going to be an awfully good team. All of those players, and certainly Tony, did a remarkable job of dealing with the terrible shock of losing an outstanding pitcher and person, Darryl Kile, to a heart attack in late June. They regrouped, made a couple of personnel moves, and kept going to a championship year. One of those moves brought in an excellent third baseman, Scott Rolen, who was an outstanding basketball player at Jasper, Indiana—he once made ten three-point baskets in a game. He was a teammate there for a year with Mike Lewis, who was an excellent player for us at Indiana and now is a graduate student on our staff here.

We had a recruiting goal right from the start: We wanted to develop a situation where kids from this part of the country—West Texas, bigger than most states—would want to come to Texas Tech. Then we wanted to reach out across the state and develop some interest in Tech basketball around Texas. It's a state that is as economically healthy as it is big. In the last ten years, the population in Texas has grown by several million people who have moved in from all over the country to the many different employment opportunities available in our state.

We're happy with the rate of expansion in our fan base. People without allegiance to any particular school—just basketball fans—have adopted Tech, I've learned from my trips around Texas. That's gratifying and helpful, because it's reflected in recruiting interest.

It helps that more of the state is seeing our games now. My son Tim is an assistant athletic director with responsibilities that include building up our TV coverage. He did an outstanding job in the first year, putting together our own TV network. The second year he achieved something big for us. He was able to get our games televised in the Dallas–Fort Worth area, which is a major recruiting area and certainly one that we want to take advantage of. Texas produces as many outstanding basketball players as any state in the country, far more than most.

We received some awards the first season relative to contributions made to athletics in the state of Texas and achievements in basketball that were very good for us in terms of recognition, things that did a lot to increase the interest in Tech basketball, not just in this part of the state but around the state. Already, our basketball program has had a great impact on the financial status of the athletic department. With revenue from television, season ticket sales and private seat licenses, the basketball revenue has increased by more than $10 million.

Tim has had a lot to do with that, too. He worked very hard at putting a TV package together and did a lot of work with our ticket sales as well. We had extremely low ticket prices a year ago—$11 or $12 for floor seats and $5 or $6 for the balcony. We've upped that to $18 and $11, and ticket sales have gone up, rather than being hurt by the higher prices. That has helped our whole athletic department, across the board.

Our women's basketball team has had tremendous success over the last twelve years with Marsha Sharp and her staff. They have an excellent program with tremendous coaches.

Just as Sam Carmichael, among the coaches at Indiana, was a very close friend of mine, so, too, is Larry Hays, our baseball coach. If I'm in town, I never miss watching his team play. He was an outstanding fast-pitch softball player, and we have had a great time talking about that sport. I played fast-pitch for several years, at a pretty good level, but not at the level Larry did.

He does a great job coaching. I get the same enjoyment watching him work that I do when I go to spring training with the Cardinals and Tony LaRussa.

Of course I was disappointed that we weren't able to play any farther in the NCAA tournament than we did, because I thought we had a great chance to do some things. A lady who had stood in line for a couple of hours at one of our book signings last spring heard me mention my disappointment at the way we finished. She smiled and said, "Coach, that's what next year's for."

It was the perfect comment—so nice and so genuine that it instantly stuck with me. As soon as I got back to Lubbock, I told it to our returning players. It was the best possible way for us as a team to go from thoughts of our achievements and our shortcomings of 2001–02 to thoughts of our upcoming season.

I didn't catch the lady's name. I don't remember which store or which city we were in. All I remember is the lift it gave me and I think our team when I passed it on to them.

It's our turn now to repay support like that.

INDEX